You'll Dig *Dirt*

The most memorable gardens—and the most vivid gardening *books*—are alive with the colorful quirks, hardy opinions, and unrestrained excesses of their creators.

In *Dirt,* style-setter Dianne Benson digs deep into her own unique philosophy to give you the scoop on what it takes to put down roots (or tubers . . . or magical bulbs), how to spend your precious gardening dollars, where to doll up your property, and how pleasurable your artful garden-making can be.

On propagation: "Artists no longer mix their paint from minerals—they go out and buy them. Why should we gardeners feel obligated to start from the revered seed?"

On container gardens: "Inane fuzzy blue ageratum, mixed with some stiff and too-popular orange marigolds. . . . This is really a waste of a container, especially if a beautiful one."

On identifying weeds: "A weed is anything you do not want in your garden. *That's* the rule."

On garden tour mishaps: "I thought everything looked perfect. To my horror, a tourer pointed out a bloated dead fish in the pond. I nearly died myself."

On tools, accessories, and clothes: "With your first-rate nursery in place, some glorious plants in mind, and a take on what part of your property to cultivate first—it is high time to outfit yourself in some worthwhile attire and acquire good tools to accomplish the task."

DIRT

THE
LOWDOWN
ON GROWING
A GARDEN
WITH STYLE

DIANNE
BENSON

A DELL TRADE PAPERBACK

A DELL TRADE PAPERBACK

Published by
Dell Publishing
a division of
Bantam Doubleday Dell Publishing Group, Inc.
1540 Broadway
New York, New York 10036

Notice: The information in this book is complete to the best of the author's knowledge at the time of this writing. All recommendations are made without guarantees on the part of the author or publisher. All products discussed have been used by the author with short-term success, but long-term effects are often unknown. We disclaim all liability incurred with the use of this information (although all information is a product of the author's experience and/or a by-product of her taste).

For ever-present Dad
and remarkable Mom

CONTENTS

Six or so years ago two major dilemmas confronted me: my much touted and very chic but financially distraught Dianne B. stores were unraveling at the seams, and in tandem, a new house begging to be gardened was staring me in the face. The house had been bought by my guy Irving (whose business was obviously much better than mine). Wandering around our new, flowerless not-quite-an-acre and arguing with myself became my new preoccupation. How was it that I, this supposed fashion *maven, dreaded* going to Paris for the next round of fashion shows? A hunger for a passion more meaningful was brewing, the glamour was wearing off and something was very wrong. Who needs a senseless fashion world where even Issey Miyake, that fine Japanese designer nurtured for over ten years in my stores, can suddenly announce that *Dianne B.* could no longer sell his clothes (even though his collection was my most important, not to mention my favorite, and he knew it) because he was opening *his own store* on the very same Madison Avenue? Who wants this? I asked myself as I considered the long, woodsy, weed-strewn path leading from driveway to the house. Issey, in the end, helped make my choice.

There was another way to vent my energy and satisfy my artistic propensity. Operating stores and designing clothes were just too prone to the vagaries of fashion. Increasingly it occurred to me a garden is unconcerned with politics—or crazes—or *who* can do *what* for you next. It will never dump you. A prized perennial might be overtaken by blight or refuse to flower, but it would never purposefully hurt you.

As I surveyed the situation, the untouched acre began to take on layers of new meaning. Perhaps it was Providence there wasn't even one stray clump of daffodils, only a beautiful tree-laden plot. We had been looking for a nice house and pool, but fell in love with an awful house and a verdant, overgrown property teeming with potential. With both predicaments at hand—sensibly trying to restructure my business or turning this property into an idyllic flowering woodland—I decided to, yes, garden.

And so began my obsession to imbue our beautiful acre with lush, excessive, natural gardens accentuated with sometimes eccentric, but always interesting objects. To wean myself away from all those frantic fashion factions. "Hell," said Sartre, "is other people." Gardening, I found, took their place.

Gardening is good. It is good for mind, body, soul, and infinitely more fascinating than fashion. Gardening generates a sense of style, an individual and specific eye, and forces a perception of color and proportion, texture and form; thereby manifesting all positive attributes of creativity and none of the dull realities like explaining to your investors why it didn't sell if it was so gorgeous. The ability to make it all look effortless and natural is the acquired icing on the cake. The gardening mode, unlike fashion, transcends trends and tiresome pretensions. Contrary to the most overworked voguish opinion, style *can* be acquired; and as the seasons come and go, instead of having to deal with the dreaded concept of being only as good as your last collection, you can enjoy a garden that just gets bigger, bolder, better, and more instinctive. As immutably as night follows day follows night, its growth and seasonal maturation become a living thing highlighting your life, creating the enviable emotion of always having something to look forward to. Quenching your increasing thirst for the natural—in a world growing more artificial each day—is an added attraction.

In a posthumously published book about her travels, Vita Sackville-West, gardener extraordinaire and great heroine of mine, describes "the agonizing delights of anticipation being replaced by the colder flood of fulfillment." Because gardening has a beginning but never ends, that static plateau of complete satisfaction is never reached—you are always on the verge, forever anticipating, and never satiated, although you are eternally accomplishing a divine thing bringing pride and reward.

Forget any frumpy, bumpkin associations you might attach to gardening. They are simply not the case. Gardening and glamour are not incongruous. Flair, allure, and an aura of excitement can all be applicable to tending a garden, like anything else. My sister Adele, an upright, American, steadfast soul, continuously applauds my ability to maintain my gardens and not fall into what she calls "the Farmer Brown mode." Forgoing the fleeting mindset of fashion, with its compulsion to reinvent itself every six months, in favor of feeling a oneness with the earth doesn't mean I've forsaken an ounce of my personal style or would be caught dead in the garden looking like an old cowhand. Spontaneously translating your own aesthetic to a garden abundant, buoyant, informal, and inviting—even ultimately overgrown and wild—is not achieved by mincing around, cutting corners, or being indifferent to any matter of taste.

Note, too, a horticultural treatise is far from my intentions. If your tendencies are toward cross-pollination or expertly having a hybrid named after you, then put down this book. Furthermore, my version of gardening most certainly does not include starting anything from an infinitesimal seed. A big proponent of what you can actually see, touch, and smell, I champion nurseries and catalogs to buy all the bountiful ingredients to create your garden image. Artists no longer mix their paint from minerals, they go out and buy them—sculptors don't sink into the quarry to hack their own stone. Why should we gardeners feel obligated to the revered seed method of starting everything from scratch to create our pictures? Mine is the fast-lane, quick-gratification approach to creating something of your own, with a lot of tips and hints about how to begin, where to go for the best of what you need, what to avoid, and what to expect. This is not about laborious toil in nonexistent greenhouses or a lifelong love affair with ecosystems. This is also, and most definitely, *not* the good old "Yankee thrift approach."

In this straightforward approach to diving into gardening there is no mumbo-jumbo or endless references to *Hortus*—not the First, Second, nor the Third. *Hortus* is the Bible of gardening and is oft referred to with the kind of reverence routinely reserved for higher beings. Of course, I *had to have a Hortus* once the gardening bug bit. Having succumbed, I will now say to you, don't bother to spend $145 on this dry and dreary tome. Don't ruin your living room with messy containers for the excruciatingly slow seed propagating recommended in most other gardening books, either—I don't care how virtuous the books make it sound. And don't be lulled into using the lurid color combinations most often proposed by the too-popular annual offerings you come across in most catalogs and nurseries.

Also stand warned that this book is probably not for someone with a hired gardener in residence or a preference for picking up the phone and contracting the classiest nursery in town to do it all for you. Much of the great joy is doing it yourself, or at least being a major participant with a yearning to be involved with the earth and plants. The heady thrill of pulling up in your drive on a day in April when the earth is exploding with life is simply indescribable. Knowing if it weren't for *you* this progeny would be nonexistent is such an ecstatic feeling, it is then you first understand why all those songs and poems about the spring have so enthusiastically endured.

And do not be dismayed if you think you are lacking a "green thumb." This is not a genetic endowment or any physical characteristic of which I'm aware. If my dear Mom had lavished huge amounts of affection on a proper perennial border instead of having made a few vague exclamations each spring about our single lilac bush, would I have been a born gardener or be any better or worse at it than right now? Of course not. Is it a product of scholarship? Perhaps a little; the more you know—the better off you are. But if you put your heart into it and *have the desire*, then green thumbmanship will follow suit. *The desire* will translate into a certain new variation of love lavished on your garden, which will, in return, recognize it and reward you. There is no English-language word for this part of the gardening art, but in Norwegian the word *Opelske* literally translates as "loving your flowers . . . bringing them to bloom and vigor purely through adoration." I wasn't aware these Nordic folk had such passion, but isn't it grand that this pertinent gardening language exists.

Another incalculably wonderful blessing is that anyone can be a gardener. It's simply a matter of choice. On the day you find yourself fretting about the first frost or ruminating over rhododendron color, the day you say to yourself, "I'm a gardener"—you are one. You need no degrees or doctorates, no accumulation of blue ribbons at a prestigious Iris Competition, no title bestowed by an intimidating gardening society, no personnel official to declare "you're in," nor any special knowledge of pH factors or compost heaps. What is essential is training your vision to see beyond what's already there; having enough strength to haul around a garden cart filled with fifty-pound bags; and money, because you can't start planting without any plants, and I believe the only way to begin is to buy them full blown. In those early gardening days, I would set out on an early Saturday morning, hit three or four nurseries, choose ten or fifteen plants with glorious potential, haul them home (a convertible makes life easier; my Volkswagen Cabriolet got very used to dirt), plant them that very afternoon, and marvel at an increased garden the same evening. Oh, it was heaven!

My objective in this book is to enthrall you with the enchanted world of gardening. There are shelves full of step-by-step gardening books to fill you in on botanical details and endless propagation techniques. Verily, each prissy encyclopedia can provide one tidbit or another. By reading *this* book, it is hoped, delving into so many dull primers will become unnecessary and instead, you will realize the interesting approach is throwing yourself into it full force. *You* want to participate in your landscape the same way you position furniture in your house, install paintings on your wall, or put clothes on your body. Regardless of your motives—communing with the earth, impressing your neighbors, exercising your creative capabilities—you'll emerge from your gardening foray richer in spirit, if not a plant fanatic. By and large you will join the illustrious crowd Vita wrote about in a letter to Virginia Woolf: "This all fits in with the theory that people who live in the country and like flowers are good."

My goal is to acquaint you with gardening in a visual and visceral sense, to force you to overcome any lack of experience (as I had to) by *doing it*. Anyone can do it, even if you've never come any closer to flowers than writing thank-you notes for them. I went from nothing—including no knowledge, no inherited arbors, no grandame granny with a garden of old-world roses, no green thumb, and no patience—to making a garden in six years that is now included on the same Garden Tour with Martha Stewart, no less. Procrastination will get you nowhere. Divine inspiration will never strike if you spend all your time looking at pretty picture-books chock-full of blooming gardens not your own. Anne Raver, the esteemed garden writer for *The New York Times*, is perfectly well-grounded in her fitting statement, "Gardening is like life. If you stand around too long, paralyzed by your lack of knowledge, then you'll never acquire any." If you are not moved to action at the end of *Dirt*, it is clear my version of gardening euphoria is just not your thing. If, on the other hand, you can't wait to get out there and dig right in—*this is how to do it.*

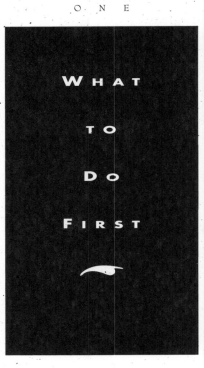

Garden Zones. Analyze.
Assess. Local Nurseries.
Caveat Emptor.

Time present and time past
Are both perhaps present in time future,
And time future contained in time past.
. . . Other echoes
Inhabit the garden. Shall we follow?
T. S. Eliot, "Burnt Norton," *Four Quartets*

Chances are, if you are reading this book you already own land and perhaps a garden. Lacking a patch of ground you are itching to plant, however, your first objective must be, of course, buying a house with property. I have no interest in writing about planting window-boxes or fighting against nature to grow things on fabulous penthouse terraces. This book is about transforming your very own property into a glorious garden dream. So be sure to acquire a house *begging* to be gardened. Preferably a nice mature property overgrown and under-realized. You don't want a pristine plot with someone else's idea of a garden, because designing your space (with a charmingly undesigned quality, of course) will bear witness to *your own* unique character and style. Our house happens to be in East Hampton and the land was devoid of even a common daylily when we bought it. Not *one* daylily. Everybody on Long Island has a few daylilies—but not this house. When we first moved in, the idea was to spend idle and idyllic weekends here. Little did I know that once the gardening obsession took hold, languid days would be a thing of the past. This slightly-less-than-an acre did come replete, however, with glorious, huge, mostly evergreen trees and, albeit small, a woods.

The house was awful. Sort of '50s and not even gracious enough to be called a ranch-style. But the property was so raw and beautiful and overgrown, we figured we could change the house. So succumb we did to all those gorgeous trees that would take someone else a lifetime to grow. We redid the ugly house, which amazingly took only six months. The Fourth of July was move-in day, and the balance of that first summer was spent sorting through myriad crates we had accumulated from all over the world the year before: dishes from Jerusalem, beds from Marrakesh, stuffed turtles smuggled from Bali, the usual. We spent days finding the perfect spot for everything, replacing deadbeat appliances, and settling into a new house with things basically all new to us. The inside took on the whimsical, if unconventional, lived-in look I was after; but the outside was another thing entirely. In redoing the house and pool, some trees were moved around and we were talked into some plantings by the local landscape guy who was a chum of the contractor. In no way was I convinced that these puny little garden areas he'd arranged were for me, and when the landscaping bills came pouring in on top of all the other bills, I screamed, "Stop at once with these plantings," although I had no idea at the time how to do better.

As I looked out upon a plot of land lacking in any cultivation beyond trees, it seemed to me the first priority was to use the natural pathways, boundaries, and visual focal points already there. Although without a clue about garden "bones" at the time, I must have had a premonition that a garden springs from what you already have, a concept we will investigate in detail in Chapter III.

GARDENING ZONES

Trying to formulate my ideas, I bought a few gardening books and quickly realized that locating your "gardening zone" was key to any foray into gardening. East Hampton is in the best of gardening zones, I believe, good old Zone 7. Actually we are at the northeasternmost tip of sprawling Zone 7, which sweeps down the East Coast to the Carolinas, stretches across the country through Tennessee and the middle of Texas, goes all the way down to the Southernmost edge of New Mexico and Arizona, then shoots up through the East of California and winds up in Alaska. Now I do not profess to understand exactly how this zoning works or how it could even *be possible* that all of these parts of the country share the same weather conditions; but I've now seen hundreds of garden-zone maps and, invariably, they are the same. Certain that plenty of research has been compiled by all sorts of experts to draw these conclusions, I don't question that all of us in Zone 7 have the same four articulated seasons, as does most of the

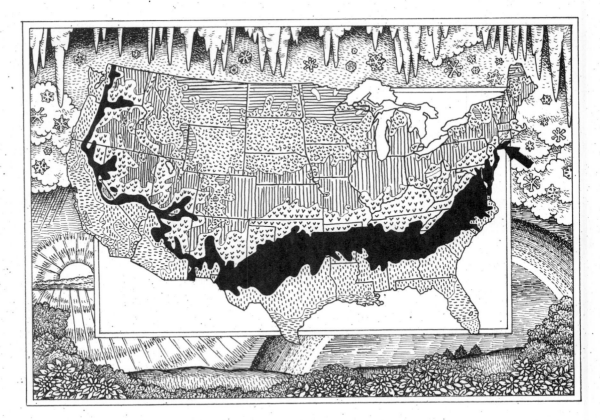

My beloved, though mysterious, Zone 7 is the blackened area. South of me are more tropical zones 8–10. North of me are the increasingly more frigid Zones 1–6,

country. The zones have more to do with hardiness (how much cold your plants can endure), however, than timing. My sister's lilies and tulips and everything else in her Eastern Shore of Maryland garden consistently bloom about three weeks before mine, even though we are both securely in Zone 7.

Gardening in the hot zone (Zone 10, where it never gets colder than forty degrees and tropical-plant aficionados in Southern California and Florida are blessed with perfect conditions) or in the freezing zone (Zone 1, where it can get colder than minus fifty degrees, which must be hell on a garden) is a completely different story about which I know little. But here in Zone 7, zero to ten degrees is as cold as we can expect and now that the disappearing ozone layer is cooking up the earth, it isn't often cold enough for even our small pond to freeze over. The rest of the zones (2 through 9) operate on a scale varying by ten degrees warmer or colder, and most of them enjoy the wondrous four seasons like we do.

DIANNE BENSON

Now that you've located your zone, we are ready to garden. Let's say it is the first glorious weekend of spring, and the only thing fresh and green stirring in your world is the envy you feel over everyone else's daffodils. Well, you can't have daffodils or tulips or any of those gorgeous harbingers of spring till next year. Planning for them, paying for them, and planting them will keep you occupied from August until Christmas, which we will delve into with great enthusiasm later in this book. But there are many other things you can do with your acre (or less or more) to give it springtime zing. Hundreds of unique situations will become apparent on your very own plot as soon as you train your impatient but eager eyes.

ANALYZE YOUR NEIGHBORHOOD

For now, walk, bike, ride, even jog if you must, around your town. Keep an eagle eye peeled for color, form, and what excites you. The big benefit here, of course, is that if you fall in love with things already growing, healthy and lush, just a mile from your house, you know that you can grow the very same things in your yard. It's a much more significant way of refining your eye than leafing through book after book full of plantings that might be totally out of place in your zone. Develop a sense of what is around you and what you find arresting, amusing, or just plain gorgeous. *Do this often* because what today looks like a bunch of ho-hum green leaves may be a beautiful flowering extravaganza a month later. Mama Nature is anything but static. Look for big things first, like shrubs and ornamental trees, which are more likely to be approachable and exposed than the flowers so often tucked away behind houses or hedges. If your house is in a new development and everyone nearby is in the same barren boat as you—venture out into the older neighborhoods surrounding you where things are already mature, or better yet, overgrown, to get a feeling of all that's possible.

Don't be afraid to ask questions of your gardening neighbors, and never be timid about snapping off a leafy twig for further identification by your nurseryman. If you really peruse your neighborhood with a fine-tooth comb, it will teach you many things. Having covered every street, every lane, every path of our town dozens and dozens of times, I've not only discovered plants, trees, and shrubs I couldn't live without, but have also watched what goes on in the neighborhood as the plants are maintained. When the showiest gardener in town cuts down his *Vitex*, I cut mine, too. My decision to plant vitex in the first place was a result of falling in love with the late-blooming blue-flowered shrub spied in the neighborhood. Having snatched a branch of this beauty, I took it to a local nursery where they confirmed it as vitex and happily sold me two of the divine shrubs.

Figuring these neighborhood gardeners know exactly what they're doing, I don't ever feel even a bit like a knock-off artist for copying their delicious combinations. I happen to love the white daffodils and *Mertensia* (Virginia bluebells that set off daffodils perfectly with their most striking inky-blue color) in my favorite garden on Lily Pond Lane; and it's incredible how the iris take over just after the poppies fade in the great garden on the Highway Behind the Pond (that's really the name). On your rounds you may come across gardeners at work and be amazed at how anxious they are to impart information, *especially* if you begin the conversation with a compliment. Although gardening is rather a solitary dedication, people are always eager to show off what they've grown. Try to catch them on the public periphery of their property, and hang onto every word they say.

ASSESS YOUR PROPERTY

After you have digested your environs, go back home and take a keen walk around your own property. Really squint your eyes and look hard at what already exists from every conceivable angle: look out your windows, stand on your deck or porch, walk every route, stroll up and down the driveway, move a chair outside and sit in the various parts of your yard while you contemplate it. What do you see? Nature is generous and abundant and no place is totally vacuous. You too must have a natural starting point somewhere. What you're looking for are the natural little niches and nooks or crannies, the serene view pleading to be isolated, an appealing corner ideal for rearrangement as your outdoor living room, a sheltered sunny focal point—spots creating the most hospitable and charming setting. These are the strong points of your garden. *Don't even consider* plunking down a predictable angular flower bed surrounded by its own predictable picket fence in the middle of your lawn and calling it a garden. What does it relate to? And, please, do not stick to a careful row of azaleas or anything else to cover the foundation of your house and hope to find fulfillment. Enhance what you have. Take everything into account. Do not impose a garden on your property like a foreign element—look for spots naturally begging for attention. Which is the area that will make the best canvas for your very first garden picture? That's what you want to find.

Think of making your garden into your own personal vision of virtual reality. Your garden is not a flat, one-dimensional object to be enjoyed from a single, fixed perspective. Your whole property is subject to becoming a 360-degree enchanted world to be appreciated from all angles. By altering it, adding to it, and moving things around, you can create a wonderland, which can be just as quirky as Alice's if you allow it.

The bases of trees are natural starting-off points. So is a gate, a wall, and any undulation of your ground even modestly suggesting a hill. They all can be capitalized upon with just a frisson of imagination. Watch the sun as it travels along its path during the course of a day, and focus on where the light is in the morning and how it changes throughout the day and affects different areas at distinct times. In every description of every plant you will encounter some mention of sun: "likes afternoon sun"; "sun or light shade"; and the dreaded (for me) "full sun." It has been my experience that everything loves sun (with the exception of those woodland wonders). Most flowering plants can't seem to get enough of it, so make good use of those golden rays where you find them. This is not to say that shady spots are to be ignored. My huge familiarity with the many remarkable things to be grown in shade is the flip side of my big-beautiful-trees coin. With no such thing as full sun anywhere, I prudently preserve my sunniest spots to grow the real baskers like iris, poppies (real poppies, *Papaver orientale*, not those common-looking, orange, annual things from California), asters, peonies, and foxgloves.

Balance this perfect little niche where the sun shines with how you use your property. What you see as you come and go from your house, its porch, deck, or drive, will most likely dictate where you put your initial energies and how you establish your priorities. It makes no sense to create an arbored path in an area where you never walk, especially if the expanse between your front door and driveway is an eyesore. Although it is wonderful to come upon a surprise garden patch where one would least expect it, that can come in time. First things first. Use the natural beauty of your land; enhance it; make it better. Your initial gardening goals are to attend to what you already have, touch it up, reinforce strengths and disguise weaknesses.

Having cruised the neighborhood and assessed your own grounds, it is now high time to make the first of countless trips to your local nurseries. Bear in mind all the dazzling things you've spotted on your plant-hunting sojourns and are dying to grow. I am in the fortunate position of having three great nurseries in my area, about six with individual strong points, and a few mediocre ones, all within a twenty-minute drive. It is very important to seek out *every one* in your vicinity before you spend one serious dime. Scout them all. Don't jump to the conclusion that the first one you see is sufficient and seems to have everything. No nursery has everything. In fact, most nurseries specialize. Though it takes more time and energy, it makes much more sense to buy your shrubs from the one with the largest healthy, perhaps homegrown, assortment than to buy your shrubs in a nursery that concentrates primarily on annuals and herbs.

The purpose of nursery hunting is not so much a matter of price, though I find some will invariably be more expensive on one thing and then, with no real pattern, cheaper on another. This I can't account for; but I do know there is no such thing as *the* best one. I hope you, too, have access to a selection of nurseries because I can't think of anything quite so depressing as being geographically stuck in a remote place with only one dreary garden center offering only the most predictable plants. Of course, you do have the catalogs, but they can never really replace the joy of buying something in full bloom at the nursery.

Because I am always looking for something singular, novel, or in keeping with my color schemes, during the height of the nursery season I visit at least three each week. You never know what you may find. On a given day, even the couture of the East Hampton nurseries (it's an ongoing race between The Bayberry and Marder's) can be fiercely lacking in, say, delphiniums when the only thing really obsessing you is delphiniums. Buckley's on the very same day, is perhaps packed with the most glorious assortment of said delphiniums you have ever seen in shades of blue in serious competition with the sky. There is no way you can have a really interesting garden with only one nursery source.

Don't be intimidated by the nurseries—they're *supposed* to be knowledgeable and you should feel free to ask questions. By the same token, don't fall into the trap of becoming so chummy with a particularly friendly staff person that you feel compelled to buy something. Of course, milk these nursery pals for any information they might provide, but don't succumb to their sales chitchat unless you are perfectly in love with a plant or convinced it is the only thing that will do for a certain spot crying out in your garden.

Your local nurseries are not only marketplaces of gardening, they can also be a vast source of information and education. In my first gardening summer, armed with my very elementary Ortho books, *All About Annuals* and *All About Perennials*, plus Nicola Ferguson's packed-with-information tome *Right Plant, Right Place*, I would arise at the crack of dawn to be at the nurseries when they opened. Up and down the rows, in and out of the beds I would prowl, and whenever something appealing was spotted, I would break open my trusty books, figure out what kind of plant it was, what it needed, and if it made any sense in my scheme. In the very beginning, I admit I didn't even know the difference between an annual and a perennial; so I would begin by looking up such rudimentary concepts. You see, I didn't even realize at the time that nurseries separate annuals from perennials—all I had was a vague notion about gardening by color and knew I detested marigolds. Right from the start, I wanted nothing to do with a garden grounded in a pastiche of different colors—especially bright oranges and yellows. In those earliest of gardening days, dreams of Vita Sackville-West's white garden at Sissinghurst had already seeped into my brain, although I didn't know at the time she was to become my gardening role model. I had, in fact, been fascinated by her long before ever giving thought to a garden. I was smitten by *Portrait of a Marriage*, an incredible account of her highly individual lifestyle written by her son, Nigel Nicolson. This book had a huge impact on me twenty years or so ago when I first arrived in New York with more than my fair share of stars in my eyes. The eccentric lives of Vita and her husband, Harold, and all their fascinating cronies and lovers were to be the barometer for the life I imagined I would lead. However, even in the heady '70s, their lifestyle was a little too unorthodox even for me, and so I made do with more conventional relationships. But I was truly taken with Vita's look, although it took me a while to realize that she was usually photographed in her gardening outfit! Ine*vita*ble, in*vit*ing *vita*l, Vita—*what a girl*!

With Vita in mind, and the sun shining most brightly in the morning on the west side of the house, I began hacking away at underbrush and unruly woody shrubs to make a garden space. Between the pool, graciously surrounded by golden cypress trees, and the house was a big bramble of unsightly overgrown honeysuckle, with a few huge old evergreen trees growing up in their midst. Instead of the bramble, I decided I would plant a white garden, just like Vita's at Sissinghurst. After hours of snipping, clipping, and pulling, however, it was clear I was getting nowhere. To boot, the guy who cuts our lawn made the discouraging comment, "The more you cut away, the more dead stuff you're going to find, and the browner and sadder it is going to get." No way was this big untidy jungle going to disappear through my meager efforts. So, with tempting visions of a new garden and an expanded property to draw him into my scheme, I coaxed my dear Irving into abandoning his fixation with televised baseball and enlisted him into the clearing mode. Well, Paul Bunyan has nothing on Irving once he gets into it. This day was the first of many rabid clearing days that eventually transformed masses of ugly old twiggy brown stuff into a pond, our hammock grove, the white garden, a second-cutting garden, my rain-forest emulation—and we're still clearing to this day.

My white garden started out in maybe thirty or forty square feet with white pansies as its mainstay (although this is almost unbelievable to me today—I have silly pictures to prove it). I also planted fleeting white alyssum, white peonies that finally bloomed after four years, and something called *Lysimachia clethroides* or "gooseneck loosestrife." I fell in love with my lysimachia at a nursery and wasn't at all dismayed when I read in one of my books it "can be invasive." This didn't mean much to me until a few years later when I realized it was threatening to overtake the entire garden. Take heart, however. Though aggressive, to be sure, it's controllable, especially if caught in the early stages. When you are beginning a garden, it seems impossible there could ever be anything growing in too much profusion because whatever you plant never seems enough, never matches the plentiful pictures, and never seems as significant in your garden as it did at the nursery. Not so with this beauty; after only one year my lysimachia was a sight to behold. Mama Nature in her wisdom has counterbalanced the negative rampant aspect of this plant by seeing to its delicacy and gracefulness—just the qualities you want tons of. Imagine a gooseneck (literally) made up of hundreds of tiny white individual florets that nod at you like a ballerina *en pointe*. I mean, what could be better than to have masses of something you really like, even if it means every spring spending an hour or two pulling it out where it's unwanted or interfering with other charming things. Be sure to buy this plant—but *not* the other lysimachias, most of which bear a homely yellow flower and look like weeds.

Mr. Gooseneck is now center in my large white garden, which spans a good six hundred feet or more. Though the garden looks nothing like Vita's, by midsummer such an extravagance of whiteness is blooming that the house it totally obscured from the pool. The lysimachia is surrounded by at least sixty different plants: most perennial, many bulbous, and very few

Struggling *Lysimachia* and *Platycodon* in the first gardening
summer (inset) grew into this beautiful flowering abundance
in just a few short years.

annuals. And so the white garden stays white, really white, from May to October. Heartening, isn't it, to know you can do this too—create something heavenly from absolutely nothing—once you learn about bloom cycles and really become adamant about filling every available inch of earth with something pleasing.

But at the beginning, when gooseneck was acquired, I knew only what charmed me at the various nurseries, which pictures appealed to me in the catalogs, and what popped out while combing through my books. For the first year or two, prose, poetry, biography—all genre of reading matter—became inconsequential in my pursuit of a gardening education. I truly knew nothing, there were no grandiose gardens in my past, not even an old family plot of peonies for me to nurture. The sum and substance of my gardening knowledge was how big was each bouquet from my current boyfriend, how amazingly Paul Sinclaire could transform my apartment for photo shoots by joining forces with some great floral designer like Michael Fenner, or which designer was trying to outdo the other with bouquet size in the scramble for floorspace in my then very sought-after stores. At the height of the Japanese fashion craze in the mid-eighties, after I opened that enormous, concrete, ultimate definition of minimalist aesthetic in SoHo for Rei Kawakubo/Comme des Garçons, so many flowers came pouring into my hotel room at The Okura in Tokyo that I needed a second room to accommodate me, all my fashion paraphernalia, and the flowers. All these flowers were certainly gorgeous, but with the exception of maybe a lily, a tulip, and a rose, I couldn't have named them, much less have known how one would go about growing them.

Now smug when faced with any bouquet, I'm as familiar with most plants as if they were old friends, and Latin names come pouring out of me like a near second language, although my pronunciation occasionally leaves something to be desired. (In discussing the Greatest Hits Plant List at the end of this book I give you the phonetics, so you too can be glib when it all becomes second nature.) The engaging thing about the Latin names is that they are one of the rare pieces of information on earth that is truly universal. Once you get the hang of them, you will find they are actually helpful, descriptive, and much more meaningful than colloquial Albanian or Sanskrit. I have felt no small elation when able to identify the myriad flowers overflowing the vase on the lunch table at, say, Club 55 in St. Tropez, and have all the worldly French waiters nod in understanding and applaud my effort when I point to *Physostegia*, *Allium*, and *Monarda*. If I said instead their common names—obedient plant, flowering onions, and bee balm—not only would it sound pathetic, it would be completely unintelligible and my gardening knowledge triumph would pass unnoticed. You will also find the Latin useful when dealing with the occasionally haughty nursery person, or if you're trying to find or describe plants in various regions where the common names vary greatly from place to place or become meaningless outside your usual beat.

Although not a certified card-carrying member of the Linnean Society of London, I much admire the wonderful and incredibly busy guy, Carolus Linnaeus, who dreamed up the extremely sensible system for classifying and naming all our plants and trees. He also extended his foresight to minerals and animals; but we won't dwell on them here. For nearly 250 years, the entire world has embraced his system because it works so well. You will notice at the nurseries and in all your gardening books and catalogs (at least, any worthwhile catalog that might tempt you to order) most things well labeled bear a three-name description. The first capitalized word is the *Genus*. This is the main name of a given plant group and usually can be traced back to the structure of the plant or has some other purposeful relationship to the thing itself. The second word, in small (lowercase) letters, is the *species*. This name is often the real clue as to what to expect from a given plant because it is usually a description of some significant characteristic or a metaphor of some sort. These descriptive species names fall into four basic categories:

1. Names that indicate where the plant came from; for example, *nipponicum* (Japan) or *hispanica* (Spain). This helps to indicate whether or not you might grow it in your yard. Obviously you cannot expect much luck with something labeled *aethiopica* or *africana* if you live in Maine. If you are in New England, you can hardly miss with *novae-angliae*, which translates as "New England." *Novi-belgii*, however, is a complete mystery—it translates as "New York"—which only proves that there are some things you just have to remember.

2. Names that describe the general habitat of a plant; for example, *maritimus* (by the sea) or *montanus* (of the mountains) or *polaris* (of or from the North Pole), and what could be more immediate than *rusticanus* (pertaining to the country) or *solaris*, which means you definitely do not plant it at woods' edge because it is "of the sun."

3. Names that describe a feature or habit of the plant. This might be color (*alba* is white, as is *virginalis*; *caerulum* is blue, *purpea* purple, etc.), or it might be size: It doesn't take a genius to figure out words like *giganteus, grandis, magnus, maximus, elephantum, titanus,* and *spectabilis* are telling you to expect this one to be large and showy; and on the other hand, what would you expect from a species called *compactus* or beginning with *micro* other than it be small. The names can also indicate something about a plant's leaves: *sempervirens* means evergreen and *ovatum* explains that the leaves are egg-shaped. And then there is a large group of miscellaneous names that might indicate scent: *odoratum* means it smells sweet, *fragrans* means it smells especially sweet, and *foetidum* (as in fetid) means it stinks. Or a name can indicate style: *pendula* is weeping, *horizontalis* means it will spread, and *muralis* means, conveniently, you can grow it on walls. Once in a blue moon, I suppose, Carl couldn't figure out any characteristic striking enough to be noteworthy and would finally resort to *ambigua* and *confusa*. I actually like those terms, as well as *vulgaris*. It makes it so much more human.

4. Lastly, there are names that commemorate people. These do not tell you much about the plant, but I'm sure the various horticulturists and botanists were happy to be remembered.

The third, unitalicized word in a plant's proper name, if set off by single quotation marks, is the 'hybrid' or 'cultivar' and refers to what man has added, and continues to add to the horticultural picture. New introductions are made every day by crossing species or existing cultivars to come up with new colors and more bounteous plants. This can be quite graphic as well, as in *Syringa vulgaris* 'Little Boy Blue'—a blue, dwarf lilac.

So, there you have it. Now instead of perceiving botanical Latin as a hodgepodge of mumbo jumbo meant to confuse you, it is my hope that you begin to see how it can set you straight and help you. Get comfortable with the Latin names of things you are growing in your own garden right away; it will give you the sense of being much more the flower sophisticate.

YOUR LOCAL NURSERIES

As you start getting comfortable with the language of plants, you must also try to get familiar with your nearby nurseries so you can more easily spot their specialties and identify the kind of plants you are looking at. At the beginning of my gardening mania, I became attached to one nursery, Joseph Hren, because it was easy to figure out—every area was clearly marked and labeled—and so I kept going back there to buy perennials because I could find what I needed so easily. Not realizing at the time that this nursery's forte is shrubbery, ground covers, and garden tools, I had no idea that their offering of perennials is nearly the mottliest in town. Most nurseries have a scheme for separating plant categories. Once you are able to recognize it, you can much better assess where to go for what.

Generally, the first plants you see flanking the nursery's street side are the freshest, the most abundant, and those currently in bloom. However, just because something's blooming in the nursery in May doesn't necessarily mean you should expect it to be in bloom the next May after it has lived a year in your garden (assuming it's a perennial, of course). Often the nursery stock has been raised in a greenhouse and forced into an earlier bloom than its natural cycle. This is another one of those things you will come to know. Perennials are usually the most unattractive of a nursery's offerings, so you rarely find them at the front. They don't have so much to say for themselves as they might be on their way to bloom or have just finished. At best, you might find a quarter of a nursery's perennial stock in bloom at any given time. This is when your picture books *really* help, particularly if you are crazy about the leaf but haven't the vaguest what the flower is like or its color. Usually you will find perennials in gallon containers and grouped together, most often on the ground, though a few nurseries put them on tables. In my first few summers, I was constantly hauling home post-bloom peonies, iris, and columbines that looked half dead, but I had high hopes they would return next summer in all their glory just like the alluring pictures. Some did. Some didn't.

Though bloom time for perennials is usually much shorter than for annuals, annuals are an every-year chore of replacement and never as substantial, while perennials become good old dependable friends. Over the years many of them increase in size and strength and will turn into something much more spectacular than any annual ever could. Also, there is a much broader spectrum to choose from, as they range in form from ground covers to subshrubs. They are definitely the mainstay of any flowering garden.

Although many tropical perennial plants are regarded as annuals here, true annuals are fibrously rooted plants with weak systems that live only through one cycle of bloom. Annuals come in flats, which are those tray-like things with subdivisions of four or six plantlings in little plastic cubes. Customarily the flats are laid out on tables, and you can spot this area of the nursery most easily because it's the most colorful. It doesn't make sense to buy less than half a flat because your display will just be too meager, which you definitely don't want. Many annuals, like the ubiquitous impatiens, bloom all summer and well into the autumn; but then that is that. Once finished, they are yesterday's news and ready for the garden trash. But they are handy as fill-ins for garden bare spots and can be used to replace spring and early summer bulbs while they are dying down. There are actually some annuals more appealing than the above-mentioned impatiens and the loathsome marigolds: Cosmos look like small white, pink and fuchsia mallows and bloom profusely on fairly strong stems (but not strong enough to withstand a good wind, so they need to be supported) and can easily grow to six feet; cleome (spider flowers) also grow quite tall and are wonderful to look at with their dense cluster of long-clawed petals; and nasturtiums have lily-pad-like leaves and pansylike flowers that come in gorgeous shades of salmon and deep dark burgundy (occasionally some orange ones sneak in too, but you can't have everything). Other annuals bearing consideration in my book are heliotrope (bronze leaves and purplish flower bracts); petunias, which come in glorious colors; celosia (cockscomb), which is intriguing with its velvety textured plume-feathered flower spikes in fantastic shapes; and if you must have impatiens, at least grow the New Guinea strain, as they sport more formidable leaves, often variegated, and bigger flowers in better colors.

Trees, shrubs, and large vines usually border the nursery and require significant attention as most will be with you forever. Depending on the extent of this periphery, which can sometimes go for acres, you can tell how serious any given nursery is about this classification. It's always best to check out this section for things in flower—dogwood, magnolias, and weeping cherries in spring; rhododendron, lilac, and wisteria a little later; hydrangeas and crepe-myrtle in summer. Always buy a flowering tree or shrub *in bloom*; it's the only way to be

Some worthwhile annuals: clockwise from upper right—cosmos, petunias, celosia, New Guinea impatiens, divine datura (actually a tropical perennial), cleome, all surrounded by a heavenly border of morning glories.

sure you're getting a flowering specimen and not a deadbeat. The stuff that really holds your garden together are these grander plants: you need them as backdrops, as focal points, to soften harsh edges, and to make transitions. Don't get so carried away with the smaller flowering plants in the beginning that you ignore this most significant and critical category, the way I did for a while before wising up. The important shrub and ornamental or flowering tree categories should be among your first purchases. You want to start them on the road to fabulousness as soon as possible.

If the nursery is well organized, the trees and shrubs should all be tagged and priced. Do bear in mind, however, that the price will increase by 40 or 50 percent (depending on the policy of the nursery) when they politely ask, "Would you like us to deliver and plant this for you?" So, be prepared: they are not just being friendly. Of course, if you want to haul it home somehow and dig the huge hole yourself, well, that's fine, and you're back to the original price plus some peat moss. However, the additional money not only saves you the problem of transporting the big thing and digging that vast hole, it also guarantees the hardiness of whatever it is you have bought—like insurance. Generally, it is worth the extra dough for really big, tough-to-plant things.

If the nursery is one big greenhouse, it will typically be most interested in selling annuals, and maybe some herbs. You usually have to poke around in the back of these greenhouse affairs to get a real feeling of whether or not there is more to it than meets the eye. Often, too, the greenhouse-types will offer potted plants for indoors, or houseplants. My affinity is not really toward these houseplants, except for my spectacular *Clivia*, because in winter the sunny parts of the house are so full of tender plants resting indoors during the cold months that there is no need for anything like houseplants—and in summer, well, then you have the great outdoors. I largely forego the unrelieved greenery of most houseplants and find it more interesting to grow things inside like calla lilies, tropical bulbs, and to maintain my passion-flower vines.

In most nurseries, you will also find a covered or arbored section. In the best of these, hanging baskets will be overflowing with cascades of tenderly beautiful begonias, and fuchsias will dazzle you with their harlequin-like shape and colors. Make sure when you are smitten by any of these things that you likewise put them in a sheltered shady spot with indirect light. At first, I must confess, it never even occurred to me that these covered shady nooks were anything more than the nursery's penchant for charming outdoor architecture. It took a while for it to sink in that another thing the nursery display clues you into is what conditions the various plants like—such as the perennials being on the ground in full sun, the woodland plants grouped together in the shade, the tenderest plants under cover or in a lath-house, etc. Take note.

Ground covers, though extremely meaningful in any gardening situation, don't seem to warrant any definite pattern in the nurseries. They come in flats and pots, are sometimes on the annual tables and often mixed with the perennials. If the nursery has segregated them, look for the unmistakable ivy and you will usually find the *Ajuga, Pachysandra, Asarum* and *Epimedium* (two of my heart-shaped favorites), with *Sedum* and *Liriope* not far off. Sometimes you might even find them kept among the shrubs. You have to look for them, but please *don't ignore them* just because they seem dull in comparison with everything else. Ground cover is like the gesso on a canvas before you paint it, it fills in all the areas between the flowers or grows abundantly at the edge of a border or woods. Many times ground covers are preferable to grass, because of their vastly more interesting leaf shapes and texture, and most bear flowers at one point or another, though these may be fleeting. We will talk much more about all the various kinds of ground cover when we get to the good part about what to actually plant in your garden.

The last thing you might want to track down in your local nurseries are herbs. This is another pretty ragtag-looking group usually; but they add that homey touch and satisfy your urge to eat from your garden without requiring you to plunge into vegetable gardening in a wholehearted way. Growing your food is an entirely different exercise than creating a self-fulfilling flower garden. I neither have the room, the sun, nor the desire; but I do engage in a little basil, parsley, and lavender at the end of the cutting garden nearest the kitchen door. These couldn't be easier, and the pooch and I both occasionally indulge in eating some leaves as we pass by.

I hope that all of these various nursery divisions will now be clear as you delve into your local offerings. If your town is on the same wavelength as mine, you will find the various nurseries becoming increasingly more sophisticated and selective each year. I read somewhere, not so long ago, that horticulture has been the fastest growing industry in America over the past five years. If cashing in on this trend means the nurseries just get better and better—well, that's fine with me.

In my initial nursery forays, the white garden was only one of the main schemes. I also had designs on a deep, dark red garden (a dramatic gesture and the closest thing to black in the plant world) and that most elusive of garden colors: blue. Though much conscientious effort has been made to remain true to blue, it has evolved into a bluish kind of mauvey, purpley, sometimes even pink statement; but the pinks are all pale and very subdued. The blue border is cool and captivating, and the challenge of maintaining its blueness is one of those fascinating garden-making fantasies.

With the nurseries as my main initial source, the rudiments of my first three gardens were created. Six springs later I still judge the progression of the season by things planted in the first year or two—many of which are now commendable, if not splendid. Others, of course, are long gone. The most excruciatingly slow and difficult development has been the blue(ish) garden, which is also the largest. Directly across from the main entrance to the house, it began as a spotty planting in front of the woods facing the main door, but has gradually and painstakingly evolved into the anchor of what I call the "serpentine border." Running almost the entire length of our land, it has now softened to blend in with the woods' edge, which has been cut back, cajoled, and altered to achieve a harmony between itself (the background) and the plantings. Three or four years of talking, planning, and digging occurred before this serpentine border actually took shape; but it is now what its name implies—sinuous and subtle as it slinks in and out of the woods.

Each year we come up with new ideas and ways to make the border better and deeper, to find new niches, to clear more woods—all part of the joy of the gardening exercise. With each season and each discovery, you realize there is always one more step to make your garden more unified, natural, and spectacular at the same time, or as the Garden Tour Guru said, "More artistic."

It is my task to emphasize that you must never underestimate the impact of your local nurseries on your garden. Of course, there are the catalogs, and later on every significant thing I've come to learn about them will be imparted to you, including how to use them, for what, which are important and vital, and which to absolutely ignore. The catalogs occupy you during winter, and there are definitely areas of your garden better served by scrutinizing, judiciously ordering, and planting some things from tubers, bare roots, and fledgling plants; but it's the nurseries that keep you going *when the garden is actually growing*. You can't fill a maddening bare spot in the middle of summer by placing a mail order for some on-the-come shrub or plant, arriving a week later at best even if you fork over the extra $15 for speed delivery. For all the glorious pictures in the fancy full-color catalogs and all the wordy descriptions in the more erudite ones—there is nothing like the tactile, sensuous event of being able to see, feel, and smell the next thing to highlight your very own yard. The nursery offerings usually cost about twice as much as the catalog's, but the catalog plants often arrive only half there (a mere ghost of the tantalizing photo)—so in terms of dollars there is an equality.

Once you've tracked down your ideal selections at the nursery, be discriminating. There will always be one plant that's bigger, plumper, and showier than the rest of the lot. Lean toward ones that are root-bound and pot-bound—their working systems are *really* in place. When you get these advanced pot-bound beauties home, it's usually easiest to cut the container away with your sharp pruner and then knead the roots apart—you know, loosen them up, let them breathe, welcome them properly into the nice earthen hole you have prepared for them. Really step among the pots in the nursery rows, scatter them around, and wade through the selection. Differentiate which are the most thriving, with the fullest growth habit. Choose those with the most buds, the healthiest leaves, and the least weeds or any other signs of weakness to bring home. This is no time to make rash decisions or to be subtle.

If you get stuck in the rut of one or two nurseries because they are closer, they deliver, you can charge there, the guy who carries your plants to the car is to die for, whatever, you are doing a disservice to your garden. It will then become a servant to that nursery's taste (or commercial nod) and not the personal vision you can create by extracting the details of your dream garden from many sources. It's worse than dressing from head to toe, right down to your underwear, in Donna Karan. At least she has cadres of minions who sort out all the fashion trends, and from this she boils down her collection into a unified, while still diversified, whole. You can bet at any one nursery there are no teams of designers slaving over color palettes or knee-deep in worldwide source books laboring feverishly to offer you the most scintillating cross section of flora to be grown in your region. Most likely, you will be subject to either what is commercially most in demand or, more interesting but still hardly covering the spectrum, the idiosyncratic specialization of a few dedicated souls. Without a doubt, the best way to insure that your garden is as diverse and robust as possible is to involve as many nurseries in its making as you can conceivably find.

Late in July, in anticipation of the judgmental visit of Mr. Garden Tour, who includes or rejects you depending on his take on your garden on the particular day he views it, I went on a desperate nursery jaunt to come up with some last-minute looks. I needed fill-ins where June bliss was long gone and the end-of-summer beauties hadn't kicked in yet: I was looking for some leafy things to plant in places where leafing was still scant and I was desperate to find color or height or cover to disguise a few glaring spots so sore they might have had neon arrows pointed at them. After all, you cannot really conduct a grand tour on less than an acre, thus everything there had to be *really* gorgeous.

At the end of July there are scarce choices at the nurseries. The mail-order catalogs aren't even functioning then. It's not unlike trying to buy a bathing suit in June when you really need one and invariably the stores are filled with suede coats and cashmere sweaters. "Slim pickings" became the byword as I went from nursery to nursery.

On the first day I scouted the furthest venues, venturing forty minutes away from home to find a pot of perfectly colored petunias but not much else, and finally wound up at Marder's where they were displaying a most intriguing patch of never-seen-before locally late-blooming perennials. Marder's is smart—it's trying hard to be a twelve-month-a-year business, or at least a nine-month one, and is succeeding in out-bayberrying The Bayberry—which, incidentally, I frequent less and less since vivacious Mario departed to open his charming shop, Casa el Patio. Anyway, at Marder's I scooped up a few really abundant ferns, a breed of *Helleborus* I'd never seen before, and three fat *Trycirta hirta*, which were about to burst into their beautiful, though transient, little orchidlike flowers.

At the same time, I noticed that Marder's had a big field overflowing with pots of *Clematis montana rubens*. The nursery must have made a very good deal on this purchase from a trusted clematis farm or severely overestimated the area's desire for this fantastic flowerer, because they had hundreds of them. I made a mental note of this deluge, figuring they would still have plenty at half-price in November. Even though *montana rubens* is among the least spectacular of clematis flowers, they make up in profusion what they lack in flower size, are one of the easiest clematis to grow, and bloom the earliest. This voracious vining capability would be just the thing to cover a big barren fence we'd recently been forced to erect around our property.

The town of East Hampton, which is always interested in keeping the local contractors busy, last summer decided to renege on the grandfather clause about fences around one's swimming pool. Suddenly, it was pronounced that "if you have a pool (and even if you have had the same pool in the same place for the last thirty years, even though you do not have kids, and even though no neighboring children exist—let alone have been on your property or, God forbid, drowned in your pool—it did not matter)—you must erect a fence."

Obviously we weren't going to build a fence right around the pool, so up the fence went around the entire back half of the property, creating a new corner which pleaded to be cleared for a new cutting garden. Well, thanks to good old Marder's half-price sale, sure enough, six fat clematis were there for the taking at $20 instead of $40, so come May we should have a back fence that looks like it has long been there, smothered in tough flowering vines.

The next day I explored the nearer nurseries, not yet satisfied that I was worthy of inclusion on next summer's Animal Rescue Fund benefit, dubbed the East Hampton Garden Tour. For the most part, the offerings at my local haunts turned out to be dregs of the same old tired stock I'd been seeing for the last three months. There was pot after pot after pot of *Macleaya cordata* (plume poppy, one you want to stay away from unless you have garden space to spare like mad), and row upon row of fading annuals not to be touched with a ten-foot pole (or even a long-reach pruner). But with an indefatigable spirit, an eye peering in every corner, and an unquenchable craving to be included on this tour, I did find some bountiful begonias at McConnell's (real tuberous ones, not those insipid bedding things), some striking white caladium, an odd dwarf umbrella pine, and one or two other little just-right-bright things here and there.

The moral of this particular story is that you must go out and get to know your nurseries. The more in your repertoire, the better. When they are all at their peak in May and June it can be especially confusing. This is why you must become well acquainted with them in the rudimentary months of April and September when it is clearer where their priorities lie. At the end of summer and into autumn, it takes much more imagination on their part to get you to part with your precious gardening dollars. If you spend them in the wrong place, you are forever lost.

CAVEAT EMPTOR

Speaking of precious dollars, don't be too anxious to establish charge accounts in every single nursery. It's easy to say, "Oh, charge it to me," instead of digging around for some cash or remembering to have a credit card that will withstand another purchase, but it's often a big mistake. I've bought too many plants on an oh-charge-it-whim that had already failed in my garden but I bought them again because it was just so *easy*. Don't be rash and do this. Once you know your nurseries really well and feel certain about which ones are for you, then establish one—maybe two—charge accounts; but no more. In my initial eagerness, I had about ten active nursery accounts and found myself hauling home unwanted things or plants I knew better than to buy. And then I had to pay for them at the end of every month.

A long time ago—eighteen or twenty years—I was a buyer at Henri Bendel when Henri Bendel was "IT," when Geraldine Stutz was the Queen of Fashion, and the Fifty-seventh Street arena was a breeding ground for all that was hip, new and fabulous, or quiet and cool in its chicness. We had a protocol: on Friday mornings we opened our doors to any vagrant persons calling themselves a designer or stylist who dreamed of seeing their clothes in Bendel. Legions of well-meaning people with true and honest intentions lined up. Some talented. Some mediocre. Some confused. Some simply awful. Often they waited in line for six or eight hours to see me or Jean Rosenberg (the High Priestess to Geraldine's Queen) or Claire or Marion. There weren't very many of us then. After all those hours of meeting designers, my taste buds began to blur, and who could tell what was fabulous and what just looked better than the stuff from the last bright-eyed hopeful with hopelessly lackluster clothes? At ten P.M. how could you tell the guy who'd persevered for eleven hours that he just didn't have a clue? It was hard, but also exciting, because once in a while somebody really great came along, like Zoran or Jeff Madfoff, or the guys from Go Silk; but usually I was so fatigued from sizing up merely okay clothes, that it became difficult to distinguish what was really good from what just had fortitude. And every now and then, a real barker would slip in. When these Friday night clothes arrived and took their place in the sacred basement receiving room, it was all too clear which had been bought in a rash of enthusiasm because they were gorgeous and which were there because I'd been too depleted or tired to make a wise judgment and it was easier just to buy them. In gardening, the product is different, but the criteria the same: "Too easy" can lead to poor choices and a static garden.

Too few sources and too many charge accounts will make you lazy. You might choose things that don't really work just because they are there and you really want to buy something. So you settle for something you tell yourself "will do." Invariably, it won't do. You are much more likely to ignore such unwise selections if you can't charge them; and even then, *caveat emptor*.

One last story about foolish garden spending:

On the first sparkling morning of Memorial Day weekend a few years ago, I was greeted in the kitchen by my stepdaughter, who was unconventionally up before me. Our Wendy has no real interest in the gardens, let alone any individual plants or their standards. In the five summers spent around here, not only has she never ventured to become involved in the digging or planting, she has seldom even been intrigued enough to ask, "What's the name of that one?" or even, "Can I cut some flowers to take back to the city?"

"Were you expecting a delivery this morning," she asked as I was struggling to wake up, "because there is a big bunch of plants and stuff in the middle of the lawn. But you know," she ventured further, "they don't look like *your* flowers, so maybe it's a mistake." Intrigued, I dashed outside to see what it was that made eternally uninterested Wendy offer such a discerning remark. Out on the lawn was the mottliest assortment of plant-life I have ever seen. Upon closer inspection I discovered that it was a misdirected delivery from Wittendale's, my least favorite nursery in town. My heart went out to whoever the proper recipients actually were. Probably some eager people who had hopes of beginning a garden on this very first official weekend of summer.

How sad I felt for them. Clearly their intention was to plant a garden themselves because along with the sorry selection of plants was peat moss and topsoil. The choice of plants was horrible; a pitiful melange of marigolds, the most common, runty-looking red impatiens (because red and orange are so lovely together, I guess), and some half-dead, leggy portulaca. Strangely out of place in this pathetic assortment was one (only one, of course) stunning dwarf delphinium in a great cobalt blue. The thought of stealing it briefly ran through my mind; but my consideration for the people waiting to receive this ambiguous, homely conglomeration got the best of me. After all, at least they should have one nice thing.

I'm sure these folks put themselves in the hands of the Wittendale's nursery people, since it's hard to believe that any homeowner or even home renter could make such a hideous choice of plants for themselves. But letting the nursery make the choice was the *easiest* thing to do. Big mistake. And not only did Wittendale's assemble, or condone the assembly, of this hideous assortment, it didn't even deliver them watered. Everything was dried out, limp and dismal. The moral of this story is not that Wittendale's is a lousy nursery (except for its sometimes interesting selection of cut flowers and greenhouse plants), but that whoever wasted $822 on this grisly array had simply not done his or her nursery homework in a town burgeoning with great nurseries. Get my point?

WHAT YOU

NEED: THE

IMPLEMENTS,

ACCESSORIES,

AND THE

CLOTHES

Tools. Sources.
Dirt Enhancers.
Mulches. Accoutrements.
Sensibly Chic Clothes.

Then all I need to do is run
To the other end of the slope,
And on tracts laid new to the sun,
Begin all over to hope.

Some worn old tool of my own
Will be turned up by the plow,
The wood of it changed to stone,
But as ready to wield as now.
  Robert Frost, "In Time of Cloudburst"

With a solid familiarity of your local nurseries in place, some glorious plants in mind, and a take on what part of your property to cultivate first—it is high time to outfit yourself in some worthwhile attire and, even more important, acquire some good tools. Though quite an array of implements is necessary, you do not need all thousand of them listed in the catalogs or on display in your fully stocked garden center. For those of you who are inveterate shoppers, however, this is the consummate opportunity to satisfy your shopping lust. Since these tools are going to come into contact with all the diverse elements, become an extension of your garden-ing soul, and must last a very long time, *buy good ones*. It makes no sense to start out with weak tools, cheap tools, or the very first tools you come across. Buy good ones to begin with because you will only wind up buying good ones in the end, after wasting time and precious gardening dollars better spent on a fabulous flowering magnolia.

This is one shopping spree you can actually feel good about because gardening tools *never* go out of style and therefore merit a serious investment. The truth is many of them have remained more or less the same since the beginning of recorded time. Think of countless drawings of cavemen laboring with shovels and clubs, plus the hundreds of ancient artifacts crowding museums which are various kinds of spades or other crude instruments used for tilling, plowing, and cultivating. Not that much has actually changed.

Much of what is interesting about gardening is the practice of honest labor. It is the rare career that provides you the opportunity to do anything really "hands on" or sweat. Yet it is this very involvement that makes the gardening process so personal. The construct that you yourself have created something with your own hands and your own good tools brings a particular kind of satisfaction.

THE TOOLS: HARDWARE

SHOVELS

The act of digging is the most profound of garden tasks, pun intended. To my knowledge, it has not been improved upon by any state-of-the-art technology, and it is the heart of all gardening chores. To do this age-old and respectable process justice, you need tools that suit you and will last.

First and foremost, you need a comfortable shovel. By comfortable, I mean one that fits *you* right. To determine this you must go to your chosen gardening center and try it on, as you would a new jacket or pair of shoes. If you have a shovel too big or too heavy, it will only overpower you and weigh you down; if it's too small, you will never get the leverage needed and will constantly be hunched over, which is not only an unattractive stance, it will wreak havoc on your back as well. For this personally comfortable shovel, definitely get one with a pointed tip, not a straight edge. The sort with the straight edge, called spades, I find much harder to use for general garden work. A shovel is what you want.

There is a right way to use your shovel and dig a hole. As elementary as this may sound, I explain it, because the digging of holes may be as alien to you as it was to me until my friend Steven Hamilton snickered at my pitiful attempt and showed me how it should be done. Steven is a poet, not a farmer, but his mother was a serious enough gardener to attain the stature of Garden Club president back home in Indiana, and therefore Steven is expert at hole digging.

So, imagine digging a hole. You don't use just your arms and back, which is how I did it before the great revelation; to really get that shovel under the earth, you use your feet. Stick the tip of the shovel in the dirt and then sort of kick it (or even jump on it, depending on how hard your dirt is) in order to loosen the earth, then repeat this process in a series of arcs until you have made a circle. Those back and arm muscles then come into play as you lift out the loosened-up dirt and pile it near your hole. It's a process like extracting the center out of a cake. Now that you've created the hole, continue to use your shovel to bail in some peat moss and cow manure, and then the shovel becomes a big stirrer to mix everything together—not unlike a whisk in cake-batter making.

Get a good shovel. Tell your local tool man you want one with a "solid-socket handle" and he'll really think you know your stuff. I learned this is the only kind to consider after explaining to the friendly Agway man how my shovel handle had irrefutably snapped in two while I was desperately trying to unearth a wanton and homely honeysuckle bush. He laughed this off, explaining I obviously didn't have a solid-socket handle.

You also will need a second, larger shovel, or spade, for grander chores like transplanting shrubs or planting trees. Surely you will not always feel like paying the nursery the additional 40 percent (or more) to plant things for you. If I can handle it and am confident the plant will survive my efforts, I plant the tree or shrub myself or persuade Irving to do a little hauling and digging, and we do it together, which is nicer.

TROWELS

Get three kinds of trowels. You need more than one, not only for the various chores requiring different sizes and types, but because they invariably get lost. With three, you have others to fall back on. Of course, whatever you lose you eventually find; but that may not be until lush summer has died back; and then, if the trowel is not stainless steel or good quality, it is rusted and dead. I heartily recommend stainless-steel tools, whenever you have a choice—no boring sanding and refinishing ever required for rust.

The three trowels you will need are:

A. the narrow blade

B. the basic standard

C. the indispensable long-handle

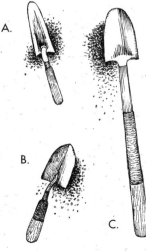

- A standard size trowel, the kind you see everywhere and use for everything. I must have about ten different versions, but my darling has a wooden handle, a black metal scoop, and is a bit oversized.
- A bigger, long-handled one, about twenty inches long, for holes not quite big enough to demand a shovel, as in planting nice healthy young perennials in four-inch pots. Also, if you are dealing with a tight spot and no room to kneel, this long-handled trowel allows you more reach. The Walt Nicke Company sells a great stainless one. (See the appendixes for more information.)

- A skinny one, the same length as the standard, about ten inches, but with a longer and much narrower blade. This is just right for crowded little chores like making the right size hole for certain bulbs like muscari and anemones and setting out bedding plants, which are annuals.

Aside from being constructed from stainless, trowels come in many configurations. There are molded ones made entirely of metal, which are okay but do not afford as flexible a feel. Wood-handled trowels in many shapes and sizes are a commodity in every worthwhile garden center and catalog. And there is plastic. The redeeming values of plastic trowels are no rust, and, because they usually come in jarring colors like bright orange and yellow, they are easier to find in the foliage. Because of my aversion to bright plastic in general, you don't find these at home in the honest environs of the Benson garden. The trowel is a tool you use and use and use, so you want quality. Try the various sizes and grip designs, because, as the shovel fits various bodies differently, so must the trowel be comfortable in your hand.

PRUNERS

The pruner is a particularly vital implement. I have two favorites. One I'm never without is a small all-metal affair painted black and operated by spring action with very fine, sharp blades. Although I first discovered it in Hong Kong, I've since ordered this pruner countless times from Smith & Hawken as I wasn't smart enough to buy dozens at ten dollars Hong Kong (which is about a dollar fifty in our dough) when the time was ripe. I've never been able to retrace my steps somewhere behind Cat Street and find that industrious Chinese man at his forge again, so Smith & Hawken it is. They don't always picture these wonderful pruners in their catalog, yet they always seem to keep them in stock and will gladly send one along if you request it by phone. Called their "Thinning Shears," at last look they were $16. Get two, since this is one of those items you use every single day and tend to misplace. It drives me crazy when I reach for it and can't find it and don't have a spare. I use this pruner for everything: deadheading, which is the rewarding job of removing faded flowers from a plant (just at the base of their stem) causing it to bloom much more profusely and not set seed; pruning, which is removing dead or unwanted branches from a tree or shrub; and flower cutting, which is, of course, the real joy of gardening. It's even possible to remove intimidatingly fat tree limbs with it, but I don't suggest this use because it's exactly how I always manage to screw up the alignment of my precious pruners, which leads to ruin. A big hearty recommendation for this superb tool.

A more sturdy pruner is needed for bigger jobs, such as the fat-limb removal just described. Felco is the Hermès of pruners. They are Swiss-made, precise, reliable, and never change. They even boast replaceable parts, twelve to be exact, and are guaranteed free repair of any manufacturing breakdown. My Felco was a Christmas gift, no less. A harried Irving doing last-minute stocking shopping was told by Larry Nathanson of the divine Grass Roots Garden in SoHo, "If she doesn't have a classic Felco No. 2, then what kind of gardener is she?" Figuring Larry knows his stuff, Irving bought this pruner although he swore it looked exactly like at least five other pruners hanging around my potting shed. Well, the Felco is so much better than the others, it is clear one Felco from the outset would have easily done the trick. So learn from me and buy a Felco to begin with, even though they cost twice as much as the ordinary brands; they are worth every one of the thirty-seven to fifty dollars that is their price range. Have a look at the whole line and choose the size right for you; they even have left-handed ones. They are easy to find or order.

Only recently I happened on the newly introduced ultimate Felco, one I had never seen for sale locally and couldn't recall seeing in any catalog; but there it was in our favorite knife, cutlery, and scissors shop on the via della Spiga in Milano. After a few hours of fashionable shopping, one understandably gets itchy, and this store is always a respite—an old-world assemblage of ivory-handled razors and peculiar scissors. We spied this fat new Felco gleaming down from the cutlery display and upon closer inspection ascertained it not only has a different blade angle (for heavy-duty and close cutting) but boasts the unique and innovative feature of a rolling, or rotating, handle. Of course, I had to have it, and it's wonderful. The handle you grip in your palm is fixed, but the other rotates as your fingers squeeze it; therefore, it is much more flexible and makes those tough limbs that much easier to remove. It is called Felco No. 7. Fortunately, you do not have to speed to via Spiga to purchase this great Felco. In the latest edition of *Garden Talk* by the Walt Nicke Company, what do you suppose is included? "Felco No. 7 and No. 10 [10 is the convenient left-handed one]: I think we paid an extra twenty bucks in Milano, but you can have it for a mere $52.95 from resourceful Walt.

the Felco lopper

favorite small metal pruner/shear

Loppers

When a cutting job is too big for your Felco, then you need a lopper. Both of these tools are correctly called *secateurs* and perform the same function. A pruner cuts smaller things, like woody vines and baby trees, and loppers are right for mature trees and gnarly old shrubs and spots you can't reach with your pruner. A lopper is basically a pruner with

the classic Felco #2

long handles and a bigger "jaw." Used with both hands, it provides more leverage and tolerance for loftier chores.

If you are attempting to cut something that is too big for a lopper, then you need a saw, an axe, or a knife. Not keen on jobs of this magnitude, I can't advise beyond suggesting you get somebody else to do your Bunyanesque chores. However, I do have a snazzy little curved Japanese saw in a nice wooden sheaf that is among the classic garden items sold by the Museum of Modern Art. It's been used on occasion, but mainly kept as a focal point in the garden shed because I simply adore the way it looks.

WEEDERS AND DIGGERS

Unfortunately you need many instruments to extract the weeds and grass invariably growing where you don't want them. Because weeds range from tiny but annoying clover to the most powerful strangulating vines that can actually achieve a three-foot growth in one week, you need various kinds of weeders. For manageable tasks, like the unearthing of compliant weeds, my preferred weeder is wood-handled with a long metal spike ending in a notched blade, called a "fishtail weeder." For dig-deeper jobs, and to uproot grass where you want to create an area for planting, there is another wood-handled wonder with a long, slender steel arm ending in a five-inch-wide, razor-sharp triangular blade. This is really good for getting underneath things with stubborn roots. It, too, comes in a left- and right-handed version and is called a "weed slicer." Smith & Hawken's seems the most finely honed. Weeders for getting between stones with a hooked end are dubbed "Cape Cod weeders." Another has a pronged end about three inches wide ideal for those really scraggly dandelions and other stubborn wretches. Last but hardly least, there is a weeder

the "U" and "V" weeders

the fishtail

the Cape Cod

the claw or "magic weeder"

the triangular weed slicer

with steel prongs like a curved fork or big claw. Walt Nicke adoringly refers to this one as "The Original Magic Weeder" and it's the best I've found to date to uproot the totally recalcitrant varieties.

There are nearly as many weeders as there are weeds, and you will find, haplessly, endless opportunities to use each. You will also find all weeders work better when the ground is soft— so seize any opportunity after a rain to put these tools to their best use and rid yourself of countless forms of unwanted vegetation fiercely competing with your lovely garden. Of course, you can go out and purchase demon chemicals like RoundUp and its many clones, but that kills everything and goes against Mama's strict principles. These chemical, blatantly nonorganic weed killers have some positive institutional uses or could be considered for clearing a clogged stone driveway, but they are not for the garden. Thwarting those weeds by digging them out with proper tools is the only way to go.

RAKES

You need two kinds of rakes: a big leaf rake and a little hand rake. The leaf rake is self-explanatory; but you also need it to smooth mulch and to level turned soil. A really good one from the dependable Walt Nicke Company is called "The Great Adjustable Rake." It is all metal and easy to adjust from a width of seven to twenty-three inches. When narrowed, it comes in handy for getting into the border or between shrubs. Fully extended, it does all the big, obvious chores like autumn-leaf cleanup.

The little hand rake is used all the time. Once you have shoveled the dirt out of a hole, there is all this detritus left over on the lawn. The hand rake is perfect for getting rid of it and for clearing remnants of mulch and so forth. I also keep a common little whisk broom in my garden cart for tidying up around rocks and anywhere there are little crevices.

A GARDEN CART

To haul your tools around, some sort of movable container is sorely needed. Since a gardening cart seemed like a nuisance when my gardening foray began, I tried to anticipate what might be needed on any particular gardening day and put it all in a chic basket to carry to that day's gardening venue. I learned quickly this never works. Inevitably the thing you need is the one thing you don't happen to have in your chic basket. You need a cart. Also, without a cart, it is impossible to manage the peat moss and cow manure or bonemeal or whatever the season dictates. The cart helps with hauling your plants around, too, and it's always convenient for carrying a bottle of Evian (or whatever your preference for intermittent garden refreshment), a good supply of plant markers, and the cordless phone.

A cart can't be too small because there must be room for many things: the two-cubic-foot bag of peat moss (which is the most manageable size), composted cow manure (which can be only found in a barely liftable forty-pound bag), and a selection of trowels, weeders, pruners, etc.

Yet a cart can't be too big, either, because the tendency to overload will manifest itself, and your burden will become so grandiose you won't be able to budge it, let alone maneuver along the garden paths. Shop locally and really scrutinize these carts. The one I did mail-order seemed ideal at that moment—right tires, black rubber body—but turned out to be as big as a tow truck. It has found its function during the autumn-mulch mode and other big chores, but a garden cart it's not.

What you want is a two-wheeled yard cart or utility cart that holds everything perfectly and is adaptable. Make sure you buy one with spoked pneumatic tires, not the kind of wheels that look as if they belong on a baby buggy because it will simply fall apart on the day you need it most.

Garden carts are not paradigms of balance, so be sure to arrange the weight inside so that the heaviest things are toward the back; otherwise, you will be faced with an overturned cart, which is a mess, a waste of time, and a total bore.

To carry your tools in an organized way inside the cart, find one of those divided wooden boxes normally used for picnic silverware or the strong polyethylene-that-looks-like-rubber "Tack Caddy" recently added to *Gardener's Eden* catalog at the astonishingly cheap price of $6.50. The box I really sigh for was pictured in an early 1992 issue of *World of Interiors*, my favorite of the voyeuristic other-people's-houses magazines. Dutifully, my credit card number was sent to Habitat in London to procure this tasteful, stained pine garden-tool-box with a lift-out tray for £25, but it never arrived. I keep expecting one of our beloved catalogs, which pride themselves on being members of the good-taste brigade, to knock it off, but so far no luck.

DEBRIS GATHERER

There is this bag called a "Bosbag" in the *Gardener's Supply Company* catalog. Despite its singularly unattractive name and bright green polyethylene makeup, you plainly cannot do without it. It folds up politely when not in use and then opens to a big receptacle of two and a half square feet that remains expanded just like you need it to do, holding all your weeds, clippings, and plant containers not worth saving.

Of course, a charming array of baskets and trugs is a more picturesque way to dispose of your unwanted garden debris; but believe me, having been through dozens of delightful baskets, not only are they never big enough, they eventually rot. All that wet leftover matter takes its toll, and the bottom putrefies. That's just how it is, so save your baskets and wicker for more winsome purposes and get a few of these ugly green Bosbags. They work fantastically well.

COMPOSTING INTENTIONS

Much of the gardening dregs gathered in your Bosbag are perfect fodder to empty onto a compost heap and produce the fabulous organic compost everyone raves about. I realize it's my moral obligation to the environment to sooner or later become one with this composting concept, but to date this has not happened. First, I can't figure out where to put the pile, especially as it needs sun—that rare commodity; second, despite reading countless descriptions, I don't really understand how compost works; and third and perhaps most significantly, it seems to me all this rotting humus is bound to attract even larger parades of slugs and other creatures I would prefer not to deal with any more than I already do. Therefore, procrastination has prevailed. I also have real concern about the compost itself containing all those weed seeds that are bound to gain readmittance into the garden—a concern also voiced by Hamlet.

> And do not spread the compost on the weeds to make them ranker.
> William Shakespeare, *Hamlet*, Act III, sc iv.

These apprehensions seem legit to me, but every time *The New York Times* or *American Horticulturist* (which is the official publication of the American Horticultural Society) writes yet another article about the virtues of composting, stirrings of guilt slither in among my conjurings of slugs. I continually toy with attempting this composting ritual behind the new fence, but my misgivings are still rather monumental.

KNEELING PADS

Besides the Bosbag, another unattractive green necessity is a foam-rubber kneeling pad. These cushions come in other colors, but the palette is nothing to rave about, so stick with green for these unsightly yet useful things. This pad fits ideally next to the peat moss in your cart and is ultra-necessary when the ground is wet or the situation smarmy, which is oddly enough the preferable time to do on-your-knees chores in the garden. All sorts of other kneelers and scooters are offered to keep you aloft from the damp dark dirt, but they all seem like excess baggage to me, especially the nineteen-pound wagonlike one fondly called "The Scoot-N-Do" by Gardener's Supply Company. The Bosbag kneeling pad works just fine.

WATERING ESSENTIALS

Water. You need it, of course. A garden needs three things: sun (which we cannot control or even augment, only make the most of), soil (which we can enrich with all sorts of products in the fertilizer, food, and mulch mode), and water. It is the most unusual of circumstances when nature provides enough of it in our domestic surrounds, so watering becomes a fundamental need. Even if you have the most sophisticated irrigation and sprinkling system known to modern man, you still need a good old pliable hose long enough to reach anywhere on your property that you are likely to plant. Sprinkler systems can break down; be chewed through by moles, voles, and all sorts of underground demons; can become morally objectionable if drought is terrorizing your region; and they simply cannot compensate when you need an abundance of water for a fresh planting. The only way to really welcome new babies into the garden is to really *soak the earth*.

Sprinkler systems are worthwhile for everyday watering, but if you are contemplating the installation of one—*Wait!* Hold off until you have a real feel for the extent of your garden, otherwise you will just keep ripping up earth to add more sprinkler lines as you become obsessed with beautifying new areas. I should know. Woody, our irrigation guy, has been patient with me. Each year as we clear new areas and plant new gardens, he reminds me that he has stretched our original sprinkler system to the max and it should be no surprise to me that some heads now spew out only scanty sprays.

So until your boundaries are more or less fixed, get a good hose and a few good Gardena sprayers. The "Four-In-One Multi Spray Nozzle" is as good as a hose nozzle gets. It does everything you need without ever having to change the apparatus. Also, it kindly clicks itself into a constantly "ON" position, so your hand does not become numb from applying all that pressure. Aside from nozzles, Gardena offers all sorts of ground sprinklers. Between the "Oscillating Sprinkler" and the "Six Pattern Sprinkler" there is no watering responsibility you can't control—and control you must.

> To enjoy freedom . . . we have of course to control ourselves. We must not squander our powers, helplessly and ignorantly, squirting half the house in order to water a single rose . . .
> Virginia Woolf, *The Second Common Reader*

Gardena is to watering tools what Felco is to pruners. Gardena is the best sprayer around and is available from many sources. It's made completely from plastic, which seems the best material for this wet exercise, and exists only in the peculiar color combination of gray and orange, but you can't have everything. Another good Gardena investment is the poetic but practical "Long Reach Water Wand." This is excellent for spritzing the back of the border and it can even reach across the pool or pond if you advance with a big, strong backhand motion. The

Long Reach Wand even comes with a clear plastic attachment for inserting fertilizer tablets (also made by Gardena, of course, as the tablets must be a sure fit), thereby accomplishing feeding and watering at the same time. Be sure to keep the fertilizer tablets dry until you use them, because once they get moist, they crumble and are useless, leaving a big mess and quite a few wasted gardening dollars.

PESTICIDE AND FERTILIZER SPRAYERS

Now that we have touched upon the watering of your coddled garden, there are other items to consider for distribution of liquid pesticides and fertilizers. In gardening, there are two dull but essential routines: fighting and feeding.

A compression sprayer for pesticides is easier to use and more effective than it looks. It is a metal can or tank with a pump and a hose attached. Avoid plastic—not only because it looks awful after the chemicals have had their way with it and it turns that horrid moldy-yellow color, but because the plastic absorbs the various chemicals and can defeat your purpose in the long run. Compression sprayers normally carry three gallons of whatever it is you need to apply, and unless you have a really gigantic area to cover, three gallons are usually more than enough. For specific jobs, you rarely have to fill it to the top, half-full will take care of a bed of twelve azaleas, sixteen holly (*Ilex*) bushes, and a grove of thirty rhododendron, and you will still have some left to splash on a flagging juniper.

Another sprayer, more finely tuned for fertilizers, is a more economical version of the aforementioned Long Reach Water Wand and attaches to your hose. Those Gardena specific fertilizer tablets don't go very far and aren't cheap (as far as I know, you do not get a good deal even if you buy in large quantity). The alternative is a plastic container with a spray nozzle built into its top that attaches directly to the end of your hose. It acts like a giant mister or a really abundant perfume atomizer. You put the fertilizer in the container—the instructions are delightfully easy to read—and the hose provides the diluting water, which means you don't have to lug around the big three-gallon thing to do the job. With the compression sprayers, you haul the whole concoction around; they even give you a strap so you can pretend it's a shoulder bag. With this screw-on sprayer, you only have to be concerned with dragging around the hose.

What fertilizers to put into these contraptions is another story. Being a perfectly honest gardener, I must admit that, with all of the time spent those first few years shopping and planting, reading and thinking about all the aesthetic considerations, I never did get around to fertilizing. Well, I did use the easy but expensive Gardena method. Subsequently, though, I became partial to the fertilizers and soil builders trademarked Roots Plus, which are all organic, applied with the sprayer that attaches to the hose, and always available from Gardener's Supply Company. Yet, early on with my huge share of successes, I truly believe Mama was on my side.

My rich East Hampton dirt (a tangible payoff for the enormous taxes we pay, though there's still no place to park for town residents) had been lying fallow for so long it probably rejoiced at being stirred up by my trowels and was delighted to share its nutrients with the plethora of new plant friends.

THE TOOLS: SOFTWARE

DIRT AND FERTILIZERS

Fertilizing is to plants what eating properly is to us. If they get too little or too much of one thing, they will be cooperative but prone to stress, just like we are. Simply put, trees, plants, and flowers need sixteen elements to photosynthesize. This is how they feed themselves using sunlight, water, and carbon dioxide. These sixteen elements, or nutrients, are the same as a balanced diet. The first three—carbon, hydrogen, and oxygen—you don't have to worry about because they come from the air and water. Provided you have a little breeze and douse your plants with water, no problems. The other thirteen nutrients are contained in the soil and are there, depending on the dirt, in varying degrees. Some are more important than others, such as nitrogen, phosphorus, and potassium—*The Big Three*. They are primary, and each does a specific job. Just as we know we need vitamin C to build up resistance and fight colds, and vitamin E is necessary for nice skin and healthy hair, our gardens, likewise, need their essential nutrients. *Nitrogen* promotes growth of the green part of the plant—the leaves and the stems (which sometimes are bronzish or golden, too). *Phosphorus* aids in the most obviously beautiful parts of the plant—helping to increase the flowers and fruit, as well as strengthen the roots. *Potassium* helps the phosphorus in the beauty business and also aids in the vigor of the plant, keeping it immune from disease and able to cope with stressful things, like freezing cold winters.

Therefore, if there is bountiful leafing and scant flowering, the plant needs more phosphorus. That's what all those numbers signify on fertilizer bags. A 5-10-5, for example, means equal amounts of the first and third life-givers: Nitrogen and potassium (or *potash* as it is often called), with twice as much phosphorus for flowering. This is really not such a difficult equation to comprehend once you have committed the three basic ingredients to heart. If you have any kind of decent dirt, these elements more or less take care of themselves. Only in extreme circumstances do you have to deal with anything more complicated than The Big Three Formula.

If your curiosity is so piqued you lie awake nights ruminating about what exactly is in your very own soil, there are a number of ways to find out. There are numerous books and magazine articles on the subject, but the easiest way is to acquire a pH Soil Test Kit which will tell you if your dirt is acid or alkaline (mine is slightly to the acid side). This answer, more or less, translates into which nutrients you have in abundance and which ones are scarce. If you want to be absolutely sure, every county in every state in our fair land is said to have a Cooperative Extension, which is a local agency of the Department of Agriculture and usually found at a local college. For free or just a few dollars, you can send them a sample of dirt from your very own yard and they will analyze it for you. My agricultural curiosity has not driven me to mail my dirt because my garden has been healthy just by design, using common sense, and asking lots of questions at the nurseries.

Though unromantic, there are certain practical concepts you need to know. Suffice to say, fertilizers are like friends of the earth, and you will probably need to use them somewhere along the line if you have a burning desire to make your 'Nikko Blue' hydrangeas really blue or crave an agapanthus bloom after a patient, but long, four-year wait. Certain flowers and shrubs favor certain elements, which you will discover as you go along. As far as nurturing, I am personally a big fan of the composted manure and organic humus in those cumbersome forty-pound bags— it goes in every hole I dig and welcomes every new plant.

DIRT ENHANCERS

My *composted manure* and *organic humus* gets dragged all over the garden and I'm convinced that ever since James Topping told me to start using it, I have a more luscious garden. And who should know better? Not only does James occasionally earn an honest dollar by trading trees and working at his uncle's Arrowhead Farms nursery but the Toppings have been around gardening and farming for so long there is even a road in a nearby town named after them. James said cow manure makes things flourish, and I didn't need any more proof than his gigantic cosmos in mid-June coupled with climbing roses, bigger and redder than you have ever seen, covering his ostrich pen. Now, to be truthful, James only said cow manure. Since the Toppings have a real farm with horses galloping and chickens clucking, maybe he meant the *real* thing, but I took it to mean the nice, clean, odorless kind you buy at the Agway.

Bonemeal comes into play when planting anything that is a bulb and with a few other specialties, like irises. I've read at least a hundred times that my dearly beloved bulbs, both spring and summer ones, are big fans of bonemeal and there's no reason to question this wisdom. I've had great luck, not only with the obvious tulips and narcissus, but with the more exotic *Fritillaria, Leucojum, Ornithogalum* and lilies of all kinds. Later we delve deeper into the fabulous world of bulbs, because it is an immense and divine story, but for now, an item in the what-you-need mode is definitely bonemeal or Bulb Booster fertilizers, available everywhere. They should contain nitrogen and phosphorus as well as bonemeal.

And peat moss. *Peat moss*, which has suddenly become controversial, is a planting mainstay. Books from all over the world advocate peat moss. My *New Illustrated Encyclopedia of Gardening*, which dates from the '60s, cites peat moss at least twice on each of its 2,646 pages. I wouldn't be caught dead without peat moss. Yet, suddenly, along comes Mark Griffiths, editor of *The New Royal Horticultural Society Dictionary of Gardening*, who says peat moss is unnecessary and a waste of time and we should all go back to the old potting recipes of the Victorians (whatever they are!). Well, my guess is this twenty-eight-year-old Brit (not that I have anything against Brits; to the contrary, I'm quite the Anglophile) felt a need to stir up a debate on one issue or another to give himself some distinction and has chosen to wage war against peat moss, of all things. Let's ignore him. As far as I'm concerned, peat moss goes in every hole, aerating the soil, giving different substance to the dirt, while conditioning it. Who wants to garden in a world without peat moss? I will debate Mr. Griffiths on the subject, if he should so bid.

So, peat moss; clean, composted cow manure; and bonemeal with its variations are my stalwarts. When my heart is set on growing a particular plant, there are times I'll buy an additional nutritious combination like a 10-10-30, or a 5-15-20 championed by one or another articles or persons I've reason to trust (which is how I decide which combination to use). Just recently, for example, I've been swayed into ordering something called "liquid humus" from a daylily specialist who insists it is unique in stimulating root growth in daylilies. Having just ordered forty-seven of them, I'm an easy mark. I mean, how could I resist this description? "Liquid humus is a natural product derived from Leonardite rock—the concentrated essence of *primordial muck*"!! Of course, I'm convinced primordial muck will be a boon to profuse flowering. How can it miss?

The one dirt enhancer you don't have to buy but should definitely encourage is worms. As they burrow through the ground they aerate the soil and keep it loose—perfect for gardening, while the food they ingest (tiny weed seeds and insect eggs) are precisely things you don't want in your garden anyway. The big bonus is the "castings" they produce (those little mounds of soil you see above ground). These piles are laden with nitrogen, phosphorus, and other nutrients garden plants just adore. Love your worms.

MULCHES

Now along with dirt enhancers and pesticides, the other software category to embrace is mulch. Mulch is not so complicated and it's much more fun, because it is decorative as well as functional. You need mulch from the onset because it makes any garden look better, especially an early garden not yet abundant, which needs cohesion to bring the bare spots into harmony. Mulch is a form of ground covering, not unlike icing on a cake, and is used wherever you have newly planted garden areas or an unsightly stark sore spot on your property. It is used around trees and shrubs, on either side of the driveway, around the house foundation, under hedges, or anywhere you want to define an area, make a comely transition from the grass, or cover the bare earth. Naked earth looks fine when it is moist and brown, like after a delightful spring rain, but for the most part it merely looks barren and crusty on the surface and is much nicer when masked by mulch.

Not only is mulch a big visual plus, it has all kinds of inherent benefits. It deflects the sun and keeps moisture in the ground, thereby helping cool the earth in the warm seasons. During the cold, it covers like a big warm blanket and insulates against the vagaries of unpredictable Mama. Mulch attracts earthworms and other nice friends of the soil, but perhaps its most true and tangible asset is really helping keep down weeds and unwanted grass. (You will find grass often difficult to grow where you want it but thriving like crazy in spots eked out for your garden. It's just one of those things.) Mulch has an abundance of positive attributes. What more could you ask of something that does so much good and looks so swell?

Choosing a Mulch

Consider here the vast variety of mulches, all with different looks and diverse functions. There are fake mulches and real mulches. The fake mulches, which are various forms of manmade textiles involving one kind of polyurethane or another, do not provide the nice nutritional benefits, and are not necessarily environmentally correct, but they are the ultimate in weed control. The real mulches, like tree bark and various beans and husks, might admit a few more weeds but their virtuous protection capabilities and ability to break down into nutrients far outweigh their disadvantages. In between organic and artificial mulches are stone mulches. They serve as a top cover and inhibit weeds to a degree, but they tend to look trite and commercial if not used artfully. Think of all of those white-gravel patches at your nearest fast-food place and you will get a sense of the look you do *not* want to achieve.

However, properly placed stone mulches can be underlayment to a rockery or a gem of a focal point around specimen trees. Granite and marble chips can add a highly dramatic accent to a given area, as they come in beautiful colors like earthy red, good dark green and almost black, but this can be seriously expensive if you envision nice fat chips laid in deep enough to make an impression. They are also not so easy to find, but anything can be had with enough cash and perseverance.

Fake Mulches

The fake mulches are most often used *under* organic or real mulches, which is a relief. I mean, what would you rather see in your landscape? A big patch of weeds or a big sheet of black plastic? Neither is a particularly tasteful prospect. For those of you who can't abide weeds or weeding, sheets of plastic or polyurethane can be put in place and then covered by something organic like pine or cypress bark. Man-made mulches come in various forms and colors and are constructed either of fiberglass or other kinds of plastic products and sold in sheets or by the roll. If you opt for man-made, make sure to use only the porous variety, as water cannot penetrate the totally solid plastic kind. No weeds (or anything else) coming up from the earth and no water going down to the earth is a no-win situation. If you really can't bear the thought of weed disorder and feel you must go with solid plastic, then be prepared to install some serious underground irrigation system like soaker hoses, the end-all of irrigation systems.

The porous mulches, which work fairly well, are generically called "geotextiles." In our Hammock Grove, with its haven of cedar trees as a perimeter, we eventually resorted to a porous mulch covered with pine chips. Initially, I was wary of the idea because I wanted everything to be oh so natural. We laboriously cleared away weeds, brush, and strangling vines, spread organic mulch on the ground, strung up a big wide hammock, put in a few French garden chairs (those ubiquitous green slatted ones) and a nice stone bench. No sooner had we finished when a miniature version of the weeds and brush began to spring up again right through our nice wood-chip mulch. Black weed-blocking barrier to the rescue! We used the fiberglass kind, which is penetrable, and topped it with more bags of wood chips than you can possibly imagine. The good news is that it has been in place for some four years, keeping the weeds and wanton brush to a manageable level.

One more good word about the ersatz mulch: you do not have to commit yourself to it for life. If you decide to change the vista where you have laid the sacrosanct stuff, simply choose the spot where you want to add color or plant an arresting specimen, cut a hole in the store-bought sheet of mulch, and dig away.

Real Mulches

The real organic mulches can't be beat, however, for they're lovely to look at as well as functional. Although they decompose quite rapidly and as a result have to be revived, added to, and replaced often (every season is likely), this very decomposition is another form of fertilizing. It adds nitrogen to the soil and improves its structure. So you see, everything about real mulch is good. Even more astonishing, in this world of ours where so little is completely positive, there is even an array of alluring looks from which to choose.

The essential category is bark. Bark chips, shredded bark, bark nuggets—these are all possibilities probably available in your area. They all hail from natural tree-bark and are therefore an honest brown color, just like dirt in its best disposition, unless you get specific and choose cypress bark, which is more gray than brown. Bark is a great natural mulch and far better looking than the less appealing concept of wood chips. No self-respecting mulch merchant should sell you bark mulch claiming any more than 15 percent wood in it. Wood is not as nice as bark in texture, it is coarser, and its color will probably be tinged with yellow, which isn't quite as viable in Mama's green scheme. Bark sells for about four dollars per two cubic feet, and since it takes about fifteen of these bags to cover one hundred square feet to a decent depth of at least two inches, it can get quite costly. The aforementioned not-as-nice wood chips cost about half as much, which is why they made sense for our hammock grove of seven hundred square feet but I would *never* use them in the gardens proper.

In a big fat book devoted to mulches I read that buckwheat hulls and cocoa-bean mulch are both quite stunning, so naturally I charged out to acquire these when the next mulching session was upon me. Upon investigation, the buckwheat hulls were alien to East Hampton, but I did find cocoa beans, and when I brought in my first twenty bags and laid them in, I was thrilled with the results. They looked dark and great, and in the heady action of application they had the pleasing smell of chocolate. Although eating chocolate does not turn me on, smelling chocolate in the garden did. Over the winter, the cocoa defied being wind-borne and stayed in place looking quite somber, neat, and, well, beany. Came the spring, however, a downside reared its unattractive head. As the beans decompose and lose their bonus of aroma, they tend to create a mold not unlike the most repugnant mildew. Not only did the beans take on a terrible rotting appearance, they gave me the distinct feeling my plants couldn't breathe. The next autumn, I switched to salt hay. Though the visually attractive cocoa beans are still among my favorites for decorative purposes in focal places in the garden, I restrain from laying them in very deeply.

Salt hay is not a decorative mulch; it is a *working* mulch. This is what you blanket your gardens with for the long haul of winter. It goes right on top of whatever fancy mulch might already be there and serves the exact same purpose as a blanket: covering the garden to keep it warm. Salt hay also makes sure the garden does not suffer too much stress when the soil "heaves." Heaving startles the soil with the real shock of freezing cold after a period of balmy days and throws the plants into a tizzy. To acclimate them slowly and achieve a nice sense of satisfaction, put your garden to bed by layering in this salt hay at about three or four inches, somewhat like a winter prayer. Imagine my thankfulness the first year we used it and were greeted with a snow blizzard on the first official day of spring.

The salt hay comes in big bales and is arranged in such a way that you peel it off layer by layer. In garden talk, these layers have the nice cognomen of "books," and they sort of undulate over the garden and look quite cozy. Salt hay stays crisp and clean over winter's duration and doesn't even get slimy, as I had feared. If you have room in your basement or a big barn, it is said you can even store it from one year to another. Make sure it is salt hay—not any old regular roadside hay or, God forbid, straw, because these can harbor all sorts of seeds that germinate and produce more weeds than you ever bargained for. Salt hay is sterile because it needs salt water to germinate; therefore, no weeds and no problems, unless the garden is right smack up against the ocean. Another plus is ease of removal. As spring begins nudging its way in, you can peel the "books" off the gardens in layers little by little; therefore, you do not jolt your sweet sleeping plants from their long winter's rest.

There are lots of other mulches to buy, and some are even free. In the former category, you can use peat moss; I also understand that sawdust is quite acceptable, though it seems to me it would fly around or remind me of some unsavory barroom floor or construction sight. There is also cork, as well as cranberry vines and oyster shells. I haven't tried any of these. Nor hops, peanut shells, or seaweed, mainly because they are not sold at my local Agway, but they might logically be more available in areas involved in pursuits generating these by-products. The latter category of free mulches is a terrific added attraction, depending on where you live and what you've got. If you have a property full of pine trees, then you've got it made. Pine needles are wonderful for flower beds as they deposit acid and allow the rain to soak through. They don't look so bad, either. Another free mulch is the great pile of leaves you spend hours raking in the autumn. They can be put right to work around the shrubbery, tender trees, and evergreens. You need a lot of them—at least eight inches thick, because they tend to mat down and decompose fast; but they are natural, easy and cheap. Also, any leaves that wander into your gardens should be welcomed and left to decay. Last but hardly least in the gratis group are evergreen boughs, which are best supplied by the aftermath of your Christmas tree and those of your neighbors. A particularly good point about post-Christmas working mulch is that you can be almost certain the ground is finally frozen, which is the optimum time for this nondecorative pursuit.

That's it for the software. Now on to a very definitive list of little, but important, accoutrements—things you absolutely must have for your garden.

GARDEN ACCESSORIES

GARDEN MARKERS

First and foremost on my list of essential accessories are garden markers, which define the plantings and serve as an invaluable reference for what's already in the ground as well as what you envision for the next seasonal cycle. They come in various materials and sizes, but only the metal ones (zinc or aluminum) are any good. They outlast all competition. Keep the carbon pencils accompanying them in a good place, because they are the only writing instruments that really work—do not attempt to use any kind of felt-tip pen; no matter how waterproof they say the ink is, it is not waterproof enough. Forget the wooden markers, they disintegrate and the writing disappears no matter what you use to write with. Ignore the plastic ones, too; they break apart, and there is no pencil or ink that adheres to them once there has been a serious rain.

The metal markers are more uniform, less ugly, and they persist. The only time I might recommend the wooden kind is for seasonal planting—for instance, to mark your dahlias for the duration of one summer—but if you are *really* hot to know exactly which cultivars are the ones you want to repeat next year, use only metal ones with a proper pencil.

I know for a fact that wooden and plastic markers don't work, having been forced to use them myself a few autumns ago. Up to my ears in fall planting of bulbs and lilies and bare-root hosta, I bounded to my deck to resupply the garden cart with metal markers and was faced with the unexpected dilemma of disturbing a bird's nest or grabbing my markers. A little brown wren, not fascinating in any way except that it was alive and a mother, had decided to build a nest and lay eggs right in the very box on the very shelf where the marker supply is kept. There was nothing left to do but repair to the hardware store, where I had to settle for lousy wooden ones.

I needed markers so badly, it was inconceivable to wait for a FedEx delivery of metal ones from Smith & Hawken (who, though generally more expensive than other fancy catalogs for standard supplies, on this item has the best price) or the slower delivery routine of my favorite marker supplier (with the best price of all), the Paw Paw Everlast Label Company (they have the best quality and a huge selection of every size and every type of marker, with prices about 25 percent lower than the others). Anyway, by the following spring the little wren had flown its nest, so there was no sentimental reminder of why I'd opted for wooden markers. I was left with just the bitter truth that I had no idea where I'd planted anything, for whatever was written on the wooden labels had long since deteriorated.

You need the metal markers for many reasons. They are reminders of what you intend to plant and what you have already planted. Come the flush of spring when you're madly trying to identify new planting you did in a flurry last fall, if you haven't labeled you will be totally lost. If it hasn't emerged, how will you ever remember the spot where you planted the allium, for example, which won't break earth till May? It's disheartening if not heartbreaking to stab your trowel into what you think is a bare spot, only to split a big beautiful bulb or root mass in two. If it does emerge, and in a million years you can't recognize it, marking is, *again*, the only thing that will save you in the precious planting scheme.

Beyond these considerations, you also need markers to remind you what it was you decided to plant in a certain spot when its seasonal planting time rolls around again. For example, splendid spring has arrived, you stand back proudly surveying your narcissus display, and you see two blank spots just glaring at you. This is when you mark for the future: put 'Cheerfulness' here, put 'Mount Hood' there. Then, when you are standing in the same spot next October (which will look altogether different) with many big fat 'Cheerfulness' and 'Mount Hood' bulbs in hand, you will remember exactly where to plant them, without destroying the already existing tableau. After the passage of summer, when your microcosm has matured, the whole scene looks so different you will never recall your intentions unless you follow my labeling advice. *It's the only way.*

In the dead of winter, as you read catalogs with the ardor of a monk reconstructing the Bible for latter-day enthusiasts and become enthralled by the notion of a light-hearted trailing vine, *Adlumia fungosa*, sprouting throughout the hellebores (Christmas or Lenten roses) in the shade garden, you should run out in the cold and put a marker there to remind yourself, or at least strongly note it on your calendar or in your journal. For when that adlumia arrives verdant and vibrant, you will probably never recall your intention of it rambling over the hellebores in the shade path unless you've marked it. At the end of July, I dug a big hole for a perfect late-blooming clematis after a last burst of nursery shopping. It didn't occur to me until too late the root I yanked out was my precious mertensia, which had died back at the beginning of June.

Let me add that you must always maintain the marker pencils with a sharp point, so you will need to invest in a battery-operated pencil sharpener, and put it in a convenient location. As you get more and more into gardening, you will find more and more reasons to label: the plant-rotation cycle, deep planting, over-planting, plus signaling favored perennials that wait until everything else has reared its lovely head before they emerge, like the lovely *Platycodon* (balloonflower).

For a couple of years I was perfectly satisfied with the marker hawked by all the catalogs usually called Perennial Plant Markers but became irked when their nameplates repeatedly unhinged themselves from the support. Through Paw Paw, I have discovered a better kind requiring a little assembly, but they never fall apart. I know the assembly sounds monotonous bordering on the indescribably tedious, but while you are out in the garden, isn't there someone inside (like my Irving, who is a big devotee of TV) who likes nothing more than to contribute to the garden in some small way like putting together garden markers? This is a rote exercise that can be carried out while watching all those big guys in arenas performing football or some other kind of ball.

At this very moment, seasoned gardener I presume to be, I am at a total loss because my tulips went unmarked during last fall's planting. You'd think I would have learned by now? This spring one patch of "lily-flowered tulips" was glorious—beautiful colors, at least thirty inches tall, all perfect and long-lasting—and the other patch of supposedly the same kind of tulip from another source was only mediocre at best—maybe twenty inches tall, half of them my least favorite color, yellow, none of them perfect. Since proper marking wasn't done, I had no idea which patch came from which source. How can I be confident in placing my order this year? The same goes for the peony flowering pink that was a true vision: Was it 'Angelique' or was it 'Pink Perfection'? I guess it was too cold, or the days were growing too short, or I was just too lazy, but now I'm stuck in another old briar patch. *You must mark everything.*

FLOWER SUPPORTS AND STAKES

As your garden begins to bloom, you will need stakes and supports to display all those beautiful flowering things you've so diligently planted and marked. This is another category of garden accessory available in a vast array of shapes, sizes, and types. I don't have a source as *sine qua non* as Paw Paw, but Gardener's Supply Company and Smith & Hawken have well-thought-out selections. Since they are all rather expensive, it hardly matters if the thirty-six-inch one with three hoops inside is fifty cents more or less somewhere else. You don't really need supports in your first year. Thinking back to my inaugural garden year, I would have pleaded to have a perennial so out of bounds it overreached itself, or grew so tall it wouldn't stay erect on its own steam, but then just one measly year later, stakes and supports became fundamental. They keep the garden in sync and upright.

I don't have much use for single-stem flower supports and can't even fathom why they aren't abandoned altogether. One of these smart catalog companies should create a support that looks and acts just like the forked limb of a tree. It seems so perfectly obvious and natural I've contemplated going into the making of garden accessories business myself.

Many good ones do work, however, like "Zig-Zag Flower Supports," which function much better than you would think from the dopey catalog illustration. These supports lift up the flowers overflowing the summer border and are also good for marking off beds during fall planting. If you use enough of these linear Zig-Zag Supports, they even help keep out the rabbits, or whatever other animals come to feast, leaving discernable little teeth-marks on the leaves and sometimes biting off the entire flower. (Those definitive little teeth-marks always catch me off guard, as I associate them with real little mouths, which are hungry, too.)

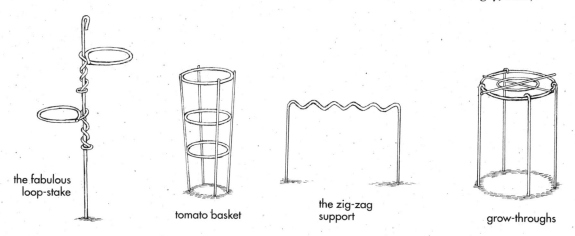

the fabulous
loop-stake

tomato basket

the zig-zag
support

grow-throughs

Then there are "Flower Support Rings" and "Grow Through Supports," which are more or less the same thing—circular metal rings on stakes that surround your unruly or drooping plants, keeping them erect and confined to the space where you want them. There are two kinds: the kind you can fold for storage, which have their legs attached by movable hoops, and the stationery kind. Forget the latter—they are too hard to store, and worse, the legs begin to break off after one season. The trick with these supports is to position them over the plant before it has broken into real growth. Even though they don't look too fabulous in the garden for the first few weeks while they nakedly rise in midair, the sun and the season will suddenly work their miracle, and the surrounded plant will burst forth, making you quickly forget the rings are even there. They work amazingly well, and you will be surprised how badly you need them when your second-season perennials sprout.

Supports are an item for which you have to plan in advance and order from the trustworthy catalogs. For some reason, supports are one thing I can't find locally, not even here in abundant East Hampton, where you can usually find anything at one price or another. One last cautionary word on grow-through things: Don't think you can impose them on your *Physostegia* or lilies once they have already thundered into flowering. It just doesn't work, no matter how tenderly you try to coax the contraption over the buds and into the ground. Only one item can save the day when something is already full-blown—Loop Stakes (Walt Nicke has these). They are fabulous for peonies and bearded iris *germanica*, as well as all the lovely lilies, or anything with a tall stem and a heavy flower. Each stake has four-inch loops that can be unhinged to admit the flowering stem and can be adjusted up and down so it fits your flower perfectly, the closest thing to made-to-measure clothes in the flower-support demimonde.

To keep the garden looking buoyant and perky, you also need stakes. Stakes are just straight old wooden sticks that usually come in green and are used with twine or "Twist'ems." If you happen to have some spare bamboo growing in your yard, then that is ideal (but how many of us have?). Sheared of all its stems and leaves, you will then have the real version of the garden stakes striving to be bamboo. Handy green gardening twine does not last forever, but gets you through the season, which is all you need. The natural-colored, stiffer twines and jute are good for heavier chores, like tying back tree branches, but not pliant enough for the flower garden. When it's time to tie the flowering plant to the stake, it is best to tie the twine first around the stake to secure it—then gently wrap, with plenty of slack around the stem. As the plant grows, the stems get fatter, so if the tie is too tight, you will defeat your initial good intentions of supporting the plant by strangling it instead.

Stakes come in many sizes; but you probably only need the multipurpose size, which is about one fourth of an inch thick and three feet long. If you intend to grow dahlias, which I heartily advocate, then you need some really beefy stakes at least an inch thick and five or six feet long. These must be on hand in the beginning of May when it is time to plant your dahlia tubers because they increase in size so phenomenally in a season, you need to set the stakes at the moment of sinking the tuber into the earth. Elaboration on dahlias comes later; but be prepared to grow them, as they are the ultimate in quick gratification while offering you an incredible opportunity to choose colors, sizes, shapes, looks, and forms. Even in a first-year garden they become a literal flowering jungle if you choose at least eight or ten spectacular ones, and there are hundreds to choose from. But for most other plants, stakes, unlike supports, aren't needed till the stems are obvious and about to droop.

Flower-Gathering Buckets

To gather dahlias and other beautiful flowers from your garden, you need a French Florist's Bucket—named by Gardener's Eden, but available off and on from other sources. My favorite twelve-inch bucket exploded last year because I thought it would be charming to fill it full of holly last Christmas and leave it on the deck near the Christmas tree. How was I to know freezing water expands? So although this is not a good use, it is an otherwise multipurpose item.

The French Florist's Bucket is made of galvanized steel, is quite chic and functional at the same time. Because it has handles, it is easy to carry around the garden in the evening, my preferred time for cutting, although it is just fine to cut your flowers in the morning when still dewy. What time of day you choose for flower-cutting is another of those instinctual subjective decisions, although the height of the afternoon, when all the blossoms are stretching toward the sun and fully open, is assuredly the wrong time. Why cut them at their most stressful moment? Better to catch them when just waking up and all perky and ambitious, or when they're ready to retire for the day and feel relaxed.

Plunging your flowers into water the

French flower buckets loaded with lilies.

minute you cut them is a logical idea. Considering that with the snip of your pruners you have just severed them from all their life-giving juices, it is only appropriate you immediately give back, at least, their water. Tepid water is best for most flowers, save the tulip, which prefers cold, cold water. Fill one or more of your gathering buckets with the correct temperature water before going into the garden. These buckets come in an eight-inch, twelve-inch, and sixteen-inch size. I suggest you need them all. The little one is good for short-stemmed blooms like dahlias, annuals, and most daffodils; the midsize is generally the most useful; and the tallest one you need for long-stemmed wonders like the late tulips, stunning lilies, and any branches, flowering or not, you might want to cut for impact. Sometimes it is charming, not to mention casually classy, to leave the flowers in the bucket, which creates a look of gardening profusion. When you do this, however, be sure to organize them in a sort of well planned, though seeming haphazard fashion.

Far-fetched as it may sound to the beginning gardener to suggest one day you'll wander your very own yard and snip a bouquet from a garden you have grown, I promise you will not only be able to do just that, but will become enraptured with the idea. An immense pride accompanies arranging a vase full of flowers you nurtured yourself. As a few seasons pass and you get the knack of it, you will even begin coordinating color and texture schemes by planting certain things you know will bloom at the same time in various subtle color combinations. An arrangement of deep, dark red dahlias punctuated with the graceful *Acidanthera* (a stylized member of the gladioli family that has white petals with a deep red blotch in the center) and topped off by white turk's-cap lilies spotted with scarlet turk's-cap lilies is a sight to behold. This is actually a much bigger turn-on than coordinating a wardrobe ever was for me.

Once I began cutting my own flowers, a solemn vow was made never to spend another dollar on fresh flowers again. Suddenly it seemed like a sacrilege to spend seventy-five bucks at a florist for some blooms that would be pleasing for maybe four days when I could use those same floral dollars to buy two columbines (*Aquilegia*), a *Buddleia* (butterfly bush), a few more hosta, plus a French Lace hydrangea, which together will yield armfuls of flowers for years to come. Yet lacking a greenhouse, I must admit, has caused me to re-embrace cut floral purchases in the doldrums of winter. Also, it's impossible to pass my favorite Korean grocer on University Place when he has long-stemmed Washington State tulips in February and the first daffodils of spring, still in their drooping bud state. But by and large, this is not how I spend my precious flower dollars any longer.

The Bulb Auger

It was a fabulous and unforgettable autumn day in the fifth year of my gardening preoc-cupation. My lungs were full of brilliant brisk late-September air, ideal conditions to greet the arrival of 750 gorgeous, fat, healthy bulbs from Dutch Gardens (the biggest of my several bulb orders that year). On this timeliest of days, out came my new bulb auger. This tool is a long steel borer you attach to the end of any ordinary electric drill in order to make holes in the earth. Why I waited so long to buy one of these things is a total conundrum, as I was even told first-hand about it by my one fanatical gardening friend, Joanne Fielder, but opted to poo-poo the idea. It seemed too—too what? Too mechanical? Too unnatural? Too electric? Too something. It was only that autumn, knowing I'd be in Europe and Asia the whole month of October, that I broke down and decided to try it. Joanne had promised it would make the fall planting go infinitely faster; but I was reluctant and skeptical.

I ordered from Gardener's Supply Company, and I put my auger to use that fine and frantic September day. Well, it is simply the most fantastic tool ever to cross my path. The sense of accomplishment achieved at the end of this day was *sans* precedent, and in the mellow evening, I wasn't even particularly tired or sore. The initial auger worked fine, but I kept thinking there ought to be one that could make a bigger hole, and then, lo and behold, the Langenbach catalog offered a Super-Auger with a three-inch-wide capability. Get the big one to begin with, it is just great.

With it you need a power supply for the drill. This is unfortunate and cumbersome, but there is always a negative with anything fantastic. You can buy a drill with a built-in recharge-able battery, but it winds down and wanes out just as you are in the biggest act of planting. A plug-in drill never quits and is the best recourse, but of course requires extension cords. To cover my not-quite-an-acre sufficiently, I need 250 feet of horridly bright orange, but reliable, electric extension cord. Thank God the house (power supply) is nearly in the middle of the property, or else it could be worse. At thirty-five dollars for a hundred feet, price is another consideration, but it is worth every dime.

Once put to use, the auger is too fab for words and allows boundless creativity. Looking around the yard with augered drill in hand, suddenly I spied all sorts of little niches heretofore too hard to reach, too root-bound, or too unchartered for me to have considered planting before. Once I got the hang of being able to bore into any place that seemed appealing, it was a snap. Too-hard-to-get-to spots became surprisingly hospitable—lift up a fern frond here—a hosta leaf there—drill a hole and *voila*! Next spring there will be tons of new flowers in amenable places. You see, the big trick is to indulge in the spring flowers and make sure something hardy will be popping up to overtake their yellowing foliage at just the propitious moment.

Having used it for planting spring bulbs (including the impossibly gigantic three-nosed narcissus), summer bulbs, even the occasional annual, the only bad news to relate is I've unmercifully chopped an earthworm or two in half, but don't they regenerate (harkening back to biology lessons I never thought would be meaningful)? Just goes to show you how every little thing you learn along the way can acquire importance. The one other thing to note is to be careful of roots of things you diligently planted. Auguring into, for example, the big fat tap root of a *Dicentra* (bleeding heart) that has performed like a dream for three years can be disheartening. Caution is the keyword in a crowded garden, but get this tool and get it NOW.

This finally brings us to an end of tools and other garden necessities you cannot live without. If you acquire everything described in this chapter, absolutely no gardening job is beyond you. You are equipped to plant and maintain your garden. No doubt you will get sidetracked by various other gadgets and accoutrements seeming irresistible, and your heart will go out to other tools that look promising, but you will find the ultimately indispensable items described here the ones you will use over and over and over again.

MUSIC

Music is certainly not an essential, but I find my outdoor speakers a particular gardening boon. If there are heavy chores to be done like digging up dahlia tubers, I sometimes turn to somber Mahler; when spring is bursting out all over, I'm more inclined to Bob Marley or some equally danceable reggae while doing my garden number; the automaton ordeal of lily planting is best accompanied by energetic Philip Glass, who keeps me in the assembly-line mood. The music mixed with the birds chirping and wind chimes chiming is the perfect extra-sensory touch. Of course, in the '70s there was quite a stir about *The Secret Life of Plants*, a quasi-scientific treatise proclaiming plants to be thinking, feeling, emotional beings. And of course, in Alice's garden, the plants could even talk.

> "Never mind!" Alice said in a soothing tone, and, stooping down to the daisies . . . she whispered "If you don't hold your tongues I'll pick you! . . .
> How is it you can all talk so nicely?" Alice said, hoping to get it into a better temper by a compliment. "I've been in many gardens before, but none of the flowers could talk."
> "Put your hand down, and feel the ground," said the Tiger-lily. "Then you'll know why."
> Alice did so. "It's very hard," she said; "but I don't see what that has to do with it."
> "In most gardens," the Tiger-lily said, "they make the beds too soft—so that the flowers are always asleep."
> Lewis Carroll, *Through the Looking-Glass*

I'd wager, anyway, the flowers like music, too, and I have deep-seated suspicions they do communicate. How else can you explain the otherwise unaccountable ability of, say, the balloonflower *Platycodon* to rise up to four feet tall so it won't be crowded out by the *Gaura* and gooseneck loosestrife—knowing this is a two-foot plant by anybody's standards? They do talk, I'm convinced, otherwise they could never be in such symbiotic sync.

DIANNE   BENSON

THE CLOTHES

> Vain trifles as they seem, clothes have, they say, more important offices than to keep us warm. They change our view of the world and the world's view of us.

That was lifted from Virginia Woolf's fabulous book *Orlando*, dedicated to and written for, our very own Vita of Sissinghurst. Vita and Virginia were great allies, raconteurs, and lovers—of each other and of mutual grandiose ideas. Their story is a brilliant version of everyone's day-to-day story: whether you are front and center at the most clucked-about fashion show, cleaning up after your pet, making an extraordinary entrance at a big to-do, or tending your garden, how one looks is an extreme matter of personal choice. You have to wear clothes anyway, so you might as well wear clothes with style.

YOUR GARDENING OUTFIT

What to wear, what to wear? Clothes, actually, are inconsequential compared to tools; but you do need gardening clothes sensible and chic at the same time. My fashion instincts do not leave me even when on my knees on the dampest, coldest, dreariest days of November planting the blackest tulips one can order. Looking tasteful and considered while gardening has nothing to do with designer labels. Instead it has to do with fashioning a gardening wardrobe of basic and basically never changing apparel, long enduring because of its usefulness. The functions these items were designed for are not necessarily gardening, but they are clothes made to be *used*. If there were one designer label to endorse for gardening, it would be Issey Miyake's Plantation because these clothes have longevity, will endure, and have nothing to do with fashion. They are pure in spirit and rugged clothes of the earth. But essentially, go with items I suggest here because they are tried and true and much more in keeping with the gardening experience.

There is no need to look like a frump, a farmhand or some inveterate railroad engineer, as the Smith & Hawken catalog might have you believe. (Ugly though I find their silly, impractical gardening clothes, they must lure someone because they devote entire editions to the subject; to me their only strong point is good pruners and the like.) Homely clothes signify everything gardening is *not* about. There are considered, even elegant ways to approach practicality and comfort, other than resorting to shapeless pants or inane midcalf skirts that get in the way. They can never take the place of the gear posited here which will always be there and you will come to love.

> On the whole, I think it cannot be maintained that dressing has in this or any country risen to the dignity of an art. I cannot believe our factory system is the best mode by which men may get clothing . . . the principal object is, not that mankind be well and honestly clad, but, unquestionably, that the corporations may be enriched.
> Henry David Thoreau, *Walden*

The Gloves

Without a doubt, the single most important element in your gardening wardrobe is gloves. Aside from the fact that they protect your manicure and prevent blisters, they also make you much braver. To say the least, I'm on the squeamish side, and the idea of immersing my hands into a hole full of mud where all sorts of unknown organisms, worms, and bugs are lurking is truly repugnant. With my gloves on, however, there is no hole into which I will not plunge, nothing I will not touch. Even been known to pluck those repulsive slimy slugs off my delphiniums without a second thought and pick ticks off my pooch as though it were second nature. But, which gloves? Without exaggeration, I've owned and discarded every pair of gardening gloves known to man, up to and including a ridiculously expensive suede pair from Hermès in the strange but engaging color combination of saddle and magenta. When I was almost at wit's end, the perfect pair surfaced, thank God. Stupefied everyone isn't on to them, as they are so good and with the world becoming smaller each day and all that; yet you still can't buy these gloves just anywhere. They're called French Gardening Gloves and you must order them from Gardener's Eden at the amazingly cheap price of seventeen dollars.

Since these gloves are French, 50 million Frenchmen are as good at gardening gloves as they are at ready-to-wear. They have figured out a way to treat the leather so it doesn't become stiff as a board once it gets wet. In fact, these gloves even like to get wet. In from the garden, gloves all squishy, crusty, and dirt-laden, I simply wash my still-gloved hands with soap and water and leave them on the sink's edge to dry overnight. Fabulous. The next morning they are as clean and soft as when they were new. They do eventually discolor a little, but doesn't everything? I have a number of pairs in various stages, and even the two- or three-year-old ones are perfectly fine.

Once available only in one shade of unobtrusive, not-too-bad celery green, suddenly there are color choices. The good old green still exists, but now you can order real red and bright blue. Probably best to stick with green, but I may opt for a red pair if the mood strikes when in my next ordering mode. If you have very small hands, you might need to wear some other gloves inside because they start at size seven; but that is a minuscule downside. As well as the normal wrist-length glove, they come in a gauntlet style, which they call "rose gloves." These are great for planting or pruning thorny roses, weeding in a bramble patch, or clearing poison ivy. These gloves have the added attraction of being the same shape as the fashionable gauntlets Claude Montana and Azzedine Alaïa always fall back on. Get both styles, and get a few pairs of the regular-wrist length. There is almost nothing quite so reassuring—in the middle of a cold, soggy March Sunday when you are up to your elbows in the dampest of spring chores—as changing into warm, dry gloves.

THE PANTS

Since gardening is a nine-month outdoor affair spanning most seasons, what one wears has a great deal to do with how cold or warm it is. But given that the most intense gardening months are spring and autumn, when it is often pleasant to cool, but sometimes drizzly and freezing cold, the basis of my standard outdoor outfit is riding breeches, which are ideal in most climatic circumstances. Do not bother with fashionable in-one-season-out-the-next spinoffs from Ralph Lauren or Donna K. Go directly to your equestrian haberdashery or the good old State Line Tack Inc. catalog and get the *real* thing. Even though they are the same price as (or perhaps more than) the pseudo-designer ones, the real ones wear like proverbial iron and are perfectly at home when dumped into an automatic wash load. The designer versions just do not have the same stamina.

In homage to Vita's most impassioned gardening photos, I started out with jodhpurs, but find them a bit too fussy with all that extra fabric flapping around my thighs. The breeches are ideal. Euro Star and Harry Hall are my favorite brands. As we are dealing here in timeless issues, notice the emphasis on *brands*, not designers. If, like me, you are not a horse person knowledgeable in the art of dressage, go right to your nearest riding store and try them all on to find which brand and fit you prefer. Believe me, the horsey types running these stores couldn't care less whether you use these clothes for riding or gardening, just as long as they make their sale.

Make sure the breeches you buy are comfortable. It just won't do to consider anything other than comfort when buying your gardening duds. Forgo the size you can barely squeeze into for the next size, which feels better. The feel-good size will make you much happier when you are up and down on your knees for the fortieth time in one afternoon. Riding breeches are obtainable in a huge range of weights, colors, and fabrics, so there are choices to be made. It's better to start out with one heavier pair in corduroy or heavy twill and then a lighter-weight pair, perhaps in drill cloth, even denim. You will be pleased to know that before the fashion community ever uttered the word "stretch," these sweethearts were made with stretch fabrics. You will love wearing riding breeches. They never quit, always look great, and are even perfect for breakfast in town. What more could you want?

GARDEN JEWELS

That doyenne of gardening, Vita, usually topped her jodhpurs with a big white man's shirt (which is suddenly the rage again, as everything great-looking always resurfaces) and either a severe black jacket or an oversize natty cardigan, which could only be English. Also, I've never seen a photograph of Vita in her gardening gear not wearing, at least, her pearls. I, too, believe

Vita in her gardening outfit and
me in one of mine—a rare day
without breeches.

Vita photographed by Evelyn Irons.
Dianne photographed by Stephanie Pfriender, courtesy of *Mirabella* magazine.

in jewels for the garden. Why not dress up a bit there, just as you do on other cherished occasions? Not really a pearl girl myself, I am still loathe to attend to the garden unadorned and never venture out without at least earrings and my Ted Muehling branch pin fixed to my gardening vest.

In the *Letters of Vita Sackville-West to Virginia Woolf*, the compilers dryly describe Vita's exuberant taste: "She strode her own grounds now attired almost exclusively in whipcord breeches and high boots, pearls and earrings." Virginia Woolf had a much more endearing take on the matter:

> I like her and being with her and the splendour—she shines in the grocer's shop in Sevenoaks with candle lit radiance, stalking on legs like beech [birch?] trees, pink glowing, grape clustered, pearl hung.
> —Jean Moorcroft Wilson, *Virginia Woolf: Life and London, a Biography of Place.* Cecil Woolf Publishers, London. 1987.

UNDERPINNINGS

I often forswear Vita's man's shirt for a cotton or wool jersey turtleneck, sometimes two turtlenecks, and if cold enough, I add the black jacket. Under the jersey turtleneck usually goes a silk one. During the most rigorous months of gardening (the cold ones, of course) silk underwear underlies the whole outfit. This is another reason not to get your breeches in the skintight size, to allow room for silk underwear. This is an age-old concept favored by hunters and other outdoor types that really works.

I'd never really given a second thought to silk underwear as a savior until Irving was seized by an unusual urge to go on a white-water rafting trip. The organizer of this daredevil affair, his pal Richard Rubenstein, who is coincidentally a producer of classic horror movies like *Night of the Living Dead*, insisted he get silk underwear for this frightful outing without fail. Irving's trepidations about it being too cold bore fruit; he never ventured on another rafting trip and has no real opinion on the virtues of silk, as his only reminiscences are of being soaking wet. On the other hand, I've become a big fan. One blustery morning, dreading facing the mean outdoors, but knowing my frantic schedule of gardening chores wouldn't wait, I spied Irving's silk underwear and thought, "Why the hell not." Now, slipping on my own silk underwear at any sign of penetrating damp weather has become almost religious. It keeps you infinitely warmer, and you can last outside much longer. It works. Thank God for Richie Rubenstein.

THE VEST

Over the turtleneck (or T-shirt, as the case may be) goes my vest with lots of pockets. Think of it as a gardening handbag. Indispensable and wildly useful, much more so than a pocketed gardening apron (things continually fall out of the pockets when you are bending over), a knapsack (can't get to it), or one of those belt-purses like messengers wear (not big enough). Two of these many-pocketed vest affairs are essential—a warm-weather one of cotton and mesh and a cold-weather one flannel-lined. My original cotton vest was bought in a Banana Republic and was a typical safari-ish looking thing. After three years of hard wear and pruners poking holes in the pockets, it was time to replace it. Banana Republic (being closer to fashion than function these days) no longer carried the vests, so a search began. I wound up at a photographer's supply house and came upon one even more perfect than the old, because it even has loops to hold those precious carbon marking pencils. The warm, flannel-lined vest I ordered from Cabela's is called a "Master Angler's Vest."

Gamehunters, photographers, and fishermen must need lots of paraphernalia like we gardeners do, because these vests work perfectly. In the various pockets go: the little pruners I'm never without, markers and pencils, some twine, a weeder, and, of course, a lipstick and cigarettes. When you're down on your knees in a tight spot, suddenly from this earth-bound vantage point you see weeds needing to be pulled, stray branches to be clipped, and flowers to be deadheaded; and it is very handy to have these tools right on you. If I'm not wearing my vest, once I wriggle out of the snug situation and go to the gardening cart to get what I need, something else distracts me and all the good things that might have been accomplished while down on my knees remain undone.

A new catalog called Wathne, which has designs on a more accessible Hermès, specializes in an up-market array of sporting gear and clothes. They offer a very good-looking "Twill Angling Vest," among other things that look garden-durable, but I haven't quite convinced myself their vest is worth $295.

The Boots and Shoes

For strolling Knoll and Sissinghurst, her two distinguished English estates, Vita shod herself in knee-high lace-up riding boots. They look so perfect in all the photographs, I was convinced they would be ideal for me and duly ordered a pair from the J. Peterman Company, which swore to their authenticity in that romantic, virtuous tone their catalog copy takes. Upon arrival, these quintessential riding boots turned out to be of leather hard as steel. Having neither the patience to think about breaking them in nor the belief they could ever be broken in at all, I returned the boots to Peterman and went straight to Bridgehampton's Bit and Bridle, the trusted equestrian store. Again faced with an array of too-stiff boots—probably ideal when astride a horse but lousy for kneeling and bending in the garden—I settled for a quite wonderful pair of rubber pull-on riding boots. In Vita's day the real thing must have been much softer, because she doesn't seem like the suffering type to me.

My favorite leather boots, reasonably supple lace-ups stopping about four inches above the ankle, hail from a little store on the other side of the Arno in Firenze called Ritz. Subsequently, I found the same boots, more or less, at a funky shoe store on Eighth Street in Greenwich Village, also called Ritz by a strange coincidence. (Ritz is not a chain, this was just a happenstance.) They are ordinary enough and it's not difficult to find versions of them elsewhere. You need something substantial on your feet for giving that good old kick to the shovel, tamping down the dirt around your new plantings, and generally for striding around your yard or estate, whatever the case may be. Only recently I've come upon the magic world of Mephisto. Never thought I'd give in to any sort of rubber soles, but what they lack in style they make up for in sublime comfort, and in black suede (NuBuck, really) they're not so bad.

Of course, when one is very cold or extremely wet, any semblance of glamour is compromised, and rubber is the only thing that will do. Either those round-toed unattractive English Garden Boots appearing in all catalogs in their greener-than-green way or my rubber riding boots. Actually, Irving and I both have a pair of the egregious green rubber boots in our respective sizes, and we keep them next to one another beyond the main door of the house on the deck. They look very cozy there side by side: one big pair he wears for his annual pond-cleaning chore and one pair not quite so big—somehow they conjure up a contented family in residence. Be advised, however, neither of these boots has a lining. Since nothing feels as horrible as cold, damp rubber, get them a size bigger than you normally wear so you can fill them with lots of socks. Make one of the pairs cashmere for ultimate warmth.

For occasions when it is very wet (rain, sprinklers, watering) but not so cold, the catalogs suggest you need footwear called "gardening clogs." Yes, they do hold you aloft from the damp earth and wet grass and provide a dryer mode, *but* they are awkward, available only in screaming bright colors, and very ugly. J. Crew to the rescue. They have come up with something better, though why there is not a version for guys is beyond me. J. Crew calls them "rain shoes," they cost thirty-six dollars, look like acceptably svelte loafers and even come in black. What more could you ask?

THE TOTAL LOOK

This is my basic outfit: boots; breeches; silk underwear for the cold; a turtleneck; white shirt or T-shirt; and my vest. It's vitally important to segregate your gardening clothes from the rest of your wardrobe, as the last thing you want to do on a gardening morning is waste time trying to decide what to wear. And *never* even consider outfitting yourself in anything you couldn't bear to get dirty.

CONSIDERATION OF OTHER SHOES AND STYLES

If you are a blue jeans and big white running shoes type, then of course your everyday outfit will suffice for the garden. Personally, I loathe those big athletic shoes and blame them for many things: For instance, wasn't America a much more romantic place when men and women wore particular kinds of shoes appropriate to the time of day and venue? Whatever happened to businesslike shoes, traveling shoes, sexy shoes? I believe these cumbersome shoes to be singularly responsible for extracting much-needed glamour out of our country. Despite how much thought or money goes into a woman's outfit, what do you focus on when she is wearing those big fat white shoes? The shoes—they're all you see, and the rest of the outfit might as well be rags. My mother always preached, "You can't be glamorous and comfortable too." I will take this adage to my grave and never succumb to those bloated athletic shoes.

I am a diehard Maud Frizon girl and thrilled to find her shoes back under the new label Ombeline. Maud Frizon is a French shoemaker who designs Italian-made shoes for women who delight in their ankles and insteps. Always the most fashionable. Usually the most expensive. Many a pair of Mauds have bit the dust in my overly zealous state upon arrival in East Hampton, after an anxious week in the city wondering whether the hosta have suddenly upturned the earth with their comely twirling phallic buds or how many daffodil hybrids have joined the show. Leaping out of the car to inspect every single growing thing as soon as we pull in the driveway, I'm routinely halfway round the garden before it hits me, "Oh no! My shoes!" But once that suede is gone from your heels, it's gone. Then my expensively acquired Mauds, or whatever, become entertaining footwear for the pleasant summer months of snipping and shearing and showing off my garden.

In summer, when gardening chores are much less rigorous than spring or autumn, I'm perfectly comfortable in a variety of warm-weather wear such as a bathing suit with sarong or a short jumpsuit or some other odd ethnic wraparound. With the exception of the occasional planting of something irresistible from the local nurseries, summer gardening is mainly mainte-nance. Although you can deadhead, stake, fertilize, water, and make plans for the next season wearing just about anything, never dispense with your gloves.

In 1871, Sarah Joseph Hale, who was the editor of *Godey's Lady's Book*, wrote in the March issue of *The Horticulturist*:

> Every lady who looks for success in gardening will provide herself with a proper dress for outdoor work—garments which, while allowing freedom of movement to every limb, will afford sufficient protection from the weather, are not injured by dust, mud or sunshine, and can withstand frequent contact with stump and stake, and brush and briar.

Hale goes on to explain how flounces, peplums, and bustles are inadmissible, which is hardly relevant to us; but the essence of what she describes is not very different from the good basic outfit I've outlined. She also mentions thick leather boots and buckskin gloves.

THE UBIQUITOUS STRAW HAT

Since the straw hat is such an omnipresent symbol of the gardener, you may wonder why I've neglected to mention it as an essential. Contrary to opinions from the usual unreliable sources, hats are for strolling in gardens, not garden-*making*. My range of gardening hats, all of which seemed like must-haves when I bought them, just get in the way. If the hat is not being blown away by the wind or caught in tree limbs, it is tumbling off as you stoop over to snatch those weeds growing among the ground cover. Also, a hat cuts off your peripheral vision, which is undesirable because you never know what you are going to spot from your various perspectives. Much more satisfying is to tie my hair up in some sort of wrapper or scarf and wear sunglasses. If you are really nervous about the extreme effects of the sun's rays and lie awake nights fretting over skin-cancer concerns—then, absolutely, wear a big hat with a huge brim; but if that is not the case, the hat is more of an image idea, if, in fact, that's how you see yourself.

Sarah Hale closes her article with a little fluff: "There need not be wanting a white linen collar and cuffs . . . or a fastening of pretty ribbon and the suit is as becoming as it is serviceable." Not unlike Vita and her pearls, or me and my omnipresent bracelets and Ted Muehling pin, it is always charming to personalize yourself. Be comfortable. Get a few good and durable basic outfits. But don't ever be afraid to make yourself as illusory or as glamorous as the garden you are tending.

The most vivid image I hold dear of a true gardener is the balmy, sunlit, uniquely English day when my incomparable True Brit old boyfriend, Timothy Andreae, took me to the Family Lodge in Hampshire to meet Mother. She was, appropriately, in her rose garden. In my now calm recollection, it appears as quite the fantastic garden, but at the time—so mesmerized by the fading, bald Persian rugs, so unattuned to their debate on dowager's cottages, so anxious to join in their breezy conversation about Oxford dons, and so unable to discuss the roses—it was her endless application of bright red lipstick (which she kept stored in her gardening apron) that enraptured me most and made a poignant, unforgettable, and indelible impression. One should never disregard the glamour.

This compilation of basic things to wear and necessary tools comes from one who knows a good thing when she sees it. All the elements espoused here are the best of the lot. They have passed the use test and are as visually satisfying as they come. It is beyond my nature to complicate things once the best situation has been found. If you consider I've not changed my perfume in twenty years since discovering Penhaligon and its natural gardenia and bluebell fragrances, then you can better grasp I am not swayed by the tides of fashion, though I must admit to being totally smitten by Issey Miyake's *l'eau d'Issey*. It's such a wonderful fresh essence (the guy's a master, after all) I may have to beg off my Penhaligon when Issey becomes regularly available, but I'd hardly call that capricious.

Though fashion was my game for many years, I never really approached it like the here-today, gone-tomorrow world of *Women's Wear Daily*. People everywhere continually comment in the most intrigued way on my scent, my style, my clothes. Feeling just as, or more, fashionable than anyone around me in most circumstances comes from my favorite things being like old friends and many mainstays of my wardrobe being comfortable things I've held onto for years and years. For instance, a few decades ago a jeweler abiding in the arcade next to the old Bendel offered an original set of Cartier three-gold-tone bracelets in their first simple incarnation and original Cartier box. I was crazy over them and had to have them, so Irving and I eventually figured out a way to pay for the bounty. Without being sentimental, I can say they are as nice today as they were twenty years ago, and not one day has passed that I've removed them from my arm. What can I say? This is not a Holly-Golightly concept. When something is good, it's good for keeps, so *trust this list*.

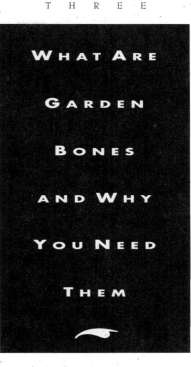

WHAT ARE GARDEN BONES AND WHY YOU NEED THEM

Focus. Fences. Paths. Trees. Water. Structures. Stone. Moods.

There is a certain standard of grace and beauty which consists in a certain relationship between our nature, such as it is, weak or strong, and the thing which pleases us.
Whatever is formed according to this standard pleases us, be it house, song, discourse, verse, prose, woman, birds, rivers, trees, rooms, dress, etc. Whatever is not made according to this standard displeases those who have good taste.

Pascal, *Pensées*

After skeletal considerations, Webster defines bone as: "ESSENCE, CORE; the most deeply ingrained part: HEART—usu. used in plural," or "the basic design or framework." Roget aligns bones with such synonyms as *render strong, strengthen, invigorate,* and *cohesion.* Essentially, these two definitions from our good old standard reference works are correct. This is what "garden bones" are all about—the garden's basic design. The flowers come later. The themes come later. The walks, walls, major trees, and structures—these are your "bones," and their size, style, color, texture, form, and position in your garden picture come *first.* Think of your garden bones like your favorite black turtleneck—the basis of your wardrobe that persists throughout all seasons. Your garden bones will be there when flowers are nowhere to be seen, in the deepest recesses of the dreariest weeks of winter, as well as when there is snow on the ground (at which time they tend to look particularly beautiful). In early springtime, when you're sure the rain will never stop and you will never be warm again, your bones will be there welcoming the earliest snowdrops (*Galanthus nivalis*). You want your garden bones to be permanent, so consider them carefully, and certainly do not think you must acquire them all at once. An adored object, a tree, a sundial at the end of a path—all bones—an Italianate fountain, rustic dovecote, a sweet thatch-roofed guest house—so many garden bones.

Steven Hamilton reminded me of a classical allusion to be recalled: In the Anglo-Saxon Chaucerian world there was no name for "body" as we know and say it, the closest word they had translates as "bone house." So the garden is like a receptacle for its bones.

HOW TO CREATE GARDEN BONES WHEN YOU HAVE NO OLD STONE WALL

How could I forget the day Irving bounded up the lawn much more excitedly than is his normal sauntering status quo and said, "Honey, stop that digging [or whatever task was at hand] and come and see a most spectacular thing right around the corner." Around two corners we went, and not five hundred yards away from us, heretofore hidden in dense woods, was a marvel. Would have thought it an apparition if not staring me in the face. On this maybe an acre or so, there stood a stone pool pavilion replete with a background wall twice the length of the pool and about twelve feet high. Picaresquely set into a hill and incised with niches holding life size romantic sculptures more Art Nouveau than classic Etruscan or Greek, but big, bold, and very beautiful. I was awestruck. It was clearly the most fabulous garden bone ever. Folks living in East Hampton in the twenties were more into fantasy than they seem to be now.

Nothing like a crumbling, but salvageable, neo-Gothic ruin to ground your garden. However, if you lack a stone pool pavilion or a millstream with footbridge, and if you are not of the mind (or purse) to acquire same—take heart—there are still plenty of ways to create your very own garden bones. Your basis can vary from a birdhouse to a treehouse, from a friendly stone pet a'grazing to a trickling fountain, from a topiary to that especially enchanting English conceit, a folly. Even a near-barren plot of land has some rudiments you can convert into your garden bones. As you assessed your property in deciding where was the ideal spot to create your first gardens, what did you consider? More likely than not, it was your walkways, your fence, your trees. Well, each of these is a serendipitous element of your garden bones. A path is not just a path or the most direct route from the car to the front door, a fence is not merely something to shield you from your neighbors, and similarly, a tree is most definitely not simply a tree.

Gardens do not spring from nowhere. They are natural progressions extending from a desire to enhance and take pleasure in the same things by which you are surrounded anyway. Each one of these bones is a starting point, the sum and substance of your gardening muscle. Now go back and reevaluate your yard one more time. Which elements can be transformed into assets once embellished a bit? With thought and money, each can become focal points from which your garden springs, and they are another way of working with nature in an attempt to improve it. What is unremarkable now, with scrutiny, can become a boon to the big scheme of your garden plan.

FENCES

Think of a fence like the backdrop of a stage set. Chain link and chicken wire are more difficult to mellow, but it's still not unthinkable to turn even them into something at least pleasant, if not a thing of beauty. At bare minimum, considering your fence as a background to your garden, you will want to cover it, or at least punctuate it, with something living and vinelike. There are many fabulous vines that know no bounds of growth within even one short season. There is always tried and true ivy (*Hedera helix*), which comes in a great many varieties once you explore it. There are hybrids upon hybrids of climbing and rambling roses lying dormant in every nursery and every mail-order catalog warehouse just waiting to meander like mad over your fence. There are even annual vines that easily take over a fence only six or eight weeks into the season. I have just bought a purple *Cobaea* to cover our new fence in its first year. This "cup and saucer vine" is reputed to bear big blue flowers cup- or bell-shaped. It has darker than green, almost bronze, leaves and is already throwing off zillions of tendrils while still in my living room waiting for the frost to abate. Getting very good vibes from this vine, which cost $15 and will only last the summer; but who cares? A mere $15 for a summer of beauty is a very good deal.

And what could be more charming, or more of an accomplishment, than a fence dripping in morning glories? Big blue fairy-tale flowers with clear green heart-shaped leaves just blossom and blossom all summer long and refuse to be restrained. True to their name, morning glories flower in the morning and last, maybe, till two in the afternoon. If you are strictly not a morning person and expect to spend most of your hours in

A wisteria-festooned fence.
Easy to achieve.

the garden as late in the day as light allows, or if you are interested only in flowers blooming in tandem with the cocktail hour—you are not left out of this plethora of beauty and whimsy because there are also evening glories, more commonly called "moonflowers." From the same family *Ipomoea*, both morning and evening glories are so easy to grow with a modicum of sun and ordinary decent dirt, and *you can even grow them from seed*. I know I've clearly stated this book is not about growing anything from seed; but there's no tediousness to contend with here. No germinating mix—no transplanting—no peat pots—no coddling—no greenhouse: none of that.

In order to revel in this feeling of progeny: You buy the seeds for a dollar. Around May, when you can be sure the warmth is here to stay, soak the seeds overnight in tepid water because the seed coat is very hard and wants to soften. The next morning stroll out along your fence and prepare the soil a bit—loosen it up—add some peat—some composted manure—stir it around a little, and stick the seeds right in the ground about six inches apart, barely covered by half an inch of soil. Then you wait. You don't have to wait long, because if you don't see little green heart-shaped seedlings popping up before two weeks, then something has gone wrong. Maybe not enough sun, maybe you forgot to water, maybe it was just not meant to be, but probably you will see little seedlings. All that's left to do is check out which ones look strongest, leave those to mature, and pull out the runts. That's it! Most likely your morning glories will thrive and their grabby tendrils will attach themselves all over your fence.

However, every seed in the two-hundred-page seed catalog will *not* do this; nearly fool-proof morning glories are an exception and should suffice to satisfy your craving to grow at least one plant from a seed. I must add, to keep a sense of balance here, if you buy a nice well-into-growth healthy morning glory at your nursery, you will get a glorious glory vine sooner, which might make you happier. I only mention the ability to do this seed thing here as my conscious bow to the traditional gardening world.

There are many possibilities, both annual and perennial, to enhance your fence and make it part of the garden. The plus side of choosing perennials is that even during winter your fence will be covered with at least a sign of something growing. Even though it may look like a tired conglomeration of brown stems and twigs, it remains there, very "Here I am" à la David Byrne, promising and comforting. Among my favorites in the hardy perennial vining, climbing category are *Hydrangea petiolaris* (climbing hydrangea, the flower is a misty wistful ecru spray, and the branches are gutsy and strong with an elegant leaf; it begins to bud very early, reassuring you of life after winter); almost any kind of clematis (this dazzling one requires a few tricks having to do with cool roots and hot sun intermittently, but you are well rewarded with spectacular flowers); and wisteria (which is really profuse and must be monitored lest it take over your whole patch, but when the heavenly panicles bloom, it is the vine divine). From these three perennials, you can create a convincing vine-covered fence in one season if you go for expensive well-started ones at your nursery. And I promise that within a few short years you will feel as if you inherited it. And who's to say you must limit your vine-covering to one sort of vine? Why not mix ivy with clematis, climbing hydrangea with morning glories, or wisteria with passion vine and roses? Thereby the same covered fence can be evergreen and flowering or have two distinct bursts of flower and color all at the same time. Good idea, no?

Now, what to do with the vine-covered fence? First thoughts will usually turn to creating a kind of border either along some portion of the fence or adjacent to it in some way. If that's the case, definitely consider building up your border/flower bed with lots of rich topsoil and your old friends, peat moss and cow manure. You will be creating a slope, a hill, or a terraced effect. Not only is this great for whatever you grow because it provides a natural method of drainage, it also gives the opportunity to plant in steps or on different levels so the sun reaches everything. This effect is also much more pleasing visually, as viewing a bed or border now becomes three-dimensional. Natural 3-D is a fabulous thing and you don't need any of those curious glasses.

Truly one of the banes of my gardening existence was my reluctance to take this into consideration when we did important things, like put in the pond. If it had been raked (as in the rake of a stage), what is now quite charming would have been sensational. The pond is on a flat piece of land surrounded by various trees, so it is only the most explicit sunbeam that reaches behind it, allowing nothing beyond hosta or ivy to grow. Had we built up the area behind the pond, not only would we have better camouflaged the not very becoming woods, but would be able to grow oh, so many things that would make the whole pond scene more lush. Let my mistake be your good lesson. So, do think about this option, in front of

A garden nook created on the slope behind the white garden. The hands are just another of my fetishes.

fences or anywhere on your property; the perceptible starting point of a slight hill is a natural.

You can think about extending the fence into the interior of your property, thereby creating a garden room or a special area. You can mask the fence with hedges, or some less formal combination of evergreens. You can make it the backdrop for a rugged furniture grouping or an outdoor dining room. You can hang planters filled with begonias on your fence if you have shade, you can rig birdhouses on top of it, you can do a million things. You can even fix it to reflect the night-blooming morning glories, when the moon is in the right quadrant, that is.

What your fence is made of will certainly influence how little or how much of it you choose to adorn or hide. Obviously, if you have installed a beautiful natural bamboo fence correct to all rigorous Japanese standards, you do not necessarily want it to serve as merely a vine support. A choice of such a definitive nature makes its own statement and most likely, if you've gone that far, you would carry the theme through with smooth river-rock pathways and the delicate sound of water dripping from some ancient-looking Japanese waterwheel. The bamboo can be split, woven, picket-fence-like, or curved. Call for the catalog of the Bamboo Fencer and you will be thrilled with countless choices.

Settling on a material and deciding how best to use it is no different from all things of option. When designing clothes, you begin with the material. If you want a soft, drapey, fluid look, you don't start out with gabardine. If you want a breezy, casual, informal garden, then you would probably be much happier with a split-rail fence than proper bamboo or rigid stockade. If you want something gracious, long lasting, and beautiful unto itself, you might go for wrought iron—intricate or just symmetrical—covered or bare. Also, very expensive, unfortunately.

Fences are the natural extension of gateways and are very handy at obscuring ugly views, unsightly bramble, garbage cans, and cellar doors. They are the best way to provide privacy, whether from the street or not especially welcome neighbors. They can also be a vain attempt to keep the dog in and the rabbits and raccoons out; but in my experience, this works only in theory because Pooch is resourceful and always finds a new means of escape and the animal menage is still abundantly with us, even though we're now all fenced in.

GARDEN WALLS

Now, and very importantly, if your fence happens to be made of stone, brick, or even poured concrete—then it is a wall. A wall is superior to a fence any day; but walls are a *big* undertaking. Though magnificent, they are expensive and labor-intensive. If you happen to have one, or the wherewithal to build one, then treasure it. I have dreamed up any number of schemes to add garden walls around here, but as of yet, no walls. A few summers ago, I actually got close to building a stone wall. The right guys were around, intrigued by the project and into drawing all sorts of rock configurations. We spent many hours at the local quarry. Well, not really a quarry because the rock is not actually hewn from the ground there—rather it is more a gigantic Rock Store. There are huge piles of rocks: dozens of kinds, millions of shapes, all sorts of sizes powerfully scattered over acres and acres. Their origins are everywhere from Arizona to Thessaloníki, and trying to make choices was incredibly hard. Unfortunately, by the time I decided on *which* rocks and finally figured out how to pay for them, the liaison with the fascinated would-be wall-builders was over, and so, never got my wall.

If you build a real wall, make sure you build it with crevices, so things can grow not only over it—but *out* of it. There are two important concepts: a more or less solid wall built with mortar, and a wall laid stone on stone without cement or glue of any kind to bind it. The cemented and sealed wall is more formal, rigid, and perhaps a bit foreboding. An unmortared stone wall is what you want, the dreamy kind you see in all those fabled overgrown English garden photographs. That doyenne of gardening, Gertrude Jekyll, who really knows her walls says it the best:

> A grand old wall is a precious thing in the garden, and many are the ways of treating it. If it is an ancient wall of great thickness, built at a time when neither was work shirked or material stinted, even if many of the joints are empty, the old stone or brick stands firmly bonded, and, seems likely to endure well into future centuries. In such a wall wild plants will already have made themselves at home, and we may only have to put a little earth and a small plant into some cavity to be sure of a good reward. Often grasses and weeds, rooting in the hollow places, can be raked out and there spaces refilled with better things.

I particularly love the part about manual work not shirked and materials the finest. Oh, to have been in England! However, at this turn of the twenty-first century in America, we seem to be re-embracing a time of respect for manual labor and preference for honest materials. Certainly I've tried using this argument with Irving, suggesting we should tackle building a wall ourselves, but he is not even remotely excited by the scope of this project. After having spent arduous days over two summers laying in beautiful big rock borders of New Mexico terra-cotta and luminescent Crystal Lake rock around my gardens, I know my back is not as strong as my sincere yearning for a wall. Suffice to say, fences and walls are really important items in the landscape, so do give them uncommon attention. They are among the most basic garden bones and can make all the difference in the world as to how your property is perceived.

Having just returned from a fast, furious, and fantastic trip to Egypt, I can report that there are walls other than those made of stone that endure. The incredibly tasteful ancient Egyptians had a penchant for surrounding their temples and tombs with walls made of mud-bricks, which are precisely that—bricks made of dried, compacted mud—withstanding thousands of years of arid desert conditions. This, like many things, could be unique to the Nile Delta and its very particular climatic circumstances; but *Fine Gardening* has just published quite a convincing article extolling the virtues of "soil walls." Rammed earth walls, they say, weather beautifully, and they even suggest you can build such walls yourself. The description, however, of mixing the dirt with binders and compacting it by ramming got a little too detailed for me. But if intriguing to you, University of Arizona Press has a book, *Adobe and Rammed Earth Buildings* by Paul Graham McHenry, that might be just the ticket.

HEDGES

Hedges serve the same function as fences and walls, but being living things, they provide a more natural shield than wood, iron, stone, or anything else. Perhaps they are psychologically the politest way of defining your property, keeping nosy neighbors out, and providing a buffer between you and the rest of the world. Hedges can be giant or pygmy and are often the best way of separating gardens within gardens because of their ability to define and highlight. Their most interesting aspect is they can be formal or wild, depending on the image you want to convey.

When thinking of hedges, the perfectly pruned privet might be the first thing conjured, but it is by no means the only way to go. Consider a hedge of weeping cedars, for example, a complete departure from clipped and manicured. Or how about rhododendron (the evergreen kind with big fat leather-like leaves) mixed with holly (especially nice if you are one of those year-round Christmas people). Stick with things that stay leafed and green the year round because what's the point of a deciduous (leaf-losing) hedge when half the year you would be staring at a bunch of twigs? Even though the bare branches would still somewhat serve the purpose of a visual barrier, they are lousy at muffling the sound of traffic and diminishing the wind. So do not remotely think of using lilacs, hydrangea, rose of Sharon, or God forbid, forsythia, as a hedge; although you would be surprised how many times books list these as hedge suggestions.

Ultimately, conifers are probably the way to go. Of course, you need a lot of them, and big ones, if you want your hedge to magically appear overnight. Arborvitae, a fine needled fir, conical in form, a dense deep green if you choose the type called 'Emerald', seem to be the fastest growing and least expensive of evergreen choices. Another in the great buys and gorgeous looks department is *Cryptomeria japonica* 'Elegans'. We bought a fourteen-foot beauty for less than three hundred dollars, planted. This has a bushier, fuller habit, which bronzes beautifully in the winter. However, if money is no object, I would suggest combining different types of conifers arranged in a staggered fashion—creating a kind of green-gold-blue tree tapestry. Nowhere is it written a hedge *must be* a straight line.

One final word of advice on fences, walls, and especially hedges. As these items usually dominate the perimeter of your property—make sure they are well *on your* property and not someone else's. Property rights are such that a disagreeable neighbor can simply chop down anything infringing or overhanging his land and that could be very disconcerting.

WALKWAYS AND PATHS

The next obvious place to look for bones is wherever you walk. These patterns create pathways, walkways, or even require a sidewalk; similarly, your approach by car requires a driveway. These are essential elements to any property no matter what its location or size. Everyone has these in one way, shape, form, or another. This element must be as closely considered as the fence or hedge forming your boundaries, as its conception is the other most provocative garden bone.

It is next to impossible to determine what is most important about a passageway: its size, construct, material, or placement. The size and siting have everything to do with how most gardens are perceived, because the major walkway on any property naturally signals its focal point and, many times, is the origin of the garden itself. The idea should now be developing that nothing is necessarily what it appears to be, and everything already existing can be enhanced. The garden is everywhere.

A narrow walkway of thirty inches and a six-foot-wide path give two startlingly different perspectives to whatever is being approached, not to mention the approach itself. The former path could be considered intimate or just plain ordinary and boring, while the latter most likely will be perceived as grander and might even suggest an *allée,* which is a wide, decorous path most usually associated with French orchards. If you are dealing with a new piece of property on which walking patterns are not already defined, do ponder the best route for your path to travel, as it is not necessarily in a beeline from the street or car to the front door. A monotonous, straight walkway with a little border of impatiens on either side is too trite, especially if set off by a white picket edging. Why do that when there are so many other wonderful choices?

Most often a walkway meandering a bit is more interesting than a straight line. This curving or zigzagging should be planned to encapsulate some part of the garden or a garden picture. Paths that cross one another create a natural point to accentuate with some sort of planting or container. Your walkways should always be positioned, of course, to show your garden assets to their best advantage, leading from one part of your panorama to another with an amiable rhythm.

As a pathway marks the transition between the house and the outside, it makes sense that the material you use for your path bear some pleasing relationship to the materials of the house or some structure in the garden. Defining whether you want wood, stone, concrete, or gravel is only the beginning. What kind of wood: do you want it to be an extension of your deck in the same material? Do you want to paint it a different—maybe artsy—color? Or do you want a rough, natural look that might come from railroad ties? If stone, do you want precut interlocking stone for a solid look, or randomly placed stone? And do you want it to be terra-cotta or slate or one of the other multitude of rock that exist? The profusion of choices is endless.

Often existing conditions will help make your choices. If there are bricks left over from building your house or new garage, then use the bricks; if your local rock seller or mason advises you that the imported stone you've fallen in love with is five times as expensive as the local stone, use the local stone and spend the extra money on stone planters to accentuate the path. It's not so much the material itself, as *how* you use it and *where* you place it. But I'm definitely all for recycling found objects.

The path leading from our driveway to the front door is made of variously colored, irregularly cut marble slabs set into the grass. Though this looks pretty great, I don't advise it categorically because it's seriously slippery when wet; but since I just happened to have these slabs. . . . After the demise of my last extravaganza of a store, there were all these beautiful pieces of marble, once its shelves, and I could hardly let them go to waste. Actually, this architectural feat of a store that eventually led to my retailing ruin was filled with many natural and beautiful elements I've resurrected in the garden. In truth, they make me much happier here than they did in the store. Some of the most spectacular elements were not exactly portable, so I was forced to leave behind the lead-covered columns, which would have been fabulous interspersed among the strong, tall treetrunks, and a brass-gilded cage that would have made a fabulous arbor. But I did manage to make off with the display racks, which were metal sculptures, each unique enough to hold its own and not look as if its only reason for being was to hold Alaïa's latest number. They are now quite commendable as my garden vine supports or *tuteurs*. In the white garden, one now props up my "Duchess of Edinburgh" clematis, two at either end of the pool support some pendulous branches of our beautiful blue weeping cedars,

Garden *tuteurs*, available in many catalogs, covered with the lovelies of vines—clematis.

and in the burgundy garden there's one between a Scotch broom and a dogwood in my version of a daylily field on which I'm coaxing *Aristolochia*. Now, you may not have left over sculptural racks from a defunct store, but *tuteurs* are generally available in catalogs, and spectacular ones can be had from New England Garden Ornaments. They are a particularly nice way to accent a pathway or give structure to any garden bed.

Tuteurs are another charming French idea. Tall, metal, and open-worked, they are usually shaped like either a pyramid or obelisk, an orb or an umbrella. Any climbing plant growing on them suddenly takes on a stylized shape and further dimension. Claude Monet was particularly fond of them and used them to arrange all those graceful flowering images at Giverny.

The very heavy metal floor with "Dianne B" incised into it (along with other mysterious hieroglyphics) now stands on its side at the far end of our deck and holds my garden tools. Why allow anything with integrity to go to waste? Absolutely use what you've got, and if nothing is around—think carefully about what you choose from the vast array of options out there. Shop around and look around; it's the same story as delving into the nurseries.

Your path can be open, it can be covered with an arbor, it can be sided with a railing or a trellis, it can lead to an enchanting pergola; it can *always be more* than just a passageway leading from one place to another in any kind of creative gardening scheme. Amazing, too, what you can do with a few rocks, some paving stones, and interestingly colored gravel.

TREES

The last of the truly intrinsic garden bones is trees. Inclusive in this category are important shrubs, as well—old broad-as-tall rhododendrons, viburnums, and hydrangeas (to name a few) can invest your garden with shape and structure for sure—but the concentration here is trees, trees, trees. As I mentioned at the very beginning, if you don't already have trees, it is imperative that you acquire some. Get any old trees if you have to, get powerful and provocative trees if you can. In creating a harmonious garden, pay paramount attention to which trees you obtain and how they relate to any trees already there. There are millions of trees, and though not a tree expert, I do know there are basically two main kinds: evergreens (which are classified as conifers and usually have some kind of needle instead of leaves) and deciduous trees (which are the huge spectra of trees that lose their leaves in winter and often bear flowers or fruit at some point in the year). This is a very broad statement and would be hooted right out of the greenhouse by any forthright horticulturist, but this big generalization is true and the first thing you must come to terms with. As trees are the most cogent element of the garden, let's deal with them in grand, sweeping ways.

Trees are the most natural, and therefore perhaps the most essential, of your garden bones. Just like perennials, annuals, vines and shrubs, they are plants of Mama's kingdom and come in many different variations; but unlike their kinfolk, they never truly disappear and are with you in one form or another through all seasons. They are living records. You can plant a tree to mark momentous occasions like the birth of a child, a marriage, the move-in to a new home, or anything you want to commemorate. Most likely, the tree will evolve and flourish. One can only hope the human drama unfurls in the same forthright and indicative manner.

Trees will not necessarily surprise or excite you like so many other things you will plant because they grow slowly and thoughtfully. Of course, "slow" is a relative term, and there are a few trees like weeping willows and poplars that grow alarmingly fast. One must take into consideration when planting a tree its eventual size in relationship to the whole space, but generally, don't worry about fifty years from now—five years maybe, but not fifty. In their comparably slower growth and mass, they command a greater presence. Although not eternal, as they can be toppled by the elements, they probably will outlive you. *The New York Times* tells me the average American moves eleven times in one life cycle. Considering that, planting trees is probably one of the most permanent things you will ever do. If you are prone to looking at the future with a "big picture" frame of reference, then you can pride yourself in the thought that every time you plant a tree, prune a tree, fertilize a tree, you are contributing to many following generations of what one hopes will be nature appreciators, if not outdoor enthusiasts. Trees occupy a proportionately greater space than anything else you can grow, and therefore, they determine the mood of any land they inhabit.

With the exception of an ocean horizon, can you honestly say you have ever seen an arresting bit of scenery not including at least one tree? Highly unlikely. Can you conjure up even one idyllic landscape not tree-ridden? I bet you can't. Come to terms with your trees. The evergreens are more taken for granted than their showier deciduous cousins. They, too, change with the seasons; but it is a highly subtle change. In exchange for their lack of spectacular flowering periods and brilliant autumn foliage, they provide a year-round presence and give permanent shape to the landscape. Whether used as a hedge, in a grove, or as a definition of space, they probably exert more importance than any other single thing because they are *always* there.

If you are blessed with a tree-covered property, think very carefully before you decide to remove any. Trees create the natural elements around which your paths meander, are a natural backdrop to any border, soften a fence or any other means defining a boundary, and they largely determine what sort of gardens you can even plan; that is, a densely tree-shaded area is no place to grow roses or anything in love with sun. Trees are the anchor of the garden.

As this particular garden book is not a study in how to spend many thousands upon thousands of dollars creating a mature forest from nothing, and not a treatise on patience required to grow trees of serious stature from shoots, I'll discuss only trees accessible, somewhat affordable, and already conspicuous. Much more into flowers than trees (given we had all these wonderful old trees to begin with which are the starting and stopping point for all the gardens), I will get rapturous only over trees I've come to know, found deserving, and heartily condone. Though our plot in East Hampton is no arboretum, as it would take hundreds of species of trees and woody plants to qualify for that nomenclatural highpoint, it is a pretty great looking place with lots of swell trees. Speaking of arboretums—it is my duty to point out one more gardening idiosyncracy. Though ultimately, how to pronounce this word is an enigma: I have heard both ar·bor·et (as in "yet")·um and ar·bor·et(as in "eat")·um and both from reliable sources. And it's true, *American Horticulturist,* the publication of the North American Horticultural Society, has in its seventy-first volume condoned seventy-four (74, that is correct) different spellings for this word describing "a tree place." The fact that you say arboriatorum and I say abortum only makes it that much more mysterious and interesting. After all, if you can choose from seventy-four ways to spell one word, then it is unlikely you could ever spell it wrong. This, too, is what gardening is all about. Endless choices that have only one determining factor in the end—does it sound/look/feel/smell right to you!

Big Trees

Either you already have them or can afford to spend a bundle to buy them. Steven Spielberg, just down the road a bit, this summer completed a guest house and literally surrounded it with a full-grown forest. The stockade fence is now bordered by two layers of trees on *both* sides, which means his new planting is four trees deep. The interior layers are maybe eighteen feet tall and the exterior layers about ten feet. Why they are all deciduous is beyond me, and they're not very distinctive trees at that, but I guess he was opting for subtle and doesn't care about winter. Anyway, my Irving has a way of extracting information and from an inside source got the Spielberg dope. To shield this little guest house cutely named Quelle Barn East from the road, he reportedly spent "between seven and eight hundred thousand." Well, this is a pretty hefty sum for a bunch of indiscriminate trees if you ask me, but goes to show you anything can be done.

Obviously we all can't or wouldn't choose to operate on this scale. So if you have a lot of stark space and want to fill it quickly with graceful, fast-growing trees, plant those speedy weeping willows, Lombardy poplars, or the most towering and least expensive of the interesting conifers, *Cryptomeria*. Other than that, for the big tree mode, it is a slow-growth idea. My best experience with an imposing tree not already on our property when we arrived is our spectacular *Magnolia*. Surrounding our sizable deck, there is a big old dense juniper hedge, and in a big snowstorm some years ago we lost one of the bushes and were faced with a gaping hole in a very focal spot. Shopping to replace the juniper, we were shocked to find buying one of any equal size was going to cost several thousand bucks. "Oh, boo," I thought to myself, "who feels like spending that much money for this ordinary looking evergreen." Luckily, in my search to fill this hole, I spotted a magnificent *Magnolia grandiflora* for under three hundred dollars. What a godsend. Placed amidst the hedge, it creates a much more interesting look than cedar after cedar and—huge bonus—it is as evergreen as any hardy conifer. Twelve months a year, it persists with gigantic, dark, leathery-looking green leaves that seem waxed, and come summer, it bears extraordinary creamy-white flowers almost a foot in diameter. This fabulous display is followed by berry-laden cones, also sensational, and a fresh summer display of even more of those lavish leaves. When we planted it, it was a few feet taller than the rest of the hedge, maybe twelve feet high. Now it towers over the hedge these few years later at about eighteen feet, maybe twenty. This is what I call a great buy. Each of its qualities is superb, and the little touch of the Ol' South is capriciously charming.

Not-So-Big Trees

Japanese maples, properly called *Acer palmatum*, are another group to put your money on. Now, a little explanation is required here because there are many kinds of Japanese maples at all sorts of prices. They have obviously become an obsession to some because it is incomprehensible how many of them are for sale in East Hampton alone in the five- to twenty-thousand-dollar range, which means someone must buy them. Even Jack Benson, Irving's brother, known as quite the astute businessman but definitely not one of the last big spenders, succumbed to a Bloodgood Cutleaf Japanese maple for his one-time Connecticut digs and forked over six thousand bucks, which we've heard about at least a hundred times. But there is no need to go to such extremes if you have any modicum of patience or some shred of belief that you will be occupying your property for at least a few years.

We have installed quite an array of Japanese maples ranging in price from eight to sixteen hundred dollars. Granted, the sixteen-hundred-dollar palmate (leaves shaped like a hand) 'Osakazuki' six years later is quite a specimen. A joy in every season: a variegated olive-khaki bark in winter; a fine architectural form when leafless; a brilliant chartreuse turning to real green as spring changes to summer; a fabulous panoply of scarlet, auburn, and gold as autumn ensues. I suppose it was worth the money, but now it has almost outgrown its milieu. It was one of our more extravagant purchases made just after buying the house when who knew better? It could have been bought years younger for maybe a third as much money and would probably be just right today and require less pruning. Pruning, by the way, wants to be done in very early spring, and the growth habit of each individual tree will dictate its need for same. Aside from removing any dead twigs, or the purposeful desire to keep the tree a certain size, you won't be doing much pruning at all as the maples have a naturally graceful proportion and seem to shape themselves.

Our very own Bloodgood Laceleaf Japanese maple, *Acer palmatum dissectum* 'Viridus', installed the same time as the 'Osakazuki' cost a tenth of what Jack paid, is now a true specimen, and looks exactly like what's for sale for many thousands. Seeming millions of delicate filigree-like leaves make up each pendulous branch,—an overall look of pure elegance. But the ultimate illustration of savvy Japanese-maple acquisition is the one I ordered for eight dollars from a catalog printed on newsprint. I remember clearly it was eight dollars, because when it arrived in its twig-state, Irving cackled and sardonically questioned why was I so carefully planting a stick.

My eight-dollar stick, planted next to our pond, even in its first season began to look like a

One view of our *Acer palmatum dissectum* 'viridus' in its sixth year.

little tree. Now I spend considerable time cutting it back because it grows at such a rapid pace it is competing with the weeping birch, which is our pond's focal point. Japanese maples are vigorous, beautiful, seemingly carefree, hardy almost everywhere, and easily occupy whatever position you accord them in a proud way. They thrive in sun or shade, although some sun is necessary if appreciation of all their fabulous color variations is what you're after. We now have six and are always on the lookout for engaging new cultivars. Japanese maples definitely merit your gardening dollars, and seventy-five dollars tops is all you really need to spend if you have even half an ounce of forbearance and ferret out good container-grown ones to begin with.

If the selection of Japanese maples at your local nurseries leaves you cold, you need not fret. A wonderful specialized catalog exists offering one- or two-year-old trees at reasonable prices. Mountain Maples nursery is the only nursery I've found that grows and exclusively sells these splendid specimens, and they seem to have covered the gamut. The catalog is divided by leaf shape, and the descriptions are eloquent enough to enable a choice, though it would help to have J. D. Vertree's proper *Japanese Maples* picture book at hand to see what they look like in living color. For an extra fifteen or twenty bucks you can go for the two-year size to make you proud quickly.

Magnolia and the maples are without question my known highlights in the tree category. Less luck with dogwoods (they don't want to flower at our house, and if they don't flower, then what's the point, because otherwise they're not that distinguished), but still maintain a glimmer of hope with a flowering peach planted bare-root four years ago. Although still tiny, it has born masses of deep magenta flowers and tiny, tiny little peaches for the last two years, which I find very endearing.

Weeping Trees

Ah, unconditionally my favorites, whether deciduous or evergreen, red-leafed or green-leafed, pendulous or contorted—I love the exotic flavor of weeping trees. Some can grow so big and weep so profusely, beeches especially, that the space under their branch canopy takes on the quality of an inner sanctum. Their width can be twice the size of their considerable height. All trees that have limbs growing down instead of up are considered weepers. Their unusual structure makes particularly grand garden bones, because their silhouette is so remarkable and sculptural. These are trees you never want to crowd. They need a position where they can show off their markedly distinct design.

Dominating the north side of my white garden is a black-green weeping Alaskan cypress. Its big dark droopy branches bear long needles that set the tone in the white garden for my preference for other pendulous plants like *Aruncus, Cimicifuga, Lespedeza thunbergii*, and my big, graceful white butterfly bush.

Anchoring either end of the pool are a pair of weeping blue Atlas cedars. Believe me, they are glorious. This type of tree you might recognize by the fact it can be trained to grow horizontally, and any self-respecting nursery usually has a few fabulous specimens that they show off. When we first planted them (at about six feet, or half the size they are now) it was our intention to train them in this horizontal fashion so one day they would meet in the middle and frame the far side of the pool in the draperylike waterfall manner they adopt. Well, staking and tying the flexible branches seemed like torture, so we decided to get rid of all the stakes and strings and let them take their own course. Perhaps one day training a fruit tree or crabapple in *"espalier"* fashion (which means deliberately pruning, pinching, bending, tying, and fastening branches in a formal design against a wall or trellis) will tempt me and I'll get more familiar with this conscious, studied exercise. However, the now unleashed drooping bows trail outward over each end of the pool and command a circumference of about twelve feet, bringing a special cohesion to the pool, lawn, and slate patio in a way best corresponding to my love for the wild and natural.

The Birches

Perhaps our most elegant weeper is *Betula pendula* 'Gracillis', the weeping birch dominating the pond. The shadows of the leaved or leafless swaying branches on the water, the silvery green leaves in contrast to the rest of the deep-greenery, always make me sigh.

Weepers and all birches are the last category of trees I vouch for and sorely wish there were more of them around here. Birches have the most distinguishable of beautiful barks and seem so incredibly pure in both their summer and winter states with exuberant white bark peeling off as gracefully as a ballerina folding into an effortless *plié*. A fabulous extra added attraction of birch bark is it can be stripped off in sheets large enough to be actually used as the most exotic writing paper imaginable. The next time you have a really sensitive letter to pen, try birch bark with real ink, and I promise you the recipient of your missive will be very hard-pressed to ignore or forget it.

THE WATER ELEMENT

Now we move to an idea less basic than walkways or trees, but likely to be the most effective asset you can impose on your garden. You can introduce water into your own landscape in many ways. Starting with the simplest, there is nothing wrong with building a garden around a big porcelain urn with room enough for a water lily, an upright water plant or two, and a few fish. This, of course, is not as nature-compatible as possessing a piece of land on which there is a natural brook or stream; but that being the rare circumstance, we will concentrate here on creating water where there isn't any. There are two approaches to water gardening: constructing a pond to fit into your landscape in the most natural way possible or introducing a more formal pool or fountain, which is strictly decorative and purposefully means to be an adornment.

The latter approach is by far the easier one, and you don't need to conjure up images of Versailles in order to think of creating a small pool on a flat piece of land. If you are building a house from scratch, incorporating a pool or small aqueduct right into the architecture of the deck or patio can be very rewarding. Assuming your house is already built and you have no natural hills, valleys, or hospitable spots on your plot to incorporate a water mood in sync with nature, a very delightful statement can still be made with a small formal pool amidst your plantings, echoing the character of your garden and house, without forcing onto it the idea it has sprung from nature. As a very straightforward statement, it can be the destination of your walkway surrounded by the same paving stones and plantings you have used elsewhere or can illuminate a woodsy edge. You will find it's amazing what the reflection of a little water and the presence of a few frolicking goldfish can do for your garden—and your spirits.

However, if you have the inclination and a receptive spot, the greatest joy is to install a pond as close to nature as you can possibly make it. I have mentioned our pond already, which sprung from nowhere but has acquired a look of inevitability as if it were meant to be there, even though the ground is more or less flat and its setting no more natural than being the transition between the lawn and woods where the long border changes from blue to burgundy. Gertrude Jekyll states quite unequivocally in her *Wall and Water Gardens* tome,

> Happy are those who desire to do some good watergardening and who have natural river and stream and pond, as yet untouched by the injudicious improver. For a beautiful old bank or water edge is a precious thing and difficult to imitate . . . it is as a canvas primed and ready for the artist's brush.

She is absolutely right; nothing beats the real thing; but take heart if you are without even a drop of natural water. You will be very surprised to discover what can be done with a plastic liner, rocks of some sort, and a little imagination.

Our pond is no rival for some gorgeous, huge man-made ponds I have seen, and certainly no nesting place for three species of gracious waterfowl, but it has changed the whole nature of our property with its fish and frog activity and that intangibly peaceful sound of dripping water. Tiptoeing around on back roads near the ocean off elite Lily Pond Lane on a rainy Sunday, Irving and I discovered a man-made pond so beautiful it made us both gasp. In the garden I'm always drooling over from the road and try to duly emulate, on this particular Sunday I brought Irving to see spring glory at its peak. Also to illustrate to him what I mean when constantly repeating I need ten times as many hellebores, hundreds of *Epimedium*, and lust after dozens of jack-in-the-pulpits instead of my three. Being much bolder than I, he wasn't satisfied to view this gorgeous scene only from the road, which I thought the intention of the sensitive owners, who embody good taste by the looks of this garden and their beautiful vine-covered chateau always seemingly bathed in a mist. So we trespassed.

Staggeringly divine doesn't come close to describing what lies beyond the road. Every inch of maybe three or four acres is drenched in the densest, most sumptuous plantings I've ever seen in a private (or public, as a matter of fact) place. Nothing left to chance but articulated in such a manner that it all seems inevitable. Primroses, which normally are take-it-or-leave-it, take on a very different meaning when there are two hundred of them in bloom in only the most desirable colors. Nurturing three little patches of *Convallaria* (lilies of the valley) for years and so thrilled this spring when my oldest patch finally bloomed, here was a field of lilies of the valley numbering in the hundreds surrounded by a profusion of the perfect companion *Polygonatum* (Solomon's-seal, truly fetching—a long arched stem with graceful frondlike leaves from under which more little white bell flowers grow). In the middle of all this loveliness, which is canopied by an immense melange of trees, there is a pond. Whether or not this pond already existed in some form or another or whether it was totally invented by them is anybody's guess; but it is breathtaking.

The pond itself must be at least half an acre and is endowed with its very own small island in the center complete with the perfect huge picturesque weeping tree. On that sublime Sunday filled with oohs and aahs, the island was populated by several kinds of ducks, some geese and a few big exotic heron-like birds that seemed very at home in this *Giardino Paradiso*. Encroaching on all this beauty, however, we did spy just an edge of black plastic, which meant the pond had a liner! See what can be done with some acreage, money, plastic, and love of all things beautiful.

On subsequent visits we discovered many things: A proper path from the side road made us think the owners, after all, were generous and didn't mind if people stepped in to view their garden. A *second* pond! This one with swans! The bathed-in-mist chateau by the road must be the gatehouse (or more likely, gardener's house) because the real house seems to lie beyond the gardens on the ocean. And an incredible progression of beauty as the season progressed. From mid-May to June, the highlight is irises, zillions of Dutch and English, then bearded Germans, culminating in fabulous Japanese varieties. Big, sweeping swathes of harmonious color. The iris display is followed by a lily display of equally grand magnitude. And, of course, there's a ravishing rose garden and a huge vegetable garden. Too beautiful for words. I'm also charmed to note there are always bags of cow manure tucked next to a tree here and there, a pile of empty nursery containers, more plants lined up in pots waiting to be planted—it is not just a static illusion, but an ongoing garden—which proves a garden is never finished and can always be improved. As summer draws to a close, it is intriguing even this Garden of Eden has holes in all the hosta leaves and the same things beginning to look ragtag in my garden are exactly the same in this one. This garden has become the barometer by which I now measure all gardens and certainly the look I strive for in my own.

Now, surely not everyone has the wherewithal or opportunity to create this sort of heavenly atmosphere; nor am I any less enthusiastic about our own in-harmony-with-nature pond because it is smaller and simpler. Ours came about totally spontaneously four years ago during the initial clearing-away-like-mad mode. The Serpentine Border was still in its early struggling stage, and there was a particularly ugly thicket of bramble and honeysuckle in the way of its next most likely progression. After a day of digging and hacking and pulling, we stood back to assess the situation, and Irving said, very plaintively and extremely decidedly, *he wanted a pond*. No sooner did this thought form than we were in L & M Nursery, as they have a really appealing small pond bustling with fish and frog activity, good trees and shrubs, and are pond-installers. The very next day their truck arrived loaded with bamboo, our weeping birch, one of our Japanese maples, some yucca plants, lots of rocks, and some very cool, muscular, attractive young guys.

This battalion of cute guys started digging and by day's end, lo and behold, we had a pond. Now I can't say this brand-new man-made-from-scratch pond looked like it had been there since the beginning of time, but it did look pretty divine, and suddenly what was just a dead spot forty-eight hours prior was now this fabulous focal point. Having this vision of our version of a teeming wildlife sanctuary, we raced to Hampton Bays to what we were told was the ultimate fish store in the Hamptons. We explained in no uncertain terms to the Fish Store Man that we had a brand-new pond to stock. Well, it is clear this guy saw us coming a mile away and encouraged my every whim. I fell in love with fab fashion frogs looking like a Jean Paul Gaultier frock at its best—a great chartreuse color with burnt orange dots arranged in sort-of stripes. When I said "Give me two," the guy said "Take four." "Absolutely," I said, picturing them perched on the rocks adding this wonderful sense of humor to the serenity. Then there were turtles; we had to have the most beautiful ones, which, of course, were the most expensive, but splendid with extreme shades of color like in old Victorian tortoise vanity sets. Then the fish. The guy gave us a big story about Japanese coy and their life spans and why every inch of their length justifiably cost that many more incremental dollars.

Very excitedly, we sped home with our bounty of water creatures. Hampton Bays, a town not normally frequented by us, never seemed farther from East Hampton than it did that day as I balanced all of those plastic bags full of breathing swimming things on my lap. Upon arrival, we dashed to the pond and very meticulously, very carefully as instructed, replaced the water in the bags with water from the pond so the adjustment of all these creatures was not too abrupt. Having done this in the most gentle and caring way, as if each of these creatures was to become as personal to us as our pooch, we stood back to survey the vision of flora and fauna created by all these life-forms. Within ten minutes, maybe less, we stood gaping as not one—*but each and every one*—of the four-legged creatures bounded from the pond we had so faithfully introduced them to and scattered to God knows where. It was then that I knew the age-old adage about the hare and the tortoise was just as false as the one about eating apples every day. I detest apples and am healthy as can be and you have never seen anything zoom and flee as fast as these turtles. We obviously never again patronized that Fish Man, who promised us we would have a grand old pond, and my suspicion that one should avoid Hampton Bays bore fruit.

The fish, thank God, can't crawl or hop, so they stayed around for as long as any fish stay; because to keep them you have to compete with raccoons, seagulls, and the necessary but evil annual job of cleaning the pond, Irving's least favorite late-spring chore. If you do not clean the pond once a year, it becomes a pestilence and provides none of the endearing qualities for which you acquired the pond in the first place. Trickling sounds drip to a halt as the filter gets clogged and fish-watching becomes obscured as the algae turns the water that horribly thick rancid green. The only thing to do is empty the pond, scrub down the rocks, bale out the leaves. Definitely the downside of the pond adventure. Invariably the biggest of the fish do not survive their overnight stay in temporary quarters, no matter how diligently we follow the best directions and how large we make their hotel room. But during the course of a year, the pond is a wonderful thing and warrants this repugnant, if not repulsive chore.

Intermittently the original planting has been added to with reliable ivy, hosta, caladiums, Asiatic lilies, which bloom despite our pond being bathed in shade, some variegated liriope (a nice fountain-shaped clump-forming plant that looks like exotic grass), and a combination of *Osmunda regalis* (royal fern) and crown-vetch (looks better than it sounds), which both have the same airy fernlike leaf and complement one another. There are the Japanese maples at either end (a graceful, dark red *dissectum* original to the pond and my rampant eight-dollar one). Crocus in the spring, colchicum in the fall, and a number of my odd *Arum* varieties for leafy form and texture complete the look.

We try to be natural as possible about keeping the pond fit, although there are certain chemicals we are forced to subscribe to when the water looks too dank or the fish seem sick. In the customary natural mode, however, each year we stock it with snails and tadpoles. These two creatures are both scavengers, so between them and the submerged oxygenating plants, our pond manages to look healthy all summer and produces enough natural vegetation for the fish to survive the winter, just as if the pond were a work of nature. The most endearing quality of the tadpoles, of course, is that they eventually turn into frogs. Unlike the fashion frogs, the ones who have spawned there actually hang around and sometimes even perform such distinctive acts as perching on a lily-pad just like all those garden sculptures imitate. Great profusions of them hop around in early spring and reappear in late summer. Where they go in between is another one of those mysteries of life.

Once the summer weather is firmly in place, the final glorious touches are added. Waterlilies—what would a pond be without waterlilies? Of the two categories, the hardy waterlilies, which actually manage to survive winter in the pond, are not the resplendent ones of

One day we cleared a thicket (top photo), the next day we had Irving Pond. This photo is actually three years into the pond exercise.

dreamy Botticellian images or Giverny's lily-gorged gardens. Though they do produce quite a number of flowers, they are diminutive and the lily-pads puny. The really gorgeous ones with the big pads are tropical waterlilies. Flowering in a much more showy fashion, they are bigger in all respects, grow on longer stems, and exist in the most enchanting shades of blue and lavender, besides the white, pink, yellow, and red ranges of their dowdy sisters, the hardy lilies. These are not cheap, especially as they have to be treated like annuals and replaced each summer (unless you have a spare sun-lit bathtub to turn into a holding tank); but they are worth every dime. Blessed with two nurseries stocking waterlilies and other water plants, we are able to pick our beauties ourselves.

If you are not so fortunate, Lilypons Water Gardens, which exists in Maryland and Texas and ships everywhere, has a splendid and consummate catalog offering everything from lilies to liners to fish food and frogs. The catalog is to be savored as a great product source as well as a textbook about pond care and maintenance. Last but never least, they are very helpful, like getting a replacement pond filter to us overnight when ours wore out, stagnating the water as it kicked the bucket. Aside from waterlilies, I have had great luck with *Pontederia* (a water plant that also survives winter and has interesting arrow-shaped leaves); water clover, which are big four-leaved affairs that add a lucky touch; and water hyacinths, which spread like mad and produce unearthly fat bulbous stems. As I saw on my recent foray to Egypt, my concept of spreading like mad and the Nile's version are two very different accounts. There the canals are so clogged with so many incorrigible water hyacinths that deciphering the liquid from the land is futile. But in this land of contradictions, nothing is usual. In the narrow fertile strip enveloping the Nile (which represents 3 percent of Egypt, by the way, and is home to 58 million Egyptians) what grows *really* grows—banana trees and date palms so stately, profuse, and prodigious against the dry, barren desertscape only yards away that they seem more surreal than their carved Balinese counterparts.

Unfortunately, without a bog (the muddy part between the water and the land in a natural pond), I've no experience with the fabulous array of bog lilies and bog iris; nor have we the hot sunny conditions necessary to grow lotus. You can imagine, with all the mystical, religious and exotic connotations they conjure, lotus are high priority on my list. I mean, on what would Buddha sit if it weren't for the legendary lotus? After no luck with lotus attempts from Lilypons (East Hampton is just not Bali, where they grow in such wondrous profusion, holding their heavenly oval eighteen-inch-wide leaves erect at least five feet above the water's surface, the lustrous flowers and seed pods doing the same dance—all true objects of beauty), this year Marder's had such a vigorous, fabulous lotus, Irving said, "Oh, honey, it's not like this would be the first $75 we've ever wasted. Buy it if you love it so much." So home it came to roost at the sunniest edge of our pond. We even vainly cut away two more levels of surrounding tree limbs, hoping to give it that extra touch of light that might do the trick. Well, it didn't die, but no manna-like flowers were forthcoming either. *However,* those legendary leaves devotedly kept materializing, one after another, all summer long—and that performance was enough for me. If you think your situation is at all imitable of the Tropics, central France (Giverny again), or like me, if those gravity-defying dancing leaves would be enough for you, then you must have lotus. But if not lotus, then waterlilies are very very nice and certainly will suffice.

So lotus or no lotus, if you are serious about your garden being fulfilling and fabulous—definitely investigate introducing water somewhere. It is the greatest sensual element you can add as it plays not only on your visual sense, you can also hear ripple and splash, you can smell it (sometimes aromatic, occasionally a bit fetid), and you can even beget a new sense of family by the addition of fish and whatever else may settle in once you've provided some water. Though less exciting than the pond or pool itself, think of the other advantages to a water garden: no mowing and no weeding.

Aren't you convinced? Your biggest problem now is to make the choice between a more formal pool, a natural pond, lagoon, or if you are really ambitious—a stream. The most beautiful private house/villa/estate I've had the pleasure of spending time in is "La Fiorentina" on Cap Ferrat, which had it all. Among the distinguishing features of this dreamworld: the house stationery—featherweight parchment neither engraved or embossed but watermarked; the erratic combinations of Pratesi and Porthault linens changed daily in each of the many guest rooms—all with fully stocked bathrooms of the finest soaps and oils; plus *two pools,* a lagoon, and a charming pond. The formal pool was not for swimming, but a long, long rectangular affair for reflecting, judiciously placed on the perimeter fronting the lower lawn of the villa and hedging the tennis court. The cheekily casual swimming pool sat on a cliff overlooking the Grand-Corniche, flanked by a Palladian pool house on one side and the Mediterranean on the other. There were flowers everywhere and, of course, a charming pond centered around an old stone well. It was heaven.

You can make *your* water look serene or wild, you can impose a real Japanese aesthetic using sacred river rocks and lengths of bamboo spouting water at just the right intervals, you can even turn your swimming pool into a water garden of sorts. Of course, this is most easily done if you are building your pool from scratch and make it a free-form natural curving shape more readily accepting of lush watery plantings. But even the most rigid rectangular pool can be softened by combining it with an ornamental water feature: a gurgling fountain, a reflecting pool, a surround reminiscent of those fabled hanging gardens of Babylon. No matter which approach you take, water is a major garden bone and will outsparkle anything.

GARDEN ROOMS AND GARDEN DIVISIONS

Do not think the idea of rooms in a garden sounds stiff, as they are in fact, very soft. They are another sure way to give structure to your garden and can be as simple as introducing a trellis or elaborate as building an iron filigree outdoor summer pavilion. Not suggesting you create garden rooms with anything like traditional walls; here you use screens and frames, lattice and trellis, trees themselves, or ultimately a unique garden formation such as a gazebo, arbor (an arch), pergola (raised horizontal beams supported by columns), or a belvedere (charming open-air house with a view). This is the decorative definition of space that goes beyond the relationship of driveway to house and fence to pool or outdoor dining room. Indigenous to the best gardens is the wonderful element of surprise.

If able to stand in one spot and see the entire gardening picture with one sweeping glance, then the subtleties of any garden are likely to be lost. The ideal is a garden that is *concealed* and then *revealed* by the use of some structure, tree, or screening device, your property then appears larger, more intriguing, and infinitely more inviting. Garden areas also provide for various gardening techniques: you can't very well place a rock garden smack up against a perennial border and expect to achieve any kind of desired effect unless there is some transition between the two.

An ultimate illustration of this method is the *limonaria* (literally lemon-house, a wrought-iron-encased, frivolous but functional glass house, home to a lemon grove), which I saw at the *Villa I Tatti*, Bernard Berenson's eccentric scholarly home in the hills beyond Florence surrounded by breathtaking gardens even fabulous when viewed in October. The function of the *limonaria*, beyond protecting the lemon trees, is to divide the terraced gardens between the flowering and the nonflowering (leaf color, leaf texture, leaf size, etc.) parcels. What a vision— what great taste—what a day! So inspired by the Berensons' magnificent overture to the Renaissance, I even impressed myself as my gardening awareness was overtly reawakened. Maybe I can't always tell a Titian from a Tintoretto, but the only one in the elitest tour group (ten people are admitted once a week arranged months in advance) who could name the blooming plumbago hedge was me! The flower on my small mound of *Ceratostigma plumbaginoides* happened to look exactly like this flowering hedge—and I knew!

Without introducing a grandiose structure like a *limonaria,* or any structure at all for that matter, garden rooms or divisions are perhaps most naturally created with pathways and permanent tree plantings. Often this can be enough to segregate space, or it can be heightened further by the introduction of screening or framing. Either way, spatial definitions are what you're after: to mask an area you want to conceal by creating a blind or barrier, to separate your garden's moods, as well as to compose a view or create a focal point.

Trellis and latticework can take on many forms and can be used in a vast number of creative ways. The French have made a real art of it and have a term for it—*treillage*. This actually refers to a centuries-old art of creating complicated and ornate architecture out of flimsy trellis suggesting massive architectural statements. On my last trip to Paris, I was never so aware of just how much of this treillage is around. Its most dominant feature is its uncanny ability to create dimension and perspective with a flat piece of intricately worked wood. Instead of boring, bland diagonally slatted strips usually associated with run-of-the-mill trellis, incorporated within the woodwork are arches, *allées,* and all sorts of interesting shapes. It is used to enclose space on the top of buildings, mask uninteresting walls, and bring focus to a spot otherwise prosaic. So taken was I with all of this treillage enhancing Paris, the already most embellished city in the world, a major trellis urge is coming on and I expect it means a new project about to be undertaken at home.

If carpentry is not your strong point and creating treillage not in your scope, it's easy to create alcoves and niches with the everyday trellis bought at your local building-supply-house, as a design device. Segregating various parts of your garden, screening the pool from the house, or hiding fuel tanks—this most appropriate way will lend interest where there was nothing or something unspeakable. There doesn't seem to be a cornucopia of sources for interesting ready-made trellis, posts, arches, and modules, but Country Casual in Maryland and Bow House in Massachusetts have the most imaginative variety.

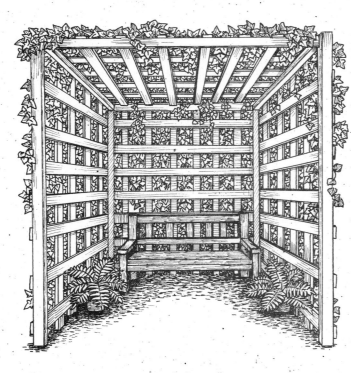

This simple structure, once vine-laden, will emerge as a heavenly garden room.

A naked trellis or lattice structure, no matter how enterprising its shape and use, will still be lacking until it is covered with twining, climbing plants: the raison d'être of arbors, trellis, et al. Here we revisit the-what-to-do-with-the-fence routine. Remember the eternal ivy and the extravagant selection of vines and climbers. Climbing and rambling roses are breathtaking when in full flower either covering a trellised wall, flowing over an arbor, camouflaging the garage, or canopying a walkway. The ramblers, the most graceful of the two kinds, have the drawback of flowering only once during a season. The climbers are a bit more stiff in their growth habit, but they flower over a longer period and offer immense choices in kind and color. Unfortunately, these words on roses are not coming to you through my own painstaking experience, but this seems to be the cumulative byword according to everything read, and James Topping—who insists ramblers are the way to go, and his exotic chicken house smothered in red ramblers bears witness to his preference. An exotic chicken house, by the way, is a normal old henhouse except it is home to fascinating foreign chickens like a Chinese red pheasant, ostriches, and an albino peacock instead of your day-to-day cluckers and egg-layers.

My choice of the vine queen: clematis is more personal. Looking out one window of my lacquered green room (my lovely office in East Hampton) in late May, I can see a fence not quite densely covered; but truly a sight to behold as six *Clematis montana* 'Rubens' are flowering and twining like mad all over the place. Yes, the same half-dead looking bunch of twigs we purchased for half-price last November are now, a mere seven months later, double in size, and each is smothered in pale pinkish mauve flowers that individually are not so large but appear lavish in their abundance. Another clematis success is with perhaps the most common cultivar called 'Jackmanii'. This big, delightful purple flower explodes here in early July. A big solitary shrub-form evergreen, nameless because it was already here hiding the pool equipment when we moved in, has taken on new meaning now serving as backdrop for three rampant 'Jackmanii'. Already in May they are twining like crazy through the shrub and producing tons of buds, and during the July flower explosion the bush literally turns purple. Also a few 'Nelly Mosers' are being nursed in hopes they will burst forth among the golden-cedars around the pool and adorning every tree trunk that backs the blue border are various blue varieties. The trick with the clematis, said over and over and corroborated by my ordeals after any number of false starts, is they need to have *cool* roots and *hot* tops. This translates to their preference for a sunny position with either a good mulch around them or an over-planting with ground cover. At the base of the 'Jackmanii' drenched shrub, there is ivy; in the white garden the glorious 'Duchess of Edinburgh' is surrounded by hosta and aruncus. These *Clematis montana* 'Rubens' smiling at me from the new fence are planted between arborvitae and deeply mulched with the chunkiest pine nuggets.

Clematis are a specialty, and countless cultivars bloom from spring throughout summer: my grand plan is to acquire a few new kinds each year and intersperse them along fences and shrubs to create continuous flowering from May to September. So, when you invest in your clematis, make sure to buy hybrids blooming at different times. In my big scheme, the visual aim is to have them fighting for space and outdoing one another with their fabulous fairy-tale flowers. Some of the later ones are particularly spectacular, with huge flowers as big as eight inches across that somehow never seem heavy, and a myriad of color. The patient clematis exercise is one of the most worthwhile.

Perfectly suited to cover your arbor, pergola, or trellis are other divine vines faster-growing and easier than clematis. If clematis is the queen, then wisteria is the grandmother of vines because of its toughness, abundant proportions, and resemblance to an antiquated hanging garden when in flower. If you buy wisteria plants young, it might be five years before they flower; but when this happens in late spring, they are a breathtaking sight to behold and well worth the wait, but they do vine and leaf like mad from day one. As they age, their profusion of tangled branches takes on the thick, twisting, gnarled look of something ancient. The flowering format is called a "raceme," an inimitable trailing bower of lilac-colored double-petal puffs hanging in abundance from long trailing stems. Wisteria are a special thing.

One Chinese wisteria is twining and leafing like mad around the deck rails behind the first cutting garden for five years with nary a flower and another in training as a standard (tree-form) has bloomed twice in three years, which gives me faith. But flower or no flower, if hours aren't spent cutting back and harshly pruning during the summer and again in winter, they'll take over the whole joint. So, if you want an airy leafy wonder that will eventually flower splendidly— throw up a latticed surround and grow wisteria. You can't miss. Whining to a few of my local nursery chums recently about why there are not more flowers on one and still none on the other did me no good. They all gave me the same tired, uninformed retort, "You are too nice to it." I'm not exactly sure what that means other than they haven't the faintest idea, because, as you know, a diligent fertilizer I'm not and my pruning is haphazard at best. So I wait, and marvel at the proliferation of other grand wisterias around town.

A combination of these and other adamant vines like *Campsis* or *Aristolochia* and a trellis of one shape or another will add immense dimension to your property. You can be casual or formal when imposing these sources of division and sight reference. Yard sales and flea markets can yield bits of old wrought iron, the town handyman may be challenged by your vision of treillage, or you can go to great lengths and build a true garden structure. This clearly will be a profound garden bone.

> The troubled voices of working machines
> Guard over useless anemones
> Given every chance but one to bloom.
> Would a symphony improve this? With earth
> Like grey, soggy paté receding behind them,
> The vines have nearly located the auxiliary
> Source of false energy. Surely anything
> That can extend itself upon our walls
> Knows more than we, with our constant but
> Surrogate loves and our horizontal harmonies.
> Steven Hamilton, "Fashion"

Almost any structure, however, apart from your main house—be it a garage, a garden shed, a pool house, a tree house, a conservatory (I wish), or a died-in-the-wool true garden room—has the potential to give your garden one of its most important structural elements. This is where the English excel with their wrought iron arbors and most fabulous tour de force—the English "folly," which has no use whatsoever but to enchant the garden.

Think of any structure you might have or think to build as a major component of a garden room. Planted all round its base, veiled in flowering vines, composing a backdrop for your sleepy hammock niche or covered picnic nook, it is an anchor. Invariably, paths will lead to it, whatever it is, and if nestled in a grove of trees, so much the better. A shrouded-in-shade little garden structure can be a woodland wonderland. Captivating and enticing garden structures tempt you deeper into the garden and invariably create the illusion of greater space. These airy edifices, no matter how simple, no matter if made of wood, metal, or stone, are decorative and useful highlights imposing progression and pattern on what otherwise might be ordinary garden chaos.

POTS, URNS, AND ANYTHING ELSE THAT MIGHT BE A CONTAINER

Now we come to the most accessible of garden bones—flowerpots. "Pot" is actually too narrow a word as it conjures up just that, a pot, while plants can be grown in almost anything you can dream up, from gutsily sized good old classic terra-cotta to a hollowed out tree stump. Depending on the character of your house and the disposition of your taste, your containers can be hearty wooden things you build yourself if so inclined; they can be metal—painted or raw, fancy or plain; they can be carved stone (my favorite); they can be old cast iron, or even a Jackson Pollackish paint bucket if you've a way with a brush. The range and scope of things you can use to plant in is mind-boggling, and how you position these planters can either create a garden unto themselves or focus an existing patch.

Pots, tubs, vases, urns, baskets, old stone troughs, your grandmother's lead kitchen sink: all of these, and any other found object you might embrace, are containers with the potential to add great dimension to your garden or punctuate the various aspects of your house. Containers may be single, on pedestals, grouped by pot shape, medium, or color, fine enough to be called a vase or grand enough to be named an urn. If you prefer neatness and clarity over a great wild sprawl—then container gardening is for you.

No matter how cozy or grand your domain, there is almost nothing can match a front door flanked with substantial pots/enigmatic baskets/filigree iron urns of flowers or plants to say, "Hi there. Come on in." Your deck, patio, porch, or pool surrounds can only benefit from containerized plantings. A plant, small tree, or shrub in a tub is spotlighted and set apart from everything else whether at the beginning of your driveway, at your gate, or in the middle of your garden. You might want to pot up and segregate a particular plant because you love it so much, to make a statement with a bizarre topiary, or because it makes sense for it to be portable (as in divine plants unable to survive winter outdoors). All planting containers are not necessarily portable, however; an old stone sarcophagus turned up at auction just as you are about to bid is not exactly movable once adorning your garden, but could be a magnificent repository for worthy plants.

Containers can be used very effectively right in the garden among the plants as well as around the pool, patio, or porch. That old stone sarcophagus, for instance, would make a fabulous nucleus right in the garden, giving it drama, depth, and one hell of a garden bone. Baskets hanging from tree limbs within the garden will add a new height dimension, as will anything placed on a pedestal. Using *meaningful* containers deliberately in your garden scheme will ultimately give the impression of a truly considered look. Even those homely cut-in-half whiskey barrels (which are my least favorite of the receptacle options) can be comely if inventively planted.

What you plant in your containers should mandate a specific theme or highlight a particularly beautiful specimen. The trouble with most containers on my rounds is they are usually planted with a jumble of silly annuals having nothing to do with anything conscientious. You've seen this muddle a million times: some of that inane fuzzy blue ageratum, mixed with some stiff orange marigolds, and to really add to the confusion, a sprinkling of pink impatiens with red geraniums thrown in for good measure. If the mire aspires to any style at all, maybe you might see a little vinca cascading over the sides. This is really a waste of a container, especially if a beautiful one.

How much more tantalizing to use the same container to show off a collection of dreamy color-coordinated begonias (a combination of cascading and tuberous upright strains is a real thrill), a magical Japanese maple, some fabulous tropical plant blooming all summer, or an interestingly pruned juniper (the spiral, conical, and poodle shapes are all titillating, but this summer Marder's had a paradigm of true gorgeousness—three stems holding aloft eighteen-inch-diameter, dense juniper balls: one blue, one evergreen green, and one golden: but at $850—sadly a little out of my container-plant league). Unfortunately, those brilliant blooming tropical things, unmatched by any annual at our fingertips, are quite precious here in Zone 7. Precious in a few ways: you must water them like mad because they are used to all that steamy equatorial humidity, you have to pay between forty and a hundred dollars for glorious ones because they are far from local and not necessarily every nursery's cup of tea, then you must try to coddle and nurture them through winter indoors.

Moderate success has greeted me with *Stephanotis* (Hawaiian wedding-flower), but I've failed miserably time after time with various breathtaking hibiscus, and am disturbed by my *Mandevilla*. In its first summer, it put on an amazing flowering spectacle. Bought in big bloom for forty-five dollars, it produced huge, just-right-pink, morning glory-like (but better) flowers literally all summer long till brought inside in late September. It seemed okay all through the barren months, but when returned outside in summer, it waned and didn't pick up any good growth steam till August and finally decided to flower in October, just in time for the first frost. I'll winter it over one more time because most likely the sixteen out of twenty rainy weeks constituting our spring and summer last year had something to do with its lackluster performance. *Osteospermum* was the irresistible one this summer, for which I paid an all-time high of eighty-five dollars. It thrived till mid-August with a surplus of surreal hombred rose blooms—each flower, of which there seemed to be no end, emanated from a deep blue-purple center to tips of rosy-glow-pink in a shape resembling a firecracker in the night sky. These brilliant, tropical, all-star lengthy bloomers need to be contained in a worthy movable container, so at least you have a chance of witnessing them over again. But I save the best for last.

Passion flowers. Not a cognomen dreamed up by a garden skeptic, nor an attempt to lure you into a lustful web. The true Latin name is *Passiflora* and represents not some lascivious yearning, but the supposed true passion of Christ. A deserved title when you consider its various parts pictorially and theoretically represent:

1. A crown of thorns or a halo—depending on which version of Christ you subscribe to (the lavish stripings of deep purple, white, and lavender of the corona),
2. the ten good apostles who stayed true (the combination of the five petals and the five sepals),
3. the five wounds (the five stamens),
4. the scourges (the climbing tendrils),
5. the Holy Trinity (the styles), and
6. the grabbing hands of Christ's tormentors represented by the upreaching palmate leaves.

Not having heard this story when first confronted by a flowering passion vine, I was already ecstatic over its eccentric glorious flower and *just had* to have it. Imagine my euphoria, good Catholic girl that I am (although all sorts of people wish me happy new year on Rosh Hashanah—twenty years on and off with Irving must have rubbed off), when the revelation of the symbolism hit home. Or you can opt to ignore all this religious chitchat and concentrate only on its horticultural wonders. John Glover, that divine actor and beyond dear friend of mine, has passion vines cascading all over his sunny California fence (tales like this almost make Los Angeles yearned for). Right here in Zone 7 grow my three unstoppable passion vines. My few mail-order tries of coaxing a tiny seedling into growth were utter failures, but once I shelled out twenty-five dollars to buy an established one, then two, then three: I hit the gardening jackpot. They live in twelve-inch terra-cotta pots—each different—all winter perched in the sunniest spots of our not very sunny living-room windows twining around four-foot vine supports (the biggest obtainable) sunk in the pots. Not a month passes when they die down; they are always throwing off tendrils and green as can be. Even when the housekeeper is not diligent about watering (arriving after a month-long absence, I have found them withered to the very last stem) all it takes is a severe cutting back and up they materialize again. As soon as it seems warm enough again, around late May, two of them move outside into prime positions in our old Italian olive jars flanking the stairs leading to the white garden. The olive jars are made of wonderful thrown glazed clay, about four feet high, and just wide enough at their brim to receive the terra-cotta pots.

The scoop on the olive urns is comely. Irving, always there to help a friend in need, attended a last-ditch-effort auction staged by some defunct would-be nightclub impresarios-on-the-brink-of-exile and paid five hundred dollars for the two. Just last summer, a pair so similar I would venture to say identical showed up in a fine antiques establishment on Main Street for four thousand dollars. Circumstances like this always give me great joy; but not so great as the passion vines budding in early June and continuing through September to throw off their mystical blooms engaging everyone who sees them. Passion vines in olive urns epitomize container gardening at its finest at the Benson house.

A cautionary word is necessary now. It is much easier to grow things in the ground than to grow them in a pot—no matter

Our fine passion vines in their olive urn summer nest.

how grand the pot. Not even deferring to nature-defying containers on a terrace twenty-four stories above Manhattan—a real comeuppance—any container gardening is cryptic and demanding. Although a variety of things bloomed here and there in my short-lived penthouse adventure, any containerized planting and gardening *in the dirt* are two *very different* concepts. The twenty-four stories up ordeal is a book unto itself as it is a sort-of approximation of gardening; but even a terra-cotta pot resting on the earth still takes things out of their normal habitat. You must provide for the interaction of all those phosphates and worms and be especially cognizant that water runs out of a pot much faster than out of the ground. It is tricky to garden in containers. Think about it. If a plant is in the earth, its roots have free reign and can go anywhere they choose to suck up the last drops of moisture and nitrogen. In a pot, those roots are bound and have nowhere to go once the pot's supply is depleted. It is also easier for a plant to bend toward the sun or resist the wind when in the ground making its own natural choices. Planting anything in any kind of pot is an extreme idea.

Things to know, whether planting outdoors in a fine old zinc tub or trying to force tulips mid-winter in your living room:

1. Line the bottom of the pot with something to help it drain and allow the roots to breathe. The classic pot-bottom liner is broken-up bits of old clay pots having seen better days. If you are a beginning gardener and do not have pails of shattered terra-cotta on hand (though you will find you acquire them quickly), then try gravel or rocks or be really extrava-

A bird's-eye view of the incomparable passion flower and its fruit.

gant and go out and buy some clay pots and hammer them. This is also good for release of tension.

2. New products called variations of names like "Instant H_2O" are available in all sincere gardening catalogs and hardware stores. Contained in jars, this "soluble water" looks like little pellets until you release them in the soil. Once in contact with dirt and water, they expand and hold the water for distribution to the plant when it really needs it. Unfortunately, the pellets managing to rise to the surface have the undistinguished gelatinous look of a piece of leftover aspic. Just ignore this scabrous detail because this stuff really works. Pots planted with the "magic water" adapt much better to an erratic watering schedule than pots without it. Without getting into what should not be watered during its dormant period and other obscure circumstances covered in the DB Greatest Hits List at the end of this book, it is the rare situation when you can water a containerized plant too much.

3. The magic water, potting soil, peat moss, cow manure, and vermiculite for good measure really want to be stirred up. A big brown unattractive Rubbermaid eighteen-gallon vat that began life as a container for a submerged waterlily has become my favorite mixing bowl. Once you've mixed the mélange really well and laid in the rocky liner, fill the pot/container/urn/jar you are about to plant not quite halfway. Assess the situation. What are you planting? If you are planting something with longish roots (like daylilies, hosta or amaryllis, for example) put in the broken crocks, then a little well-mixed dirt, then the rooted thing, then more dirt so it surrounds the roots in a natural way. What you want to avoid is trying to shove the roots into the already too-compacted dirt. If you are planting a tuber or a bulb (like calla lilies, hyacinths, or dahlias), fill the pot more than halfway, place the bulbous root on the concoction and then add the rest of the dirt. General rule when planting tubers and bulbs (whether in the ground or in a pot) is there should be as much dirt above them as the space they take up.

4. Water. Plants in pots or tubs or baskets or old stone urns like to be watered. The more iconoclastic you get with containerized plantings placed throughout the garden and property, the more obedient you must be remembering to water or making sure that the house watcher is in peril of losing a job if he/she continually forgets that the 'Silver Dust' English ivy looking so natural hanging from its branch in the Shade Grove is really in a pot and *needs water.*

5. To insure the life of what you have planted in your given container and make a nice visual statement—*do not fill the container to the brim with dirt.* You must allow at least an inch for water, and then you will want to mulch your container so when the dirt becomes hard and dry, the sight is not quite so offensive. It looks better. And it helps preserve moisture. I find "orchid bark" is just the right thing for my pots: not too big, not too small for a pot mulch. You

can also use pine chips, cocoa beans, river rocks, or almost anything, but mulching what's containerized is the way to go.

Even though it requires both foresight and afterthought, you will find happiness with your potted things. Even the discipline required is characteristic of the appeal of these times when nothing is easy and everything demands something. Do not confuse putting things in pots with growing "houseplants." There is nothing wrong with houseplants—my Daddy made quite an art of them—but containerized gardening is different and takes concentration and time. Like all good things. Think it through, and plant the right charming thing in a significant old pot. You'll like it.

OBJECTS OF STONE, OTHER STATUARY, AND FURNITURE

Conceived properly, well placed, and not silly stone objects *et al.* portray your intentions and strengthen the attitude of your garden. It is of utmost consideration that any items you acquire have a look of *permanence* and be consciously placed in the garden scene. Only furniture, objects, and statuary that can withstand explosive Mama Nature are under consideration here; it can hardly be considered a garden bone if you have to coddle it by taking in its chintz cushions when it rains, or if it can't withstand years of weather and tough things like ivy roots. Make sure you don't go astray when culling your garden bones, think of *big* grand things before deciding what you want. Exemplar of what must be avoided at all costs are trite objects like plastic pink flamingos perched on one leg. These will be as out of place in any kind of earnest garden as permed dreadlocks on pampered white girls.

Stone. Stone, Stone. Nothing is as good as stone. There are a few things perhaps as impermeable and impenetrable; but none of them acquire that wonderful weathered patina like stone. And there are so many divine kinds of stone aside from gems, jewels, and geodes that make permanent, not to mention preternatural, garden bones. Marble, certainly, in all its fabulous variations, limestone (the stuff of most Egyptian temples standing strong after five thousand years), granite (so many beautiful colors), sandstone, schist (metamorphic crystalline rock), quartzite, basalt, anorthosite, exquisite alabaster, and of course any good old plain nondescript stone.

Now it's necessary to digress to Guatemala. Yes, Guatemala—for there I went on a real garden bone binge. So much did I want to be in East Hampton the last weekend of May to witness the first big bearded iris breakthrough and possibly the first peonies, I actually arrived at La Guardia sans passport. Sometimes the depth of the roots of my gardening subconscious startle me. Why Irving had to choose *this* weekend to have his company convene there for its big meeting really stymied me. He had to pick the last weekend in May???

This particular vested interest Irving has in Guatemala is, however, well founded considering his trade. Do note, all Korean clothing manufacturers not anxious to keep apace with the spiraling economy of Seoul, have picked themselves up—bag, baggage, and sewing machines and moved to Guatemala. Their reasoning is as sound as it gets. To begin with, it is *always* spring, and proper secretaries make two thousand a year, meaning the factory labor works for a real pittance—yet everyone seems happy and that dreary pallor of poverty is nowhere to be seen.

Fresh for adventure on the second morning, I was whisked to the engaging primitive colonial settlement of Antigua. Lumbering across mountain roads in some curious cross between bus, car, and van—out the corner of my left eagle-eye was spied not one, but *four* garden statuary vendors along the winding road. This was pay dirt. I knew it. Suddenly, the Guatemalan experience took on new meaning. As Susan Sontag so aptly conjured in her romantic novel, *The Volcano Lover,* "To travel is to shop." And now, I'd found something fabulous to buy.

In my few trips to Brazil, on the road between Rio and Buzios (sort of the Saint-Tropez of Brazil), I've been frustrated by my absolute inability to get anyone to stop for the myriad potters, wrought-iron makers, and statuary vendors along the road. Always too hot, too impatient to get back to Rio; but I staunchly refused to allow the same lack of interest in my garden-bone acquisition to happen here. After much nagging, persuading, and insisting, "Of course they can find a way to ship it," I finagled the afternoon into a situation to get close to these potential garden bones as I was convinced they would be the buy of a lifetime and was sure the shapes looked strange but sophisticated. Nobody in her right mind would think of buying garden statuary in Guatemala, so these can't possibly be tourist prices, right?

There are at least three grades of "stone" statuary before you reach the ultimate marble and granite. There is the lousy sand-based kind, which makes for chipped-off corners leading to complete erosion. There is the pre-cast stuff which holds up adequately, but never looks . . . well, real. Then there is the concrete-based kind, which is as close to real as you can get and what this Guatemalan find was made of. Of course, it is not as good as the *real* real stuff made of pure stone, but for a few hundred bucks, you can't have everything, or hardly anything at all when it comes to stone garden bones.

Upon closer inspection, it got better. My first purchase, totaling 115 U.S. dollars, included a coiled six-foot pedestal reminiscent of uniquely Venetian doge-palace style, three smaller sister coiling pedestals cum garden seats, two ancient looking Mayan creatures, a few big imposing pots, and a smallish grazing lamb. The guy across the street with an even more eclectic inventory was more difficult. He kept insisting everything was "*vendido*," but my cohort, Alex-the-Korean-come-to-Central-America, did some fast Spanish talking. We then struck a deal for ninety-five dollars, and to my cache was added a funny, wonderful, gigantic stone alligator bench, two elephant stools, and a fabulous elephant-trunk birdbath.

Five months later, after many faxes and much quibbling, amusing news arrived: Now the arduous trek of the weird conglomeration from Guatemala to Miami had been completed, *but* the shipment had been seized by U.S. customs and was being held in Miami pending the arrival of a U.S. customs specialist from New York, no less. It seems Floridian customs were convinced my find was "Mayan Artifacts" and had no intention of letting this big heist pass through their fingers. Clearly they had never encountered an obsessed gardener before. Ho-hum, well, this only reconfirmed how good this cheap stuff looked and my new anxiety, now I knew my bones were actually in the country, was would they arrive intact?

The final delivery to our driveway was a real scene. The night before, a frantic phone call from the trucker was received requesting assistance on hand as the driver couldn't possibly unload the truck himself as the shipment weighed *2,600 pounds*! Well, even after rounding up the Morgan brothers (my good faithful guys who take care of all big yard jobs), even more able bodies were required for the final lifting, but lo and behold! There it all was, right in our very own yard. The birdbath lost three of its four elephant trunks and the Mayan creatures' heads had separated from their bodies; but otherwise it was perfect and looked fabulous, including the absurd 750-pound gape-mouthed 'gator bench requiring five husky guys to move it into position.

It crossed my mind I might be beneficent and give a few pieces away because all of it might overwhelm our acre, but once these guys lugged things around, it was surprising how conducively the woods and trees received their new accoutrements adroitly placed. Bones. Bones. Bones.

The trick is to find just the right nooks, crannies, and little niches for these, or any, assortment of garden bones. It won't be long until my Guatamalan menagerie weathers and looks even better with a little lichen clinging, and it is amazing how well they blend with my various other stone adornments—benches from England, buddhas and geese from Hong Kong, a series of rabbits and pigs from all over, pressed fern statues from the Philippines, concrete taborets from a neighboring Hampton, and pots and urns from everywhere. You must always be on multi-alert, even in improbable places, so that *you* will never be indifferent to a great opportunity to vitalize your garden with substantial bones.

It is highly understandable if alligator benches don't sound like your cup of tea, but in the big world out there, there must be something to amuse or satisfy you in your garden. Perhaps it is gargoyles that turn you on—if so, there is quite the reputable firm, Design Toscano of

Chicago, which specializes in the often-sweet beasts. Though I've ordered no gargoyles to guard us against various evils, the group we've collected is dearly loved without containing a creature that looks out of place, hackneyed, or overdone. All our animals and objects have found comfortable nestling places and after even a few months, seem part and parcel of the garden scene. Others are strategically placed for reasons like keeping the hose from uprooting the hosta or highlighting the tiny cyclamen in the rockery.

Topiary is to be importantly considered here as well, as it can take on such unique form and character as poignant in the landscape as any life-size muse or piece of garden art. If Edward Scissorhands does not live in your neighborhood, this might be an engrossing pursuit to take up yourself. Just imagine turning some old overgrown shrub into a fabulous sphinx! On the other hand, just recently saw some gigantic topiaries at Urban Archeology, a store indigenous to SoHo (New York). The quirk is these affordable topiaries are made from Astroturf and are bizarre and charming at the same time.

Of course, if you are an ardent art collector, nothing is better than true sculpture that can withstand the outdoors. I'd give anything for a rotund bronze Botero or a languid Henry Moore. A striking modern piece by Donald Judd or a Jim Dine Venus would suit me just fine too. Gladly I'd trade my Petar-made leftover-from-the-store sculptures for a tall gangling Giacometti to peek out from the bamboo; but as no dealer is about to make this barter and the others are not in my realm—I'm perfectly satisfied with my various exotic and eccentric garden bones.

Whether your intentions are to landscape in the grand manner or create a small, cheering garden for diversion—whether the ultimate goal is theatrical and spectacular or composed and halcyon—decorative garden bones and furniture play an integral part in completing your vision. Be it a bench or a balustrade, be it rustically hewn from wood or carved from fine stone, each introduction into your garden sends off signals of your own taste and personality, as well as affording your flowers, shrubs, trees, and lawn a counterpoint. Bear strongly in mind, six sunshiny months of the year your garden bones are just *part* of the gardening picture—during the other drab winter six they are the *entire* picture and focus.

Don't be daunted by these special, considered pieces and don't feel their very introduction is pretentious nonsense. Perhaps statuary is too grand a word, maybe sculpture sounds too significant, garden ornaments too trite: what you want are things that reflect you, your house, and your style—features to complete your garden picture or emphasize your own individuality.

Garden furniture of one kind or another will ease the transition into garden rooms, and you can take heart because most garden furniture is pretty standard stuff, ostensibly oblivious to any fancies of fashion and generally not as provocative as other whimsical objects you might acquire. The latest thing on order is a terra-cotta-colored monkey-based concrete table from

House Parts—but by now you realize the standard stuff is not what I search out to fulfill my garden-bone fantasies.

Garden bones. Some you already own but just haven't looked at in this frame of reference—your trees, paths, and perimeters. Others you will want to acquire or build. Your garden needs its bones. If you don't get comfortable with this idea and find the modus operandi suiting you, your enterprise will be lacking—missing its inner core. Without well-thought-out garden bones, it is difficult to formulate a vision that really works—and the last thing you want your garden to be is an enigma. Take pride in your garden bones. After all, they are the heart and soul of the garden and the epitome of your personal stamp.

Stone 'bones' guarding the pool overhung with our fabulous weeping blue Atlas Cedars in command.

FOUR

Color. Shakespeare.
The Religions. Designer.
Specimens & Specialization.
Rocks & Troughs.

JUST

HOW

DOES

YOUR

GARDEN

GROW?

He had always been passionately fond of flowers, but during his residence at Jutigny, that love had been lavished upon flowers of all sorts; he had never cultivated distinctions and discriminations in regard to them. Now his taste in this direction had grown refined.

Simultaneous with the refinement of his literary taste and his preoccupations with art, permitting him to be content only in the presence of choice creations. . . . his love for flowers had grown purged of all impurities and lees, and had become clarified.

He compared a florist's shop to a microcosm wherein all the categories of society are represented.
J. K. Huysman, *Against the Grain*

Now you know where to plant, are gathering your tools, and have recognized the irrefutable importance of garden bones. You are ready. Now, what exactly to plant? Which kind of garden do you want to grow? How to weed out the plain, redundant, tedious, and dull? This is the next and probably most exciting decision—the way to avoid winding up with a pointless patch of disjunct annuals bringing no real reward. I won't go so far as to say garden specialization is the only way to attack mediocrity—but almost. The next logical plateau (if you have any *real* ambition about your garden) is to choose the method with which to unify your garden—while defying blandness, conquering run-of-the-millness, avoiding the hodgepodge, odds-and-ends approach, and ultimately leading to your very own garden style. Still encouraging you to be flexible and always allow room for inevitable change—determining which distinctive kind of gardens you want to espouse will not only heighten your gardening experience, but put you on the right track.

Choices are vast. Your garden's theme might be determined by existing conditions: a rocky slope could be well utilized as an alpine garden or rockery; a torrid climate might suggest a wild tropical garden resplendent in orchids; or your hard clay soil may not serve a perennial border but would be perfect for a maze of geometric English box and topiary. Furthermore, and fortunately, history has provided us with a great store of fodder from which to choose, and the modern world is packed with possibilities. Certainly you will find one definitive criteria suiting your taste, your place and your means. Particular concentration is required here—time to make decisions—time to select your style—time has come! Of course, you can be general: deciding you want a symmetric formal garden, a wild-meadow garden, a romantic garden filled with old-fashioned plants bathed in soft, hazy light—any of these choices will do, but *you must make a choice*. Certain garden styles may strike the right chord in you: ornate Italianate, composed Japanese, or even American colonial. Surely there is something for everyone.

Certain basics are to be considered at this point. Few have the space for seasonal gardens; those requiring plenty of room for their arrangement and devoted to one spectacular flowering category (like spring bulbs or iris) with pathways assigned to the dedicated areas that bloom gorgeously for maybe one month in twelve. When that month ends, you simply no longer use the path leading to the corner of the garden that was spectacular in June but looks pitiful in July. In choosing your style you must remember it takes hard work to maintain an interesting idea *and* a progression of bloom. Flowers are, unfortunately, a fleeting thing. None of them last forever and very few of them last for more than a good three weeks at most.

GARDENING BY COLOR

Therefore, in choosing a scheme, one must think it through so it is viable and pleasing *throughout* the gardening season. Good design and simplicity often walk hand in hand, so let's begin with the uncomplicated and unpretentious concept of gardens orchestrated by color. As you know, this quest was my first gardening exercise and so my knowledge is first-hand regarding the sequence and maintenance of such gardens. My first foray into garden-planning was fortuitous and I'm still challenged by keeping the white garden white, the burgundy garden dark red, and especially the blue garden blue, or more precisely—bluish. The Queen of Hearts is not the only fanatic in town.

A large rose tree stood near the entrance of the garden: the roses growing on it were white, but there were three gardeners at it, busily painting them red. Alice thought this a very curious thing . . .
"Would you tell me, please," said Alice, a little timidly, "why are you painting those roses?"
Five and Seven said nothing, but looked at Two. Two began, in a low voice, "Why, the fact is, you see, Miss, this here ought to have been a *red* rosetree, and we put a white one in by mistake; and, if the Queen was to find it out, we should have all our heads cut off, you know."

Lewis Carroll, *Alice in Wonderland*

Pitiful before
and promising
after—the
'Bluish' Border.

The white garden is the most classic of the color choices, made so respectable by Vita's Sissinghurst, and so evocative of elegance—purity and pristine obsessions—moonbeams and magic. For a better understanding of what it takes to keep a one-color garden that color for a whole season—or more precisely, a white garden white—let's embark on dissecting my very own. Let me also add this purity of vision does not necessarily include strictly white flowers— shades of gray (everything but those awful hairy lamb's-ears), silvery-green, as well as ivory and

DIANNE   BENSON

ecru are perfectly at home in any respectable white garden. My white patch is not flush with meandering paths or encapsulated rooms, but has become lush and large and passes through approximately ten mutations in one season. The first signs of white are the earliest spring bulbs planted the autumn before: snowdrops (*Galanthus nivalis*) appear first in late February and are followed by their bigger cousins *Leucojum* growing up amongst the ever-white ground cover *Lamium* 'White Nancy'. The *Lamium* anchors the ever-present white garden's bones: a big, serene, marble white Buddha head; the thirty-inch-high white porcelain hands found in an antique sanctuary in Sag Harbor (once the dies from which industrial gloves were made); metal clematis tuteurs; and the white-edged Mexican rock bordering the garden. Real substance is provided in March and April by *Pieris* (better known as *Andromeda*, which covers itself in drooping panicles of lily-of-the-valley-type flowers on its always charming evergreen shrub base), *Dicentra spectabilis alba* (those old-fashioned but endearing bleeding hearts, which just get bigger and better every year) and *Pulmonaria* 'Sissinghurst white', both perennials. *Viburnum* and *Deutzia*, both shrubs that become totally obliterated by masses of tiny white flowers follow in May. Nestled amongst these are all sorts of white (*alba*) spring bulbs: *Crocus, Muscari, Pushkinia,* scads of various tulips, and of course, daffodils and miniature narcissus (the dimunitive but really-white 'Thalia' being my favorite). The beautiful but difficult *Sanguinaria canadensis* makes a fine brief show of dainty, double white flowers in May, which are happily followed by winglike, undulating, leatherish leaves having real character of their own. Lilies of the Valley and Solomon's Seal light up a shady corner at the same time. A brilliant patch of peony-flowered tulip 'Mount Tacoma' and white hyacinths make a startling statement at the base of the weeping Alaskan cedar. As soon as the tulips die down, they are yanked out and replaced with calla lilies (*Zantedeschia*) and white caladiums to take over this prime spot. For a few years, I was perfectly satisfied with the ground cover *Houttuynia* surrounding this picture, which broke dormancy at end of May, about the same time as the interim between tulips and calla lilies, producing scads of single and double white flowers throughout summer—but this menace has managed to devastate my white garden. The sad and alarming tale will be related in the next chapter, rankly dealing in the least rewarding gardening circumstances.

Coming up in the main section of the white garden as May becomes June are my sensational series of spiky feathery things that get better each year. First, in early June come the sprays of *Rodgersia* and almost simultaneously, the big leaved *Aruncus*; just as these two harmonious flowerings are beginning to turn—up pops the *Astilbe* x *arendsii* 'Silver Queen'—and no sooner are they in abundance than the wondrous sprays of ten-foot-tall *Cimicifuga racemosa* take over the whole scene, persisting from mid-July through mid-August. My spiky things are a fabulous look and once the cimicifuga starts to wane, the *Buddleia davidii* 'White Knight' arrives to produce the punctuation of height and white in the same sort of racemelike way. This progression is so great I must applaud it myself.

To give the white garden added punch in the spring/early summer transition, there are lilacs, the superb double white *clematis* 'Duchess of Edinburgh', and the appreciated alliums. The *bulgaricum* strain of allium is quite a fantasy with its individual hanging white bellflowers trimmed in crimson, and *Allium neapolitanum* (recently renamed *çowanii*) 'Grandiflorum' is nothing to sneeze at either. Grounding the June white garden are a few species of *Aquilegia* (divine columbines), *Paeonia* (including one very expensive tree peony labeled white by The Bayberry which turned out to be pale pink, to my horror because everyone knows once you plant a peony it must never be moved), and the exquisite iris—fancy German bearded and later, the subtle *tectorum* (Japanese roof iris). Irises don't last as long as I'd like, but close on their heels and surrounding them are *Digitalis* (foxgloves, never truly white-white, but such a homespun beauty their place can't be denied), *Ornithogalum saundersiae* (a brief but beautiful bulb bearing sterling white petaled flowers with a distinct black eye), and the first blooms of an extravagant hybrid tea rose that goes nameless but has been blooming in rare abundance for four years, very content in its spot.

At this juncture we have only reached early mid-July. Do not get despondent over this series of sequential bloom. Obviously you cannot accomplish this cycle in your first summer, but as you get into it, the rhythm falls into place. This is where your local nurseries really play an important part—you are cultivating this white garden, for example, you've coaxed it to this point; suddenly your white garden is all green and almost nothing is blooming—it's now you dash out on a maniacal run of your suppliers and without doubt, stumble on all sorts of white things that fit right in. Just on the come are the breathtaking tuberous begonias, later blooming clematis, the many white *Campanula*, and *Valerian*.

As July tolls its bells toward August and you begin sniffing just one scent of summer's end in the air, a fabulous panoply of extravagant lilies that I add to each fall (the Asiatic have come and gone, now it is time for the fabulous Chinese and Oriental), *Platycodon* (that sublime "balloonflower"), *Physostegia* (the poorly named "obedient plant" much better appreciated in the south of France than here), a few kinds of late-blooming white hydrangea, and *Chelone* (commonly called "false turtle-head" because its inconspicuous flower looks just like a demure, well, turtle head) take over. The crowning glory of this moment is *Pancratium* (an exotic tropical summer bulb with magical long spurlike petals), planted only a few months before. Through all these intervals of the season, I've managed to keep the white garden white and feel positively ecstatic.

Intermingled with all of these white *flowering* things are other plants suggesting whiteness either by their silvery foliage or their green leaves rimmed with white. Usually, and unfortunately, when these things finally flower, the flower tends to be a mauvey color—but the flowering time is short compared with the comparative whiteness the foliage lends to the garden. White-edged hosta *crispula* and 'Thomas Hogg', variegated iris *pallida*, and a mystery variegated-leaf hydrangea all lend a white blush to the garden over the long haul, but when in flower it's simply a matter of arising early to cut down their disturbingly colored blooms to fill another vase somewhere in the house.

Then comes the challenge of summer's end and inevitable beginning of autumn—bringing with it the remainder of *Lysimachia clethroides* (the "gooseneck loosestrife" about which you have heard so much), *Gaura lindheimeri* (the valiant perennial producing a minute white flower at the end of a very long wandlike stem), and the substantial 'Royal Standard' hosta that regally sends up more and more sprays of its seldom remarked on but habitually important white flowers each year. Mid-September arrives before you know it, but securely I rely on *Anemone japonica* (formerly called *Anemone hupehensis*) 'Honorine Jobert' to take up the white-blooming flag and strut with it, fall-blooming *Colchicum alba* (which are much more interesting than crocus, though they dwell in the same family), my lovely *Lespedeza thunbergii* (here I cheat a little because it is slightly pink, but so mystical, glorious, and unknown that it suffices), my late-blooming conical-shaped *Hydrangea paniculata* 'Grandiflora', and the only thing still in a flush of white bloom in November—my old faithful hybrid tea rose that never quits. So you see, maintaining a rhythm in a chosen mode of gardening-by-color takes planning and doesn't miraculously happen overnight.

But with a little patience and a great deal of love, it can absolutely be achieved. Mentioned here are a great number of plants acquired over the years making up my white garden. As one comes to know them it will not seem quite so overwhelming as it must this very moment dutifully reading this list of forty or fifty plants for the first time. Because this book is a truthful exposé of gardening, I confess there are at least another dozen or so unmentioned fill-ins making up this vision of white enduring from March till November; but it truly takes at least this many items to make a specific garden really good with a few things constant like the white stone Buddha et al. Easy it's not to create a theme garden persisting throughout the better part of the year; but it is thrilling, rewarding, and an achievement one can't deny. Of all my gardens, the white is my favorite. Thinking back only six years to when the mainstay of this garden was white pansies, I feel really proud about the insistent plethora of white.

A SHAKESPEARE GARDEN

The summer's flower is to the summer sweet,
Though to itself it only live and die,
But if that flower with base infection meet,
The basest weed outbraves his dignity:
For sweetest things turn sourest by their deeds;
Lilies that fester smell far worse than weeds.
William Shakespeare, "Sonnet XCIV"

So we proceed to what sort of garden suits you. Color is, of course, not the only way to go, though perhaps one of the most obvious without being trite. If one tends toward the literary, a Shakespeare garden is a fine consideration. How classic can you get? I've a real penchant to indulge in one myself if I could just find the room. The room, the room, my kingdom for more room!

This garden can be extremely abundant, quite beautiful, and even contemporary (if you choose to include the modern hybrids he inspired) as the Bard was very generous in his mention of flora. Hark back through your Shakespearean studies and contemplate his predilection for gardens and flowers. Shakespearean scholars will be the first to remind you William was a knowledgeable gardener, much more so than Bacon, Marlowe, or those other Elizabethans. His imagery is chock-full of gardening lore: and his mention of plants is endless: violets, narcissus, ginger (which actually merits a √√√ on the hit list as *Hedychium*), *Asarum europaeum* (a fantastical woodland ground cover—my most treasured), columbine (*Aquilegia*—a pronounced favorite of mine, with its magical spurred flower looking as if it is always ready to take off and soar), my beloved *Fritillaria* (especially *meleagris,* the diminutive snake's-head frit). There are many herbs as well, including some of the most virtuous— jasmine, lavender, thyme, rosemary, rue, and mint, the classically beautiful *Paeonie.* And there are even ever-faithful daisies, all sorts of lilies and daylilies, *Endymion* (English bluebells), *Eglantine* (sweet briar), *Oxalis* (wood shamrocks), quince, cyclamen, plus countless trees: pine, elm, horse chestnut, palm trees, firs; and we mustn't forget peaseblossom and mustardseed: then of course, musk-roses, crimson-roses, damask-roses, roses, roses, and more roses. The list goes on and on and on.

Much of the allure of a Shakespeare garden is not even so much in his mention of numerous plants, but his incomparable use of metaphors employing gardening images. *A Midsummer Night's Dream, The Tempest,* and *Othello* immediately spring to mind, but every play is chock-full of exacting oneness-with-earth ideas. The following are but an example, and all from *The Life and Death of King Richard III,* if you can believe it:

Why grow the branches now the root is gone?
Why wither not the leaves that want their sap?
Act II, scene ii

But we will plant some other in the throne, . . .
Act III, scene vii

Small herbs have grace, great weeds do grow apace:
And since, methinks, I would not grow so fast,
Because sweet flowers are slow and weeds make haste.
Act II, scene iv

—and of course—

Now is the winter of our discontent
Made glorious summer by this sun of York;
Act I, scene i

This is all pretty remarkable, but the only Shakespeare Garden I've actually seen is one of the many specialized plots of the ever-so-renowned Brooklyn Botanical Garden and on the days I've inspected, it was extremely intriguing but not that truly gorgeous. Must have something to do with its necessarily containing only old-world plants and the BBG being a stickler for authenticity. None of the fabulous hybrids developed in the many centuries since William sat upon the banks of the Avon and penned his classics even existed then.

In our modern times, many hybridizers have harkened back to the Bard in their nomenclature, so you might intersperse all those enduring old-world ideas with the very fabulous 'Desdemona' and 'Othello' strain of *Ligularia* (a big, bold, bronze-leaved affair bearing stalks of deep dark gold—shading to the best orange clusters in deep late summer, the only thing I grow in my garden maintaining any relationship to the color yellow besides daffodils), *Eremurus ruiter* hybrid variation 'Cleopatra', *Rudbeckia* 'Goldstrum' (the choicest version of the sunflower), and without question—the Red Rose of Lancaster and the White Rose of York. There is almost nothing you can grow not Shakespeare-correct if you really dig around and use your imagination.

This bud of love, by summer's ripening breath,
May prove a beauteous flower when next we meet.
Romeo and Juliet, Act II, scene ii

Surprisingly, I have not uncovered any strains named after Hamlet or the Henrys (although Wayside Gardens touts an Oriental lily called *henryi* but doesn't go into any interesting detail), but that doesn't necessarily mean they don't exist. A Shakespeare garden is a pursuit, like any worthwhile endeavor. You must be dedicated to the idea. Willing to research it, pursue it, afford it, and coddle it. You cannot expect to hit one nursery and browse through one catalog to come up with a garden beautiful, and scholarly as well. But then again, isn't that half the pleasure?

like an untimely frost
Upon the sweetest flower of all the field.
Romeo and Juliet, Act IV, scene v

A BIBLICAL GARDEN

Staying in this time-honored vein of classic and old-world, you might be more intrigued by the religious than the literary and feel spellbound by the idea of a biblical garden. Whether tea-drinking and mass-going, or an outright spiritual fanatic, if intrigued by this but questioning its practicality because the Bible is not exactly committed to heart, fear not! The Bible now exists on an incredible computer-chip driven device and all one has to do call up a phrase—or flower, as the case may be—type it on the keyboard and *voilà*—this machine will scroll you to exactly the appropriate place in the Bible. Fabulous, no? This might exist for Shakespeare too, come to think of it, but I've not seen it.

Anyway, now it's so easy (I saw this computerized Bible in a Radio Shack, for $59.95) to access which flowers are and are not included in the Bible, you can devote yourself to searching out celestial and heavenly statuary, if not hallowed and holy. I mean, why immerse yourself in a religious garden, without a few really biblical stone bones? Of the many theme gardens within the unspeakably beautiful Magnolia Gardens in Charleston (a formal herb garden set within the framework of a boxwood knot, a maze garden fashioned after Henry VIII's sixteenth-century Hampton Court but planted with *Camellia sasanqua* and holly instead of diehard Brit boxwood), there is an intensely intriguing biblical garden. Upon entering this sanctuary, via the many plaques, you were reminded Genesis 1:11 tells us the grass, the herbs, and the trees followed the heaven, earth, and seas, but preceded the fish, the fowl, Adam and Eve, you and me, and everything else. The Garden of Eden must have been spectacular.

So, how to bring this inspiring nirvana and fittingly spiritual mode into your yard, that's what you want to know, right? Well . . . at Magnolia, the biblical theme is ensconced within a wooded grove and anchored by two large beds. *Get this now:* the one containing plants of the New Testament is in the shape of a cross that has twelve sections identifying the twelve disciples. The Old Testament bed also has twelve divisions—embodying, of course, the tribes of Israel and takes the form of (wouldn't you know it?) the Star of David. So, how's that for symbolism? These beds are punctuated, as can be expected, with two highly dramatic suitable religious sculptures. Most of the flowers planted within both are obvious and honest ones— "lilies of the field," "rose of Sharon," hyacinth, crocus, anemones, and so on; but, of course, there are infinite other exotics you can embrace. Heavenly manna, I learned, is actually the drippings of the tamerisk tree, while frankincense and myrrh are fragrant herbs. You will also be correct, in the biblical gardening sense, should you choose to grow willow, allium, rue, or quince. Never thought much about quince before, but have come to adore it, having seen it in full bloom for the first time this past spring. And what would a biblical garden be without passion vines?

A FABULOUS SOUTHERN GARDEN

My visit to Charleston last May was the godsend culmination of an otherwise lackluster trip (save the sighting of schools of smiling dolphins) up the Intercoastal Waterway on a boat too small to suit my tastes or accommodate my luggage. After three prolonged days in the great American South, we arrived in Charleston on a perfect Sunday evening. Having never been there and not knowing much more about it than its prominent role in that most passionate of wars, the Civil (which began in Charleston with the firing on Fort Sumter), I was open to a romantic vision.

Along the Intercoastal, not much impressed with St. Augustine (too gimcracky), or Hilton Head Island (looked like a big mall), I found Charleston *another* story altogether. The city is so engaging and saturated with well-maintained remains of a more gracious time, it seemed to have dedicated itself to its own preservation and transcends just being another historic curiosity. I loved the fact that it was not glossed-over, rebuilt, renovated, and permeated with silly souvenirs and neon-described food, but was a real true lovely old magnolia-ridden, vine-covered enduring town. Admitting I plowed through *Scarlett, a Sequel to Gone with the Wind* like a mad fiend only some weeks before (on an otherwise unadventurous stay on Nevis save for two hours spent with an expatriate American doctor showing off his highly entertaining and exotic Orchid and Other Rarities Garden in between many drinks), I made close friends of taxi-drivers and waiters all just so willin' to show me the very house on the very proper street where Rhett's mama lived.

Being in the charmin' city of Charleston on a comely May day did bring out the Southern belle in me—my Daddy's family bein' from N'Orleans and all that. Immediately immersed in this fine Southern city, I perused the tourist paraphernalia a little further and came up with accolades toutin' a fine old plantation called Magnolia Gardens as the reputedly eldest in America still in glorious tact, and honey, welcomin' visitors every single little ole day; but listen to this:

By 1900, *Baedeker's Guide* was recommending Magnolia Gardens, along with Niagara and the Grand Canyon, as one of the three major attractions in America. In Kew Gardens in England, a sign beside the *Indica azalea* reads: "Azaleas in their highest glory are to be found in Magnolia Gardens."
Peter Coats, *Great Gardens of the Western World*, 1963

and especially this:

I specialize in gardens and freely assert that none in the world is so beautiful as this. . . . Nothing so free and gracious, so lovely wistful, so richly colored, yet so ghost-like, exists. . . . It is a kind of Paradise . . . a miraculously enchanted wilderness . . . it is otherworldly.
John Galsworthy, *Century Magazine*, 1921

Well, the combination of "enchanted otherworldly wilderness" being rated alongside the Grand Canyon really got to me, so, obsessed gardener that I am, what choice was there but to rearrange plans and hightail it out to Plantation Country? To the credit of Magnolia Gardens goes the singular achievement of introducing the adored azalea to America. This is a pretty big deal when you think of the reverence bestowed on the azalea today by all the societies and garden clubs devoted solely to its propagation and cultivation. Just what would the nurseries sell on Mother's Day if the refined Reverend Drayton had not introduced azaleas into Charleston way back then when it was called Charles Town and before anybody ever thought about anything so illogical as a Civil War? Life at Magnolia appeared to be quite divine and civilized to me after my day of roaming the patently preserved and lovingly coddled grounds.

Magnolia Plantation sits right on the Ashley River, no less (very fiddle-dee-dee). Amongst abundant breathtaking acres of moss-laden live oaks and cypress, massive bountiful plantings of brilliantly flowering azaleas, camellias, roses, hibiscus, lilies, wisteria, dogwood and more, zillions of magnolia trees reflected in dark dreamy lakes spanned by graceful and harmonious white walking bridges, there lie many specific and specialized gardens. Beyond that, there's a children's zoo loaded with lilies and a big old alligator swamp smothered in every big-leaved perennial I've ever seen pictured. Bountiful, fabulous, suffused with the most above-reproach, genteel gardening ambitions come true. I loved it.

FASHION GARDENS

Moving from fixed-in-time gardens to the contemporary, and speculating that you might be aligned to certain fashion dictums, I suggest that following the lead of your favorite designer might influence garden theme inspirations. What kind of clothes do you wear? Or perhaps better put, what kind of clothes *would* you wear if you chose to spend your money on them rather than on your house and garden? A certain fanaticism toward one style or another might induce interesting, eccentric, or gregarious gardening methods, allowing you to set your own personal perimeters about your gardening style. Elan, technique, and charm are the keywords here.

In the fashion mode, if you like Armani today, you probably liked Saint Laurent and Halston before, respect Galanos, and most probably find Zoran, Romeo Gigli, even Donna Karan agreeable. If being on the edge suits you more than these tending-toward-classic refinements, then your path is more varied. If it's Jean-Paul Gaultier at his best or the Japanese designers you like, then read on—I can advise you. If it's Mr. Gianfranco Ferré and his seductive white shirts, I can empathize. If the strange symbolism of Vivienne Westwood or Jean-Charles de Castelbajac turns your head, then we are in the same garden. But if it's Mr. Versace with his ill-advised bugle beads joined with leather, Thierry Mugler at his most scabrous peak, or vulgar Madonna-wear that turn you on, we have little in common and you may not be entranced by any fashion-garden idea suggested here.

If we weren't speaking the same language, it's unlikely you would have reached this page—so on that positive note, let's begin with fashioning a garden from the Armani mind-set. I don't wear Armani but like it, and if most of my life were spent in conference rooms of various kinds, I'd probably buy it. Fashioning a garden with the same aesthetic would naturally turn up something harmonious, sleek, tailored, and subdued. To achieve this, concentrate on a garden picture created from the various forms of conifers—evergreens, fir trees, the substantial, lasting varieties. They exist in an amazing assortment of subtle colorations beginning with a dark brown-green. This "breen" (as it's known in the fashion world) works its way into a burgundy sort of brown that never really gets red, but can be a crimson-copper shade Giorgio might use in the occasional *accessoire*. To contrast with these brown-based colors and highlight the many shades of green are the beautiful blues of the spruce family. This stately category will lunarize any garden scene. As if this were not enough, then consider the junipers in their vast array of yellow and golden tones for just the right bit of emphasis. These charming and cooperative junipers can be ground-hugging and horizontal or sky-bound and vertical, providing hosts of harmony. Not only do you have classic and chic color to work with (although there is no plant I've ever seen that is actually Armani taupe), you have a chimerical choice of structure and form: pyramid shapes, weeping shapes, arching shapes, and almost any other shape you might envision can be achieved by adroit pruning—which is an intricate and precise mode unto itself. In the long run, however, the most Armani characteristic of the conifer approach is its timeless nature. As ageless and evergreen as Barbra Streisand's lyrics; an Armani garden is classic, permanent, disguises things best kept hidden, and is a very good investment.

A lover of the avant-garde might also appreciate this Armaniesque devotion to subtle color, shape, and form—but find it too easy. Like the best Japanese designers, your instincts would embrace the Armani look to the tune of eschewing glaring color and relying on elusive harmonies of size and shape, but you would be drawn to the oddest and rarest species to spotlight your garden: all the plants the classy catalogs refer to as "bizarre" or "conversation pieces." Unexpected associations and a sense of assymetry, that beloved penchant of the Japanese designers resulting in twisted hemlines and out-of-balance lapels, can be achieved with, for example, the twisted corkscrew-like branches of a shrub called *Corylus avellana*, more commonly known as Harry Lauder's walking stick. *Morus bombycis* (contorted mulberry) will achieve the same discriminating goals. Both of these are true to the counterbalancing act of Issey Miyake. A shrub having a mystical now-you-see-it, now-you-don't quality is the *Cotinus coggygria*, more easily remembered as purple smoke-bush. This glorious plant has rich purple-black leaves and stems throughout the season, and at summer's end bears a flower not like a flower at all, but more a mauvey mist shrouding the plant in a mythical way. This one is very Rei Kawakubo (Comme des Garcons). She would also be drawn to the dark-leaved *Ligularia* and my sacred Indian lilies, *Sauromatum guttatum,* as well as the eclectic and fantastic *Fritillaria* group of spring-blooming bulbs, especially the species *persica adiyami* with its bell-shaped blackish-plum flowers adorning long arching celadon stems. If these designers are your bent (as they are definitely mine), then you must keep your eyes peeled for the odd, different, and engaging. You will also be entranced by a biennial named *Angelica gigas* conjuring a fantastic sexual growth pattern culminating in a swollen bulbous stem that mysteriously breaks into an aubergine tufted flat flower rising six feet aloft its gigantic serrated leaves. Another intriguing plant is *Poncirus trifoliata*, the hardy, inedible orange that smothers its strange, spiny, thorny, twisted branches in fragrant white flowers in spring. And most likely you will not be able to live without a horse-chestnut tree, as it is the ultimate in sureality.

A sense of the sculptural will appeal to fans of Claude Montana. This can best be translated into the garden by those plants that leaf in such a fabulous way the flowers become a secondary consideration. Aside from the much revered and ever present hosta, particularly the big bold *sieboldiana* types, there are tons of choices. Other big impressive leafy plants are *Crambe, Gunnera, Macleaya,* and *Rodgersia*: all seeming like they need severe shoulder-pads to support their upright stance. The first has a long, slender, sophisticated cabbagelike leaf, but unfortunately flowers like *Gypsophilia*, which is the commonly called "baby's breath" ruining so many otherwise perfectly acceptable flower arrangements. The plume poppy (*Macleaya*) is a pleasing gray-green in color, sports an imposing, immense leaf, but has the unwanted quality of producing a root system impossible to dislodge once it really digs in—you really have to like this one and have a lot of space. The last, *Rodgersia*, is the real charmer. It is perennial, has no bad habits, flowers like *Astilbe,* and has divine, imposing palmate leaves setting it apart from everything else. In the sculptural Montana garden of significant leaf forms, canna lilies would be a natural (not the trite green ones seen in so many institutional plantings, but the divine aubergine-leafed *edulis* species commonly called 'Black Velvet' or 'Red King Humbert'), as would *Colocasia esculenta*. Like *Gunnera,* they make an incredibly imposing statement with their huge, respective heart-shaped and oval leaves that can attain widths of nearly two feet.

For the Karl Lagerfeld diehards there are many excessive and showy choices like hollyhocks, big French marigolds, forsythia—one of my least favorites, but you see it everywhere—phlox, and the most blatant chrysanthemums. Though I am not enamored by them, him, or that din created by all that cloying clanging Chanel fake-gold jewelry, many French public gardens are the epitome of Karl style—big color, big flower, big chic—but not much substance, lots of things obvious, little implied. However, in my youthful fashion enthusiasm, my head was turned by a quote in the then-revered *Women's Wear Daily,* "I like bad taste. It's so much better than no taste." That was uttered by Jacqueline Jacobson, better known as Dorothée Bis. This was a capricious remark voiced in her heyday that left a marked impression on me. Equating it with my own elusive cosmic values, I therefore have a certain oblique kinship with all that over-the-top stuff.

GARDENS DEVOTED TO ONE FABULOUS GENUS

If you find fashion frivolous and can't relate to it (understandable) or aren't smitten with any garden themes already described—take heart. Specific gardening can be accomplished in a most honest and sincere way relating only to the plants themselves, with all outside influences curtailed. This type of gardening is more plant-oriented than people-oriented, because instead of creating a big picture, you are obliged to plumb the depths of creating exactly the right site and conditions for your *precise* plant pick. Embracing one genus of plants—provided you choose one with enough variations worth embracing—can be a consuming and rewarding pursuit. You can decide to make your game iris or cyclamen, for example, and you will encounter many intricacies and a plethora of variations. Never fear that you will be alone in a pursuit such as this, as there are legions of devotees as enthralled by your plant grouping as you are. For very nominal dues of ten or fifteen dollars annually you will be welcomed into the American Iris Society, American Rock Garden Society, the North American Lily Society, or even the Semipervum Fanciers Association, or the International Ornamental Crabapple Society, to name a few.

No calling, no matter how particular, is overlooked assuming you have chosen an interesting group of plants with bloom times interspersed throughout the year and plenty of adaptations and mutations to keep even the most discriminating gardener interested. When you plumb the depths of any one given species, you, by nature, become a supreme specialist. Your objective is a plant choice allowing enough variety to keep you occupied over a span of, at least, three months. Or immerse yourself in two or three groups to provide for the entire growing season from March till October.

TULIPS AND LILIES

For example: your spring specialization is tulips and your summer emphasis is lilies. You scour the bulb catalogs and cover yourself in every classification of tulip. Therefore you start the season in March (maybe even earlier in some places) with the earliest blooming "botanical" or "species" tulips—often referred to as "wild" ones. Not the florist's variety you are so familiar

A bucketful of exotic tulips plucked from the garden in mid-May.

with, these are shorter-stemmed and generally smaller, but come in a fascinating diversity of dissimilar shapes, colors, and sizes. *Kaufmanniana* and *Greigii* tulips bloom in March and are also very different little darlings than conventional tulips; many add very interesting mottled-with-purple leaves to their repertoire, and because they're low-growing, you get the sense of a natural little bouquet. Quite a sight in the midst of blustery March and all of these earlier tulips have the distinction of being more or less perennial. Next are the spectacular *Fosteriana* tulips that overwhelm you in early April when they burst open with the biggest flowers of any tulip—flaming, flamboyant, huge red petals grounded with a profound true-black center. Breathtaking. Now the tulip season really begins to pick up steam and your eyes feast on the balance of the thirteen classes: single early, double early, triumph, Darwins (the ultimate in the stately florist's "French tulip" category—some waft on stems nearly three feet high), single late, to end with the sensational lily-flowering (real aristocrats, with graceful pointed petals) and parrot tulips, with their twisted, ruffled, bizarre petals either wildly multicolored or solid, which bring the tulip season to a resplendent, dramatic close. Glorious bloom from March through early June is the result of a tulip devotion.

Your second arena of enthusiasm is lilies, which begin to bloom as the tulips wane in June. All lilies, like tulips, are bulbs; but unlike tulips they have no protective covering around their fleshy, scaly selves and are more vulnerable to drying when out of the ground (so plant them right away—none of this refrigerator storage will do) and drowning when underground (so they need good drainage). Also, like tulips, they will reward you whether planted in a sunny spot or not. Asiatic lilies and a few species Turk's cap lilies blossom first in the last weeks of spring; classic Easter lilies, if cultivated in the ground, bloom in summer. Asiatics, definitely the most abundant and easiest of the early lilies, unfortunately are a bit stiff and sport colors never particularly subtle, except for mauvey "Unique" and the white ones. However, the stems are strong, never need staking, they come in quite a range of all warm colors of the spectrum and bloom incessantly for at least a month as each stem carries many many flowers.

On their heels arrive a resplendent assortment of trumpet (or Aurelian) and Oriental lilies. Between these two groups you get awe-inspiring blooms from July through September and these are the ones which are the stuff of lily dreams. Sometimes towering seven feet over the garden, they nod and sway like an architectural triumph as their submarine-shaped buds swell to the point of flower. They can either be full-blown like the trumpet after which they're named, curiously in-curved, or wildly, widely petaled and suffused with a powdery spotting. The most romantic, fascinating, and strange need the most time to mature and reach their crescendo in early September. Between tulips and lilies, with dogged and determined dedication, you can be graced with glorious flowers from March till September—more than half the year—a more than worthwhile pursuit. To round out the seasons and your gardens, sure, you might (and probably should) bathe your lilies and tulips in appropriate companions, but if you are rigorous about these two genera, then a very proud gardener you will be. The concept here is to really get *into* each of these classifications, come to know them in all their depth, and delight in your special knowledge of their preferences, foibles, idiosyncracies, and efflorescence.

Iris

Harkening back to the iris as a perfect example of a genus to enthrall you, there are unexaggeratedly thousands of horticultural varieties. Iris fall into two main categories: those that grow from corpulent rhizomes or tubers, are planted in late summer, bloom the following June through early August, and are the most magnificent; and those bulbous, planted in autumn to bloom primarily throughout the next spring. There is no other single kind of flower that spans the color spectrum like iris and few so classic as to be the prototype of the much-heralded fleur-de-lis. The shades of color range from every conceivable tint and hue of pink, salmon, blue, lilac, purple, yellow, and orange, and although there is no true red (but there are fabulous maroons and burgundies), there is even white and black. Upon close inspection, some glints of purple may be found in the black, but to find them you have to really scrutinize, and iris-black is as close as you are ever going to get to a black flower. Iris are so unique they have their own set of nomenclature to describe their parts: standards, styles, beards, and falls are characteristic only to iris.

The many species of iris occupy nine pages of small-print, big-page *Hortus,* so I will give you only a sampling of how absorbing this preoccupation can be. You can begin to appreciate your first irises at spring's inception if you have duly planted your *Iris reticulata* in the previous autumn. These first iris are diminutive, not more than six inches tall, but these miniatures are a marvelous study of microscopic charms, and forerunners of all the spectacular iris yet to come. They whet your appetite. There is a four-month buildup between this early first iris show and the culmination of the phenomenon that waits until July.

The autumn-planted iris growing from bulbs are classified as Dutch, Spanish, and English, and bloom in that order during May and June. The earliest Dutch resemble a classic orchid to a degree, come mainly in shades of purple, yellow, and white, and follow right on the heels of late tulips. The last to bloom, the Spanish and English, are more abundant than Dutch, have larger flowers, frillier petals, and come in more divine colors—from bronze to true blue. Catalogs and books preach that these need sun, but I've been lucky with them around the pond and under trees where there's not much sun at all and they have persisted over three or four years now.

The next group to bloom and fascinate are the herbaceous iris, growing from tuberous roots. These are the real show-girls of the iris family in form and color and have numerous classifications beyond the differentiation between bearded and beardless iris. Bearded iris are the obvious ones most associated with iris and unto themselves can become an addiction because the choice of color and kinds is staggering. The 72-page full-color Schreiner catalog offers *only* bearded iris! Among the huge range of colors are even color patterns such as bitone, bicolor, blends, and plicata—so the color-coordinating possibilities are endless. "Beard" refers to the fuzzy patch on their falls, which are their lower-drooping petals that look much more interesting than they sound. They thrust their big show in June.

Following them in July are the beardless—the pinnacle of beauty in this group being *Iris ensata,* the Japanese iris. Although tough and hardy once established, their overall appearance is delicate because of the wondrous crepelike texture of the blooms coupled with subtle fluctuations of color called "veining" or "penciling." They have a completely different form than all other iris as the bloom somehow resembles a cushy, pillowlike cloud—velvety, icy, billowy, heavenly—and can be as wide across as ten inches. Even if you decide an iris specialization is not for you, you *must* grow this one. Other good late-blooming iris in this group are Siberian (need a cold climate, as you would expect by their name, but are elegant and often referred to as "the butterflies of iris"), Louisianas (wide-petaled and particularly perky), and

Pacific Coast Natives (which, of course, need hot, dry conditions). Once again, wherever you dwell, Mama has made sure there is an iris for everyone.

Iris pallida 'albo-variegata' has a nice lavender flower appearing in June, but more importantly, it flaunts handsome white-banded erect leaves that shine in the garden eight months a year. *Iris tuberosa* is a weird and arresting one, more of a curiosity than a charmer because of its near-black flower accented with chartreuse in a strange form giving it the common name of "snake's-head iris." Then there is the endearing *Iris tectorum* or "Japanese roof iris." One legend insists its name derived from the Japanese propensity to save space. During hard times, the Japanese tore up their gardens to plant food but couldn't let go of this one beloved iris and so transported it to their roofs. Another legend states it isn't Japanese at all, but Chinese, and was used as a living binding for their thatch. Whatever the story, it's a must-have for its foliage alone, which forms broad, neat fans of ten-inch high, deep, pleasant green leaves lasting most of the year with a completely distinct look. At the edge of the white and blue gardens, these Japanese roof iris are loved by all.

A CUTTING GARDEN

A cutting garden is an absolute must, in addition to any other theme or topical gardens enchanting you! Marring the picture in the borders and color gardens by cutting the most exquisite blooms is close to unthinkable, yet to not have vases full of your own garden's progeny is illogical and unacceptable during bloom time. So you *must* establish a cutting garden. My first cutting garden came about when a terrific windstorm knocked over a huge hedge on the south side of the deck. Perfect opportunity, thought I, to take away *all* the hedges from this singular passably sunny spot and create a cutting garden. A few years later, wanting more cutting blooms, we cleared away yet more woods and now have three cutting-garden areas.

Ideally, your cutting garden should be tucked in a spot not focal to your big gardening picture. By virtue of its purpose—to provide you with exquisite cut flowers—it should never look very beautiful, as the time to cut flowers is just before they peak. So think of your cutting garden like a closet where you keep your clothes, which are usually not on display and serve mainly to organize your array (unless, of course, you are into retrospectives). The flash comes when you take the clothes *out* of the closet and the flowers *out* of the garden.

> Methought that of these visionary flowers
> I made a nosegay, bound in such a way
> That in the same hues, which in their natural bowers
> Were mingled or opposed, the like array
> Percy Bysshe Shelley, "The Question"

The annual rotation goes something like this:

Spontaneity is a fine concept, actually my favorite, but in late autumn, just as the dahlias (which have been blooming like mad since July) peak, you must make a plan and replace them with scads of gorgeously color-coordinated, properly-timed, well-planted tulips and other enchanting spring bulbs. After all, what is more beautiful than a vase of, say, white, single late tulip 'Maureen' on their magnificent long stems blended with a smattering of almost-black/purple tulip 'Black Diamond' along with a few fantastic 'Black Parrots' thrown in? Or a vase full of burnt-orangish Daydream tulips accentuated with a few *Fritillaria imperialis* (crown-imperial)? Almost nothing I can dream up. So, the fall-planted spring-blooming cutting garden consists of the whole range of amazing tulips, *Fritillaria persica adiyami* and *Fritillaria imperialis*, as well as a smattering of the minor bulbs and perhaps a special corner reserved for hyacinths and daffodils (of course, the most enchanting ones—nothing run-of-the-mill), which persist year after year and deserve devoted choosing and planting because they endlessly bloom to perfection.

As May arrives, all of the early and mid-season tulips get dug up and discarded, as I'm not a believer in keeping tulips around that unfortunately lose their stamina in the second and third year. They are worth the expense and effort of replanting each year because they are singularly the most divine flowers. Also, a tantalizing creative uplift comes with deciding new color schemes and flowering types each year. Then the artfully chosen dahlias, gladiolus, acidanthera, and calla lilies are planted in stages in the same space where the glorious tulips were; as the tulips get dug up week by week, the summer flowers go in the ground—also extending their bloom time. This rotation takes place in the original cutting garden.

The new cutting gardens are less work season after season, but just as divine, as they are devoted to permanent plantings of iris, lilies, peonies, *Dicentra spectabilis* (bleeding hearts), *Eremurus robustus* (gigantic and spectacular foxtail lilies), foxgloves and *Physostegia*. None of these needs to be replanted each year and instead become stronger and more profuse with each season. Also relegated to the cutting area is my struggling rose garden. Although not as exquisite and certainly no rival to the fabulous variety of color and form found in lilies, iris, *et al.*, it's nice to make space for the more robust and important annuals like cleome, cosmos, and felicia, but these are mere pretenders compared to the *real* thing.

AN HERB GARDEN

Perhaps an herb garden is singularly the most common garden of all, but it's fundamental, not boring. To boot, the majority of herbs are quite charming, some even perfectly suitable for flower borders, like *Nepeta mussinii* (catmint) which is one of my favorites in the blue garden (gray-green mint-leaf foliage and smothered in tiny lilac-blue flowers from June till September). It is used as edging as it tumbles over itself in the most tidy manner. I would venture to say everyone—from the most floriferous estate gardener to the humblest farmer—has some version of an herb garden or, at least, is growing a little parsley and a few chives in some corner. You need to have only the slightest bent toward the culinary to find interest in this one, and you can participate in some small way in eating what you grow without turning over vast patches to vegetables (and the inherent tribe of smarmy suckers that follow, like cabbage loopers and squash borers).

My herb garden, albeit diminutive, services all our favorite menus and conveniently occupies the end of the cutting garden nearest the kitchen and barbecue. Three kinds of basil are the mainstay, including an exotic purple-leafed one that doesn't taste so great but looks smashing; an Italian and a Chinese parsley, oregano, and marjoram. Adding a touch of shrubbery is classic *Lavandula munstead* (lavender, which even looks nice in the winter in a ghostly way) and two wonderful clumps of *Thymus citriodorus* (thyme that smells like lemon). Find a nursery with an array of herbs, sniff out the ones most pleasing, and arrange an orderly herb patch. This is one time when you don't want wild profusion and might even consider adding a few dwarf conifers or shrubs to border it and give substance and form. Your salads will seek a new level, for sure.

For those of you really obsessed with the culinary, you might consider the super specialization of "menu gardens" to bring the growing of edibles within bounds. The French gourmand might plant *haricot vert* (green beans), *courgette* (zucchini), petit carrot, butterhead lettuce, chervil, and French tarragon with a *treillage* background. The Oriental cook could go for snow peas, green onions, daikon radishes, Chinese cabbage, etc., using a wok as a planter or a bamboo fence to set the theme. The variations are measureless.

A GARDEN OF GRASSES

After all these exuberant pursuits, here is a method of gardening to entrance the most elusive of you gardeners, a defining statement that outlasts every trendy whim: growing ornamental grasses. The one totally-devoted-to-grass garden I've known was a knockout and made me question seriously why I, in the same neighborhood, wasn't exhibiting the same nonchalant brilliance. This grass garden was on the property of fanatical daylily enthusiasts who sent out invitations to perfect strangers (must have made the list after the Garden Tour, because I have no idea who these people are) but I found the lure of "A Rainbow Garden at Dusk" irresistible. Their daylily garden (another fine and viable pursuit) was the stuff of obsession. Rows upon rows upon rows of every kind, color, diploid, tetraploid species and hybrid of daylily surrounded a house looking lived-in and well thought-out, and behind the house—a huge field of daylilies being crossed, hybridized, bred, and nurtured. Proudly displayed was their "Distinguished Display Garden" plaque bestowed by the American Hemerocallis Society. Although a believer in and lover of daylilies and fascinated by their garden, what really struck me (wedged in an area between the proper gardens and the coddling gardens) was their grass exhibit.

On this late July evening, I saw huge clumps, (I mean *huge*, thirty feet in circumference and ten or twelve feet high) of maybe twenty different kinds of grasses—all looking glorious in that effusive, weeping habit they acquire and crowned with long waving "foxtails," which are their flowers (also called panicles, spikes, or inflorescences). It reminded me of an exuberant English maze and made me realize how impressive and graceful grass upon well-arranged grass could be. Also, how the singling out of any one genus can heighten the excitement of any garden. To achieve this splendid looking apparition, you need a sizable plot (at least twelve by twenty feet), and sun. Our grasses growing behind the pond are not much to speak of after many years there because we have no sun, but the three kinds of grass growing around the pool where we have our closest approximation to full sun are a very different story. The clumps double in size each season, and the plumes appearing toward summer's end get statelier and more colorful each season.

All grasses, including the stuff in your yard, as well as bamboo, belong to the same family *Gramineae* and when you consider this group also contains all the cereal grains, it is easy to understand why the Brooklyn Botanical Garden states "it represents the most important single plant family." Here, however, let's forget the dull, homely grasses, the life-sustaining grasses, and of course—that meanest of weed—crabgrass, and delve into only the majestic ornamental grasses you might choose to make your theme garden statement.

Among the many enhanced ornamental grasses, you will find irregular ones, mounding, open-spreading, and tufted grasses, as well as upright-arching, narrow, and open. Ranging in height from one to fifteen feet, they go by such charming cognomens as "striped giant reed grass," *Arundo donax* 'Variegata', pampas grass (really tall and can be had in white, pink, and black—referring to the color of its plumes) which is *Cortaderia*, fountain grass (self-descriptive *Pennisetum*), zebra grass (striped and easily located as *Miscanthus sinensis* 'Zebrinus'), and small but special, *Festuca*, or fescue grass (a really adorable low fountain-shaped variety that comes in blue, olive, and bronze). *Imperata cylindrica rubra*, Japanese bloodgrass, is one always waxed didactic about—many cite its particular ability to bounce the sun off its blood-red blades; but after two or three honest trials I've yet to witness this phenomenon. At a Horticultural Society lecture on ornamental grasses, however, John Greenlee (eminent grassman and author of *the* book on grasses), swore that a mass planting of bloodgrass ranked with the angels when it comes to heavenly looks.

At this same lecture, this cute young guy (who attracted an unusually attractive young crowd as far as the gardening lecture circuit goes) stressed that grass growing could be compared to drawing with the "big sixty-four-color box of crayons." Grasses can be had in a huge rainbow of color: chartreuse, yellow, gold, blue, gray, pink, red, burgundy, purple, and white, most of which will deliver an autumn color bonus of orange, brick, russet, and biscuit. He was especially adamant about the inherent rhythm and diversity of grasses—resolute in stating "nothing adds movement to a garden like grasses."

Bamboo is a category unto itself and can certainly command its own garden. There is something magical about a mature grove of bamboo (*Phyllostachys* or *Bambusa*), the way the wind whistles through it, the way it commands the same presence as a tree without the bulk of a trunk. Bamboo, which is a woody grass, can be clumping or running, from timber to pigmy size, as well as hardy or tropical. The bamboo shoot, or cane, which is synonymous with all things lithe and Oriental and a mainstay of garden decoration and support, is such a unique idea that it, too, commands its own nomenclature. The hollowed-out, jointed, familiar stem of the bamboo is properly called a "culm." There are imported noninvasive kinds, but for the most part these culms dig down into the earth and form long, strong rhizomes that rise up around the parent plant to produce more and more bamboo. This sounds enthralling, does it not? But you must be aware that the prolific bamboo may overwhelm your area and your idea. So, either grow it on a patch of land whose boundaries are very loose, or contain it, either by potting or curbing it with serious substances like sheet metal or concrete. However you do it, you must remember that it likes water—lots and lots of water—and is persistent and will be with you for a very long time.

If an entire garden of grasses or bamboo doesn't entice you—hark back to the last chapter and think what glorious partitions you can create with grasses. Abundantly there in the summer, persisting through winter in their "dried" state, the only time your grass dividers are absent is the few months of spring when you cut them down near to the ground. Lovely curtains for your garden rooms, those swaying reedy clumps.

AN ALPINE GARDEN

Suggesting an alpine garden is a natural since it was one of Vita's fixations.

I have been making a tiny garden of Alpines in an old stone trough—A real joy. My botanical taste tends more and more towards flowers that can hardly be seen by the naked eye—shall I make an even tinier one for you? in a seed pan, with Lilliputian rocks?
— Vita Sackville-West (Letter to Virginia Woolf of 2 September, 1925)

This is a perfect choice for those of you interested in becoming intimately acquainted with diminutive plants exuding miniature charms. Literally, Alpines are plants growing on majestic mountaintop locations above the tree line in a rocky or gravelly soil protecting their root-run. These conditions can be simulated in either a rock garden or in containers. If you think you can justify a microclimate on your property imitating the Alps, and you feel fondness toward tiny miracles often exhibiting relatively large flowers, there are societies and catalogs devoted to this exercise where you can acquire the fodder to feed this indulgence. If meticulousness is one of your characteristics, you revere restraint, and anal-retentive applies to you, Alpine gardening should be right up your alley—or in your trough.

By now it must be evident that there are many specialized gardening paths for you to stroll. Any one of them will make your gardening activity more interesting. The last thing you want to subscribe to is being an obsessed gardener with nothing to talk about. If your days in the dirt are

My fledgling version of a rockery in its first year.

spent tracking down a ubiquitous but unattainable old-world peony cultivar to round out your Shakespeare garden or importing that final, fabulous, just-right, golden-green *Chamaecyparis pisifera* 'Golden Mop' to accentuate your Armani conifer border, then your chitchat at the dinner party is likely to be far more engrossing than the chick at the other end of the table who plants loads of impatiens in front of her hedge or along her walk and bores the party into doldrums. Specialized gardening makes *you* special as well as your garden. Think seriously about the *kind* of gardens you want to grow and become expert. Your toil and tedious attention will be well rewarded as your garden distinguishes itself from the rest of the hordes. By planning a garden with your own personal interpretation of a fixed theme or goal in mind, whether you apportion space in acres or yards, whether your fixations are narrow or wide, focused gardening is the only sure way to add dimension, atmosphere, imagery, and interest enough to keep them awake while the rest of the table has yawned itself into dreamland.

Weeds. Pests. Predators.
Rigors. Solace. Solutions.

My peonies have lovely leaves
but rarely flower.
Oh, they have buds
and plenty of them. These
grow to the size of peas
and stay
that way.
Is this
bud blast?

What ails my fern?

I enclose a sample
of a white disease
on a leaf
of honesty
known also
as the money plant

My two blue spruce
look worse and worse

What ails my fern?

James Schuyler, "What Ails
My Fern?" *Selected Poems*

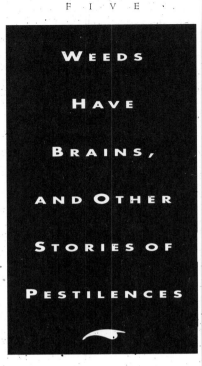

WEEDS

HAVE

BRAINS,

AND OTHER

STORIES OF

PESTILENCES

Dreaming up idyllic rapturous gardening scenes and indulging in satisfying integrity-ridden shopping sprees are surely the stuff of which garden fantasies are made, but like all things in life, nothing is total pleasure. It's my obligation as your gardening friend to introduce you to the deep, dank, dark underside inherent in gardening, as well. However, you must view this nether side in the context of the Big Picture—nothing following is even remotely significant enough to be a true deterrent to gardening pleasure. Don't even consider fretting, because to every problem there is an answer. Some problems are more overwhelming than others—but I haven't yet come across a pestilence that couldn't be beat. Of course, people say I'm lucky, but I believe that with a positive attitude, you can always put yourself in control of a situation that otherwise might provoke panic and lead to hysteria. We will deal with the bugs and slugs shortly. First, this chapter's perhaps bewildering title should be explained. There was a time when I, too, would have dismissed weeds as totally acerebral, simply a nuisance and an eyesore, and that would have been that. Not the case, however.

WEEDS

This truism, "weeds have brains," has been coined because I believe they absolutely do. How else could you explain their cleverness? Of course, some are oblivious, ugly, brainless, and stick out like sore thumbs wherever they grow—these are the lower class of uneducated weeds, *not the sophisticated smart ones* that exist only to outfox and frustrate you. One balmy early September day with signs of summer's end saturating the air, I was roaming around with my Felcos to give a clip here, a trim there, in preparation for a month's departure from the garden. Being away for such a stretch of time at the beginning of crucial autumn normally wouldn't be a consideration, but our trip down the Nile with all its attendant sphinxes, pyramids, and antiquities seemed like an adventure not to be missed.

WEEDS PARADING AS PLANTS

Anyway, Felcos in hand, I approached a divine *Hydrangea paniculata* 'Grandiflora' in full panicling flower planted last summer and now at least doubled in size to about four feet. Beautiful creamy-white dome-shaped flower heads, florets encircling tiny little sprays of flowers (referred to as corymbs) tipped each branch—a gorgeous specimen. At any rate, the shrub has a very definitive elliptic leaf shape (with an attenuate base and a cuspidate tip, to be exact), so when I noticed one branch out of sync with the shape of the plant and growing too tall, I simply thought it needed pruning because the leaves of the abnormally high branch *were exactly the same* as the rest of the bush.

The oddity was its largesse, yet it ended in no flower, like 90 percent of the other branches on the shrub. So I stalked about and looked really carefully at the leaf on the tall branch and the other leaves—the same. I turned them over to better see the veining on the reverse—once again, identical. Even the color and size of the stem, even that sort of reddish tint

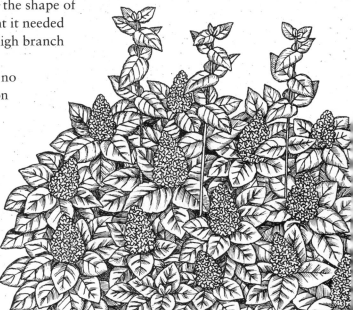

The wily weed among the hydrangea.

where the stem meets the leaf—one was absolutely indistinguishable from the other. "This is too weird," I said to myself, then proceeded to get down on my knees to examine the base of this beautiful hydrangea and found this tall stalk *not attached* to the trunk but growing on its own out of the ground. AHA! A weed! One of those very brainy weeds that know to grow among fine cultivated things and mimic their very same pattern and form. How do they manage it? How did this one *know* to pop up in the middle of this hydrangea where it has been camouflaged the entire summer instead of materializing next door among the *Crinum* lilies and *Physostegia* where I would have spotted it immediately? *How* did it know?

They know, they just know where to grow, how to dupe you, and how to camouflage themselves among the perfectly respectable plants, *they just know*, and therefore, I've concluded weeds *must* have brains. They have also figured out exactly where to hide so they will receive full benefit of your composted soil, devoted watering, and fanatic fertilizing, and these tricks of theirs have been going on for a long time unabated. How else could Hamlet have discerned, in his indulgent exhortation to his mother,

And do not spread the compost on the weeds,
To make them ranker.
Shakespeare, *Hamlet*, Act III, scene iv

Now I'm aware of these ingenious and wily weeds everywhere, sidling up to their cultivated counterparts, emulating emerging muscari, feigning phosphoresences, imitating ivies. They're especially crafty in spring when all that glorious green is bursting through the earth. Shrewd weeds seem to think they are just as entitled to their space as any other plant.

So we naturally must ask, just what *are* weeds? Well, this could be a long story, but I won't allow it because weeds are not interesting enough to dwell on. Even though Anne Raver in the *Times* extols the presence of many edible ones and whole books have been written about their classification, as far as I'm concerned if you did not *deliberately* plant it, then it's a weed.

As if the last great annoyance uniting us
Was gone, the dandelions perished.
And we were all a bit stunned.
Of course, other breeds remained
Weeds even more difficult to eradicate
Than our favorite, our yellow terror.
But they were less obvious, almost too elusive
To make your interest more than dalliance.
Steven Hamilton, "Thoughts of a Country Boy"

Armed with this data about how bright and brazen some weeds are, it stands to reason that the next thing you want to know is how to be cleverer than they. Well, once you look upon them as part of the exercise, you must steel yourself to out-persevere them. In Chapter II, I've described a profusion of weeders and diggers by which you extract them from the dirt. When using any of these implements, it is vital that you do not just pull off the top growth, but get out that persistent root. Though some are stubborn, with long taproots, most weeds are weaklings when it comes to their root systems. It is one of their distinguishing features, actually. If you don't recognize it and you can pull it out easily, then it is most likely a weed.

Weeding is frustrating, repetitive, boring work. There are a few tips, however, to make it easier:

1. Do it after the rain, after you have watered, after the sprinklers have sprinkled—anytime the ground is soft.
2. When you do weed, get rid of the whole weed, all its parts and all its seeds. It's those weed seeds you especially want to destroy.
3. Examine any container-grown plant arriving on your doorstep by mail-order or bought at your nursery carefully before planting. A too-large percentage of the time there will be weeds well started in the soil along with the lovely you plan to plant. Get rid of them.
4. You already know how I feel about good tools. The proper utensils to rout out the weeds are high on the list.
5. I have recently uncovered a theory in the 201st edition of *The Old Farmer's Almanac* that seems a bit impractical, but quite logical and even romantic:

By performing all soil-disturbing operations after dark, they [the Germans] discovered that weed germination could be reduced by as much as 78 percent. Weeds typically covered only 2 percent of night-cultivated test strips, while adjacent strips cultivated during daylight were 80 percent covered with weeds. Sounds crazy. But a recent test in Germany has shown that gardens cultivated on cloudy, moonless nights produce 78 percent fewer weeds!

In the event you view this as a panacea, perhaps you want to procure for yourself one of those "miner's hats" with battery pack and a big beam on top. Just the thing for moonlight cultivation. Irving actually gave me one of these hats as a sort-of joke present (he had read somewhere that beleaguered Prince Charles used one for his nighttime gardening) and thought it was just the thing I had to have for planting autumn bulbs, as I'm continually cursing the dreaded Daylight Losing Time that abruptly shortens further the already-too-short autumn days.

PLANTS THAT SHOULD BE CLASSIFIED AS WEEDS

When is a true flower a weed? That seemingly beautiful perennial ground cover *Houttuynia cordata* described in the last chapter as the perfect transition between spring and summer in my white garden is *worse* than any weed known to man. No self-respecting nursery or catalog should ever sell it without a HUGE WARNING ATTACHED. Here is the sad and alarming tale.

The Depressing Days of the Downfall of the White Garden

September 1, 1992. Would I have been better off never subscribing to *The Avant Gardener*, a monthly pamphlet held dear, and going about my days in perfect bliss, only occasionally sidetracked by the unusual aggressiveness of the *Houttuynia cordata* planted as ground cover along with *Lamium* 'White Nancy' in the white garden? "Beautiful but Vicious" was the lead line of an article in the July 1992 issue and the departing point of the demise of much of my gorgeous overgrown white garden. It is gone. My white garden is . . . mostly gone. All those years waiting for the peonies, all the money spent on those exotic *Pancratium* and *Hymenocallis*, my eight-foot-tall white tea rose that blooms until November. Unbelievable as this sounds . . . it is at least half gone.

The Avant Gardener quotes Harold Epstein, one of America's foremost plantsmen, as saying

> It [*Houttuynia*] is a vicious weed when planted in most gardens. The species is common in all islands of Japan but seldom cultivated there except in pots as a show plant. The roots are very fine and stoloniferous and wander irrespective of wet or dry conditions. It is almost impossible to eradicate except with strong weedkillers such as RoundUp. I recall being shown a huge patch of it on a rock garden slope at Willowwood, the garden of Ben Blackburn in New Jersey. A bit of it had been planted and within a few years it had taken over the entire slope, overwhelming all other plants.

Well, I have no intention of sitting back like this Ben Blackburn, whoever he is, and allowing this to happen. Who knows how many acres is Willowwood, but I venture quite larger than my .94 acre and I refuse to be defeated by this goddamned alien ferocious weed and allow it to overrun my beautiful focal white plot. After getting down on my hands and knees and really scrutinizing, the sad truth is that the two four-inch pots of this stuff planted some three years ago had spread at least twelve feet in every direction and had begun to suffocate everything in its path. Time for action! I got Irving in on the act and together on a scorching August Sunday we began the deed of digging up this dog. After three hours, it was clear we were getting nowhere, as the roots were everywhere, twined around everything, and went very deep. I sought HELP! and watched with dread while two husky guys and the collegiate son of one of my favorite nursery families, the Buckleys, came at my request to extirpate this stunning but deadly *Houttuynia*. Uprooting the better part of my garden became the only solution to rout out the mendacious, insidious, ugly, infiltrating roots.

You can't imagine the breadth of my emotions while my glorious garden was being destroyed. Dennis, the young son, was almost too sympathetic. He said, "God, are you sure you want to take out those beautiful Royal Standard hosta [which just happened to be in full bloom]? It takes years to grow them this big." *No kidding*, who knows this better than me, but, "Yes! Out with them," I screeched in angst, remembering a particularly cold fall day laying them in bare-root some five years ago. Sure enough, the twelve hosta root systems were riddled with this perfidious, furtive, strangling weed I once thought a divine perennial ground cover.

Oh, it's sad now crossing the deck in this direction. Usually I exit the kitchen, stop to admire the exotic pot, glance over to the bird feeder to see what delightful creatures are chirping and chomping away, check out the passion vines in the big glazed Italian olive urns flanking the stairway to the lawn, where I'm then greeted by the wonderful vista of the white garden. As of this afternoon, this stroll curtly ends by the confrontation of a raw dirt patch: dug up, rototilled and drenched in some terminal toxin said to kill everything it encounters.

The days pass, frustrating days spent puttering around to find spots to replant all the dug-up bulbs (some I can name and others—not a clue), salvaging what perennials were not completely choked by the mendacious roots, making an all-out effort to transplant the miraculous white hybrid tea so happy in its spot—now fearlessly cut down to its wood for any chance of survival. My latest daily ritual is a scrutinous examination of the bare patch, looking for signs of this heinous dog being bold enough to reappear.

Does the exquisite expensive weeping Alaskan cypress have to go too? That's the next step to be taken should the beast rear its ugly head again.

~

September 15. Oh, it's so disheartening. I was beginning to hope beyond hope that we had licked it, but knew deep in my heart there were still a few profligate stolons to be dealt with because already reappearing was a heinous leaf here and there. So again I coaxed Irving into taking long trowel in hand and everywhere he poked—in every patch we dug—there was more and more and more of this monster weed parading as a highly interesting ground cover from Japan. What a treacherous weed it is. Now that it has been dug and poked, rototilled and poisoned—the evidence is in. *You can't beat it.* One tiny little sliver of root left in the ground regenerates several new shoots within fifteen days.

What to do?

Defeat has never been a part of my vernacular. I refuse to succumb to this Japanese weed parading like a floral achievement and proudly for sale in fine nurseries and catalogs.

~

September 20. Okay. New word is in. We are not digging up the Alaskan weeping cypress to untangle the vile thing from its roots. In addition, forces have come together and agreed it was a big mistake for the husky boys from Buckley's to have rototilled, because each and every little fragment has these aforementioned huge powers of regeneration. It is said the singular solution

The heinous white roots of the *Houttuynia* invading the perfectly polite rootball of a *Platycodon*.

is demon chemicals, and harkening back to the *The Avant Gardener*, the only product to do it is RoundUp, which works in a very peculiar way now well-explained to me. To begin with, the hotter it is when you apply it the better (so, no good in autumn, of course, which means an interminable wait). It is applied to the foliage of the plant, and once it kills the greenery, it then lethally works its way down into the root system.

Therefore, drag of drags, we must wait till next summer when it eagerly and viciously rears its head again to zap it. I've already tried drenching it in double-strength RoundUp, but the cool weather does not seem to be doing the trick. The consensus, from George Morgan, our tenured lawn and other heavy-job man, who swears he has done extensive research around town about ridding us of this horror, and Kenneth Pascual of The Bayberry, who seems to know his stuff and sold us the weeping cypress in question, is if we really want to slaughter this atrocity—waiting till next summer is the only way.

So I'll use the space as a tulip cutting garden to mark time between now and the advantageous moment next summer to really slay the beast. An ultimate example of exactly the sort of ruthless monster you *do not want in your garden*, and a sad, sad tale.

Other plants to watch for which have a tendency to become so invasive they should be considered weeds are *Lysimachia* (the *clethroides* Mr. Gooseneck version is okay because it's beautiful and shallow-rooted, as you know, but avoid at all costs the yellow flowering kinds), *Monarda* (good ole "bee balm"—not only does it truly attract bees—its aggressiveness is such that it will climb right over and crowd out anything less vigorous), *Symphytum* (comfrey, which bears a charming true-blue flower like Virginia bluebells but is a literal *wild*-flower and produces so much foliage it can overshadow many other plants), and *Macleaya* (the plume poppy, rather fetching with its big pale celadon leaves that all the nurseries were hawking this summer; but don't be fooled—it has mean roots that really work their way down into the ground and it spreads like mad—why, it nearly wiped out a hydrangea, but thankfully, I got to it first).

Convallaria, precious lily-of-the-valley, is rumored to be incredibly invasive ("invasive" is the catchword to watch for) but not in my experience to date. I have two struggling patches of the plant, which I've coddled for years, and nothing would please me more than if they got incredibly out of hand, but so far there's been a modest 10 percent increase a year. On the other side of the what-to-watch-for fence are wild strawberries. We have some that appeared out of nowhere a few years ago and are now taking over the place. And clover. Unlucky three-leaf clover is manifesting itself like mad everywhere I turn. Where all this clover and these strawberries have come from, I can't begin to explain. Maybe carried home in another plant, maybe they just picked the Benson garden because they like it—who knows? Just another of those idiosyncrasies and small crosses to bear. As much time was spent last summer pulling out these two newcomers as all other weeding combined. You must stay on top of these rampant ones or they will drive you crazy.

THE POISONOUS ONES

Famous poison oak, ivy, and sumac are as much a part of my woodsy arena as they probably are of yours. Personally, I don't get too terribly afflicted, but other members of the family and guests have come down with some seriously consequential rashes. Take heart! For this there is a veritable cure. A product called Tecnu is as good a healer as there is, and you can order it from many catalogs and find it locally. This magic mixture of chemicals impossible to pronounce and wood pulp (which sounds friendly, anyway) does the trick. Apply it on the rash when your skin is dry, and give it a very vigorous rubbing in. I'll wager after two applications, your poison-whatever rash will be gone. There are special concoctions at your local supply store to slay the plant itself.

SMALL FURRY CREATURES

Though weeds are a drag, they can be conquered. If you can't bear the thought of digging them out, you can murder them with all sorts of chemicals if they exist somewhere other than right in your garden among your precious plants. It's the other creatures in dear Mama Nature's spectrum that threaten our gardens but require the steeliness of a cold-hearted cur to condemn to death by poison, which is just not in my makeup.

In the excess of spring, madness is not uncommon to the gardener who has deliberated for weeks about what bulbs to order, has finally made decisions, spent considerable dollars, toiled endless hours in planting, and spent months counting down the weeks anticipating the first signs of life, only to have all hopes and dreams (not to mention work and money) of the last nine months thwarted by some unknown predator that dines on the long awaited darlings just as the buds have swollen to their plumpest state and are about to bloom!!! It doesn't matter whether you are a devoted animal lover and the "criminal" is the sweetest bunny rabbit in town. It doesn't matter whether the pestilence is an elegant deer eating the sweetest portion of the garden from the top, or a less graceful groundhog, mole, or vole satiating itself from underground—this is definitely the stuff of *garden madness.* You simply cannot take the glory of the flower for granted, and it is necessary to prepare for minor battles before the final victory can fully be appreciated.

Now what to do, as a proper friend of the earth and environment, about these creatures who find your tulip bulbs, lily bulbs, or crocus petals deliciously irresistible? Well, basically there is nothing you can actually do that is acceptable or conscionable to *really* get rid of these, or any, animals. Gardening, at one point or another in the vast spectrum of Redfordesque love of the earth, its rivers, and progeny, insists you choose sides, take a stand: it's the rabbits, the posies, or me!

Without going overboard one way or the other, I've tried silly measures like sprinkling all the tulips with red chili pepper, suggested by *The New York Times,* no less. Not only did this not stop the rabbits, it made the tulips look like they had developed some dreadful rust disease. I thought perhaps the East Hampton mandatory fencing in of the property would help keep out some of the creatures, and it did for maybe two months; but those especially hungry bunnies and other small, sweet, scurrying animals abound again. Of course, there are gardens literally caged in with wire mesh screens, but to me this looks so atrocious I would rather sigh over eaten flowers than endure these garden prisons—the antithesis of the wild and natural look we aspire toward.

So what can you do to dissuade our animal friends from using your garden as their dining room? Naturally, don't replant the very same thing in the very same tasty area—find a new spot not quite so hospitable and not already on their beaten track. You can try the dubious red chili pepper, talcum powder, wood ashes, or blood meal worked into the soil around the plants: these are solutions advocated by many. I've even read that mulching with human or dog hair actually works—although I can't imagine how, and once again may prefer the eaten-flower routine, especially as the groomer who tends to our pooch, Dylan, nearly hooted me out of his joint when the inane suggestion was made.

Naturally, I've tried the ultrasonic sound devices marketed in all the gardening magazines. Supposedly, these battery-operated stakes you bury in the ground emit a noise inaudible to humans (although I could hear it buzzing perfectly fine) but maddening to gophers, squirrels, and moles. After placing six of these around the property, which was twice as many as was recommended, I didn't detect the decrease of our small furry animal population by even *one* percent. Do not waste your money on these. And of course, there are traps, but traps within the traps abound. If you choose the humane route of "live traps," the kind that cage the animal but don't kill it, then what do you do with the little living furry thing? Release it into your neighbor's yard to eat his flowers? Drown it? Bring it to the zoo? I have no answer to this question. Then there are lethal traps, but the last thing I want to be faced with is the disposal of dead animals. A trapper I'm not.

As you know, vegetable gardening is not a part of my routine; knowing that it's the *really* preferred feast of all small scurrying creatures is another reason I've avoided a food patch. We do have a resident raccoon, but it seems mainly interested in birdseed (which we now keep locked away in the gardening shed), and I venture it has feasted on more than one fish from the pond—how else to explain the utter disappearance of a particularly nicely marked coy? Somehow our squirrels are rather well-behaved and don't seem to challenge the gardens, only the bird feeders. (There is no such thing as a squirrel-proof bird feeder, I've come to learn; but they have to eat, too.) Our gophers wreak havoc with the lawn, leaving holes and tunnels all over the place; but don't seem to disturb the gardens. Of course, some precious bulbs that never surface could be in their bellies—but that is the exception, not the rule.

Fortunately, we can boast of having seen divine long-tailed pheasants on our property and, more than once, a family of ducks floating in our pool; but have no tales of porcupines, skunks, coyotes, or dear God help us, bears. The big story engendering many sagas of woe at the nurseries around here have to do with not-too-distant neighbors being plagued by deer, which supposedly constitute the most horrific gardening menace. But again, guess I'm lucky, as my only run-in with a deer has been spying a supremely statuesque one standing tall and proud in the middle of the road about a quarter-mile from our house, which I found more thrilling than threatening. The gals at the nursery, however, insist the only thing that keeps them out are exceptionally sturdy eight-foot fences.

For those of you not as fortunate as I whose gardens are being attacked by all of the above, try a book, *Bugs, Slugs and Other Thugs*. It bills itself as "A Down-to-Earth Gardening Book" and takes into account everyone's best environmental intentions, while giving practical explanations and answers on the age-old preoccupation of waging war against garden pests.

THE LOWLIEST OF LOW: SLUGS

I, personally, had never come in contact with a slug before my gardening obsession took hold. They do not seem to be very interested in a simple grassy lawn, no matter how green and perfect, but give them abundant and thriving circumstances—moisture, big leaves, or delicate flowers—and just watch as they materialize out of thin air. They are bold and disrespectful, ugly and slimy, and they *love* gardens. They just love them. Stomaching and suffering many heretofore rejected ideas has become part and parcel of my gardening experience, but these slugs still make me yelp and scream when the unfortunate moment arises of encountering one unawares. One main reason to *never* approach the garden without your gloves.

These horrid mollusks, classified thus even though they have no shell to hide their ugly mucousy features, are not to be confused with worms. Worms are good to the garden, while there is not a single benefit to be attributed to a snail or slug.

Imagine. It's early evening. An ideal sort of light, soothing, summer rain has just moistened your world. You walk out to your garden feeling motherly because you know this sprinkling of real rain has been more beneficial than any man-made watering could ever be. Breathing in the heady air, you feel like some besotted earth person . . . and then you spy them . . . dripping from the delphiniums, hanging from the hosta. It wouldn't be so bad if they just left that disgusting unattractive trail of slime behind them; it wouldn't even be so bad if they were just repulsive to the touch and to the eye; *but* they inflict terrible damage on the garden to boot. They like humidity, wetness, and shade and seem particularly fond of my magnificent array of hostas, which are all over the property, and they have managed to track down every single one, chewing them full of holes. Any leafy ground cover is a perfect habitat for them: I've also watched them munch their way through my *Asarum* (lovely heart-shaped-leaved European ginger), *Lamium*, and countless tender young plants which then never reach adulthood.

News reports have elucidated
Your current predicament with slugs,
But, can this really be so difficult?

Consider our position:

Last week alone eight of ours
And two of yours departed
For the Forbidden Territories, and let us
Assure you: all positions and enticements
Afforded by the linear thought patterns
At our disposal were Fully Employed.

So what else is new?

Other would-be Species report similar tales
Of rebellion, insult, and in one case,
Rumors of extinction preceded by lassitude.

Now, outrageous squirrels in heat
Have nearly stripped all bark from
The hickory whose leaves, as you well know,
Provide the last refuge between here and
The invidious betrayal of pure sunlight.

Steven Hamilton, "To the Field Force"

Once again, what to do? Definitely *not* the beer trick. I've read and heard many times that the sure way to slay a slug is to set out shallow dishes or empty tuna cans filled with beer. Supposedly slugs are drawn to fermented lager yeasts and will drown themselves in these tins of beer set into the soil. Well, the aftermath of this practice is so hideous—a fetid tuna-tin of beer filled with dead slugs—and so futile—for every slug drowned it seems six dozen more come to seek revenge—I abandoned it after two weeks of suffering through the disposal of the drunken dead slugs. After trying everything—diatomaceous earth, sprinkling salt, vinegar sprays, and any number of products from local stores—I finally read in *The New York Times* about Ortho's Deadline Bug-Geta, Liquid Snail and Slug Killer.

This is what you do. You buy appropriately huge quantities of Ortho's Bug-Geta and diligently squirt it around the base of all slug-attracting plants once they have emerged about halfway in the spring. Then sometime around the beginning of June, you lift up leaves and hunt down nooks and crannies and apply again. Although in itself the Deadline is curiously unattractive, looking not unlike the slime-trails of the slugs themselves, *it works*! I don't know why it works and all the other products don't, but why question this magic? I figured if it could fell a slug, might it not be harmful to the dog? But a phone call to the source assured me it was safe, and after two years of use, that seems to be so. The strange problem about Deadline is it is difficult to find, at least around here. None of the local hardware stores or nurseries has it, though they carry millions of other Ortho products. Finally good old Agway tracked it down for me, where I bought a case and even got a discount. I promise you, this past summer, where I "Deadlined" there were no devoured leaves, where I forgot to Deadline, the same old ravaged results. This is a chemical I heartily advocate as it is custom-made to kill the salacious slugs and nothing else. No environmentalist in his right mind could possibly criticize you for wanting to rid your garden of slugs.

BUGS

Still just luck I guess, but I've had the good fortune to not be invaded by legions of lecherous insects—save the ubiquitous Japanese beetle and the occasional earwig. For some reason, weevils, locusts, thrips, other beetles, borers, and aphids seem totally uninterested in my garden. I like to think my efforts at weeding, eradicating the invaders at the first sign of any ailing plants, and my general attempt to keep everything charming and tidy are the basis for this godsend. *Bugs, Slugs and Other Thugs* says, "Simply put, healthy plants in healthy soil do not attract insects or disease organisms." A newsletter from the Begonia Society elaborates, "The disease triangle states for any living thing to have a disease there must be a disease-causing organism (a pathogen), a suitable living thing to attack (a host), and the right conditions for attack to take place and be successful." It's clear pathogens of one kind or another are all around us. The hosts can be any of the dear plants in our lovely gardens but surely, my insistence on growing no food is also a boon to my insectless and mildewless garden presence. The absence of vegetables obviously doesn't invite cabbage or pea aphids, Colorado potato beetles, corn rootworms, squash vine borers, tomato hornworms, carrot rust flies, or any of their cousins or friends. For this, I am exceedingly grateful. It's the third side of the triangle— *providing clean, weed-free, healthy* circumstances—we must continually practice to keep the bad guys out.

Another habit to promote is my annual purchase of the good-guy insects by mail from Gardens Alive, "the environmentally responsible, organic products for a healthy garden" catalog. Get this catalog because it has a solution for every scourge; they even claim to have something to keep the deer at bay if that's your tribulation. I order from them lovely black-spotted orange ladybugs, charming green lacewings (aptly named), and fragile, ethereal praying mantis. The fact they don't return each year because they can't find enough around here to eat, I guess, reconfirms my good fortune in not having many predators. But now I'm used to their colorful and playful addition to the garden, so I usually order them before spring along with the tubers and roots, *et al.* But if you have aphids, mealybugs, whiteflies, or thrips—these symbiotic creatures of Mama's kingdom should do the trick. If you are really inundated, you might want to consider installing a "bat house." That's right, a house to attract bats. One bat supposedly can devour up to a thousand insects per day, so think what a dozen might do if they were snuggled up in your very own bat abode?! My only bat encounters have been their insistent descent the minute night falls in Bali, and although I found that terrifying, should I suddenly experience an onslaught of ravenous insects—who knows?—I might consider bats.

The earwigs, which are chompers not so different than slugs, seem to be able to be subdued with one light seasonal spraying of a carbamic acid–based compound called Liquid Sevin, so that's not so bad; but Japanese beetles are another story. The one big advantage is you can spot them in a second because their habit is to feed in direct sunshine, so no need to use your imagination or don your miner's helmet to figure out what is disfiguring the roses, no roaming around with flashlights in predawn to catch them in the act. There are two ways to get rid of these persistent iridescent creatures. The first is easy. Put on your most supple pair of gardening gloves and go into the garden with a can of either sudsy warm water or plain old cooking oil. Simply pick the beetles right off the plants and dump them into either of those concoctions. If you have not the time or tummy for this, the only other thing I've found that works to some degree are the singularly unattractive Japanese Beetle Traps. Although disheartening to have to live with the white plastic gathering bags that necessarily hang from them to collect the bugs gracing your garden, the curious bait they contain—a combination of food and sex attractants (a sure come-on if you ask me)—seems to lure many of them into gliding blithely into the white bags and deter others from hanging around. Since you can buy these lure traps everywhere, I guess they work for everyone.

The most important concept to bear in mind when you are faced with an attack of any sort—on any level—is to *stay cool*. The compressor mentioned in Chapter II works the same for fertilizers, pesticides, or any organic combatant applied by spray. Don't be daunted by this apparatus but on the other hand, don't run out and buy one until something assaults. I've only used mine the few times under siege, but those few times were momentous; *and* the disease or offending insect actually succumbed to the treatment and disappeared! Also, don't worry about choosing between the hundreds of insecticides and pesticides available until an invasion actually takes place. When that happens, *stay calm*, cut off a branch or leaf epitomizing the scourge, and bring it to your favorite garden center. With unnatural or mangled leaf in hand, give your best description of the attacking bug or offensive circumstance. It is highly unlikely you will be the only one in your neighborhood with the same problem, and as this story has probably been heard *ad nauseum*, you will be told exactly what to buy to combat the pestilence. Simply bring it home, follow the directions, and haul out your compressor or whatever spraying mechanism suits you best. Don't endow this dilemma with any advance thought, and do not even dream of laying in supplies.

RIGOROUS GARDENING BENEFITS

If you are not a body builder, aerobics queen, or gymnast supreme—you might find the degree of physical stamina required a bit more demanding than you had bargained for. Up and down, on and off your knees an easy fifty times on any vigorous gardening day is not unusual. To the best of my knowledge, cow manure comes only in forty-pound bags, and peat moss and mulches are not exactly lightweight items either. Digging deep trenches to lay in a few hundred fat narcissus will affect every muscle in your body, as will those days of turning over the cutting gardens or struggling to clear for a new planting bed. This exertion, I find, is better looked on as a bonus than a detraction. As one who loathes organized exercise, gardening alleviates any second thoughts I might have about joining health clubs or checking myself into Canyon Ranch with its built-in workout reward. What more could you ask? A beautiful garden and a healthy fit gardener all from the same exercise.

Therapies to be derived from gardening other than those physical are the beneficial mental mind-sets you might acquire from either the serene or labor-intensive tasks. It can be quite easy to drift into a dazed trance, forgetting every single thing nagging at you from the outer-reaches of your mind, when strolling at sunset cutting down a mass of strident blooms to fill your favorite vase.

> Meanwhile the mind, from pleasure less,
> Withdraws into its happiness;
> The mind, that ocean where each kind
> Does straight its own resemblance find;
> Yet it creates, transcending these,
> Far other worlds, and other seas;
> Annihilating all that's made
> To a green thought in a green shade. . . .
>
> Such was that happy garden-state, . . .
> Andrew Marvell, "The Garden"

On the other hand, when feeling disconcerted, pent up with outrage, or totally exasperated over things not in your control—what better release for your anger than weeding! or clearing brush to make a new look! You can attack those stubborn dandelions with all ferocity musterable, you can get under the stalk of one of those big weeds parading as plants—wrench it out of the ground with passion—call it obnoxious names—vent all your pent-up fury—and you will have accomplished the gratifying task of beautifying your garden while burying those distasteful impulses which otherwise might send you scurrying to the shrink. All those dollars spent lying on a therapist's couch could be put to much better use on a new trellis for the clematis or several more hosta for a shady nook. My skepticism about shrinks accelerated threefold when the fulfillment of my garden became by far the best therapy I'd ever found.

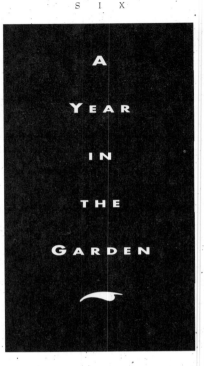

Summer, Fall, Winter, Especially Spring. The Garden Tour.

"I only have twenty acres," replied the Turk. "I cultivate them with my children; and work keeps at bay three great evils: boredom, vice and need."

. . . "I also know," said Candide, "that we should cultivate our gardens."

"You are right," said Pangloss, "for when man was placed in the Garden of Eden, he was placed there *ut operaretur eum*, to dress it and to keep it; which proves that man was not born for idleness."
François Arouet de Voltaire, *Candide; or, Optimism*

A chapter describing the Gardening Year beginning in chronological January would be illogical because nothing about the garden begins in frostbitten, dreary January. As I see it, as opposed to the zodiacal or fiscal year, the Gardening Year really begins in July. July is high summer, when there is little more you can do to the current season's garden. What hasn't already been nurtured, planted, coaxed, coddled, and cajoled will just not be part of the prevailing gardening scene. All you can do in July, really, is maintain what you've got, and *plan* for the next, more glorious year.

I can't imagine a more invigorating Gardening Year than the one preceding the inclusion of my garden on the big deal 1992 Animal Rescue Fund East Hampton Garden Tour. Already alluded to in Chapter I when describing my frantic search to make a late July garden growing limper every day look inspired enough to entice the Great Garden Tour Guru, I bring you back in time.

Having seen the 1991 Garden Tour of six East Hampton gardens, my attention and ambition were aroused. Two of the gardens were on grand estates. The old-world twenty-seven acre estate of a Mr. Frankl was statuaried to the hilt with a beguiling combination of modern and ancient art, replete with an Italianate vine-covered sunken pool, a small zoo, and a vast, dense bamboo forest housing a mysterious children's playhouse and railroad; even though the guy died single and childless and left his estate to the town. Clearly a man with a spirited imagination. The New World estate boasted fabulous sloping lawns which led to a perfect perennial border of maybe four hundred feet fronting one of the comelier town ponds; a cutting garden so dense with flowers it resembled a jungle; and a serenely sensational Zen garden of boulders and perfect Japanese specimen trees along the lawn nearer one of the gentlest modern houses I've ever seen.

Two other gardens were more careful and studied, but enviable in their own individual ways. One was charming and homey with vegetable patch, rose garden, vines and pergolas everywhere, plus a great cutting garden; the other devoted to three ideas only—a staggered property-bordering hedge of every imaginable conifer in particular groupings by color and form, a woodsy back area faithfully planted with at least two hundred different species of hosta, and a hibiscus obsession set forth on the deck in summer and housed in a slate-floored glass room in winter.

The other two were earnest, I suppose, but mediocre at best—and that is a generous description. One of these was a surprisingly stimulating house, very artsy use of mosaic, good fountain—but a silly jumble of annuals passing for an inane garden. The last I mention was just lacking in any sort of particular vision—house and garden both without charm or character.

Hmmmmmm, I said to myself, if these lackluster two are good enough for the Garden Tour, why not mine? So, after a little investigation as to who exactly curates this tour, I fired off a letter to Howard Purcell and offered up my patch. Cultivating my gardens to measure up to this tour, I thought, would be the perfect antidote to the what-do-I-do-now dilemma and would justify my life after begging off the fashion game—or its begging off me.

Following is the month-by-month journal of the anxious year spent in preparation for the Garden Tour. The seasonal pointers are applicable to all gardens in any year and I hope will help guide your gardening efforts.

JULY

. . . O'erstep not the modesty of nature: for anything so overdone is from the purpose of playing, whose end, both at the first and now, was and is, to hold as 'twere, the mirror up to nature; . . . .
William Shakespeare, *Hamlet*, Act III, scene ii

Gregarious Mr. Purcell finally arrived with his jovial companion late in July and pronounced my garden "tourable" and "artistic." Believe me, it was all I needed to hear for promises to pour forth that by next summer it would look twice as grand. Even though the gardens weren't as fresh in the waning days of July as a month before, there were some divine statements highlighting the teeming gardens: the incredible magnolia was blessed with three huge blossoms, the *Yucca glorioso* (which hadn't bloomed for the past two years) was a spire of powerful flower, my adored *Platycodons* (the valuable balloonflower, whose name refers to its thrilling puffed-up bud shape) were in abundance everywhere, the pond was blessed with not one, but two madly blooming waterlilies, the pickerel rush were in flower, and the begonias were dripping with pale pink and salmon double flowers.

By this time, at least 85 percent of the fall planting catalogs had arrived, and I was knee-deep in making determinations, considerations, and largely concentrating on next spring. Now, spring took a backseat to early summer—June is the keynote, Mr. Purcell had said, sometime in June! I need iris—I need lilies—I need summer-blooming bulbs!! Thorough search became the order of the day, for it was mandatory I grow every appealing thing for bloom next June. My next concern, of course, was money. Now I needed much more than the considerable amount usually spent on fall planting. Damn, damn, damn, I thought; why has my birthday just passed? Why did Irving have to pick this year to be so extravagant? I would've gladly forgone the longed-for, simple Piaget watch for a few extra thousand to spend on the next-year garden in the crunch of this critical moment.

Perusing the plot took on an entirely new meaning once the future garden tour was a fact of life. Maintaining the existing garden, scheming about how to turn the new fenced-in area into a wonderland in eleven months, and scrutinizing the daily-arriving catalogs went beyond obsession. July and August—especially this hot, dry July and August—required rigorous watering. The morning sprinkler's sprinkling is clearly not enough when the plants start to wane by five P.M. Usually I'd just ignore this tendency, knowing the combination of dew and sprinklers would perk them right up tomorrow morning—but somehow, suddenly, this didn't seem acceptable. Almost none of my normal routine seemed adequate. Everything had to improve. . . .

Every other evening (you don't want to *over*do it), there I was, with heavy, cumbersome hose in hand, watering, and feeding fertilizer through the Gardena system with a fervor never before known. So many plants and flowers needed to be added, it was inconceivable to think about losing anything already there. Always a believer in deadheading, I was never more meticulous. The moment the bloom started to fade, off it came. Staking anything slightly drooping became a mania. Transplanting anything ample became the mode of the day. Wouldn't the overflowing *Lamium* look perfect under those trees bordering the path to the garden shed? Now that the *Ligularia* are throwing up at least ten different distinct branchings, why not dig and divide some to fill up the bare spot where the driveway turns? The sanctified garden books do not revere transplanting in the midst of summer, but I have found it works *just fine*.

In my woodsy setting, it is at this time of year that you can ascertain just which branches of what trees are blocking the light, overhanging too heavily, or just generally look twiggy and out of harmony. It's much easier to prune mature trees at this moment—when you can see exactly what's happening—rather than when dormant and you have to imagine which branches are heavy with leaves and creating the biggest shadows or shielding some focal point. Get out your long-reach pruner or lopper and *do it now*. The trees don't mind as long as you make a nice clean cut and give them a few kind words.

July Pointers

- Prime time to make a scrutiny of local nurseries, flower shows, the neighborhood, and any garden tours available to you. Note what is flourishing and pleases you, and *make plans* to grow the same in your garden next year.
- If your garden is young and inundated with annuals, shear them lightly or forcibly, depending on how widespread their growth. The last thing you want to wind up the summer with is leggy, pitifully flowering annuals.
- Scratch in some bonemeal around the late-summer-blooming bulbs and lilies; spray and fertilize everything.
- Deadhead everything as soon as it withers, but especially snip any roses back to their next outward-facing bud religiously.
- Time to prune the wisteria. Each stem will have borne myriad branches. Choose the longest and most robust, find their base, and count the first four or five buds—cut back to there and begone with the rest. Also check the base for suckers and get rid of those. You can do this again in six weeks, but definitely do it now while there is rampant growth.
- It is never too soon to begin disbudding the dahlias.
- Waste not another moment—*order* your iris *now* for planting next month, and if it's autumn-flowering bulbs like colchium and autumn crocus you're after—order without delay.
- Pay attention to your vines—make sure anything needing help reaching the sun is tied or secured to ease the climb in the direction you prefer.
- If summer maintenance is not enough for you—it's the perfect time to try your hand at topiary on an overgrown box, privet, or any old hedge looking dense enough, or how about coaxing some ivy around those hollow topiary forms you can order from the catalogs.
- Assess your checkbooks and credit-card limits to figure out where the money will come from for your fall-planting orders. Midsummer is on us and planning next year's garden should be your overriding occupation.

AUGUST

Though the energetic freshness of early summer has gone and the radiance of autumn is still on the come, August is the least tiring, most bountiful month of summer. The foliage plants are swelling to an incredible lush size, and the most rigorous chore is cutting and arranging the plethora of flowers at their peak. This bliss does not quite take into account the kind of August that bore down on us last summer with the apocalyptic arrival of a hurricane boringly called "BOB." Believe me, there was nothing insipid about BOB. The sixty-foot cedar, our most elegant and largest specimen, standing at the heart of the white garden's end, toppled—it's gone. Historic East Hampton town trees—elms that had been here for generations, if not longer—uprooted like so many twigs with huge twenty-foot-diameter root-balls standing on end right on Main Street. All over town devastation, but amazingly in the garden many stubborn plants withstood the crisis. Hydrangea, platycodon, hosta, lespedeza—well, once the sky cleared they appeared hardly fazed by the onslaught. How could that be? The dahlias didn't fair so well, but for the most part the gardens proper were merely littered with all the detritus of the pounding storm, which felled a total of six stately trees on our little property alone. This August is very tame in comparison and my concerns about the Garden Tour seem humble in contrast.

But the catalog deadlines are hovering more insistently, admonishing and nagging that the time is now—you have to PROJECT: design, devise, and draft those orders. It is unthinkable for anyone with the gardening spirit to pass up this opportunity to decide exactly what will greet you next spring and summer. There is no way you can produce next April's splendor if you don't decide now. It is futile to expect you can go out next April or May, spend $12.50 or more for eight already pot-grown, fairly presentable tulips; transplant them in your own yard and hope to achieve the effect of springtime. I don't care how many pots you buy—this will *never* work and, thank God, fall is also ideal planting time for bare-root poppies, peonies, daylilies, and hosta—none of which will flower for the tour but all of which will add to the profusion. As bulbs and bare-roots can be planted at the same time, order forms are being filled in like mad.

The high summer garden is giddy with growth: hydrangeas in their glory (always feel I want more of them), magnificent lilies drooping from their stems (no matter how many there are, I want more of these, too); it all makes me feel like a greedy, insatiable child—so discipline is my fundamental preoccupation now. This is no time to go out and spend like a madman on things which will not contribute to the halcyon floriferous picture envisioned for the Garden Tour, although one old-fashioned white hydrangea with large, flat flower-heads unlike any I've ever seen before was too irresistible to pass up. All other money, however, is targeted straight for the catalogs and every version of appealing early-summer bloomer I can find.

The highly anticipated big box of plump iris tubers arrived from Shreiner's, and I joyously went about creating heart-stopping color schemes. Having decided to share my iris fixation with the neighborhood, I proceeded to dig a new bed in between the driveway and the hydrangea screen, in front of the junipers and under the horizontal branches of our old cherry tree. It should be a knockout. Surrounding three 'Soft Jazz', which are an astounding combina-tion of rich purple-black falls topped with creamy-salmon standards, are variations of other purple-black and pale salmony-colored wonders. I hope that the joggers, bike riders, and dog walkers will take note of this flamboyant display and at least give a nod.

Once again summer's end is nigh and the blue garden is without *Gentiana.* No matter what route is taken in planting these dazzling blue flowers—mail-ordering from my favorite sources, lovingly planting potted beauties from the nursery, even examining cut ones from the florist looking for a sign of seed—they just fizzle out in the Benson garden. Not enough sun, I fear. So, no gentians, but the *Echinops ritro,* or globe-thistle, and their companion sea holly, are finally divine after a three-year wait—the blue of their spiked, round flower-heads is almost metallic. The late *Clematis paniculata,* which resembles clematis in its glorious full-petaled blue flower but doesn't vine and is shrubby, has come back strong. The *Aconitum* (monkshood) has never looked better; the most pleasing of all asters, *frikartii,* 'Mönch' (sometimes spelled 'Moench') is just beginning its discreet display; and the *Angelica gigas* is stupendous! No one, not the most jaded gardener nor even the most blasé of our visitors, can pass it by without a gasp and a "What's that!" At a good five-feet tall, it has huge divided leaves on purplish stems forming a bulbous, sexy, plump section from which a five-inch flat head of aubergine florettes emerges. Truly astonishing.

The would-be rain forest has finally taken on the luxurious and profuse character longed for in my tropical fantasies. Though I ache for more of everything, the *Colocasia* now look like their cognomen "elephant-ears"; the leaves of the bold *Gunnera manicata* are an easy twenty-five inches across; the bronze/burgundy *Canna* x 'Red King Humbert' is a formidable five feet tall; and the *Peltiphyllum peltatum* has done exactly what Marder's promised—produced nonstoppable gigantic round, indented leaves. The *Campsis* vine is cascading over the fence full of burnt-orange trumpet flowers, while the *Aristolochia* just keeps climbing and climbing. At the bases of trees are good old stupendously big-leaved hosta—many in flower, myriad ferns, and *Ligularia dentata* 'Desdemona' sporting its burgundy-tinged heart-shaped leaves, completing the exotic, unusual, steamy effect sought after in this area.

Once over this Garden Tour preoccupation, I'm going to concentrate on my rain forest. There are all sorts of plants that will make this expanse even more romantic and strange, and you can be sure that sooner or later they will be dug in: variegated grasses, more *Rodgersia* (every kind I can lay my hands on—promising to be more thrilling than the pleasurable palmlike *pinnata* species now with us), *Rheum palmatum* 'Tanguticum' (a six-foot-tall beauty with giant maplelike leaves, still not located), and something called *Hedychium gardneranum* that has been ferreted out in the recently discovered Jacques Amand catalog (with leaves like canna and flowers like a very airy hyacinth). I foresee an architectural, tropical profusion and am having a terrible time being patient until concentration can be directed more decidedly next year.

Big-leaved lovelies clockwise from lower right: thrilling *Ligularia dentata* 'Desdemona', super-reliable *Hosta sieboldiana* 'Elegans', and *teriffis Rodgersia pinnata*.

- At this growth highpoint, assess your yard and note all keen observations in your journal—remember you will *never* recall your intentions unless you write them down.
- As you are diligently tallying your spring bulb orders—*do not* mince around and wind up ordering a few of this and another few of that—you will not be pleased with the results unless you get *at least* multiple dozens of each kind—anything less is meager and cannot be considered a clump. The old adage "Less is more" does *not* apply to flowers.
- Conclude and mail your bulb and perennial fall-planting orders *before* Labor Day—time is flying.
- Continue watering, deadheading, and staking—I bet your tall, fabulous lilies really need those Loop Stakes you should have on hand by now.
- Particularly important to keep all gardens weeded now, as this is when the little buggers begin to bear seeds, and the last thing you want is more weeds.
- Iris tubers, roots of oriental poppies and peonies, as well as autumn-flowering bulbs like *Colchium* should be on your doorstep. Do not consider leaving them there for one second—plant posthaste!
- Good time to plant those biennials, especially endearing "foxgloves" (if *Angelica* sounds like too much for you), to insure next year's bloom.
- Pot up calla lilies now. Leave them outside for the next four to six weeks so they get full benefit of the sun in starting their roots before bringing them inside for winter bloom.
- Major time now needs to be spent in disbudding the dahlias so those ending up in your vase are showy and spectacular.

SEPTEMBER

> the spring, the summer,
> The childing autumn, angry winter, change
> Their wonted liveries; and the mazed world
> By their increase, now knows not which is which.
> William Shakespeare, *A Midsummer Night's
> Dream*, Act II, scene i

Aaah, September. You begin to sniff a change in the air, see a variation in the quality of the light, and though much of the garden is still going strong, there is an imperceptible winding down and phasing out. This subtle waning reminds me of the frenzied fall planting that will soon take place. The last thing wanted is to inadvertently unearth some sturdy grower now approaching dormancy but invaluable to the entire garden picture come Tour Day, so never has my perennial labeling been more meticulous. Knowing that the plants will all soon disappear, I got seriously down on all fours and checked everything for a label, and wouldn't you know— there were at least twenty plants unmarked! No longer! They now all have their cozy metal markers sunk into the earth as close to their main growing stem as could be placed.

September, though not a much touted time in the garden, is actually quite rapturous. The big-leaved beauties are stretched out as far as they will go, the *Caladium* are in their prime of size and intricate color, the huge spotted Chinese lilies are breathtakingly wondrous, while the *Lespedeza* and *Buddleia*'s arching branches are clothed in flower sprays.

We can never have enough of nature. We must be refreshed by the the sight of inexhaustible vigor.
Henry David Thoreau, *Walden*

It seems the perennials that wait until now to flower are among the loveliest and most refined. Smitten as I am with *Anemone japonica hupehensis*, a very different plant than the spring anemone, it's a true delight to see my white 'Avalanche' finally match the vitality of my other subtly pink ones—darling genteel flowers perched above strong erect stems with a special look of cultivation. The *Physostegia* patch grows stronger every year and the *Tricyrtis hirta* never cease to astound me—the already beautiful pendulous branches dotted with wonderful opposite architectural leaves are an advantage all summer, but now, covered with tiny orchidlike flowers begging to be observed, are overwhelming. Though not in the same category as the just described elegant and sophisticated perennials, even the big mallows with their ten-inch crepe-papery flowers are finally in bloom and warrant their space in a plebeian sort of way.

As the month progresses, preparations begin in earnest for the vast autumn planting task ahead. Enough of the out-of-control annuals in the cutting garden—I rejoice in digging up the cosmos, the cleome, and definitely the various impatiens and geraniums earnestly brought to me by well-meaning summer houseguests. The gladioli and acidanthera leaves are beginning to yellow, suggesting they, too, will soon be ready for digging up. It's clearly time to send Hugo, our pool man with pickup truck, to the Agway to bring in bags and bags of peat, composted cow manure, bonemeal; bales of salt hay; and bottles of Wilt-Pruf. With all these things at hand, the arduous task of preparing the planting beds for fall (and spring) planting begins. Rake. Dig. Enrich the soil. Rake some more. Dig some more. Do a little edging. Get rid of any sign of weeds. Dig in that peat, manure, and bonemeal. Dig. Dig. Dig.

Although the begonias are still in beautiful flower, they seem tenderer than everything else requiring digging up, and the nip in the air reminds me an early frost is possible so I'm a bit stumped as to what to do with them. Three nurseries had three different opinions, just as every book dealing with the subject contradicts the other. Left to my own impulses, I decided to be safe rather than a sorry begonia-less gardener and so proceeded to unearth the choicest six and bring them indoors, where they replaced the amaryllis recently moved outdoors to dry out. I used to be an advocate of the Brooklyn Botanical Garden "school of amaryllis maintenance," but after two years of following its system (which is certainly the easiest—never let them go dormant and tend them as you would a house-plant) with less than glorious results I decided to return to the old standard method. So, late in August all amaryllis were dutifully rounded up, brought out to the garden shed, and turned (in the pots) on their sides to dry out. The begonias in their place look much splashier.

The ultimate sign that autumn is on its way in full force is the arrival of your first bulb order. The sight of these boxes fills me with the odd combination of inspiration and dread. It also throws me into a tizzy trying to recreate the brilliant schemes envisioned while ordering. This year, in my Garden Tour panic, I didn't make copious notes in my garden journal or in any one place, but in the margins of the catalogs themselves. This method is better than no method, but it has forced me to spend half a day laying out all the catalogs to attempt deciphering all those lovely pictures once so poignantly in mind. After much deliberation, I was ready to sort out my first delivery. First things first: examine all your bulbs, make sure they look healthy, at the first sign of them being shriveled up or mildewy go straight to the phone and demand a replacement.

The tulips go straightway into refrigeration, as these com-

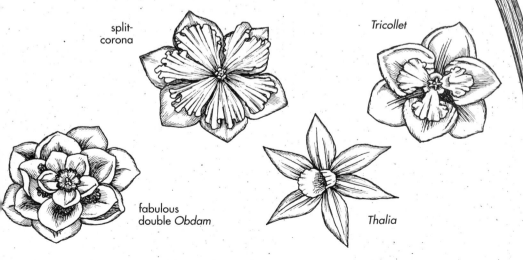

split-corona

Tricollet

fabulous double *Obdam*

Thalia

Why settle for ordinary yellow daffodils when you can choose from hosts of divine and different specialities.

pact, nearly foolproof bulbs are the last to be planted since they can't go into the ground until it has cooled anyway. Those big, winged narcissus bulbs, which take the most work, go in early, as they need as much warmth as possible to build up their root systems before cold, wet winter steps in. Although there is a lot of talk in the catalogs about buying bushels and mixes of daffodils, this is not for me. If you throw a big concoction of various daffodils in the ground, when they emerge you will have a hodgepodge of yellow and white with nothing looking specific or unique. Planting your daffodils (the ones with more pronounced trumpets) or narcissi (those with flatter "faces") in groupings of separate kinds makes a much better show and gives you the opportunity to better appreciate their striking differences.

Daffodils are not my favorite spring-flowering bulb, but my collection of over twenty varieties attests to my interest in them and their many forms. Arranged in groupings along the driveway and our street-facing side (and eventually all overtaken by daylilies) are clusters of remarkable single, split, and double daffodils. No ordinary yellow 'King Alfred' for me when there are so many specialities from which to choose. The absolute first bulbs in the ground are the important and fabulous *Fritillaria* because the bulbs are big and tender and the last thing you want is for them to dry out. Also, their adroit placement warrants prime attention. Next are the daffodils. Once they are in the still-warm ground, devote yourself to the other specialist bulbs, the ones not so dense, snug, and compressed: hyacinths, *Muscari* (grape-hyacinth), crocus, *Leucojum*, the early iris—Dutch, Spanish, and English, *Galanthus, Scilla*, and *Endymion*. Oh so much to plant before you even think of digging in the tulips.

September Suggestions

- Be totally prepared for fall planting—lay in supplies and dig those beds.
- Don't forget *Fritillaria*—no matter what else you've ordered—even if you've succumbed to Van Engelen's insistence on hundreds of tulips, daffodils, crocus, and *Muscari*—if you haven't filled in the blanks for most fabulous *Fritillaria*, do it now, you'll love me for it and dig them in without a second's delay upon arrival.
- Madonna lilies arrive earlier than all the other lilies. Plant them the minute they arrive—don't allow to dry out! All lilies need good deep holes smooshed around with plenty of peat, bonemeal, and composted manure. The only *exception* to the lily-plant-deep mode are Madonna lilies, which have the peculiarity of wanting to be planted shallow, just under the surface.
- Ideal time to plant peonies, also good for roses, ferns, grasses, all types of evergreens, and bare-root hosta, daylily, etc.
- Most tender plants should be brought indoors before the end of the month: fushias, *Stephanotis*, passion vines, hibiscus, mandevilla, etc.

- Pull out the bonemeal and scratch it in good around the peonies and iris before they retire for their long winter nap.
- Bring amaryllis to a dark, cool place and stop watering.
- Those paper-whites (narcissus) you need to give hope in the bleak months are especially affordable at Van Engelen, fifty for twenty dollars, which is a far better price than you will ever find when you go out to buy them at a premium locally in the dead of winter. It's still not too late to order.

OCTOBER

Spring passes and one remembers one's innocence
Summer passes and one remembers one's exuberance
Autumn passes and one remembers one's reverence
Winter passes and one remembers one's perseverance

There is a season that never passes
And that is the season of glass
Yoko Ono, "Season of Glass," 1981

Now the work really begins, the arduous task of laying the foundation of all your future garden fantasies. During a serene and balmy mid-month day, I accomplished many things. With all the elements in hand to make a gorgeous picture, six nonstop hours of toil created a triple-planted new bed that should be glorious. Faced with forty-five obese bare-roots culled from a daylily specialist, the entire basement refrigerator brimming with tulip bulbs, and the dining room table groaning under the weight of about five hundred other spring and summer bloomers, it was high-time to get arty and make a delicious garden picture.

The vision will not necessarily serve the Garden Tour, as it will peak in May and July; but who could resist sweating a little to produce this vision. Dug many big holes—each about fifteen inches in diameter and as deep. At the bottommost layer I laid in fifty daffodils (a peach/pink mix—the "Big Buy" from Dutch Gardens this season), followed by the fabulous fat daylilies interspersed around the edges of each hole. Digging one hole for each daylily (or any bare-root thing) the way the usual instructions indicate is just too laborious—I find a nice wide hole will accommodate three or four bare-roots if you dig it deep and roomy and lay the roots around its perimeter just so.

So, with daffodils in and daylilies around the periphery, I returned a few inches of dirt and planted two dozen triumph tulips, 'Apricot Beauty', which should complement the daffodils perfectly. Three or four more inches of coddled, composted dirt were added to the hole, then stuffed masses of *Muscari* (my adored grape-hyacinths) in between. Standing back to envision the end result next spring, I savored the portrait of the unnaturally pink daffodils popping up first, surrounded quickly by the salmon-pink tulip and azure hyacinth display

they call me the hyacinth girl
T. S. Eliot, *The Waste Land*

and then, just when the daffodils and hyacinths begin to look tawdry, the daylily growth will emerge with force, overtake the wilting, yellowing foliage of the spring things, and produce a spectacular show of black-red-burgundy flowers countered with creamy-white punctuated with coordinating dark-red eyes (centers), investing the whole scene with the stuff that sighs are made of. It also feels good to know 45 roots and 174 bulbs are in the ground and not in my kitchen.

Another day, after much rain and grayness, the ground is pliable and rife for "digging up." My enterprise is to dig up all my exotic heat-loving, big-leaved tropical beauties not able to withstand the winter onslaught of Zone 7. Of course, you can just leave them in the ground to rot if you have no interest in perpetuity or can afford to think of them as annuals and go out each season and repurchase the same over and over again. Granted, in the early years I did just that, because the idea of digging and storing was as alien to me as the old seed-starting technique. Eventually digging-and-storing became a rhythm I've come to trust and suggest it as a practice all should embrace. It's not difficult, not outrageously time-consuming, and extremely rewarding. Not only because you don't have to spend the same money time and again, but more importantly because the bulbs/corms/tubers increase each year in size and with the next planting you have bigger, bolder, even more excessive versions.

Plants instilling passion in me requiring this dig-and-store routine are:

- *Caladium*—big veiny leaves in breathtaking dappled colors; also glorious white.
- *Zantandeschia*—calla lily justly made famous by Camille and Katharine Hepburn.
- *Colocasia*—those fabulous, aptly named elephant's-ears.
- Wondrous tuberous begonia.
- *Acidanthera*—the finest version of gladioli, in fact, a stylish white bloom with a burgundy center and architecturally drooping leaves making them fine enough to be isolated in that uniquely Japanese flower-arranging method of *kenzan.*
- *Crinum*—a beautiful late-summer-blooming amaryllis-like flower.
- *Canna*—those underrated gigantic leafy affairs too often positioned in public places with no thought, which can be had with beautiful bronze leaves instead of ordinary too-green-green.

- *Haemanthus* and *Sprekalia*—both of these odd and interesting beauties of the nether hemisphere.
- *Glorioso rothschildiana*—a fleeting, but divine, flowering vine.
- Dahlia—with trepidation. My apprehension regarding dahlia storage is simply because I'd rather replace them every year as they don't fall into the same *easy* category of the rest; their storage needs special conditions and lots of mollycoddling or they tend to rot and turn themselves into a soggy, gooey mess; also it's much more fun to select a new look each season from so many dizzying choices.

Everything else mentioned is a cinch. Carefully dig them up. Shove that shovel in a good five, or six inches away from what you think might be their root or bulb/tuber perimeter and *gently* lift out the growth mass. *Leave as much dirt on them as clings*, and put them in cartons lined with peat moss (you might also add sand) that you've saved from your latest mail-order delivery. These can be any cartons, just so long as they are sturdy enough to hold the weight of the peat, the dirt, and the tuber or bulb—some of which will have grown shockingly huge and heavy over the summer. Make sure to mark the carton's contents clearly, because next spring one big old dried-up clump of dirt will look just like another. You then bring these cartons to live in the basement or garage or any place that's cool—*but not cold*—for the duration. It's actually easy, just takes a little muscle, inclination, planning, and a whole October day once you've amassed plenty of these exotics.

During the last three dismal days of rain or near-rain and grumpy skies, lilies seem to be arriving by the ton: 250 various lilies to be exact! These all must be dug deep and firm, and planted immediately because they are not compact bulbs like *Muscari*, narcissus, and tulips, which are solid. These are layered and have a tendency to dry out, so *instantaneous* action is required. But then again, they are not fleeting like tulips, so at least your efforts are rewarded year after year with lilies (so far, they've recurred for three seasons for me).

Okay. So with 250 lilies on hand, some which may coincide their blooming with the Garden Tour, it's time to be creative. What spots need the perfect summer's-end lift of lilies fabulously flowering? A scrupulous tour of the garden uncovered myriad new niches hiding among the early clematis, peeking out at the edge of the rain forest, in and out of all the curves of the shade paths. Happily, I found spots for 150, planted them deep, and finally dug big trenches in the cutting gardens for the remaining 100—expecting an end-of-summer lily fantasy.

- Cartons of plant life should be arriving now—make room in your fridge or garage for an organized arrangement of your bulbs.
- All narcissus should be in the ground—plant the remainder of the bulbs more or less in the order which they flower: *Galanthus*, crocus, anemones, hyacinths, and *Muscari*, spring iris—save tulips for last.
- All tender bulbs and tubers requiring winter storage should be out of the ground and snug in their peat-lined boxes—providing you with even more exotic versions next year without spending one new dime.
- Cut to ground all exhausted perennials except those attractive in the winterscape like some *Astilbe* varieties, *Sedum* 'Autumn Joy', and *Perovskia* (Russian sage, which has nice, white winter branches).
- Get rid of any tired annuals before the inevitable frost turns them black and oozing.
- Food for the birds is in short supply—they will truly appreciate being fed now.
- Buy a product called Wilt-Pruf and spray it on broad-leaved evergreens like azaleas, rhododenrons, magnolias, etc., and newly planted needle-evergreens—it is an anti-desiccant (prevents moisture loss) and makes a big difference in how they tolerate the shrivelling winter winds and cold (this is a terrific product—also good at combating mildew on everything from begonias to bee balm).
- Record frost dates to better familiarize yourself with next year's time and action.
- You can begin mulching roses and anything particularly young and tender.
- Take time on an indolent Sunday to walk or drive and observe the rich luster of burnished autumn reigning over the earth.

NOVEMBER

Oh, Adam was a gardener, and God who made him sees
That half a proper gardener's work is done upon his knees,
So when your work is finished, you can wash your hands and pray
For the Glory of the Garden, that it may not pass away!
Rudyard Kipling, "The Glory of the Garden"

Balmy days, balmy days, we pray for them in November. November is spent planting, clearing, mulching, planting, clearing. An unremarkable first frost has struck, and 'most everything left standing couldn't look more dreadful. Yesterday all the dahlias were cut down and dug up because I just couldn't face them any more in their depraved state, though this is one of my least favorite jobs. Vita calls it a "blackened death that nothing can redeem." On this freezing morning I decided to do a pleasant chore first and optimistically went out with a big basket to cut off all the dried hydrangea blooms. Only yesterday they were a fabulous combination of mottled colors, inspiring me to think an artfully concocted big Thanksgiving basket loaded with the different types of flower-heads from all the various hydrangea bushes could be arranged. Too late! The frost fell in a frenzy last night and even ravaged those stalwarts of cold—the hydrangeas. Now it is still freezing, the hydrangea hopes are gone, and I'm looking at 670 tulips left to plant along with what seems like a thousand other chores.

What better way to perk oneself up than to go shopping? What better time to shop than at fifty percent off? I couldn't care less about shopping for discounted, picked-over clothes; but "On Sale" nursery shopping is another story. You must keep your eyes peeled in your area for the announcement of the *big price slash*. Around here, as early as October, you begin to see a few discreet "20% off all perennials" signs, but a few weeks into November at fifty percent is *really* the time and "*all* nursery stock" is the sought-after message. Never ones to miss great opportunities—this is when Irving agrees we go *all out*. Not bothering with the little stuff— forget the forlorn perennials and leftover mums—it's shrubs and trees we're after during this momentous bargain mode—*the big stuff*, the enduring things that make the big difference. As Vita says in *The Illustrated Garden Book*:

> Gardeners who desire the maximum reward with the minimum of labor would be well advised to concentrate on flowering shrubs and trees. How deeply I regret that fifteen years ago, when I was forming my own garden, I did not plant these desirable objects in sufficient quantity. They would by now be large adults instead of the scrubby, spindly infants I contemplate with impatience as the seasons come round.

> . . . they will give far less trouble than the orthodox herbaceous flowers, they demand no annual division, many require no pruning; in fact, all that many of them will ask of you is to watch them grow yearly into a greater splendor, and what more could be exacted of any plant?

What Vita doesn't tell you is that buying these important statements on sale allows you to have a bounty twice as big (or spend half as much). We had been eyeing a divine weeping white pine at The Bayberry all season—a big beauty at least ten feet tall and fifteen feet wide from its sloping trunk to the tip of the farthest weeping limb. What would have cost eighteen hundred dollars in season (inclusive of planting and guarantee) we got for nine hundred, planted. Now, mind you, nine hundred is a hefty sum—but this is a dramatic, mature tree and just the thing to first plant in our newest cleared area as its focal point. At Marder's, we did even better with a fabulous deep, dark green, droopy-branched, alert-needled *Picea abies sherwoodii* (simply a Sherwood spruce) so wide and dense it nearly covers the pool equipment suddenly crudely apparent—this mother-lode for only four hundred fifty dollars. A few weeks later we returned to complete the scene and found another plump *Picea pumlia nigra* 'Pom Pom' (a fat and funny Norway spruce) charmingly planted on a raised mound called a "berm." Now, in situ, it looks as if it has been with us forever. I just love bargains.

The final stop was Warren's, where we made another fantastic haul: Three white-flowering Japanese wisteria, big old tangled ones, for the newly revealed fence for only twenty dollars each! Plus a divine barberry, a red spirea, an 'Aurea' cypress for the golden border, and a big evergreen shrub with a sort of burgundy cast to it that is its autumn hue. Anyway, all gorgeous and probably nothing we would have ever bought at full price, at least to be in place next spring.

The great seasonal calendar is flipping its pages at record speed. Only one week till Thanksgiving, but finally arrives a fine brisk day with clear sky and temperature a degree or two above fifty—a definite inspiration to get back to my chores. With Keith Richard's new great second album, *Main Offender*, in the background, I get the last of the tulips in and must commend myself for some exceedingly inventive plantings. Roselike peony tulips are in the rootless parts of the rose bed to give spring suggestion of what's to come; a ribbonlike drift of big, bold, fantastic parrot tulips outlines the shape of the new weeping white pine; and the bereft white garden will at least be in flower for a few months with a checkerboard of white and as-black-as-you-can-buy tulips of all kinds. Relieved elation follows tucking these six-hundred-plus sweethearts in the ground, even though I had to resort to the old digging-of-trenches method, as my precious auger hit a huge rock and bent so seriously it became impossible to use. Thank God for the agreeable day and my good mood.

Still waiting for me were twenty-four ferns, fifteen grasses, one flowering quince, three *Gunnera*, and six *Kalmia* (a May-flowering eventual tree not only shade-loving—it actually *blooms in* the woods near here)—all of which arrived looking plump, lively, and extremely promising from Forest Farm, that reliable source. Thought the twenty-four ferns would do the trick in the would-be rain forest; but although make their mark they will, it's clear I could use about six times as many if I want to even begin to emulate my all-time favorite garden on Lily Pond. The grasses are extraordinary—four pink and four white pampas grasses arrived in a crazy long carton to accommodate their five-foot length! For $2.95 each! Pretty exceptional, if you ask me. Must plant these quick before temperature plummets. Oh! for another good day. . . .

Thanksgiving festivities past, time has come for ardent clearing to make way for laborious mulching. Six bales of salt hay have been staring at me for weeks now, but I'm reluctant to lay it because of this bizarre mutable weather we've been experiencing. When to apply your winter mulch depends on when you deem the cold really here to stay. My trusty *The New Illustrated Encyclopedia of Gardening* says, "it is better to be somewhat late than too early," and so I pause. Remember, this winter mulching is not so much to keep the plants warm as it is to keep them from undergoing stress due to violent fluctuations in the weather—so you don't want to smother and hide them from the waning winter sun until the time is just right.

NOVEMBER POINTERS

- Last chance to plant!!!! Get the rest of those bulbs in the ground! Plant those fabulous shrubs and trees you hopefully got at a great bargain price—water new plantings religiously if there is no rain.
- Plant the lily bulbs the minute they arrive, and remember, tulips can wait till last, but must be in the ground before it freezes.
- Pruning of summer- and fall-blooming shrubs and trees should be finished now—be careful with any spring-bloomers that are already forming their buds—take off only sickly or awkward branches.
- Perfect time to pot up tulips, hyacinths, freesias, and lilies indoors (most catalogs note which are best for forcing) for dormant winter sleep in your cool basement or garage (soak them good at the beginning and *keep them watered*). Usually takes twelve to sixteen weeks for healthy growth to appear, then it's time to move them gradually into a sunny window for an early breath of spring.
- Continue to check weather and phase in mulch.
- Get out the rake—pile all those leaves around shrubs and hedges for a natural (and free) winter mulch.
- Check your tender tubers and nonhardy bulbs recently put in storage for any signs of new growth—if you should see such a thing it means it's *too* warm—so open a window or something.

DECEMBER

> At Christmas I no more desire a rose
> Than wish a snow in May's new-fangled shows;
> But like of each thing that in season grows.
> William Shakespeare, *Love's Labour Lost*,
> Act I, scene i

Mid-December has arrived and though it's not paralyzingly cold yet, a tour of the neighborhood has revealed a few of my favorite, admired gardens already mulched, and so I go about the arduous job finally with confidence. Irving kindly pitches in by strewing the big salt-hay bales around the various parts of the yard and clipping the fat wires holding them together. Salt hay is at last piled high around the roses, the magnolia tree, my young Japanese maples, the *Crinum* lilies I've decided to leave in the ground under great heaps of mulch (as I haven't succeeded in getting them to bloom in pots or by digging, storing, and replanting, I thought I'd try this). Laid carefully over the perennial borders, I'm very particular the salt hay doesn't suffocate the iris or asphyxiate the still-leafing foxgloves. You never want to cover anything not completely dormant. If you see little rosettes of new growth forming, let them breathe. With each layer of mulch I lay, not-so-silent little prayers accompany each covered thing, "Please, let these columbines sleep well so they will still be abloom in June. Make my clematis pure for the Garden Tour." After a solid afternoon's work and much invocation of the gods, the mulching is done.

As the urge to garden does not necessarily subside with the rest of the greenery, you must satisfy yourself in winter by gardening indoors. My first attempt at forcing delightful bulbs met with pitiful results. Though I kept them in the basement during their dormancy, it just wasn't cool enough and what emerged were spindly, sad versions of the tulips and daffodils my heart was set on. The next year I wised up and convinced Irving to help me create a temperature-controlled space in the basement. What he figured out was elementary but did the trick. A huge sheet of insulated plastic (like overgrown bubble-wrap bought at the hardware store) covered the access to one corner of the basement with two windows. He arranged it in an overlapping manner giving me and the dog just enough space to squeeze through. A big thermometer was bought to record temperature, as the bulbs need ten to twelve weeks of chilling (forty degrees or below) to simulate a dormant period. Many trips were made up and down the stairs opening and closing windows to keep the temperature at bay, and sure enough—it worked! My indoor-forced narcissus, hyacinths, and tulips took on a real life of their own and now I'm a committed indoor-forcer. You, too, may want to find an area somewhere in your house or garage to designate as your "cold room" so you can enjoy the same bounty.

December Intimations

- Buy a balled evergreen instead of a chopped-down Christmas tree and light it up and decorate outdoors on your patio or deck; keep it watered and this method, unlike the traditional one, will result in a new evergreen addition to your yard—but do note, this works only if you *never* bring the tree inside.
- Scrutinize your property for evergreens, berries, interesting branches, pine cones, seed pods to gather for holiday embellishments—decorations from your own garden are the most endearing.
- If it's been cold for a steady ten days, the ground is probably frozen—mulch now.
- If you've been remiss about potting bulbs for winter forcing—it's not too late.
- If your amaryllis are still dormant, bring them in and repot in fresh soil—water sparingly until new growth is well underway.

- Give your friends and family garden gifts for Christmas: a potted amaryllis, sharp new Felcos, a gift certificate to an unfamiliar nursery or catalog, and most positively—this book.

JANUARY

Forget not the bees in winter, though they sleep,
For winter's big with summer in her womb,
And when you plant your rose trees, plant them deep,
Having regard to bushes all aflame,
And see the dusky promise of their bloom.
        Vita Sackville-West, "The Land"

Well, the least scintillating gardening month for sure is January. But even in the depths of January, I caught a first sign of spring just yesterday, the twentieth, to be precise. You must look for spring everywhere, you see, because it gives you hope. Walking the pooch right on our own Ninth Street block in Greenwich Village, he hopped inside an otherwise unremarkable but wrought-iron fenced-in street tree so mulched it had obviously been planted. I'm never phased by his penchant for sidling up next to a tree because I understand his need to do his thing around trees and not fire hydrants—Dylan indeed being a country dog at heart. Anyway, as I bent down with plastic bag in hand to rid the mulched plot of dear doggie's poo, I spied something. Yes, it was *a green thing* nobbing its way up from the earth. The First Sign! Days are gradually growing longer—even in January you can detect the days lengthening since they passed their epitome of shortness on that bleak, brief, day of 21 December.

There is such a dearth of real gardening to be done now it even becomes satisfying to set out bowls of paper-white narcissus around the house—the single most predictable of all flower exercises, but saved from banality by their vigorous growth habit and reliable bloom. Amaryllis should be flowering as well to keep your senses piqued.

On bearable January days, it's a perfect time to appreciate the evergreens. What would winter be if not for them? I love the way the conifers gild themselves in a kind of burnished glow. The cedars, blue spruces, and all junipers are particularly impressive now as they stand up to Mama's most biting extremes. The *Cryptomeria* is to die for as it becomes more pendulous, besotted as it is with bronze berrylike cones dripping at the tip of each branch, as are the pines.

The red-twig dogwood planted two years ago as a fill-in at the entrance of the driveway is most engaging now with branches really truly red. I had read about it in some catalogs and then found a big old overgrown clump of it in the neighborhood peering out over the bleak winterscape, which convinced me some red-twig was needed to help get through these months.

One more particular to be thankful for in January is berries, most every berry-producing plant is fully laden at this very moment. The holly has never been redder and pulpier; it didn't look half so good at Thanksgiving when I sheared vasefuls off to bring indoors and make a festive statement. Even the usually homely cotoneaster surrounding Irving's green marble horse head under the three sculptured round pines is awash in ornamental red berries. You must search out every little nuance to tingle your gardening senses in this less than heady duration.

January Guidance

- It's time to start digesting the information in those catalogs again, remembering all the things lacking last summer you duly recorded.
- Plant the Christmas tree, or, if you have insisted on bringing the tree inside after all, and have killed it—at least trim its boughs before you discard it and use as mulch.
- If inundated with ice and snow, don't use that terrible salt on your driveway and walks if they are anywhere near plantings—it is lethal—sand or ashes from your fireplace work just as well and harm nothing.
- Although not a fanatical garden-tool maintainer, I always take my Felcos (both pruners and lopper) to the hardware store at this time of year for sharpening and oiling.
- Keep checking and watering your forced bulbs—when there is two or three inches of growth, it's time to act.
- Lily-of-the-valley pips are another charming way to get through January—they should flower indoors in twenty-one days and can be moved to the garden in spring. Order from John Scheepers.

FEBRUARY

In February, if the days be clear
The waking bee, still drowsy on the wing,
Will guess the opening of another year
And blunder out to seek another spring
Vita Sackville-West, "The Land"

Aha. There is life after winter. Though Mama is still primarily busy working her miracle underground, things are beginning to stir. Buds are growing fatter and even though my *Galanthus nivalis* haven't reared their perky little snowdrop heads on this second day of February, just a few blocks away they are blooming like crazy in what must be an old, strong patch at the beginning of some nice spring-conscious person's drive. Knowing it won't be long before my very own snowdrops begin popping gives me heart, and I've already been out to check on the beloved hellebores, which have sprouted new leaves (a sign! a sign!) but still resist flowering. Even though both the Christmas and Lenten rose varieties abound, and even a Corsican one, the earliest never manage to sport their beautiful blooms for me until the end of this month at best. Oh, but what a reward when they do bloom—I consider them the first real flower of the season with their mottled purple-green, purple-cream, or greenish-white tender flowers. Just after the gardening bug bit me all those years ago, attending my first New York flower show, I was greeted by a great bank of hellebores as I entered and was magnetized. Seeking out hellebore sources became an immediate priority. Most growing strong now were acquired from good old Montrose Nursery—each season I order three, four, a few more, until now nearly every tree in the hammock grove is encircled with them. This grove is bordered by one of the shade paths now completely dormant, save the glorious hellebores that manage to give growth and hope at this desolate moment.

But finally, a month has arrived when there is actually something to do outdoors. A few of my favorite late-summer bloomers, *Buddleia davidii* and *Lespedeza thunbergii*, prefer a pruning at this unlikely time of year. With my newly honed Felcos in hand, I shear the buddleia from its ten- to twelve-foot height down to an even two feet, and the *Lespedeza* in both gardens are brought right down to the ground, as they produce on all new wood. Well, this happy chore didn't take enough energy and my feet, nose, and fingertips have a way to go before frostbite, so I roam around, find nothing to do, really, and finally succumb to cutting down some forsythia to force into bloom in the living room. I despise forsythia generally, but anything in bloom is better than nothing during this cheerless time. Do note, our forsythia growing amidst the woodsy surplus on the north street side is the single thing we inherited when we bought this property. Would never dream of planting any, but at this time of year, I'm glad it's there.

The forcing of spring branches indoors is a real treat and so easy, my only wish is having more forcible branches to choose from. You need only to chastely cut them from the tree or shrub (cut on a slant), bring indoors and give plenty of water. The budding branches can't differentiate the heat from your boiler or radiator from the warmth of spring, and hasten to blossom. Great things for forcing are quince, apple (crab and otherwise), and the early magnolias, especially the dogwood magnolia with its rich fat buds—none of which I have yet. What I do have and have forced inside with great luck are branches from our old cherry trees, some unknown vines from the woods, last year a few branches from the *Deutzia* in the white garden, and that ubiquitous forsythia, which at least shows signs of life only days after you bring it indoors. And then there

Bountiful *Buddleia* and prolific (big, but dainty) *Lespedeza* like to be pruned hard in February.

are pussy willows. I haven't gotten around to growing them for some reason, although last spring Buckley's had a beautiful weeper we passed on for some reason. But the cut branches are easy to buy and so cheap. Two great bunches are in charming wispy bloom at this very moment in my Manhattan living room—a good six feet high and quite a dramatic statement—these dear pussies cost no more than $2.99 a bunch right next door at the usually over-priced Korean grocer.

The greatest thrill of February, however, especially the closer it comes to its denouement, is to behold the BUDS! They are everywhere: the *Hydrangea petiolaris* looks like it is going to leap out of its skin, the Japanese maples become more fertile every day, the lilacs are beginning to straighten up and wave their plump buds, while the andromeda (*Pierus*) and *Stewartia koreana* are rampant with promise. Subtle though it might be, spring is finally in the air if you really sniff it out.

But certainly, this is a month when you can confidently dismiss yourself from the garden. This year brought us to a magical place in the western Philippines called El Nido, a dream for divers like Irving and ingenuous snorklers like me. Certainly there were no fastidious gardens to report on, rather a general wild blooming of exotic and unfamiliar islandy things and an abundance of what looked like that elusive nonstop bloomer mandevilla, but oh! what wonder there was under the sea!

What is so incredible about undersea gardens is that neither you nor I nor any man has had anything to do with them. The greater beings saved this nether "garden" for themselves—perhaps as a lesson to we who are stuck on earth. To dive into water even warmer than the air, to swim among designer fish out-chicing any fashion configuration I've ever witnessed, to attempt coming to terms with an idyllic scene so captivating it is hard to believe so many art directors, illustrators, photographers, great imaginative journalists, and voguish minds spend hours, days, and great amounts of money endeavoring to duplicate nirvana when it can never be equaled on celluloid in some urbane attempt to outwit the real world.

Talk about texture? A mastery of proportion? The comeliest palette of color? I've never seen anything to match this. Such glorious rhythm in the sea banks of coral parading in the most stylish shades of black, camel, and taupe—interspersed at just the right moment with an aubergine sea fan or an olive-green barrel sponge to give the scene just the right touch of diversion. What gardening lessons there are always to be learned from majestic Nature. She didn't miss a trick.

So I return from this glory to the coerced tulips, an array of forced-fabulousness fine for this waning day of February. I try to push El Nido from my mind and concentrate on spring's harbingers and the splendor now working its way up through the ground. By the end of February, anyway, I find I begin to breathe again and the urge to immerse myself in the catalogs is again at fever pitch. After all, imagined June bloom and the Garden Tour are only three months away.

- Serious attention must now be paid to the catalogs crowding your kitchen. Start ordering *now* for spring planting, summer tubers and bulbs.
- Pruning is in order for what you're sure of: big old overgrown things you might have inherited, or even your newer lovelies—get rid of any branches crowded, damaged, clearly dead, or growing in the absolute wrong direction. Do not—under any circumstances—prune anything that blooms in the spring.
- Prune back severely shrubs that flower on new wood, such as buddleia and vitex.
- If you forced tulips, freesia, hyacinths, or any spring bulb—at some time during this month it should be time to introduce them into the heat and light of your warm, cozy house. If you have really bright windows, make this a slow transition—you don't want to shock the poor darlings.
- Check on your stored bulbs and tubers—get rid of anything withered or mildewy before it infects the others—you can divide your canna tubers now if you are itching for something to do. Each piece you sever should have an unmistakably strong growing point.
- Pay attention to everything growing indoors—water, fertilize, and don't forget to continuously rotate the pots so the sun reaches all parts evenly.
- If you didn't have any *Dicentra* last spring, those underrated heart-shaped Alice-in-Wonderland-like "bleeding hearts," order some fleshy bare-roots immediately—plant as soon as your ground is pliable, and you, too, will be enchanted by these living valentines in a mere matter of weeks.
- If above forty degrees, soak the appropriate outdoor plants with Wilt-Pruf again.
- By now, it is definitely time to start feeding the birds again.

MARCH

A soothsayer bids you: Beware the ides of March.
William Shakespeare, *Julius Caesar,* Act I, scene ii

Patience is not one of my virtues, and this month is surely the most difficult to get through because everything is just on the verge, and the maddening wait through those damp, cold weeks for *it* to happen is beyond frustrating. But now, there begins to be very much to do. Remember the digging and storing of all the exotics last October?—Well, it's a good thing you marked those boxes because it's time to unearth them. Oh, you could wait until late May if you don't want double work; then you simply welcome them from their winter domiciles and replant directly in the ground in all likely spots. *But* with this one-step method, the wait to bloom is much longer and therefore, the glory of the flower shorter.

If you are particularly anxious, however (and who isn't?), for early leafing/flowering, then the double-work mode comes into play right now at the beginning of March. It's the perfect time to haul out the boxes of bulbs and tubers and start them up in your brightest windows. Mix up a new clean potting soil, manure, Instant H_2O or vermiculite, and peat combination; dust off all old dirt from the tuber or bulb, now caked and crumbly and easy to remove; and get out those nice four- and six-inch plastic and poly pots you've saved for occasions just like this. Fill the pots with the soil mix and bury the sleeping beauties. Place these pots in your sunny windows on strong plastic trays (after all, you don't want to ruin your house while you engage in this early liberation of your plant's pent-up life), label, and keep them well-watered. That's it.

If you make this choice, big leaves and flowers will greet you about one month earlier (late June instead of July/August) than if you took the easy/lazy one-step method of planting directly in the ground. Adopting this system (which I did for the first time last year) will engender earlier results and bigger plants. When warm enough to plant out at the end of May, well-started-into-growth, thriving plants are immersed in the yard, not some tuber not even awake yet. If summer is on the come and no threat of *one last frost* is in the air, they will quickly develop and astound you. An easy but conscious exercise, it is well worth the effort and works splendidly for canna, colocasia, calla, caladium, and especially begonias. This year I'm going to see if I can't get some dahlia specialist to ship me early as I want to start them indoors too, if I can figure out more space. Oh, for more sunny windows! Or better still, this is the time of year I long for a greenhouse.

Imagine what I could display on this Garden Tour if I could sneak everything into bloom under glass just when it suited me? What would be better?, particularly in this year when our first serious snowfall arrived on the first official day of spring. To be sure, it was a gorgeous whiter-than-white sight—and did produce a dazzling winter portrait of pooch under the snow-laden prostrate cherry tree perfect for our next Christmas card—but on the first day of spring! Only the snowdrops seemed appropriate—yes, they finally bloomed.

Outside things are definitely happening. Vita puts it so aptly in her long poem, "The Land":

> Sometimes in apple country you may see
> A ghostly orchard standing all in white,
> Aisles of white trees, white branches, in the green,
> On some still day when the year hangs between
> Winter and spring, and heaven is full of light.

Buds are increasingly swollen, the hellebores are struggling to open, and scant signs of crocus early in the month are intensifying. I know that crocuses are a world-revered gardening conclusion, but unless you can plant them in drifts of hundreds (better yet, thousands, like the parks of London) don't expect to be bowled over by their beauty. The whole idea is that these small, rather inconspicuous blooms, work in blankets—six here and six there will give you hardly a momentary thrill. So plan to go all out or just content yourself with one or two patches of *at least* fifty bulbs each.

MARCH REMINDERS

- Start peeking under the salt hay, or whatever mulch you've used—it's not time yet to remove it with abandon—but where you see new growth or anything stirring—begin to lift it little by little as the month progresses—there is no tried and true timetable to abide here—use your best judgment.
- Pot up, pot up, pot up—that is the main theme of the day: colocasia, caladium, the fabulous tuberous begonia, canna, calla lilies, plus dahlias—if you have any hanging around with good "eyes" staring at you.
- Are you ready for spring?—check supplies of labels, plant supports and ties, fertilizer, bonemeal, potting soil, mulch, et al.
- The wind and rain of winter has twisted and turned your shrubs and trees—clip, thin, and shear to renew them.
- Regarding clematis, definitely don't touch the early-blooming *montana* varieties, but the summer-bloomers should be checked now—prune broken stems and generally prop them up to look for buds—if they're discernible, cut back to a pair of buds—if not, cut back to just above the base of the old growth.
- Now is the time to cut nearly to the ground (leave four inches or so) your glorious grasses—all of them—as well as *Liriope*—even ivy, if it looks ravaged.
- Wind up your spring planting orders without delay—and don't forget summer bulbs.
- Dig in the Miracid or any of the brand names for "miracle acid" around the hydrangeas now, if you want them to be really truly blue—and don't skimp!
- Get really energetic and dig 5-10-10 into all your shrubs, ground covers, clematis, peonies—bonemeal, too; they all like bonemeal—the plants and trees are hungry after torturous winter—feed them.
- The heartier bulbs you forced inside—true hyacinths and daffodils especially—can be planted outdoors for bloom the following year (but don't waste your time with tulips or paper-whites; they're finished).
- For those of you desperate to plant something flowering—dash to the nearest nursery to immerse yourself in pansies. The almost black-burgundy-purple groups touched with gold, the first real shot of color at the nurseries, are always seductive. Pansies are

wonderful to skim the earth on top of late-breaking perennials, around late-leafing shrubs, *et al.*—but don't expect to retain them throughout summer—succumb now—but out they go in June to make way for grander ideas.

- The big month for flower shows, see as many as you can as they are inspiring as well as informative; but remember—combinations like hydrangeas and tulips, flowering cherry trees and lilies are a product of greenhouses and you can't produce these displays in your garden no matter where you live or how hard you try.

APRIL

> All Nature seems at work. Slugs leave their lair—
> The bees are stirring—birds are on the wing—
> And Winter slumbering in the open air,
> Wears on his smiling face a dream of Spring!
> Samuel Taylor Coleridge, "Work Without Hope"

Counting the days till this month arrives is a March preoccupation. Sensational spring is just around a bend in the path. Everyone loves the spring. Bob Dylan whines about it, where he sings that *she* was born in spring but *he* was born too late. Shakespeare blames all irrational behavior on it. Songwriters blithely croon on and on about it. T. S. Eliot shrouds it in contretemps—though I've never understood "April is the cruellest month," I adore every other line of the poem. Springtime is that most alive time, a time of resurgence. There's a quickening, a faster heartbeat, a new breath—all that natural energy harnessed into the blessed event turning the world green and bringing us Mama's glorious munificence. It deserves to be so clichéd.

> I dreamed that, as I wandered by the way,
> Bare Winter suddenly was changed to Spring,
> And gentle odours led my steps astray,
> Mixed with a sound of waters murmuring
> Along a shelving bank of turf, which lay
> Under a copse, and hardly dared to fling
> Its green arms round the bosom of the stream,
> But kissed it and then fled, as thou mightest in a dream.
> Percy Bysshe Shelley, "The Question"

But this April, of all Aprils, we've been cheated of spring. The April weeks are inscribed in this year's garden journal as: more rain, still raining, endless rain and cold, and finally, cold and dreary. Believe me, these are not fanciful Gene Kellyish "April Showers" nor Portia's gentle rain from heaven dropping—this is teeming, cold, mean rain. Not a good omen for the impending Garden Tour, no matter how you measure the drops. But despite the boring, bleak conditions, miniscule but charming *Chinodoxa* and the bluest of hyacinths, 'Blue Jacket', followed on the heels of the crocus, and the mystical mottled flowers of the hellebores are finally with us. Not until mid-month did I see the first tulips (some beautiful *greigii* like white waterlilies, but lasting a scant two seconds before major rabbit attack) and finally daffodils, 'Ice Follies' and the marvelous 'Tricolette'. Finally, by the very last week, despite the bitter rain (maybe this is the sort of April T. S. Eliot was invoking), undying hope sprang up with the baby blooms of the bleeding hearts, the darling Virginia bluebells, *Brunnera macrophylla* (one of the fetching perennial forget-me-nots), the beginnings of *Muscari, Leucojum aestivum,* two more kinds of daffodils and at last, the incredible *fosteriana* huge cupped tulip, 'Red Emperor', which never ceases to amaze with its blacker-than-black eye. Not a peep from my beloved various *Fritillaria* yet; I am full of longing for them.

And now, now there is work. Because of this insipid weather, the winter mulch didn't get whisked away. Sadly, when I wanted nothing more than to tear it all up and behold daily progress of each and every precious plant, it got wheedled away bit by bit, slowly, torturously. The persistent rain, however, didn't stop the UPS man from delivering the bounty of roots, seedlings, and all varieties of garden matter so ardently ordered in February and March. Well, at least the ground has been soft, if not soggy, and laying everything in was relatively easy. Digging those bare-root daylilies into the rocky edges of the driveway was no effortless chore, though. But the soft ground was perfect for starting up the herb garden, so in went the parsley, oregano, and basil, which should be fine if it doesn't get washed away.

I am at wit's end with Garden Tour rapidly on the come and no sign of spring in the air. Rarely prone to a state even remotely resembling depression, I find myself succumbing to nagging doubts about this being the start of some weird new millenium in which Mama goes on a sabbatical and the heavenly process just never happens. I simply keep planting and praying.

APRIL ADVICE

- By the end of this month, there should be no more winter mulch—no matter what the weather—and at the same time as you are baring your garden, pull out any weeds immediately at their first sign.
- All your ground covers are looking particularly scraggly right now—shear off all their wilted leaves and top-growth—also a perfect time to plant ground cover.
- A good general fertilizing will be much appreciated by all inhabitants of your garden now, when it is in rampant growth.
- Absolutely the most rewarding time to lay in any decorative mulch—your wood chips, shredded bark, cocoa beans, or whatever you prefer—while the earth is still exploding and there are still scads of inevitable bare spots.

- This is perfect timing for any dividing (maybe you have some old *Laminium* or *campanulas* you would like to spread around) or transplanting (move that Japanese maple you know you put in the wrong place) on your agenda—do it now before too much growth develops and while it still has time to become accustomed to its new home before the real season kicks in.
- Keep a watchful eye on all things potted up in your sunny windows—there should already be noticeable growth on your tuberous begonias—keep everything watered.
- The birds will eat everything you can possibly give them, and if you've succumbed to a pond—it's time to feed the fish just waking from their hibernation.
- If you want to move any recurring bulbs around (crocus, daffodils, snowdrops, anemones if you can get them to grow for you), do it as soon as they have finished flowering.
- This is the perfect time to start a garden journal.

MAY

Rough winds do shake the darling buds of May,
And summer's lease hath all too short a date: . . .
William Shakespeare, "Sonnet XVIII"

Glorious springtime convened with the first merry days of May and brought with it overriding anxiety—less than two months till the Garden Tour! How plump do the peonies look? Why haven't the *Baptisia* burst forth? How come the Scotch broom is practically budless when I am counting on it as a mainstay of the Burgundy corner? Frustration abounds but is happily—finally!—overwhelmed by the glories of springtime. Untameable, capricious, marvelous, monarchical May ruling over the season. Surrounded by so much beauty, the Garden Tour toil is a delight. All I need do is wander over to either patch of my beloved *Fritillaria*—the *persica* or overwhelming *imperialis*—and my senses are blasted by their sublime colorations and incredible regal stance. I nearly swoon over the pale silvery-gray-green of the whorling *persica* leaves arching on thirty-inch stems topped off with generous black-purple lampshade-like blossoms, and in the very same family, the strident erect stem of the *imperialis* crowned with fairy-tale flowers and surrounded by soft yellow and sienna Fosteriana and triumph tulips. I have decided these are so beautiful and so unfamiliar to most that next year I'm going to dispense with the tulip display in front of the drive and lay in *Fritillaria* for all the neighborhood to enjoy. Not to be dismissed either, the graphic heart-shaped flowers of *Dicentra* coupled with the reverse coloration of 'Anna José' tulips is pretty fantastical too.

But oh, the toil . . . rigorous is not a stern enough word. On any given day so many hours are spent in the garden that even the balm of bathing in my vulgarly huge Jacuzzi doesn't relieve the soreness in my upper calves and shoulders. And yet, if not for those hours of toil, would I be beginning to see the light as I seem to be? Without fail, each one of the ten or twelve Hamptons' habitués arriving here on any given day take note and lay on particularly heartening compliments (and that includes vociferous nursery guys who must be sick of seeing gardens).

A rock border around the white garden is finally laid—digging the trench and sizing up the big weighty New Mexican terra-cotta rocks so they lie in harmony next to one another is no easy feat. I planted more big leafy basics in our new clearing left of the white garden, which I determinedly want to keep woodsy and green instead of another flowering garden; I'm really into this size-and-texture mode. Transplanting six hosta already in place for at least three years, therefore having shot out substantial root systems, was a true achievement in digging and prying apart. These hosta, by the way, were originally underplanted around my beautiful cut-leaf maple to "set it off." But now the very same maple has totally overwhelmed its hosta planting and needs nothing to show it off as it has spread far beyond its original width and is a thing of beauty unto itself. Now the six hosta buried beneath its graceful branches are part of the once struggling, now captivating, bigger than ever hosta patch interplanted with poppies and magnificent bearded iris.

All the canna and colocasia, etc. nurtured indoors since early March, creating an obstacle course in our living room, are now outdoors—dug deep, planted firm, and already a good eight to twelve inches above ground. At the end of the day, realizing the two days of summer we have finally experienced after literally no spring have brought the tulips to their knees prompted me to cut down masses of them while

My adored *Fritillaria*. From grandest to most petite: Crown *imperialis*, *persica*, *meleagris*, and *michailovski*.

still in their prime. This, of course, creates another chore besides finding enough tulip-worthy vases to flaunt all the fabulous blooms. It is now time to rid the beds of all tulip remnants—except the Darwin Hybrids I have been convinced can be perennialized. With faithful fertilizing and a sunny spot, the Darwin Hybrids do continue to make quite a show for at least three years. But these are the *only* tulips to leave in the ground as far as I'm concerned. The rest get yanked out and tossed away because they simply do not endure from year to year and return a listless, weak version of their fabulous former selves. If tulips were not so extraordinary a flower, I'd say why bother with all the work and expense of replanting them each year—but they merit every ache and every dollar. Besides, each year the artistic exercise of coming up with new color and planting schemes is a big turn-on.

Aaahhh, fabulous days in the garden—the best sort of fatigue. When I scrub the dusty dirt off my face and neck, then waltz out into the evening and inhale the scent of everything bursting forth combined with air so fresh you cannot only smell it, but actually taste it—my gardening obsession renews itself again and again.

Why oh why can't the Garden Tour be right now? The six *Clematis montana* 'Rubens' seem to sport at least a hundred new flowers each day, while overlooking the last, but best, of the tulip cutting garden—the fantastically eccentric parrots, the dignified lily-flowered, and the incredible multilayered peony ones. I have matched *Incarvillea* (deep magenta-pink hardy gloxinia) with nursery-bought, more deeply colored, strangely veined petunias, and it looks like heaven among the columbines. The daffodils are finished except for two abundant patches of 'Geranium' that are just coming into their own and exude a most fabulous scent as you enter the driveway. The *Ajuga* is in full blue flower and as it's used as ground cover in the blue border and around the pond, it's a rapturous backdrop to the blue columbines, *Camassia, Scilla,* and *Polemonium* (Jacob's ladder, one of my first planted perennial patches, growing stronger each year). The Japanese painted ferns with their wonderful subtle silver and burgundy coloration are the standout among their less brilliant fern cousins in the shade paths and give an other-worldly counterpoint to curving Solomon's-seal and my especially favored *Arisaema*, which are magnificent jack-in-the-pulpits. Now boasting only the common, native *triphyllum* variety, I've come upon an English catalog (albeit incongruously named Jacques Amand, decidedly Gallic, but hailing from the honest address of Clamp Hill, Middlesex) that actually does export and offers a whole roster of exotic ones. Next year . . . next year . . .

FOR MAY

- *Do deadhead* all your spring-flowering bulbs as soon as they begin to wilt.
- *Don't cut down that yellowing foliage!*—leave it intact. The spring iris, daffodils, scilla, muscari and all hyacinths, plus those glorious *Fritillaria* must be allowed to yellow and

wither so they can build up steam for next year. Make sure you have other plants in the planning or brimming with life to hide this not-so-attractive scene; but even if you must spend precious gardening hours braiding the dying leafage because you just can't stand the way it looks—do that—but *never* cut it down.

- Don't mow the grass where the crocus bloomed if their leaves have not yet died away.
- This is the moment to plan next spring's garden, while everything is in bloom—*not next August* when you are knee-deep in catalogs *but now* when you can see the gaps, bare spots, any glaring mistakes, and certainly any rapturous successes you want to capitalize on—either record in your garden journal or use your markers to remind yourself what you envision right now—don't be timid—make grandiose plans; you can always scale them back if you must as next spring's bulb orders encroach on four digits.
- The cutting garden is begging to be planted. The old rule of thumbs green and otherwise is to wait until the maple trees leaf to set in the first dahlia tubers. On a bright warm May day, maple leaves or not, in go the first round of dahlias, gladioli, and *Acidanthera*.
- Once you perceive the warmth is here to stay, set out in the garden all plants you have been nurturing indoors just waiting for this day: the *Canna, Calla, Colocasia, Caladium, Crinum, Sprekea, Gloriosa,* and your spectacular tuberous begonias.
- Treat yourself to a major statement or two—the nurseries are chock-full of spring-flowering trees and shrubs that will light up a dull corner of your garden for decades to come—maybe a heavenly scented lilac, a weeping cherry in blossom, an elusively colored rhododendron or two, or a divine spring magnolia—buying them in bloom allows you to come up with the comeliest color combinations.
- It is not too soon to begin staking tall growing perennials and setting out your "grow-through" supports and "peony rings."
- If huge, rather than many, peonies are what your heart desires—pick off the side buds and force all growth into one glorious flower per stem.
- If you have surrendered to a pond of any sort, the distasteful job of cleaning it should be apparent now.
- There is no more heady time to visit a botanical garden, an arboretum, or even your local parks than mid-May. If it is inspiration you seek for next year's planning, you will find exhilarating clumps of it all around you just for the ferreting out.

JUNE

What is one to say about June, the time of perfect young summer, the fulfillment of the promise of the earlier months, and with as yet no sign to remind one that its fresh young beauty will ever fade?

Gertrude Jekyll, *On Gardening*

May has catapulted itself into June as I return from Guatemala and rush to East Hampton just in time to catch the change from reluctant, but eventually polite spring to precocious early summer. Could this veritable jungle of flowering and leafing really be the same restrained residence of tulips, narcissus, and *Scilla* withdrawn from only twelve days ago? Astonishing indeed. What to look at first? What to *do* first? I couldn't take it all in so just wandered around for the first twenty minutes, keys in hand, bags on shoulders, proper city shoes gone to the dogs one more time. The gardens looked so lush they were unfathomable—yes! the Garden Tour will be a resounding success. Now I was sure.

The first thing to do, it seemed clear, was make a breathless call to Howard Purcell to ascertain exactly *when* is this Garden Tour—as there had been some consternation about the tentative date of June 13. June 27 was the reply, and the list of great gardens to be included on the tour was revealed as well. I was delighted to hear the roster. Martha Stewart! The venerated queen of all things perfect herself was to be on the agenda! My God, now there really is a lot of work to do. Of course, I was more than pleased that my did-it-myself garden and Ms. Stewart's were both on the same tour. It would have seemed out of the question to me some months back, but the truth is I'm tickled pink. There are to be eight gardens—and I'm determined to make mine measure up to the best.

A mad week is spent all over the property with frantic trips to every nursery in a twenty-mile radius. Am I becoming too persnickety, fussy, jaded, picayune? Almost nothing seems good enough. Looking for breathtaking items to bridge the gaps in the new rockery becomes a fixation supreme. Finally I settle on six more magical Japanese painted ferns; two wonderful dwarf junipers resembling confused corkscrews; some old big leathery-leaved *Bergenia* in honor of Gertrude Jekyll (one of her favorites); and I'm praying the tuberous begonias are literally dripping with enchanted multilayered blooms by June 27.

Each day in my travels I manage to find a startling something here, two things there and invariably arrive in my weed-ridden driveway (another thing to address) with a car full of plants. Casing the joint, deciding where this would make the biggest splash and where that would turn an otherwise homely corner into a look, I continually notice my father-in-law, who is visiting from Miami Beach, appraising the situation in his own unique way. Now, Morris Benson is quite a guy—nearly ninety and just flamboyantly remarried to a lovely lady nearly half his age who enjoys his travel and dancing manias as much as he—but I can perceive him calculating. And sure enough, when Irving arrived this weekend, the inevitable father-to-son chitchat was overheard: "Ay-yi-yi, I hope she never has another one of these Garden Tours. She is spending a *fortune*." What can I say? He isn't wrong.

Just this morning, my overwhelming desire to have a big patch of blue delphinium dominating the east half of the blue border got the best of me. So I set out with a delphinium goal and found one here, another there, and by the end of the travail had garnered ten gorgeous delphinium just on the verge of bloom that should be perfect on the appointed day. It made me sad to note that the many delphinium previously planted had clearly not returned—no matter what I do they don't want to "perennialize" here—but this newly created patch was planted hip-to-hip and a few weeks from now is going to look like it had always been there. (An afternote is many astonished gardeners on the very day sought me out and beseeched I share my secret of managing to grow these beautiful delphinium because *they have tried and tried with no luck?* Far be it for me to corrupt or deceive true, devoted neighboring gardeners; and so I reluctantly admitted they were all planted only two weeks before.) Such is the stuff that drives fathers-in-law crazy.

An agonizing week passes in the city . . . .

Why is it the Garden Tour is June 27, and on June 14, the original weekend, my garden is full of blooms that can't possibly endure two more weeks? The blueish garden is as blue as it is ever going to be, inundated with several subtle (and a few flashy) true-blue bearded iris, Jacob's ladder still going strong, fragile *Geranium* 'Johnson's Blue' (the real thing, not those omnipres-ent *Pelargonium* everyone mistakenly calls geraniums), *Allium christophii* and *karataviense* (both produce bold flower-balls made up of hundreds of starlike florets), not to mention the two astounding 'Globemasters', a striking pale blue clematis spiraling round a focal tree, and the *Baptisia australis* looks like it's going to pop any minute.

The burgundy garden is awash in peonies, and we know they don't last. Thank God for the burgundy-leaved things—the *Heuchera* 'Palace Purple', the dark red *Sedum,* and the purple smoke-bush; and waving over it all, the *Cytisus scoparius* 'Burkwoodii' (the fabulous garnet-flowered, slightly edged in gold, Scotch broom that is suddenly smothered with bloom even though I doubted it so much just a few short weeks ago). The white garden is at its zenith, and it would take an illusionist to get it to stay exactly this way.

Not being a magician, it's impossible to explain my anxiety about what will be in bloom and what buds about to burst just won't manage to make it on time because there is simply *nothing* one can do to stay the whims of nature. Not one single thing. My cavalier attitude is colored by all the forces of Mama's unpredictable impulses. Feeling helpless is one of my least favorite status quos, but there is little more I can actually do.

Of course, the choice of this date, June 27, befuddles me. This is regarded as late-early summer—or early-late summer, or something; but anyway, it is a moment when nothing of any major value is in bloom (except perhaps Martha's calculated rose garden, which I think had great bearing on Howard's final-date decision). The peonies are finished. The spectacular iris are over. The spring things seem light years gone, yet the major clematis, most fetching daylilies, glorious Japanese iris, arduously planted lilies, and the grandest of perennials are still on the come and definitely won't be in bloom at the end of June. I am thoroughly convinced a garden tour should be held either mid-June or mid-July—this transitory moment is a crazy choice!

It is about eighty hours before the momentous morning. I am gardened out. I've haunted every nursery on southern Long Island and planted till I'm green in the face. I've known since last summer that I'd give this tour everything I've got, but I never dreamed it would become *this* obsessive. This last burst of energy and desire for perfection must have something to do with Martha's ability to turn her garden mania to profit. Being a career girl at heart and totally unenthused by clothes at this stage of my game, I would like nothing better than to be a gardener for sure.

Since the celebrity factor of the ARF Garden Tour this summer is so potent, Howard Purcell has made a very deliberate change on the posters and flyers all around town right now. Last year it just said: ARF Garden Tour. Rain or shine. This is where to buy your tickets. This is how much it costs. This year, the very posters and flyers are a list of exactly *whose* gardens you can visit for your mere twenty dollars. Of course, Martha leads the list. Jerry Della Femina and Judy Licht are second, being quite the important people around town (both the Big Town and this one). The third entry on the list is me, and imagine my distress when I saw my name misspelled. Dia*nn*e with only one *n* has always bugged me, but it's my fault for not specifying, or believing my old *Dianne B.* logo left such an indelible impression. After that, no name was recognizable except Howard's as the final stop. It's a good thing that I didn't realize until the day of the tour that the fifth garden was landscaped by *the* Rosarian of the Brooklyn Botanical Garden, no less. Then I would *really* have been intolerable and totally monstrous to live with.

Anyway, in this down-to-the-wire mode, it seems appropriate to count my blessings. I am thankful we are on the cusp of the longest day of the year and as much light prevailed as could ever be hoped for, not being in Finland or Sweden. When I could no longer distinguish the dirt from the cow manure, I threw down the pruners at nine P.M. There's only so much a girl can do.

Who cares how much money these fellow Garden Tour–gardeners have got? Or how many gardeners they employ? Undaunted even by reading in the local paper of Martha engaging not one, but *two* gardeners in Connecticut, who fly down with fresh produce *every* weekend from her bigger garden up there. So, if this chick has two gardeners aviating with the radishes, just think how many she has nipping and tucking a few streets away to get her joint into shape for the big day. One reassuring thing, at least, is the knowledge Howard Purcell also tends his splendid garden himself. He was kind enough to give me a private tour last summer and explain his bountiful flowering acre was thirty years in the making; this news made me feel much better in the face of his overflowing floral dreamworld.

So his place will look glorious, and though I can be my own harshest critic I know mine looks fine but, will *they* be satisfied with it as a stop on their twenty-dollar ticket? These tickets not only allow one to be a horticultural voyeur—but the proceeds help give cute stray dogs new homes. Howard told me a gruesome tale about scoundrels parading as nature-enthusiasts and summer-lovers who arrive in these Hamptons on Memorial Day—glibly move into their rental houses and buy a dog to make it seem like home. Then the harsh reality of Labor Day arrives all too soon. They pack up their Sapore di Mare outfits, their Hampton T-shirts and toothbrushes, and suddenly—there is *still* this *dog*. The lovable pup they couldn't resist only a few short months ago is evidently not darling enough. These same people who hog the parking spaces, act like the Grand Café (the favored breakfast spot) belongs to them, and generally assume a Hamptonian air—fall dead short when it comes to pooches and somehow have no qualms about dumping them in front of the ARF shelter as they head out of town. He told me phantasmagoric stories about how the limited, mostly volunteer staff returns after Labor Day to find maybe twelve or twenty or forty howling hungry hounds. Disgraceful.

And then, suddenly, the morning of the Garden Tour arrives. It is inconceivable to me that my involvement with the earth has taken such priority that I never considered—not for one split second—just what I was going to wear. Although fashion has ceased being the end-all of my existence, I confess that I think about how I look just to go into town for supplies, and my self-perception is yet a major driving force. "There is life beyond gardening," I kept repeating to myself, wavering between the cleanest version of my gardening outfit and something a bit more befitting my old avant-garde reputation. After settling for something comfortably in between, I greeted the clear, bright, Godsend morning. Everything looked perfect. To my horror, a tourer would later point out a dead fish in the pond. I almost died myself.

How could I have known what to expect from the long-anticipated Garden Tour? Last year I attended a lecture by Mr. John Sayles, England's chief garden advisor to the National Trust, given by the stoic Royal Oak Foundation. One of those affairs where you can't quite decide whether you are pleased or bored to death to be the youngest person in the room. He emphasized "the summer sport of visiting gardens in England, as it is the principal creative expression of the English." This did not prepare me for the hundreds and hundreds of garden zealots who made their way around our little plot with a general enthusiasm never imagined and certainly unexpected.

Though inconceivable a year ago, after worming my way onto the roster of this tour, that garden devotées who had already seen Ms. Stewart's roses (roses, roses, and more roses—that was about it, except for a not particularly inventive perennial border in back of the house) and the considerable and artfully done Della Femina oceanfront acreage (you even got to stroll through their house), would say *to me*, "Oh, now this *is* a garden," or, "Absolutely my favorite!" Stirring remarks, those! It seemed to me the tourers expected to find the first two celebrated gardens looking exactly like impeccable pictures in flawless magazine spreads and there were just no surprises. My garden, as you know, is filled with surprises.

As I paced up and down on my hedge-concealed deck, sadly abandoned by Irving, who couldn't say no to a golfing invitation at the fancy new Atlantic Club, most everything being

A smidge of the mysterious 'Broken Pottery Path', with elegant *Athyrium nipponicum* 'Pictum' in the forefront.

said by the thousand-plus tourers who were roaming down below reached my ears. I was most charmed by comments such as, "It's so different," "They certainly must travel a lot," "I can hardly tell where the woods end and the garden starts," "Well, at least this one has a sense of humor." Lots of words like artistic, creative, personal . . . and invariably, "What do you think all this broken pottery *means*?" I would peek around the ten-foot-high cedar hedges and check out the particularly engrossed tourers—then, and only then, would I stroll down to the lawn, name a plant or two (always first in Latin, followed by the common cognomen), tell curious tourers that the green marble geese came from a guy in Hong Kong who drives a hard bargain, confirm that we got the Buddha babies at either end of the pool in Bangkok, and earnestly explain why I'd chosen to create the broken pottery path. This shady path is carefully littered with a Japanese vessel here, an upturned Mayan object there, an obviously freshly thrown splintered vase at one end, an enameled Florentine (tourist) plate at the other, etc.

As these shards and fragments are merely a product of my reluctance to throw anything away I really love, I explained each time a coveted prize from a far-off land bit the dust—instead of tossing it in the recycling bin—I simply half buried it along this woodsy walkway so as not to forfeit it completely, even though it could no longer serve its original intention—perhaps an ashtray, a flower vase, a salad bowl. This seemed to amuse everyone. Oh, it was a gleeful group touring my garden that inexplicably rare day.

So they came and they wandered, the garden tourers; some actually stayed around quite some time—sitting in the hammock grove, going back to the same spot for another look two and three times; a few left and even came back for seconds. I must admit, though, at the end of many of their forays, the overriding sentiment seemed unanimously to be, "This *really* took a lot of *work*." If they only knew.

June Pointers

- Last chance to plant summer-blooming bulbs: try *Crinum, Galtonia* (summer hyacinth), *Orinthogalum* (Star of Bethlehem), *Trillium, Hymenocallis* (spider lily), and calla lilies.
- Last chance to fill up bare spots with annuals, or preferably something lasting.
- If you must grow something from seed, now is the time to dibble the morning glories into the ground.
- Best month to haunt the nurseries for bountiful perennials.
- Pinch back the asters (and daisies, if you have them) at least twice this month in order to have dense, bushy plants come autumn.
- Train any vining thing growing on trellises or fences with those nifty flexible metal "English garden nails."
- All plants still languishing in the house (except ones preferring the house like gorgeous *Clivia*) should be moved outside by now.
- Don't wait any longer to trim untidy hedges—as the new growth hardens it becomes a more difficult chore.
- It is hot enough now for dastardly chemicals like RoundUp to put an end to unwanted weeds and grass on your terrace, driveway, or patio—soak them good, and in about three weeks they should disappear.

Before the blink of an eye, July has come again, and your garden should be proudly sporting the fruits of your year's labor. Contemplating next year's garden should be done with even more conviction and focus, and you will find year after year the pleasure increases along with your garden's progress. As is abundantly clear by now, the thrills of springtime, the joys of a garden, the wonders of rearranging nature, just do not come to those who sit and wait.

THE

GARDENING

CATALOGS:

HOW

TO

CHOOSE

Which ones. For what. Statistics. Alarms. Money. To Journal or Not.

I have of course never said that the cash is constant.
Ezra Pound, "Canto XXXVIII"

or to paraphrase Dolly in *Hello Dolly*—

Money is like manure:
It's not worth a thing unless you spread it around [encouraging young things to grow].

Deluged with dozens of plant, flower, seed, and tree catalogs vying for your dollars, you may find that deciphering what is *what* can be difficult and depleting, as few ever come right out and elaborate their strong points. Instead, each catalog invariably touts itself as being the *sine qua non* of all it is attempting to sell you, no matter how diverse or singular its product. This, of course, can't be so—in the vast arena of flora-furnishers-by-mail you will find schmoozers, sycophants, specialists, those too good to be true, and some that should be booed and hissed right off the mail-order map. Through much expensively acquired experience, I've come to know many of the catalogs intimately and unearthed quite a few juicy tidbits on my way to reaching a level of confidence about how and when to use the plethora of pages competing for my cherished gardening cash.

Once you've distinguished yourself by joining the ranks of insatiable plant fanatics, for which you can qualify simply by placing a few orders for a couple seasons, you will find reams of pamphlets, lists, and all-out books *en masse* in your mailbox as the catalog genie governs a huge network and is bound to decree your address eminently mailable. The unsolicited catalogs piling up in droves however, are not necessarily the ones to which you want to entrust your dollars. The ones posited here, you can count on. How do you go about receiving the *right* catalogs? If you have a good gardening friend, you might ask him or her to take a few extra minutes while placing the next batch of orders to advise favorite catalogs of your name and address (I've done this for my sister, our handyman, even a few people on the Garden Tour). Or you take the addresses presented at the conclusion of this book and write quick notes, or send fast faxes requesting your name be added to the mailing list. Even though it takes a little effort, it's well worth it.

Mine is not the most extensive list, but if it doesn't sufficiently cover your gardening needs, I can't imagine what will. *Gardening by Mail* lists at least one thousand plants-by-mail sources; but Barbara Barton, the author, will be the first to tell you it's merely a list and she rates nothing from hands-on experience. My bravos and boos, commendations and criticisms are either first-hand or based on experienced intuition. Read on and you will find there is method to the madness of catalog buying. In the summer when you're arranging your fall planting, catalogs are the exclusive route to gratifying results. But there's a *right* way to spend your gardening dollars in the tempting dead of winter as well, when it's all too easy to be swayed by irresistible images and confident copy.

The catalogs, you know, can be wickedly suggestive, and there's no time when you are more vulnerable than in the pernicious months of February and March. With colored pictures so alluring, captions so enthralling, the promise of a brilliant yard so compelling, they remind me of Noel Coward's condensed credo, "Strange how potent cheap music is." The catalogs share this cheap potent charm—having the power to persuade you to abandon all rational thought—compulsion mingled with coercion. Though catalog perusal, assessment, and purchase is a worthwhile, if not the most captivating winter sport for us gardeners, it is highly important you heed my warnings regarding self-control. It is, oh so easy to order more than you have room to plant—to be moved by a description so irresistible you duly charge it even though you know it hasn't the remotest opportunity to flourish in your scheme. It's equally as indulgent to convince yourself somehow the conditions in your garden are going to change and deter-minedly order fabulous flowering things with absolutely no chance to succeed in your zone. The winter-doldrum dream-mode plays funny tricks on our minds. There is nothing worse than receiving a huge box filled with living things having no place in your yard or, after their planting, succumbing to the first harsh signs of unpredictable Mama.

Here I give you lots of earnest catalog-buying tips and hints, unselfishly introduce you to my *precious* sources (though the fear of exploiting them does nag at me), and hope to point you toward the right way to purchase so you can feel great about the money you spend and each year have a garden peppered with more and more substantial plants. What I cannot do, however, is hold your hand while you defiantly order things that don't make any sense because you were overpowered by the tantalizing, enticing images. Take my word, and don't part with your valuable funds for plants you can't possibly hope to grow, because

- you don't have enough sun (or shade).
- you don't have enough space.
- the wall, pergola, or trellis needed for the vine doesn't exist.
- your soil is all wrong.
- your zone is all wrong.

Having made all these mistakes, I urge you to quell the same irrational desires. One winter, smitten with bog plants, which are those that grow in the muddy ground at the edge of a natural pond or stream, I persuaded myself bog lilies, papyrus, and *Sagittaria* were definitely for me. Sitting inside on a freezing day I talked myself into believing the edge of our pond—where the plastic liner meets the earth, no less—could be turned into a bog and suitably went about ordering dozens of bog plants, fool that I was. You see, no matter how desperately I wanted a bog, there is simply not a bog nor will there ever be a bog, so those days of scheming and all that dough went down the drink. Don't let this happen to you. It is all too easy to be led down the wrong garden path and suddenly find your rose-colored glasses are all fogged up.

Once you've mastered the delicacies of control and restraint necessary to make catalog purchases that suit your garden, there are certain **Golden-Brown Ground Rules** to be taken to heart:

Buy from the Specialists

You need not be on the prowl for rarities or a master of a particular genus to order from the experts of a given plant group. The more specialized the catalog, the more plump, healthy, and vigorous your plant will arrive. It stands to reason, yes? Daylilies from a daylily grower or iris from an iris farm, you can bet your life will be fatter, fresher, and more fecund than the same item from a catalog who sells everything from petunias to privet hedges. And naturally, their selection will be lustier and almost inconceivably diverse. The livelihood of these veteran specialists is derived solely from one intense obsession with a single kind of plant. Whenever possible, give them your precious ordering dollars, and you will be on the receiving end of a gratifying package satiating your hunger for whatever specific item you're after. There are many good general perennial catalogs, but when it's iris, dahlias, daylilies, roses, peonies, Japanese maples, or *any bulbs or tubers* you're after, order from the connoisseurs for sure.

RARELY BUY FLOWERING PERENNIALS FROM A CATALOG

Why not, you ask. Well, why should you? Unless you live in an area so remote you have scant local nursery resources or have reached such a level of expertise and sophistication you're beyond your nurseries' offerings, then why? No matter how much you pay in the catalog, what you will receive is something barely started into growth, while perennials purchased at the nursery are full-blown and often flowering. You can see exactly what you've got—you don't have to waste time and money planting something with a scarcely started root system—you don't have to worry about one last frost that might be its death—and you don't have to speculate about its eventual size being too much or too little for your garden. If you unfortunately live in an area where few nurseries exist, there are fine perennial catalogs to order from; but if you can avoid it—you are much better off.

DO BUY YOUR NONFLOWERING PERENNIALS BY MAIL

Nonflowering perennials are an entirely different story. Grasses, hosta, ferns, ground cover: these items are best bought by mail because the selection is far greater, the inherent value much better, and your likelihood for success almost assured. These are not so finicky as flowering plants, their root-stalks are tougher, their outcome more predictable. With the exception of hosta, which can often be as expensive by mail as in the nursery (though not if you follow my advice and order from fine people at Holbrook, Crownsville, or Forest Farm), grasses, ferns, and ground cover are inordinately cheaper, and as these are the very things you need wads of to make a plentiful statement—mail-ordering usually makes much more sense.

NEVER BUY SPRING OR SUMMER BULBS AT YOUR NURSERY

With scads of good catalogs specializing in bulbs, *why* would you want to make rash choices at a nursery, garden center, hardware store, or anywhere but by mail? Bulbs are bulbs, the ones you receive from the UPS man and those for sale down the road will most likely all look the same if you order from any legitimate source—it's how, when, where, and especially *what* you plant that makes the big difference. How can you possibly hope to create divine gardening visions standing in front of a counter, loaded down with shopping bags, worried about the dog panting in the car—where concentration is futile and you are likely to settle for their prepacked mix, rather than taking time to carefully contemplate your grand spring looks. By ordering your bulbs, you have the opportunity to sit with your various catalogs—ponder your gardening spaces—customize your critical spring selection, and not be stuck with the same old dreary, predisposed potpourri of the too-too obvious. Furthermore, the much more advantageous cost factor will afford a denser, more divine garden. A significantly designed spring garden takes preparation and thought—the wondrous bulb catalogs allow this luxury—your garden center can't begin to compete with their grandiose extensive array—so why bother?

ORDER FROM PEOPLE, NOT COMPUTERS

Since the growing of a garden is so personal, I always feel put off by flagrantly machine-oriented catalogs. Human contact between my plants and their source seems like an inherently proper proposal—that there is someone on the receiving end of my order who is going to go in the field and actually dig my plants, not some giant claw-robot machine matching my order up to a computer-designated multidigit number by techno-magic. Naturally, you can't expect everything you order to arrive with handwritten notes, but when this does happen (and it has, many times), invariably what you receive is in top condition and sizable. At the very least, beware of catalogs without a personal introduction from the grower and *never* order from a catalog listing no personal contact or direct phone number.

DO NOT JUDGE A CATALOG BY ITS COVER

Invariably, some of my best buys have come from the least slick lists, although there are the occasional exceptions, like the full-color 72-page Schreiner's Iris Gardens. Customarily, the specialist catalogs, probably because they deal so stably in one explicit preoccupation, can afford a showy catalog with lots of pictures and not skimp on quality or charge exorbitant prices. Some of the most homely catalogs, with paper covers, locally done artwork, and newsprint pages, yield the most cultivated output: for example, Montrose Nursery, Forest Farm, Bedford Dahlias, Trans-Pacific Nursery. I've known divine results from nothing more than a few mimeographed pages. Mama never specified a great gardener also had to be a sublime art director, after all.

AND ESPECIALLY—NOT BY ITS PICTURES

Do not be disheartened upon receipt of a catalog with nothing but words—many times these are the most genuine source and make a point of letting you know they forgo fancy books in order to offer you high quality at good prices. If your botanical vocabulary is still limited and you want to partake of these honest values, just spread your catalog out next to your favorite full-color gardening books (or the fancy catalogs) and cross-reference like mad. The added effort will also help better familiarize you with exactly *what* you're ordering and make the options more meaningful, and at the same time you save some dough. The Crownsville Nursery, Niche Gardens, and Van Engelen, Inc., are examples of this type of catalog.

Now, don't get me wrong—there's nothing wrong with full-color picture displays; and, of course, in the right catalogs I prefer them, as it makes the selecting endeavor much easier. More than once I've gone astray when immersed in a long list of wordy descriptions of color and form and overlooked my ultimate goal. Part of the trick is using a little instinctive intuition as your catalog-judgment guide.

A WORD ABOUT PRICES

The adage "you get what you pay for" is apt here as in most things, but it is particularly important you understand *what exactly* you are ordering. Don't expect a blooming-size shrub or an already remarkable tree for ten dollars. And if somewhere in the catalog, if not right in the description—it isn't made clear what you can expect—i.e., size of pot, numbers of eyes on the root, etc.—think twice!, or even three or four times. You will find the prices do not vary greatly among the straightforward, honest catalogs.

To prove my point, I've just consulted five catalogs on the item *Baptisia australis,* a particular perennial favorite since Steven Hamilton pointed out its apparent lack in my garden, and I found it difficult to locate at nurseries. We-Du Nurseries, Forest Farm, and Niche Gardens all offer it in the $3.50–$4.50 range, and the ever overpriced White Flower Farm and Wayside Gardens sell it for $6.50 and $5.95, respectively. You will find this pattern repeating itself over and over. The conspicuous, upscale "W" catalogs (White Flower Farm and Wayside Gardens), share a penchant for excess, not so different from the fashion "W" and its counterpart, my least favorite read, *Women's Wear Daily*, (the dreaded *WWD*). Now, two or three dollars' difference may not sound overwhelming to you—maybe you think it easier wasting a few bucks here and there and ordering from the big, glossy giants—but it's *not* simply two or three dollars—it's actually many multiples of two here, three there, and by the time you're finished placing a reasonable season's orders of perhaps fifteen new plants to introduce into your garden at minimally three plants each—the few dollars become hundreds of dollars, and so on.

On the other hand, don't be charmed into ordering a thirty-five-dollar iris because you've fallen in love with the picture on the catalog cover. These very expensive irises, daylilies, roses, dahlias, etc., are for veritable horticultural aesthetes and priced so expensively not because they're better, but because they're new introductions and rarer, with merely a nuance of difference. Unless you're lusting after winning flower-show awards judged by practiced, erudite types: avoid the specialties. You can grow equally beautiful flowers sticking with the older cultivars, which are definitely just as fine—the only difference is they've been in circulation longer, are more easily available and, therefore cheaper. It's a fact, too, some catalogs are just more expensive than others because they think they can get away with it, like the various "W" crowds.

Do Not Stray Too Far from Your Zone

If you live in New York, it's not Floridian and Hawaiian catalogs that should be your first choice for planting your very own garden. Likewise, gardeners in Zone 10 should stick to the opulence of tropical-plant catalogs available to them. I'm not saying never stray from your zone, but use good judgment and more or less don't stray too many zones away from your own, particularly when dealing with rooted plants shipped in leaf. It stands to reason what was propagated in Zone 6 will probably do fine in Zones 5 and 7 too, but it doesn't make any sense to buy your nursery stock from Zone 2 if you live in Zone 8, right? Of course, if your obsession is tropicals or orchids and you have a version of a greenhouse, you evidently will be drawn to ordering from diverse climates and not be bound by the ground and weather like we ordinary outdoor dirt gardeners.

Complain Vociferously If Your Order Is Not Worth Planting

Remember you are *always* right. The last thing any catalog company wants—no matter how large or small its operation—is your return of mildewy bulbs, dilapidated tubers, or dead seedlings crowding its warehouse, especially after having made the round-trip excursion from them to you and back again. This traveling time interests no sane supplier, and never will they suggest you return it as proof of your dissatisfaction. They will take your word and trust your tale. At the root of every catalog is a true gardener—all flora-furnishers, no matter how commercial they've become, were humble gardeners once and constitute a league of earth-loving enthusiasts. All catalogs are willing to face facts and own up to their inadequacies—I've never yet run into a scenario where the supplier reneged on its promise of quality.

Of course, if you don't phone immediately with distraught voice or post an agitated, if not frantic, letter—you will be stuck with whatever junk the supplier chooses to send you. All of them—even the most pretentious, not to mention the most provincial—never want to be wrong or be accused of taking advantage and will always wind up agreeing with you *if* you complain. Without exception, when I've taken the time to register my dissatisfaction (with the exception of a few conundrums soon described), replacements far superior to the flawed flora in question were the appreciated result.

Be Suspicious If a Catalog Overlooks Botanical Names

A catalog so inconsistent as to use only common names—ones varying from region to region and sometimes dialect to dialect—instead of the appropriate and precise *universal* language are to be avoided. You will most likely find their quality to be as unprofessional as their nomenclature. Which basket would you rather store your eggs in: Pincushion Flower or *Scabiosa columbaria* 'Perfecta'? Coral Bells or *Heuchera americana* 'Palace Purple'? You be the judge.

Specify Your Delivery

Nothing worse than a package of living things languishing on your doorstep (or God forbid, at the post office) while you are off on a grand tour of the south of France or even in the next town visiting your family. Most growers will be happy to comply with your instructions if you remember to include them. No self-respecting nursery ships live plants throughout the year regardless of Mama's cycle; but many have definitive sequences based on the needs of the plants. You will surely get your iris tubers in July and August, and most Oriental lilies at the end of October, unless you specifically instruct otherwise. The catalogs can't possibly have your personal agenda emblazoned in their souls—it's up to you to dictate your shipping/receiving/planting calendar (within the bounds of the natural cycle, of course).

Don't Wait Till the Last Minute

Many of the best suppliers are not huge plant-producing factories. Quantities are truly limited in many circumstances where the source is actually the grower, as in receiving your order and proceeding to the field to dig it—so the sooner you order, the more likely it will be *you* on the welcoming end of exactly your latest yearning. I always say "no" on the line of the order form questioning "Will I accept a substitute?" I'm sure they'll try their best to come as close as possible to the original urge, but inevitably hesitation hovers over the concept they might find yellow equally as charming as white and send me the yellow—so I always say "no" to substitutions, but endeavor to place my orders in a timely manner so as not to be left out in a chilly ambiguous garden patch. On the other side of the shovel, my despair at being advised "supplies are depleted" of a plant my heart was set on follows me around for days.

Beware of Gimmicks

More than once, I've been swayed into ordering from Michigan Bulb Company because their "Gardener's Sweepstakes" somehow seemed legit to me. Irrational thought tugged as I mused, "Well, since so much money goes into the earth, isn't it right some should be returned, which of course, I promise to put right back in the garden." Forget it. I despised the quality of what I got. They also ignored my shipping instructions, and sent everything through the post office. I also think it's highly unlikely you will ever win the pot of gold.

Also, be wary of "buy one—get one free," those ubiquitous plant "grab bags" (why on earth would you want the leftovers nobody else wanted), and especially, prepackaged "gardens." These raise in my soul a fastidious furor. Occasionally, the bulb suppliers apprise us of a preplanned bulb garden not sounding too bad (like Dutch Gardens's 'Pink Proposal' or Van Engelen's incredibly well-priced 'Collection' selection mentioned at the beginning of the book), but for the most part, these ever-more-popular prearranged gardens send chills up and down my spine. Almost without exception they consist of plants clashing in color, have no understanding of anyone's particular whim, and would look extraordinarily halfhearted if planted out as they suggest. "Lamp-Post Gardens," "Ring-Round-the-Tree," and "Colorful Mailbox Garden" will surely *look* even worse than they sound. Please, don't fall into this crappy trap.

ORDER FROM CATALOGS THAT MAKE SENSE TO YOU

If you are an avid gardener, but a beginner, sophisticated catalogs listing hundreds of botanical names and nothing else are not for you. This doesn't mean these catalogs aren't good, but they rely on the advanced experience of their audience to translate their offerings, which still may be an enigma to you. I've recently received two begonia lists so academic I can't tell which leaf is up. Stick to the fine catalogs that give good and lengthy descriptions—ones including the positive and negative aspects about their plants—you can count on them to deliver an honest product you can interpret. Any catalog claiming every single thing it sells is easy to grow! will grow anywhere! blooms all summer! no maintenance! is not worth the paper it's printed on. There are plenty of wonderful catalogs dotting the horizon between the banal and the scholarly. Surely you can do justice to your yard by finding the ones meaningful to you.

THE CHALLENGE OF THE NEW

Finding sources for less common varieties of plants, shrubs, and trees can take on the proportions of a treasure hunt. I've written and phoned, joined societies and scoured flower shows, and have cultivated quite a list; but if my suggestions are not enough for you—every strata of known plant-life has a devoted following. Could you ask for more specialization than the Sempervivum Fanciers Association, the International Ornamental Crabapple Society, or the American Gourd Society? You name it, and I'll wager it exists. Once you join any of the various societies (which is usually as easy as sending a ten- or twenty-dollar check), you are automatically apprised of myriad obscure growers of your particular obsession by their bulletins and journals. Though the minutiae of a given plant's idiosyncrasies are of surprising interest to many people, I actually find the various bulletins rather droll, as they are so obsessed with propagation and hybridizing and just too maniacal in their guidelines and competitions; but they are invaluable founts of information as far as providing sources to doll up my garden. All the horticultural societies are listed in the *Gardening by Mail* book, and appear regularly in the erstwhile gardening magazines—some of which you subscribe to already, I'm sure. Once your desire has become great enough, you will find your venue—it's just one more thing taking time, patience, devotion, and love.

Now let's talk turkey, or tuberoses and *Tiarella,* as the case may be.

To the uninitiated and willing, there are scores of sources and recommendations begging to be tried. Consider that the National Gardening Association released retail sales figures as far back as 1990 of more than twenty billion dollars for lawn and garden materials, with sales increasing a whopping 10 percent each year. Although this twenty billion must obviously include a vast array of working farms and zealous tomato growers along with we flower lovers; you see, you are assuredly not alone. No matter how the roots are divided, horticulture is abundantly on the rise.

If you cannot believe *National Geographic,* who can you believe? In their May 1992 issue they inform us eight million households placed orders from the very prominent flower catalogs: namely Park Seed, Wayside Gardens, and White Flower Farm. Furthermore, they detail the rise of Smith & Hawken from a forty-thousand-dollar business in 1980 to one worth seventy-five million today and growing every year. That's a ton of orders and plenty dollars pouring into these upstanding and incorruptibly moral companies.

The Sacred "W" Catalogs

Wayside Gardens and White Flower Farm are the most omnipresent and seemingly omnipotent of all the catalogs by virtue of their size and the plentitude of their offerings, but they can't possibly grow themselves all those things they sell to so many people. Plus they blast your mailbox each year not with one spring and one fall catalog like my most treasured sources, but with at least *two* fall issues—*three* spring issues, and assorted other in-between editions like The Complete Rose Catalogue, A Bulb Book, A Guide to Easy Gardening. Do you realize what it costs to print and mail all these lengthy, full-color creations to what must be an enormous mailing list? It costs plenty, which is why, you can be sure, they are both overpriced and overrated. A few illustrative true stories:

My sweet mother was visiting over the New Year when Irving and I spontaneously decided to remarry. (We have been together in varying states of fusion for nigh on two decades—

sometimes nuptially correct, sometimes separated, a few ups and downs here, on-again off-again there, and once actually divorced.) At the moment of renewal of our marriage bonds I was poring over one of the many Wayside catalogs, entranced by two Japanese maples. A terrifically expensive *Acer palmatum* 'Aureum', called a "golden full moon maple," a beautiful round-leaved (I'd never seen this whirling-leaf look before) chartreuse at eighty-four dollars, and an *Acer Palmatum* 'Dissectum Crimson Queen' for fifty-six dollars had me at fever pitch trying to decide between them. Mom seized the opportunity and insisted she buy both maples as part of her wedding gift. I quickly sent off my order with Mom's check and not long after was greeted with the news they had sold out of the lusted-after "golden full moon maple," which was reluctantly replaced with three *Stewartia koreana*, "Korean splendor tree," sounding perfect to fill out space behind the white garden.

What eventually arrived were veritable twigs with nary a sign of bud. I called and complained vociferously and was shipped another delivery of twigs—figurative and literal twigs. I was finally bored with fighting this issue, so the various spindly twigs were lovingly planted and a miracle prayed for. Four months later, Mom's summer visit was impending, and not being able to bear showing her the listless feeble specimens her hundred and fifty dollars represented, I repaired to one of my favorite nurseries (McConnell's) and bought a three-foot, fully leaved, important-looking maple 'Okushima' for thirty-eight dollars. My Mom, nearing eighty, couldn't really remember the original coveted trees and was tickled pink when I out-and-out lied—pointing out the freshly planted cheaper, and far better, local one as her gift. Meanwhile, seething inside because by this time this fancy catalog pontificating should not have caught me off-guard, I undertook a serious maple-by-mail investigation.

Now absolutely sure Wayside Gardens is not all it's cracked up to be, dear reader, be convinced your money is usually better spent elsewhere. From two sources, I ordered the exact same cultivar, *Acer Palmatum* 'Crimson Queen'—as a "graft" from Forest Farm for $9.95 (not a typo—that's the price) and as a two-year tree from the specialist Mountain Maples for $39. Need I tell you the rest? The Mountain Maples entrée arrived a strong stem full of buds and was planted with great confidence last autumn. It already looks like a tree, not a twig (note, $17 cheaper). The Forest Farm "graft" from which I wasn't expecting much for $9.95, arrived looking *better* than the Wayside twig, but no match for the Mountain Maples specimen. Do you need more proof?

Likewise, two summers ago when first bitten by the upright tuberous begonia bug, I simply *had to have* the Blackmore & Langdon strain touted by White Flower Farm "for their exquisite forms and colors putting lesser strains to shame." They extolled it as an extraordinary variety from England not offered elsewhere, so surrendering to their chat, I ordered one $27 wonder and a few "Exhibition Seedling" versions at $9.95 as well. Sure more of this heavenly flower should grace my garden, I spied some very plump-looking begonia tubers already sprouting eyes at the Agway. At $1.49 each, I thought, "What's to lose?" and bought six. When potting them up I carefully marked which were the WFF expensive beauties and which were from Agway, although it crossed my mind this marking is probably unnecessary because the WFF ones will speak for themselves. As it turned out, this was not the case—*all* the begonias grew into remarkable specimens. The $27 one was no more spectacular than the seedlings, and the $1.49 Agway ones were *just as sensational*. A dozen more plants from Agway would have made a much more sensational show in my garden that summer than this single over-praised expensive disappointment.

These are only two instances of many disappointments I've had with both the big-time catalogs. Over and over again, the plants are puny and the prices high. However, they both are to be appreciated on some scores. Because their offerings are so diverse and because both truly seem to be interested in exclusives and introductions, they occasionally offer what can be found nowhere else. Last season my WFF order evolved because of my desperation to find *Sanguinaria,* or "bloodroot," and hadn't yet discovered it in Carroll Gardens. This unique wildflower, smothered in double white flowers early in spring against brilliant bluish-green leathery foliage that stays beautiful most of the summer, is focal in one of the old plantings at The Bayberry where I fell in love with it, but they insisted it was "no longer in commerce." Along with the *Sanguinaria* last autumn went a healthy order as well for some gorgeous tulips.

I even must admit I'm tempted to give Wayside Gardens another try as they're offering that full moon maple again and have lowered the price to fifty-eight dollars, but I think it prudent to try out Mountain Maples first. There's usually something irresistible from either or both of them, but I limit myself to only these things and order much more extravagantly from my many other sources. However, it's important you subscribe to and pore over both catalogs because they are founts of information (especially Wayside; the hyperbole of WFF's Amos Pettingill is a bit much for me), provide some of the best pictures, and are a great educational tool. I just wouldn't give them your money—or at least, not much of it.

Throughout the chapters, I've touched on many catalogs dear to me, but will now enlighten you on which to use for what. Because the big "W" catalogs are so easy to fall for and wind up on every budding gardener's doorstep, my antagonistic bit about them is qualified. Making more negative remarks or inviting additional adversaries by droning on and on about all the other catalogs I deem lousy is not the point of this book. You will have to judge for yourself if you come upon intriguing catalogs not espoused here, *but* if it's a catalog *at all* conspicuous or prominent most likely I'm highly aware of it and chose not to endorse it because either I've had a dismal experience or just believe these other sources to be better. I personally vouch for the discrimination and caliber of all of the following:

The Best Bulb Suppliers

Bulbs are a category like no other because the results aren't immediate and you can really evaluate a supplier's performance only after the fact. If your bulbs arrive looking healthy (no mildew or rot, not shriveled up, sizable, and well-packed) it is most likely they will bear flowers true to name and variety if planted properly. What to look for in bulb suppliers is interesting selection, timely deliveries, and of course, good prices. Price is a paramount issue in ordering bulbs like no other plant group because you can simply never have enough flowering spring things (or summer things, for that matter), and it's oh! so easy to fill up thirty or forty lines of a good catalog form. Unfortunately, it's less easy to come up with the hundreds of dollars necessary to pay for this fantasy, so I scrutinize prices like crazy. In any given season, it takes as many as six or eight suppliers to fulfill my dreamy garden visions. These are the bulb catalogs I believe in and hold dear, in no particular order of importance.

Dutch Gardens and Van Engelen are the mainstay furnishers of my considerable fall-planting needs. The Dutch Gardens book is awash with full-page knockout pictures, a far better than average selection, a preprinted order sheet so all you need do is fill in your quantities (a real boon, if you ask me), terrific prices, and quantities small enough you needn't be overwhelmed. Their shipping is timely, their packaging is well-marked (though only paper bags), *and* Mr. Howard Purcell, after thirty years of gardening, proclaims this the best source and the one from which he orders *all* his bulbs. Watch for their Year Special—it's always a great deal and usually quite a delectable item. They even have a very formidable spring-planting-for-summer book, though their dahlia and canna selection is not quite exotic enough for my taste.

Last summer my friend Shaun Casey-Held was with me during bulb-ordering time and, lamenting over her disappointing tulips and daffodils purchased on the spot in "mixtures" from Smith & Hawken in Mill Valley, where she lives and gardens in a newly acquired grand old overgrown stone-wall-enclosed wonderland she's dying to improve. To begin with, I advised her *never* to settle for those hackneyed mixtures, and proceeded to pull out a nice preprinted Dutch Gardens order form for her perusal. On a quick jaunt through the book, I checked off exactly what would make her ecstatic next spring. The obligatory months of waiting have passed, and although my first crocus appeared only today, Mill Valley is in full spring blossom. Shaun breathlessly phoned to exclaim over her tulips, "I never knew there were so many kinds and shapes," she shrieked, "it's so beautiful I could just die." Her husband Billy even got in the act and called especially to say, "I never knew there were *black* tulips." You, too, will have the same reaction once you delve into this catalog.

Van Engelen has an infrequent sketch or two (so use your other catalogs to get the full picture), an astounding selection, fine communication, fabulous packaging (everything comes in a heavy cardboard box, which can later be used for storing of tender bulbs and tubers), and absolutely and unquestionably the best prices. The hitch is you're required to order all the obvious bulbs (tulip, daffodil, crocus, hyacinth, *et al.*) in huge quantities of fifty or one hundred, usually one hundred. So, as I don't have the space to plant fields of flowers, each year I carefully consider which flowers for the biggest splash should be ordered from Van Engelen. Last year it was tall, oval, creamy-white-with-blue-stamens *Tulipa* 'Francoise' and

Only a fraction of the tempting fall-planted, spring-blooming bulbs: clockwise from upper left: hyacinths, *Scilla* (or *Endymion*), *Erythronium dens-canis*, Crocus, *Puschkinia*, and anemones in the middle.

the great "collar" narcissus, 'Tricollet'. In the ground now waiting to burst forth, are one hundred new narcissis, 'Cheerfulness' (a great white double you can never have enough of, millions of flowers, and it tops off the spring cycle by waiting late to bloom), and two huge plantings of giant Darwin hybrid tulips. No need to be discouraged if you think you can't handle these lofty quantities—because there are still the fab offerings at the back of the book. A sensational selection of allium, the most important *Fritillaria*, calla lilies, many miscellaneous bulbs, *and* a terrific lily selection—all requiring quantities of only five or ten—and you need at least that many anyway. Another thing I always order from Van Engelen is my season's supply of "Holland Bulb Booster" (a whole case for $27.50, and you don't have to worry about lugging it home) and my autumn/winter supply of narcissuses for forcing indoors during the bleak months (you can't beat fifty lively bulbs for twenty-one dollars). And if it's amaryllis you're after, they stock huge bulbs at the best prices ever—you can give very impressive Christmas gifts by ordering your amaryllis here—buying some clay pots—and splurging on luxurious ribbon.

Most recently I've rounded out my spring-flowering selection with the following:

Holland Bulb Farms—They have the blackest Darwin tulip I've discovered, and another Darwin beauty, 'Picture', which has a form unlike any other—a pure rosy pink, much taller than they describe, flaunting a wavy (maybe correctly called incurved?) petal that made it appropriately spectacular as the very last tulip to bloom last spring. If you have to wait, it may as well be for this.

John Scheepers, Inc.—This is the couture of bulb catalogs. Prices are high as they get, but bulbs are referred to as "estate size," whatever that means. However, I'm drawn to this catalog because of the famous Mrs. John T. Scheepers tulip, which you will find in any self-respecting catalog. It was originated by this family, so you know they have longstanding credibility. They also were the esteemed original hybridizers of Hybrid Darwin tulips. Exotic things like *Glorioso rothschildiana* in the summer usually typify my choices from them and I've always been pleased with the results, but this year am a bit piqued. Having placed an order for only one item, *Corydalis solida*, I had my check promptly returned because the order wasn't big enough. Oh well . . . . get the catalog anyway for a look and a comparative measure.

Van Bourgondien—This one always turns up with something either unavailable elsewhere or requiring too large an order from Van Engelen. This year I wanted to add to my *Leucojum aestivum* patch (a delicate white pendant bellflower with charming green markings at the petal tips on tall stems), but had no room for Van E's minimum order of one hundred, so bought a nice dozen here (a hundred for $25.75 and a dozen for $10.95, but what are you going to do?), as well as my favorite *Allium siculum*—a real beauty—and tempting Spanish June-bloom iris with great markings not found elsewhere.

McClure & Zimmerman—This catalog was a new and exciting find. Though the prices are somewhere between the grandiose and the best buys, the selection was terrific. You are able to get into special hard-to-find tulips at a minimum of only six (the prices decrease with quantity in small multiples)—like a pink 'Emperor' and lily-flowering 'Ballade', which is crimson-magenta with a fine white border. Usually, in a selection of fifty mixed lily tulips you will get two of these and the other forty-eight all look sad in comparison. But mainly, it was their "Miscellaneous and Other Bulbs" category that sent me into a spin: a rare pendant allium, another try at anemones in the new rockery (very rarely do you find the crepey old-master true anemones available on a per-color basis and not a mix), two new *Fritillaria,* one more try with *Lycoris radiata* (fabulous spider lilies, usually pink—this one crimson with out-of-this-world protruding anthers), and the pièce de résistance—*Cardiocrinum giganteum,* a huge and striking member of the lily family I've drooled over in various breathtaking English garden books. Although woodland conditions are supposed to be their métier, at $19.95 each, I ordered only one. After all, they warn you of a probable wait of some years till flowering and once done, they are spent and die; but who can deny grandiose lilies on a stem so vital Nepalese hill people make musical pipes of them??

To wind up the season, I confess being smitten with a few tulips from good old WFF, a big ruffly double named 'May Wonder', an irresistible china rose, thirty-six inches tall, 'Boccherini', etc. Not only that, a little money was forked over to Wayside, too, because I couldn't bear to be without *Fritillaria imperialis* 'Argentea Variegata'. The catalog copy said, "Although it has been known for 50 years, this rare, striking variegated-leaved plant is available for the first time in modern times!" Given my weakness for *Fritillaria,* how could I resist? And to put in a good word for our friends, the big "W" books—neither seem to be quite so overpriced on bulbs as on plants.

The Indisputable Specialists

Some years passed before recognizing the overwhelming superiority of the specialists. Since I've begun to place orders with many of them, and subsequently compared their iris, their lilies, etc., to other plants before received in the same category—well, there is just *no* parallel. How can you not differentiate? Entire farms, acres and acres of land, totally committed groups of people make the growing of one decisive thing their life's work. The preparers of a catalog (like most) that supplies fifty, or one hundred, or five hundred various plants might be well-informed, might deliver fine products, might be totally dedicated to the earth; but how can they understand the intricacies of say, a peony, like those who do nothing else but grow peonies? Because all their efforts and entire operation are devoted to one thing, it is their natural aim to supply the most excellent version. So, from these determined and distinctive folks you can expect the very best—the pick of the lot—the cream of the crop, so to speak.

Invariably, the selection is the most expansive, the prices are as good as the others or better, the attention the most rapt, and the plant is usually seasoned with at least a few years' growth. I've not yet come across specialists for every category, but my eyes are always wide open. Just a few months ago *The Avant Gardener* (the newsletter that has informed and warned me of so many things) published a "Source Guide." Out of 432 entries, 69 are for seeds, 40 for vegetables, and 59 for fruit trees and nuts, totaling 168 uninteresting to me; 39 evergreen, tree, and shrub entries; 14 azaleas and rhododendrons, and 22 for herbs—yes, I'm concerned with these categories but feel you're much better off at your nursery to purchase same. Surprisingly, only 27 listings for bulbs, corms, and tubers (most of which I know and the best of which I've extolled); 61 perennials and 29 wildflowers and ferns (surprisingly not including some with high marks on my list); and finally, the point of the exercise: The Specialists:

14 rosarians,
18 daylily growers,
12 iris fanatics,
5 chrysanthemum madmen (mums are nowhere on my Hit List), and
4 each for dahlias, gladioli, and peonies.

You see, there isn't such a huge bevy of souls so dedicated, so while we still inhabit a world peopled with gardening gourmets—it will serve us and them to give our consistent support. These have been exceptionally important to my garden:

Iris

Unfamiliar with half of the twelve touted above; but it's impossible to improve on Schriener's Iris Gardens. In the world outside gardening, I notice deterioration at many levels (if I can find linen sheets they cost a thousand bucks, most everything "fast" doesn't suit me, domestic air travel is a nightmare in any class), but Schreiner's conjures old-world caliber as its product is such a bountiful treat—perfect in every way. A seventy-five-page gloriously colored catalog dealing in nothing but fabulous *Iris germanica*—spectacular bearded iris—specialization at its peak! If it's this wonder of June you favor (and I can't imagine what kind of garden couldn't use these somewhere), order here and nowhere else. The bulbous plants arrive tingling with life in August, allowing you to plant them with utmost conviction—by autumn they've shot up an abundance of new fans, and by next June—just as they are in glorious bloom, you kiss your new Schreiner catalog and figure out how to make space for more. If at first you are put off by the prices—read the not-so-fine print explaining it's all actually half price once you spend a mere thirty dollars.

Rivaling bearded iris in beauty—actually they are *more* delicate and subtlety beautiful—the Japanese *Iris ensata*, too, have their devoted nurserymen, and thank God—because they're oddly difficult to find in season. Although in color they can't touch the diverse palette covered by bearded iris, the best of iris colors abide in the Japanese iris with the astounding distinction of their truly breathtaking almost horizontal form, as if floating. They epitomize all the best delicate as well as intricate qualities of Oriental art. Place yourself on the list of Ensata Gardens and become bewitched by this extraordinary offering. Only placing my first order now, as I've just found this formidable source; *I know* I'll be beholden for life. Making my choice was akin to an erotic dream—do I want violet rims or cream ones—veins or veinless—single or double sepals—splashing, mottling, or stipling??? Oh decisions, decisions . . .

Another fine iris source specializing in Japanese, as well as Siberian, Louisiana, and other iris species (all which follow the bearded variety in bloom time) is York Hill Farm. These folks speak to you with handwritten discourse, send an honest catalog cheaply printed but expensively thought through, and deliver an obviously doted-on product. They offer a few other specialties, like hosta and skillfully described daylilies.

Daylily

The world of daylilies is clearly another obsessive one: remember my story about the visit to the Rainbow Garden? Well, there are daylilies and then, *there are* daylilies. In my first few gardening years I didn't appreciate them properly, equating them with some common thing to be found everywhere, not particularly distinguished—too easy—too ordinary—too orange. Always the first to admit my own mistakes, I've developed a new deep devotion toward *Hemerocallis* for its many forms and varieties. For starters, they are as dependable as daffodils—once planted, they never quit, they just increase.

Schreiner's offers 72 full-color pages of the dazzling bearded Iris.

Plus they burst forth at precisely the right late-spring moment to overtake all the wilting, yellowing foliage of our precious bulbs. Not a few hundred, or a thousand; but 32,000 cultivars have been registered. Granted, it takes a keen eye to discern the difference among diploids and tetraploids, recurveds and triangulars, or crimped and ruffled; but it doesn't take a genius to appreciate the astonishing range that makes daylilies so delectable—my most recent planting of salmon/cream petals with maroon centers grouped with salmon centers and burgundy petals should be a real killer. And once you begin obtaining your daylilies from proper sources like Daylily Discounters—there's no end to the backbone you can create for your garden.

I'm sure all eighteen sources recommended by *The Avant Gardener* are fine, but my real knowledge extends only to two: the one nearest me—Saxton Gardens of Saratoga, New York, and the aforementioned unattractively named Daylily Discounters. Upon receiving the catalog, impressed by the vibrant color pictures and great descriptions, but less taken with the prices as the order form began to fill, I deliberated as the total swelled to many hundreds of dollars. Drastically cut back, the order was mailed and the settled-for conclusion drawn, "Who needs so many daylilies anyway?" The first order arrived just as daylilies were on the come—so robust, with roots so fat, in such big clumps it threw me into a deep depression for days for not having managed to afford more. As I scouted the nurseries the same season—yes, there were, of course, many potted daylilies—some pale and elusive as the ones suggested in the catalog, ruffly petaled, mauvey colored, insistently flowering—but all twelve and fifteen dollars—and *then* you have to dig them out of those difficult root-bound pots and plant into arduously hewn-out huge holes. Feeling in the midst of a big dilemma—suddenly gracing my doorstep was the Daylily Discounter "Planting Extravaganza" brochure—50 percent off!

How excited was I? The 50-percent-off clumps arrived just as hefty, husky, and vigorous as the mere few regular-priced ones, and it was clear daylily nirvana had been found. To boot, the healthy root-stocks planted last autumn are among the first to show signs of life this spring— even before some daylilies I've had in the ground three or four years! How's that for potency? These specialist growers really know how to make a gardener happy. What a source! And this, is where you can ply yourself with the primordial muck. (Maybe it's responsible for this early spring vitality?) Heaven. Daylily fulfillment comes to those who wait; but if you can't live without, say, 'Black Plush', "a classic from the heyday of spider breeding . . . velvety very near black 7″ blooms on sturdy 28″ scapes . . . surrounding a commanding star-shaped golden throat," then you must pay $9.95, or five for $47.95, because this beauty didn't make it to the "Extravaganza" sale. But I bet you won't find Mr. Black Plush at your nursery.

Lilium—Real Lilies

You've noticed, I'm sure, the lily as a distinct standout in the panoply of fabulous flowers and rightfully endeared to legions of devotées. Perhaps the N. A. Lily Society doesn't have quite as many chapters as the American Iris Society, but they are both flooded with throngs of followers. Say it were fiddlehead ferns (as nice as they are) engrossing you, it would be more difficult to find an audience and less fascinating to track their every mood—but given a subject like lilies—then there are many fanciers, countless choices, endless varieties—shocking *The Avant Gardener* doesn't give them their own heading in the "Source Guide." Naturally, you don't get the same heady thrill of a thriving plant shooting up greenery when you order lilies because, once again, you receive a bulb—though a far different bulb from the rest, as it is made up of conspicuous scales and should have visible roots at both the top (the stem roots) and the bottom (the real basal roots). Lilies can be planted in spring, but it's much more advisable to plant in fall so the roots can dig in over autumn and winter. They love the cold and are very hardy.

Although Van Engelen and Dutch Gardens have admirable lily offerings, if you really want to plumb the depths of the Asiatics, temples, trumpets and aurelians, Oriental hybrids, and species lilies, then it's Rex Bulb Farms or B & D Lilies for you. You can't beat lilies for size, substance, and elegance in the mid- and late-summer garden—providing the sought-after crowning-glory touch once the iris have passed—and you can't do better than these sources. It's crazy to even consider planting potted nursery lilies for at least fifteen dollars each, when for the same fifteen dollars and a little forethought you can have three or even six lilies brightening your landscape year after year. As the summer progresses, the lilies get more and more fabulous. You start with the upright-flowering Asiatics, which are a bit stiff, but what they lack in glamour they make up for in number—sometimes as many as a dozen flowers per stem—so from a patch of a mere dozen bulbs you can expect continuous flowering for an entire month. And then they really pick up steam as the reflexed Turk's-cap lilies come to the fore, followed by the dramatic outfacing or pendant trumpets, often on six-foot stems, and culminating with the intricately marked and colored Oriental hybrids—the last really grand show of summer. You will want to acquire many many lilies, so get your sources in order posthaste.

Dahlias

If dahlias are your thing, and I strongly suggest they should be included on your roster of "things," Swan Island Dahlias is a catalog to drool over. Trying to decide whether to go for early bloom, longer stems, or arcane color combinations sends me into a heady spin each February as I pore over the catalogs. As they span the color spectrum from the coolest to the warmest, and seem as genuine in shades of lavender as they do in the more sensational ranges of screaming red and burnt orange—one year it might be the deepest solid colors I'm into, the next may be a vision of bicolored, dark and light blends, and variegated colors with strong tendencies toward apricot. Then there is the choice of what kind of flower??? With the exception of pompon or ball dahlias, which I detest because they remind me of the dreaded marigold—there are endless choices to be made: spiky forms that have an overall surprised quality about them (cactus dahlias); softly petaled forms (anemone or waterlily types); the curving twisting petals of the formal and informal "decorative" division, which become flashier as you look carefully at their myriad layers; or my new favorite, collarette dahlias, which have a sensational bicolor layered look. As if all this were not enough, then there are size considerations, from AA—which are the big showy giants with flowers as wide as twelve inches!—through A, B, and BB, which are the quieter four- to six-inch sweethearts.

Deciding the dahlia cutting garden each year is one of my most anticipated tasks as there is so much wondrous stuff to choose from—another reason I don't store my dahlia tubers—it's much more interesting to dream up a new image each year, and they're not really so expensive. As they are among the elite of cut flowers, it is here I plan the color feeling for my vases full of summer flowers. The singular drawback is my sunny cutting garden space has room for only twenty dahlias, and forcing myself to contain my array within this parameter requires a stubborn self-control not natural to me.

Collarette

What you receive, however, from Swan Island Dahlias or any of the other dahlia growers is a nasty-looking thing like a wrinkled, shriveled, phallic potato. That a fabulous dahlia bloom materializes from this homeliest of tubers is as mystical to me as the strange meta-morphosis of a caterpillar into a butterfly. The emergence of something exquisite and poetic from something so humble and unprepossessing is one of the more fabulous miracles of good old Mama. Both begin their cycle of life in extremely modest circumstances, devoid of ornament, and with no particular clue to the beauty abiding within. Fascinating when nature is at its most *super*natural, isn't it?

Waterlily

Vast varieties and a plethora of color nearly un-matchable is the phenomena in store for you once you've placed your dahlia order and done your proper planting, which is not very difficult, with results nearly foolproof. Few flowers have the

The wrinkled tuber explodes into: Semi-Cactus

Informal Decorative

stamina of the dahlia, remaining erect and showy under their great bounty of petals, although a harsh wind can do them in if not appropriately staked. Within their ten major classifications, incredible subtleties have been defined, and thousands of named dahlias exist—many available to you at the stroke of a pen on the order form of Swan Island Dahlias, Connell's Dahlias, or Bedford Dahlias—all perfectly reputable, but Swan has the glorious pictures.

No reason to buy any of the above flora categories from anyone but these specialists, or you are doing yourself and your garden a disservice. Also, there are many good rose growers, Jackson & Perkins being the most obvious; they must be the best because every single nursery in town stocks J & P roses. I've listed a few others in the appendix whose catalogs look good, though untried by me (you know me and my blue thumb when it comes to roses). Also scan the appendix and you will unearth various other specialists, including a gladiola person, a ground-cover man, an ivy source, and one fabulous clematis grower with a big problem, poor guy. Imagine my distress after poring over this gorgeous catalog, Steffen's Clematis, gasping over 'Belle Nantaise', *texensis* 'Duchess of Albany', and 'Alpina Willy'—only to arrive at a letter explaining there would be no shipments this year or next, as some dreaded contaminated chemical destroyed 85 percent of the crop. But my distress must've been minuscule compared to that of Arthur H. Steffen himself. What does a clematis grower do without any clematis? This would not be so painful to the sell-everything nurseries—if they lose a crop here or there—no big deal—they just concentrate on their other myriad plants. But when it's only *one* genus of plants you dote on and disaster strikes—it must feel like a steamy hothouse version of hell on earth.

Subsequently I read in more detail about Mr. Steffen's plight in a very sympathetic article in *The Avant Gardener* (of course, this monthly pamphlet is absolutely on to every inkling of gardening news) and decided to write him a little letter, butter him up with compliments, even apprise him of this book, thinking it could persuade him to fill my desperately desired order from whatever inkling was left of his crop. The reply was immediate and gracious, but no dice—you see, he said nothing could be sent that would be representative of the quality he stands for. You've got to defer to his honor, so I'll patiently wait, positive it will be worth it.

THE PERENNIAL CATALOGS

As long as we're in a phase of melancholia, this section begins with another morose tale—however this time, fortuitously, it's dismal only for us and not the good grower. From Montrose Nursery has come some of the most cherished and interesting things in my garden. Lucky enough to stumble onto this godsend early on when the only catalogs at my beck and call were the big flashies, it opened my eyes to the variety of venues beyond the slick ones and cheesy ones. Pat Mason, the venerable and distinguished broker of all desirable lower New York town houses, was miraculously flipping our ill-acquired double-house on the MacDougal-Sullivan gardens—once lived in by Bob Dylan and Sarah, no less—to Francesco Clemente. Dashing to her Cornelia Street office to sign yet another paper, I spied an engrossing flower catalog on her desk. Having never quite seen one like this before—all words and no pictures—I figured if she was reading it so thoroughly and marking it up so diligently . . . there must be something to it. Every other entry was a plant never heard of, plus the prices were amazingly cheap. Pat let you know in no uncertain terms she was a serious gardener, making a point of insisting not to call her on weekends in the country until sundown because she was in the garden and did not want to be disturbed—no matter how big her broker's commission. So, I noted the mimeographed address and begged a copy forthwith.

Deciding how to confine my order to their not-long-enough order sheet was a rapturous ordeal. Also thrilled because there were no cumbersome computer numbers to fill in—only the correct names—these tried and true nurseries that glory in digging their own plants don't need all those elaborate inventory-keeping methods. Always impressed by no complicated XZ1372B1s, it signals to me a real hands-on connection. Descriptions fantastic, offerings adroit, and prices half as much as those of the fancy folks. Once Nancy (Montrose's proprietor) knew I was really into her nursery, handwritten notes would arrive with every order; eventually we even spoke. Her voice was older than expected, as I had envisioned a frail young romantic gardening sylph traipsing about in North Carolina with her new guy Doug, whom she so lovingly introduced what seems a few short years ago. I had a forceful feeling this was an extraordinary pair—tilling their gardens—coaxing their cyclamen—reaching out to all their devoted clients. Whenever planting anything from Montrose Nursery, I made sure to scoop out every last particle of dirt from their lovingly packed containers because it was somehow strangely revered and I felt sure it would bring a new buoyancy to my garden.

So many faithful plants in my garden sprang from Montrose Nursery: my adored *Lespedeza* (a charming member of the pea family), most all the wondrous hellebores, my faithful *Lamium* 'White Nancy', and, of course, my anxious cyclamen—just to name a fraction. So, a few months ago, upon receipt of their latest catalog, I was astounded to read right on the cover the eerie, creepy, spooky, weird words, "Our 10th and Final Year." It seems Nancy and Doug have been beset by personal tragedies among their friends and relatives and have opted for some leisure time to enjoy the gardens they so tenderly have nurtured. As no mention has been made of their turning over the nursery to anyone else or it being for sale, my very favorite perennial source will not even be in existence by the time this book is in your hands. So sorry you'll miss it.

But never fear—there are a number of other great ones. I'm not sure what's in the air there—or more likely in the dirt—but Oregon and North Carolina (Maryland, too) seem to be home to an abundance of my preferred sources. Aside from Montrose, North Carolina (part of which is one zone warmer than mine, but most strangely exactly the same) boasts Niche Gardens (a particularly friendly concern—they even send a newsletter and publish pictures of the gardening staff—like one big happy family), Holbrook Farm (many of my enduring perennials hail from Holbrook), and We-Du Nurseries, the one I'm really depending on to take over when Montrose goes under, as they have a kinship (Montrose mentions We-Du as its source from time to time). Wayside Gardens, by the by, is only one state south (half Zone 7 and the other half toastier Zone 8).

Oregon (a sliver of which is Zone 7 and the balance of which is variously a zone warmer and a few zones colder), revels in many great plant suppliers: Trans-Pacific Nursery and Siskiyou Rare Plant Nursery, Russell Graham, the esteemed Jackson & Perkins, and my beloved Forest Farm—plus the most blatant of specialists—Swan Island Dahlias and Schreiner's Iris Gardens. For some reason these few states have more or less cornered the market on winning/responsible garden sourcing and the Oregonians must have a direct line into Mama.

Forest Farm is a real enigma, with unconventional methods toward everything. To begin with, they have assembled the most peculiar nomenclature for their shipping style: you either order by five gallons, one gallon, or "tubes." Faced the first time with this small-typed, 250-newsprint-paged, one-half-inch thick, hard-to-read catalog—I almost put it down, thinking, Why bother? But on closer inspection, it seemed smarter to immerse myself in its language and order hardy things like ferns, the magical shrub "select purple smoke-bush," and more *Aruncus* for the white garden.

Who knew what to expect from this idiosyncratic catalog interspersed with quotes ranging from

I think the eminently respectable Hollyhock must be doing a little bootlegging, for I have often found a humble bee completely undone within the capacious cup—the morning after.

L. B. Wilder (whoever that is)

to Japanese haiku, to

We are united with all life that is in nature. Man can no longer live his life for himself alone.

Albert Schweitzer

And what the hell was a tube? Well, a tube turned out to be a really substantial cylinder of dirt containing amazingly massive rooted plants. I was in a satisfied and pleased state of shock. Of course, this singular source has become a backbone of my garden, and with each delivery, time after time, thriving plant stock greets me at negligible prices. I turn to them now for all multiple buys of basically leafing things like ferns, *Astilbe, Spirea, Gunnera,* and of course, grasses—I told you about that splendid dispatch last autumn.

Holbrook Farm is another substantial, reliable grower, and as usual when it comes to these things, another family affair. They give you little tips and hints right on your invoice so you can hardly miss them, wish you well, and thank you—moreover, the product is consistently wonderful. I've ordered everything from *Enkianthus* (a wonderful shrub that flowers before it leafs) to foxgloves. Their catalog is easy to read, even has a few photos, and is spiced up with all sorts of very personal descriptions.

The two big "C" catalogs from Maryland, The Crownsville Nursery and Carroll Gardens, both weighty, serious tomes with no pix, no kicks of any kind, but in-depth selections of ravishing robust quality. Perhaps I favor them a smidge as they hail from my home state, but wherever located, I'd be just as excited about their quality and about currently ordering my sought-after *Sanguinaria canadensis* 'Multiplex' from Carroll Gardens (The Bayberry growing beauty I'd been unable to track down except at unfavored WFF). And what do I spy scanning the clematis list? That's right—glorious *texensis* 'Duchess of Albany' that understandably despondent Arthur Steffen can't ship. Hardy in my garden are many fine things from The Crownsville Nursery: *Chelone lyonii,* that shy, heavily blooming perennial known as "false turtle's-head" because the flowers sort of peek out from under a hood; various grasses; a wonderful *Buddleia* (butterfly bush), 'Nanho Blue'; and the first plot of my cherished Japanese painted ferns. Three or four years ago, there was a big buy of six *Acanthus mollis* from Crownsville that refuse to perish no matter how I treat them. In a vale below the once-too-too-elegant, still pretty nifty, Splendido Hotel in Portofino wildly grows a gargantuan patch of *Acanthus.* Now, all the catalogs and books say these babies need sun, and as they are so associated with sun-baked Corinthian columns in Greece, you might tend to agree; but in this dark overhung dell there is no sun, so I thought "bear's breeches" would be perfect for me. In an effort to duplicate this dreamy Italian valley—which, as you know, is impossible on my relatively flat little acre—I've moved these *Acanthus* around the property maybe six times, but they refuse to quit, and finally, settled into the would-be rain forest, they seem happier than ever.

In the **Golden-Brown Ground Rules** beginning this chapter, I warned to be wary about buying your perennials by mail, but as you can see, I've done a great deal of just that—even here where nurseries are so abundant. It's isn't necessarily not practicing what I preach—you see, many of my old faithfuls don't get nearly as big an order from me (or any at all sometimes) as my garden becomes fuller, but I used them like crazy until good sense decreed for most flowering perennials, nursery shopping is the way to go. But then, there are always the odd things discovered in books or old plantings I can't track down here, or most often—the uncommon (often curious) species unearthed by the earnest plantsmen themselves that sound better than all the run-of-the-mill stuff at the nurseries.

Perhaps the best way to make my point is to run through what's being ordered right now. Admittedly I'm late—the mulch is up—all those provocative green protrusions are thrusting from the dirt, and I'm reminded March is on the wane and only one scant order has been placed to the new-found Brit supplying rare wildflowers and heart-stopping gingers. Who knew writing a book would be so consuming as to cause neglect of my all-important spring planting orders? Shocking.

But I believe the orders are off just in the nick of time: Placed the usual whopper with Dutch Gardens: a mixture of pink-tinged poppies and peonies for some comely corner in the newly cleared patch behind the dark-red garden—a few multiples of their great "Hosta Hit Parade Collection" (much more scarce and interestingly colored than it sounds) and also for the new, barren, leveled land (to begin to give it character, and you already know you can never have too many hosta); and finally for *the* exotic pot—color-coordinated white or white-flushed scarlet/purple various Peruvian daffodils, *Nerine, Acidanthera, Eucomis* (pineapple lilies, which are homely in the ground, but great at eye-level) to be highlighted against swarthy dark canna. Must make the exotic pot really outstanding this year, because James Topping clued me in on a friend's "fabulous garden pots" book that is in the making and told me to make sure I had an exemplary fabulous one. With this challenge at hand, and the particular and focal spot the big pot demands on our deck anyway, this year it gets a whole new scheme, without relying on any of my dug and stored sweethearts.

Initially, I intended *really* exotic canna and duly filled in the form for the special Kelly's Plant World 'Intrigue' with uniquely lance-shaped purple leaves, but then thought better about it. I mean, thirty-five dollars for one canna tuber! Even though I could rationalize that in the course of just one season the tuber will multiply to probably at least five of these singular canna tubers, still—it seemed excessive, especially with Montrose Nursery offering 'Wyoming', dark purple leaves, Nancy assures, for only six dollars.

How could I not order from Montrose in its last spring shipping season??? There was no way. Aside from the purple canna, new irresistibles from Nancy and Doug include *Nepeta sibirica*, promised with bigger blue flowers and more compact growth; three more wonderful Japanese roof iris because they maintain they've improved it (although my original ones are pretty great); and for old time's sake—something called *Campylotropis macrocarpa* they say is a relative of *Lespedeza,* which they introduced me to and so, I feel beholden.

From their North Carolinian colleagues, We-Du and Niche Gardens, I ordered a bevy of woodland plants: two varieties of a never-encountered-before *Pinellia,* a member of the sexy *Arum* family and related to jack-in-the-pulpits—one of my darlings; only one *Hybanthus concolor* because they limit you to one and call it a collector's item; *Asarum arifolium* to keep company with my lovely *Asarum europaeum* because this is supposedly larger-leaved and evergreen; *Pulmonaria officinalis* 'Sissinghurst White' because I'm a sucker for anything named after Vita's garden—but more so, because they suggest pairing it with Japanese painted ferns, which I'd never thought of and sounds like a terrific idea. Out of the woodland to fight for my precious rays—two irresistible varieties of *Sarracenia*—eccentric "pitcher plants" seen last summer at Marder's, but maddeningly already sold; 'Striped Giant' reed grass, variegated and said to grow to eight feet; and a baby *Magnolia virginiana*, which is simply a four-dollar experiment. Who knows, it may one day be a grand tree.

From my revered specialists: Bedford and Connell's got my dahlia orders this year. After much deliberation, I decided on a clean sweep of showy tinged tips, blends, and bicolors—most in the collarette and waterlily form—in varying shades of scarlet, cerise, and plum.

Ensata Gardens captured a glorious Japanese iris order. This is not a cheap, conscientious addiction, mind you, a hundred thirty-five bucks for fifteen rhizomes after avoiding some of the most expensive is no great bargain—but come summer the awe-inspiring crepey canopy of splashed, tufted, and haloed blooms will make a hundred thirty-five bucks seem like so much manure.

B & D Lilies didn't get a lily order, as they're best ordered in summer and planted in autumn, but it did hook me with its 'Ashia' strain of *Alstroemeria* (Peruvian lilies). I've endeavored before to raise these lovelies, often among the handsomest cut flowers at the florist, but have failed miserably with tiny mail-order seedlings and, for some strange reason, have never seen them at any nursery. Figured if B & D is making a special point of offering three different strains in a catalog otherwise devoted to lilies, they must be on to something that I want to be in on too.

Gilson Gardens, the ground-cover people, got some business, since starting up a new cleared area especially calls for ground-cover. Some *Ajuga* 'Bronze Beauty', 'Curlytop' ivy, and 'Red Carpet' *Sedum* will certainly not do the trick, but will be a beginning. Prices here are very interesting, especially when you order twenty-five or more of an item (which is very probable when dealing in ground cover), and they specify exactly what you're getting, i.e., two-and-a-half-inch pots instead of the scarcely rooted cuttings usually received when ordering in the ground-cover category.

Kurt Bluemel, a specialist in ornamental grasses, bamboo, ferns, etc., ensnared me with two items: *Rodgersia tabularis,* described as shieldleaf, but looks to me more lotuslike with scalloped edges as gloriously pictured in *Large Leaf Perennials;* and two extravagant (to me, twenty-five dollars each is very lavish) *Cimicifuga racemosa* 'Brunette' never seen, but simply couldn't resist the description: "White flowers with almost black leaves/fabulous specimen." If I'd experienced no luck growing *Cimicifuga*, such mad splurging would not have come down on this bit of exotica, *but* since my four-year-old *Cimicifuga* thrives like mad and towers over the white garden—I have a feeling this is a groovy move.

The catalog of Trans-Pacific Nursery, Collector's List #7, took some real pondering and poring over to perfect an order, as so many entries were virgin territory. Beguiled by the drawings and general attitude of this extremely specialized grower (they make a point of everything being propagated right there in McMinnville, Oregon), I was impelled to try them out. Not only are there no burdensome computer numbers to deal with—there aren't even any prices! Except an occasional "a steal at $4.00." Not until the back of the booklet does one zero in on the never-before-seen words, "Unless listed otherwise, all plants are $3.00 each." I venture overhead doesn't run too high in McMinnville, and never before were choices made with such ease—the preconceived idea everything is only three bucks allows your imagination to take over, without having to constantly look at price, compare, calculate, and generally get yourself in a dither over the dollars. Especially eager for this delivery as I've a feeling it will be fabulous.

Succumbing to their various challenges—I opted for the following: *Tetrastigma voinicrianum*, a rapidly-growing "chestnut vine" endemic to Vietnam of all places (it's a wonder anything survived), with foot-long shiny green leaves. They say it won't survive the winter, but for three bucks, who cares if it just lasts the summer??? Whatever uncommon summer bulbs not already ordered from my Brit, Jacques Amand, are coming from here; as well as *Sollya fusiformis* (*fusiformis* sort of speaks for itself, don't you think?), "a trailing twiner bearing drooping, long-stemmed, intense blue flowers all summer." Some *Platycodon grandiflora* 'Fuji Blue' (sure, there are balloonflowers in every nursery, but I love them and never have seen a light, dusty blue); a couple of *Juncus effusus spiralis* (how's that for easily understandable Latin?) portrayed as "just about as outrageous a plant you can get on planet Earth"; three *Cordyline australis*, either green or purple (a strap-leaved beauty planted for the first time last summer [green] from Warren's that may or may not have survived the winter, still not sure) and, of course, chose purple; and tried something named *Asarina procumbens* or "snapdragon vine"—what better than a vine drooping creamy-colored snapdragons (one of my few favorite annuals—love the way they "snap") hardy to eighteen degrees. Making this order was an exercise in fantasy and so easy to revel in at the trifling three bucks—for sure you won't find these around the corner or in the fancy "W" catalogs—and if they do come up with one or two eventually—they definitely will not be three mere dollars.

From the less special but still endearing Van Bourgondien, I jumped on four *Glorioso rothschildiana* lilies for only $10.95! (usually twice as much, and since it's a bulb, how bad can it be?), some lavender calla lilies (which may have been a mistake), and a fantastic striped amaryllis. That's it. My last-minute ordering frenzy complete, I feel freed of an onerous obstacle blocking the path toward another yet more fulfilling summer. Have you detected the method in my madness? Nearly everything ordered is specific: either a distinctive plant I'm unlikely to find locally—a particular grouping of plants for an exacting area or exercise—or a comely addition to accentuate plants already thriving in the garden, and most from specialized growers or those I've come to wholeheartedly trust.

Yet, with all orders in I've still not made peace with a few furtive quests. Begonia growers just don't want to accommodate me; what I'm searching for are more subtlely colored, double- or triple-flowered variations on my already thrilling tuberous begonia collection, or maybe some forms more obscure than the easily available ruffled, camellia, or rose types; but the begonia growers insist on proposing all these complicated *Rex* types, cane types, thick-stems, shrubbies, and *semper*-somethings—none of which are about flowers or what I seek. These are leaf-oriented ideas most suitable for indoor growing and discriminated to a degree going beyond any obsessions of mine. Kay's Greenhouses of Texas lists more than a few hundred, but not one of the fantastically flowering kind eluding me; and the Fairyland Begonia Garden, presided over by Leslie and Winkey Woodruff doesn't list *any* begonias at all—only lilies— which I find very strange and think Winkey would be well-advised to change the name of his business.

And nowhere—simply nowhere can I find *Rheum palmatum.* I've taken to adding a note at the end of each order—

Hello—I'm looking for *Rheum palmatum*, please. Any idea where I might find it?
Thanks.

Maybe someone will rush to the rescue, because I'm dying for it after having spotted it highlighted in not one, but *two* recently caught-my-fancy books, *The Adventurous Gardener's Sourcebook of Rare and Unusual Plants* and *Large-Leaved Perennials*. Hundreds of catalogs and not one offering this *Rheum,* and certainly I've never encountered it locally or it would've been snatched up without question. It's only a humble ornamental rhubarb—it just happens to have huge—make that gigantic—red stems (edible if you so desire) and mammoth red-veined, palm-like leaves. The perfect subject to include with my other elephantine favorites. What to do but repair to Marder's and ask them to grow it? The old friendly local nursery routine, often saving the day when you're all cataloged out.

In order to organize your catalog and various nursery purchasing in terms of how successful which sources have been from one year to the next, the tuned-in gardener will probably desire to keep a journal of some sort. Said journal should also be the jotting-place to remind you of all the strategic ideas you had the year before. Of course, it also should serve as a time-and-action trigger to keep one step ahead of the myriad seasonal chores. My cumbersome but somewhat effective system has seen me through five years, and though I refer to it constantly, I wish it were sleeker and, most definitely, easier to read. A big (3½-inch spine) black three-ring notebook snitched from the production office of Cygne Design was designated as my gardening workbook/journal. Carefully I inserted solid alphabetical arrangers with triply-strong hole mounts so the whole thing wouldn't be falling apart every time I turned a page. Each page is labeled with headings:

WHAT	SOURCE	BLOOM	REMARKS
Botanical & common name	where it came from and when	what to expect & the record of what actually happens	words of wisdom from the experts, as well as my comments, reminders

and left what seemed lots of space between each entry so I could keep abreast of the development of each new plant. Each time something new went in the ground, I'd haul the bulky volume out and duly record (often still do) where it came from, what to expect, and what were my intentions—and would duly file in a side pocket the confirmations of my myriad catalog orders so it would be easy to reference what came from whom. The idea, unfortunately, degenerated as the book became thicker and thicker to the point of unwieldy—and the catalog confirmations, well, they just got completely out of hand until a new system was devised of filing them right with their catalogs in a segregated space on the sagging gardening bookshelves.

As for the alphabetical flower journal itself, where I left the most space to record my thoughts, invariably the plant died or interest was lost or something. Those items I'm desperate to chart always seem to be crammed four to a page, and inevitably, I do my journal catching up when I've had too much to drink or after too long a day, and my lengthy scrawl obliterates the very information I subsequently need most to know. But in the long run, this overblown scheme is better than no strategy at all, and without it, I'd be literally lost. Each of us must seek our own level.

Another hot tip is *never* dispose of your catalogs once you've placed an order. Some months later when the plants arrive you will need them for reference to help you figure out just what is *Adlumia fungosa* and what color is *Lycoris squamigera* anyway. It's advisable to keep the catalogs from which you've ordered separate from those you've only perused—also making it easier to put your hands right on them when the confirmation comes—which you should staple or fix right to the catalog (unless you've figured out a more organized way—this is the one currently working best for me).

If you're not into the do-it-yourself mode, there are good prearranged journals usually organized by the calendar year, although not one of them known to me allows enough room for proper recording of thoughts, strategies, or inspired new ideas. Of course, the trick is to not only record the fab idea on the day it strikes you—but also when the best time comes to act on it. That the blue border needs more Nepeta might overwhelm you in August when there's none to be found—make a note in March of next year to track it down. Particularly fetching among these weekly/monthly journals is the *Gardener's Five Year Record Book* published by The

Royal Horticultural Society. Albeit still not having nearly enough room per page, it is sprinkled with charming literature and provides fascinating facts such as seventy paces × seventy paces is the gardening way to measure an acre, and you can determine the height of a tree by positioning your eyes at a forty-five-degree angle from its top, then (supposedly) the distance between you and the tree is the height. Who am I to question such distinguished data? Another fairly workable book is *Three Years in Bloom* by Ann Lovejoy. It is not quite so erudite as The Royal Horticultural Society's journal, but it has the biggest format I've come across and lots of space for notes, plus graph pages for planning, as well as blanks for photos. Both books are bound, which I consider a boon.

One way or another, it is paramount you dig up a way to chart your progress, your garden's needs, all the triumphs and flops, your grand plans and nitpicking bitty reminders. Just like the imperative labeling of the garden—you must devise your own version of a notebook, chronicle, calendar, log, journal, diary, or you will never really figure out which end is up. Establish something workable for you—in this very personal undertaking it is inconsequential if it be a treatise, a trial-and-error memo, or simply a big calendar on which you record your sightings, longings, and hard-learned knowledge. Find a way. The last thing you want is not to be able to remember whether the flourishing clematis came through the mail (and from whom), was bought on a whim at the Agway for $4.99, or was precisely planted by the nursery for 45 percent extra. Just as you will never remember where you planted those late-breaking, expensive *Allium* unless you've marked it—you won't remember the scads of important details either. Trust me. Keep a book.

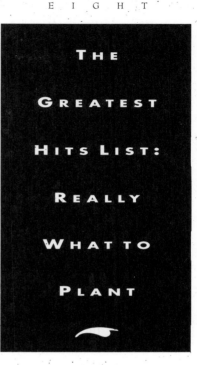

THE GREATEST HITS LIST: REALLY WHAT TO PLANT

Failproof. Discriminating.
Deliberate. Sophisticated.
Beautiful.

There has fallen a splendid tear
From the passion-flower at the gate.
She is coming, my dove, my dear;
She is coming, my life, my fate;
The red rose cries, 'She is near, she is near;'
And the white rose weeps, 'She is late;'
The larkspur listens, 'I hear, I hear;'
And the lily whispers, 'I wait.'
Alfred Lord Tennyson, *Maud*, Part I

Of the zillions of plantable things from which to choose, my greatest hits are formulated from what I've found to be the cream of the crop. If you choose to grow only plants included here, and you live in any hospitable part of our great America (not vouching for Alaska, nor the hottest spots like Baja), then you will have a gorgeous garden. This compendium has as its guideline purely my personal taste and experience—so it is, by nature, a great hodgepodge of shrubs, trees, bulbs, perennials, even annuals—organized only by alphabet. Not surprisingly, you will find a concentration of dark and bronze-foliaged, big exotic-leaved, and cool-color and white flowering plants not needing extraordinary amounts of sun, as that is how my garden grows. Everything exceptional or noteworthy ever crossing my gardening path, be it a shrub as standard but sumptuous as a *Hydrangea macrophylla* or a plant as obscure as my sacred lilies of India, *Sauromatum guttatum*, is included in this scant six-year compilation of what I've come to know, love, and usually trust.

By now you know what a wonderful garden is all about—a marvelous dense and diverse mixture of things overlapping and interplaying—and the magical serendipity of it all coming together as *your* personal statement. Each entry will not necessarily be the most definitive or exhaustive survey on said given item (no *Hortus,* in other words) but will reveal what really needs to be known, i.e. the Dirt! About each gorgeous bit of flora I'll relate the following as it has acclimated itself in the Benson garden, become familiar in my not-very-long seasoned exercise, and made itself known from my ever-expanding gardening library:

1. How to pronounce it, so you'll never feel like an ass when ferreting it out. There's nothing worse than the occasional snobby nursery-person who delights in correcting your pronunciation. Also an indication of compatible zones taken from diverse sources ranging from fine catalogs to The American Horticultural Society's *Encyclopedia of Garden Plants.*

2. Any good stories attached to the plant; from the fable of Narcissus to the sacred stature of the Lotus. It's fun to be aware of these tidbits, and knowing them makes a tour round your garden much more interesting to your friends and more significant to you as you're planting and observing.

3. How it differs (if it does, and if not, then the essentials) from normal horticultural practice in my experience; in my no "full sun" environs, for example, what right have I to be the benefactress of glorious iris and exotic South African bulbs? Also when to expect it to bloom or peak.

4. The best way to buy it (no one ever explains to my liking why one plant is better started from a bare root and another will save you years of aggravation if you buy it full grown; they are always too preoccupied detailing how to grow it from that ubiquitous old seed!); how to plant it (this will cut through myriad idiosyncrasies), and what time of year yields the most immediate results. As well as how much or how little you need to make a robust statement.

5. Particular things to note, e.g., what to do with the plant in autumn (or at the end of its growing cycle, which occasionally diverges), what to do in spring (or at the beginning of its growing season, if it is one of those odd, but important, plants that differ, like hellebores); and what to watch for, as in the case of late-breaking perennials like beautiful balloonflowers, *Platycodon.*

6. Any last appropriate words to the wise: often there will be one little trick connected to a plant making the difference between a beloved thing and a dog (as in wretch or mark-downs—surely not pooches).

When faced with plants on this list, you will not be forced to stumble around in shady forests, waste your time wading through scores of books, or find yourself in a mystifying leaky greenhouse. So here's your definitive how to—why to—when to—and what not to do—and, rest assured, not one entry is tasteless, trite, trivial, tired, or trying—each is significant (if not extraordinary) and will set your garden apart from the ho-hum herds.

By no means the end-all, be-all, this list is an ongoing experiment. Surely five years from now, it will change greatly, be less cursory, and will acquire a different energy and economy. It's a "movable feast," a product of evolution requiring additional vantage points and ever-changing cultivated information. I'd be most pleased if you more erudite gardeners would write to me—answering my many questions—advising me about wonders of which I'm still unaware. Gardening never stops—like life—like art. For sure, my endemic reportage is ongoing and always open to mutation, rotation, and innovation. Your gardening endeavor should be no different.

If it occurs to you there is an obvious omission of something divine and impossible to consider hackneyed, like *Veronica* 'Sunny Border Blue', perennial *Salvia, Lupine,* or *Gentiana,* it's because it's languished in my garden after numerous attempts to nurture it. After all, a plant isn't glorious *unless you can grow it,* and I figure if it's hard for me with my great dirt and unflagging enthusiasm—it might be hard for you, too. Other glaring exclusions include all chrysanthemum and phlox (because I detest the beasts), most everything flowering glaring yellow and orange, and a huge group of normally acceptable plants not considered by me to be garden-worthy because the flower is small or ditsy, the habit scraggly, the leaf ugly, or I just basically loathe the way it looks, like *Dianthus* (those silly "pinks"), *Amsonia, Alchemilla* (a weed if I ever saw one), *Liatris, Lychnis, Anchusa, Penstemon,* and the billowing "baby's breath," *Gypsophila.* So why bore you with my failures and aversions when there is so much to enthrall you—most easy to grow and all far more rewarding.

To make this list as accessible as the Michelin guide or the movie's star-rating systems, I've devised a ranking system, too:

√√√ ☐ This particular entry is absolutely enchanting, incredibly seductive, or will add massive amounts of drama to your garden, the plants for which you will most appreciate this book; you *must* check them out once your garden gets going as the epitome of authentic personal expression.

√√ ☐ These entries are the sum and substance of your garden, the ones to buy and try first, totally rewarding, handsome to stunning, nearly foolproof—the mainstays, and the kind of which you can never have enough; check into them *immediately.*

√ ☐ These items might be fleeting or more of a curiosity, difficult to cultivate but worth it, less tricky than anything else blooming at the time, or lastly, not appropriate to the other two categories but fine enough to make their presence known in your garden; check on them wholeheartedly.

HM ☐ These honorable mentions are wonderful and worthwhile plants that are all represented in my garden and should definitely be considered for yours as well, but inspire in me only diffident love as opposed to outright passion.

The cultural tips and hints contained herein are again, a mere product of my limited experience to date. What works for me I hope will work for you, but the mutability of nature is a well-known theme, and its vicissitudes might hold in store many surprises—both kind and mean, good and bad. Assuming it's understood this is not meant to be *the last word*, but a very helpful beginning—here dawns your entry through the gates to Botanical Heaven.

HM *Acanthus spinosus* (a-**kanth**-us)
Classic perennial. Zones 5–9.
The spiny, shiny leaves were the architectural inspiration for many Greek column plinths and the high spires of dense funnel-shaped cream-hooded mauve flowers in June are divine. Growing in a shady dell in Portofino refutes the notion they must have sun. Grand.

√√ *Acer palmatum* (**ay**-sur pahl-**may**-tum)
Beloved Japanese maples, most hardy to at least Zone 5. [See Chapter III, pp. 76–78.]
Aside from the fact they can be small or large, bushy or low and mounded, spreading or upright and columnar, I've already waxed didactic about these superb classic ornamental specimen trees, except whatever time has elapsed since that last rhapsody in Chapter III and now, has just made me love them more. It's solidly mid-spring and they're all laden with buds or just exploding into intricate leaf. I did break down and order the "golden full moon maple" from Wayside Gardens, as Mountain Maples surprisingly didn't have it, and it happily arrived looking pretty good and is already set out in the golden border, as Japanese maples can be planted spring or fall. The ground receiving it was dug deep and amended with all the nutritious elements in my weighty garden cart. Even threw in a little extra acid, as they like it so much. The leaves are unfurling in a sublime way, looking a bit like knife-pleats.
As I wander around each day, I stop to rid each maple of its spent branches, which look gray instead of healthy brown-red and can be simply snapped off with your fingers. Just last weekend we saw a breathtaking maple at Marder's. Big and lush, with *two colors* on one tree. Slashing through the middle of the burgundy palmate leaves is a grand swathe of chartreuse— pretty amazing what these grafters can do. Anyway, Irving has his heart set on it, and far be it from me to deter him if he decides to take the expensive plunge. An ongoing love tryst with Japanese maples will grace your garden and buoy your spirits for a long, long time. [See photo in Chapter III, p. 77.]

√√ *Acidanthera murialae* (a-kid-an-**the**-ra **mewr**-ree-el-eye)
Corm to be dug and stored over winter. Hardy only in Zone 10.

A beautiful flower native to tropical Africa, but easy to grow. Its cycle and cultural practice are like that for gladioli, but the similarity ends there. Where gladioli are often too stiff and floriferous for their own good, this delicate flower makes everyone sigh, and at eighteen inches it's just perfect. Beautiful enough to be highlighted as a specimen, its graceful ornamental leaves and arching stems are worthy of commanding their space and setting a mood. Setting a few out on our most focal table a few years ago (in a weighted, spiky *kenzan* that allows flowers to stand erect and be noticed), our good Japanese friend Yuki demonstrated how the placement of a few sizable, smooth rocks just touching the base of the flower's stem makes all the difference in these sparse but sublime arrangements. The lovely white flower rises slightly above the leaves and is blotched with a tempting maroon center.

Definitely not one to overlook, acidanthera are available in most bulb catalogs, not very expensive, and worthy of buying at least fifty. You'll want to pot up minimally a dozen in a suitably austere container for pleasure on your patio or deck and grow the rest in your cutting garden—this is one you can't have enough of. If space is limited and it's a choice between acidanthera and gladioli—forget the gladioli.

They like sun, but perform beautifully for me. Like all bulbs, they favor bonemeal—so mix plenty of it in your pot or garden when you plant in spring, cover with four inches of soil after the last frost. It will bloom in July onward and is incredibly long-lasting (it smells good too). When the leaves turn yellow/brown in autumn, carefully dig up and cut off the foliage. Dry the corms on a tray in a warm part of your house for a week or so. You will notice a separation between the spent part of the corm and the new part—remove the crusty old part and dust the corms with "Bulb Dust" (at least that's what it's called at our Agway). Place in a mesh bag and hang in an airy place in your garage or basement. You will also find lots of baby corms have developed, these little cormels could be collected and propagated and will attain flowering size in a matter of years—but if you want to increase your stock of acidanthera—it's much easier just to buy more. A discreet beauty.

The Acidanthera, isn't it lovely?

√√ *Aconitum napellus* (ak-oh-**ny**-tum)
Valuable perennial border plant. Hardy Zones 3/4–9.

To explain the diverse common names of "monkshood" and "wolfbane," you must consider different properties. "Monkshood" must clearly refer to the helmet-shaped flower, and wolfbane derives from its poisonous aspect (imagine setting it out to attract and then slay wolves—the cute guy in *An American Werewolf in London* probably hadn't mastered this simple solution)—as it's poisonous in every part:—stem, flowers, leaves—the whole plant. Good for witch's brews, if that's your thing, but no good for kids or pets. At first, I confused aconitum with delphinium because they share the same leaf habit and growth proportions. But have discovered delphinium come in many more varieties, are infinitely more beautiful in flower, and bloom much earlier; *but* aconitum isn't bad and *much* easier to grow. Blooming in late summer, flowers are like little purple cloches arranged on an upright spike that last weeks on end.

They don't need full sun and are happy in any rich, well-prepared, *moist* soil. Cool nights (like on the teeming werewolf-strewn moors of the English countryside) really turn them on. Buy them at the nursery or from a catalog that ships big plants (like Crownsville or Niche). A group of six or more will enhance any border. Good drainage is a requisite, and some staking may be required, but if you plant them close enough together, they reach out and thrive on one another for support. A favorite of mine. [See p. 249 for illustration.]

HM *Adlumia fungosa* (ad-**lum**-ee-ah fung-**oh**-sa)
Delicate flowering vine, supposedly biennial. Zones 4–8.

This "biennial" has persisted for me for three years. Pale green tiny leaflets on pliable stems meander in and out of the shrubbery in the hammock grove in a curiously pleasing way. Thrives on shade and moisture. A gardener's delight.

√ *Agapanthus praecox/orientalis* (ag-a-**panth**-us **pry**-koks)
An African herb like no other. Not hardy except in Zones 9–10—pot it.

Whether or not to include this fabulous flower on my list put me in a quandary, as my luck with it hasn't broken any records, but God, it is a beautiful vision. Starbursts of electric blue-mauve blooms—big round umbels of them—rise high above straplike leaves on strong stems and last from June to August. I see it in all the nurseries profusely in flower—why, tell me why, won't it bloom for me? Supposedly any soil will do, and it needs lots of sun. *Crowded roots* potted up are its nirvana, so they say. Years ago I obtained my thick, fleshy roots from Corys Heselton's esteemed but defunct Gladside Gardens (now two-year plants are available from Crownsville and some others), crammed them in a ten-gallon pot just like advised—the rhizomes barely covered with a half-inch of soil. Every year I watch and wait, hauling them out in spring and back into the living room in winter. Determined to make these babies bloom, I stubbornly refuse to buy a nursery plant in flower, which is probably what you should do and save yourself this aggravation.

Placed on the sunniest part of the property when outdoors (at the pool's edge), mine leaf like crazy (which means they're very much alive), but *never* bloom. Native to the southern tip of Africa, the geographically incorrectly named "lily of the Nile" has become a true enigma to my gardening spirit. Irving, who adores this plant and eternally comments when caught in bloom somewhere other than our house, is threatening to toss it out if it doesn't produce this summer. Last year talking to it and fertilizing did no good; over this winter—after garnering several new opinions—I tried the new approach of withholding water and any nutrients and just generally being "mean" to it. The foliage seems to be more robust than ever—we'll see whether this summer is *the* one of glory or demise. I hope the former, finally. (It finally bloomed. Bravo.)

√√ *Ajuga reptans* (uh-**jew**-guh **rep**-tanz)
Great ground cover in the mint family. Hardy to Zone 2. [See Ground Covers, p. 267.]

√√√ *Allium* (**al**-lee-yum)
A huge group of bulbous flowering onions. Many hardy to Zones 3–4.

An incredibly diverse group of plants, some of which smell just awful, others which are absolutely beautiful and hardly reek at all—or look so great, you just ignore the stench. The name actually means garlic. I'll not delve in-depth into the wide-ranging spectrum, but will tell you of the most delectable. They all love sun, but seem happy enough here, though I'm careful never to bury them at the back of the garden. These are planted in autumn with plenty bonemeal worked into the dirt and must be well-marked because many species are late to emerge in spring, but faithfully return year after year.

Starting with the biggest and showiest first, there is a relatively new (Jan Bijl received the patent in 1986 after coddling it for twenty-two years) allium on the market called 'Globemaster', and even from Dutch Gardens it costs $15.75 for each bulb! Unable to resist the allure of a description detail-

Worth-waiting-for *Agapanthus*.

ing a ten-inch sphere covered with *eleven hundred star-shaped florets* and lasting for a month on forty-inch stems, I ordered two and surrounded them with a half-dozen *giganteum*, which are more or less the same thing but not as spectacular, and only four bucks each. Well, fantastic they were, standing as proud as peacocks during the Garden Tour (in fact, all of June) and the two 'Globemaster' were unquestionably outstanding. Instructions say to give these big alliums space and plant them a foot or more apart, but that would look absurd. I left about three inches between bulbs positioned together, center in the blue garden—they looked perfect.

My near favorite allium, however, is listed two ways: either *A. albopilosum* or *A. christophii* 'Star of Persia'. What a beauty. Produces a huge flower-head, like the 'Globemaster', ten or more inches across, but instead of being dense, it is airy and light and covered with a dreamy shade of silver-violet starrier florets. Only about two feet tall, the strap-shaped leaves are a divine celadon color, and when the pubescent bud emerges it is ever so sexy. Once flowering finishes, the leaves are unfortunately a mess, so be sure to plant among ample perennials, daylilies are especially good, to hide them.

*bulgaricum
or siculum*

My absolute favorite allium is another with two names, either *A. bulgaricum* or *A. siculum*. This dreamboat is entirely different in form than the others. Growing to almost three feet, it blooms later than the others in July. Native to the south of France and Italy, it has been hardy here for two years. Rather than a big flower-ball, it produces a dense, but loose, cluster of nodding bell-shaped flowers in the surreal color combination of creamy white washed onto pale-green and suffused with beautiful burgundy markings. An absolute standout—you'll love it.

*albopilosum or
christophii*

All alliums like as much sun as possible and are great for cutting as they last in the vase a long time, if you don't mind the slight odor. Plant deeply (at least three times the depth of the bulb) preferably in autumn. They're easy, and the ones mentioned here are a delight. Forget *A. moly* available everywhere—too small and too, too yellow.

giganteum

*pulchellum (my
most recent favorite)*

Alliums are great garden punctuation.

HM *Alocasia* x *sandersei* (al-oh-**kay**-see-uh)
Tropical arum relative to be potted and brought indoors for winter.

Exotic eighteen-inch-long, wavy, arrow-shaped leaves of a metallic, glossy, deep blue-green—totally edged in white (like designer piping) are the highlight of this tropical plant. Roots don't like to be crowded. Very stylized.

Amaryllis. See *Hippeastrum*

Andromeda. See *Pieris*

√ *Anemone coronaria*, 'De Caen' group (a-**nem**-o-nee kor-on-**air**-ee-a)
Classic wind poppies. Bulb. Treat as annual in Zone 7 and north.

Invariably remind me of a Rembrandt painting—colors so rich—texture so dense. These beautiful spring flowers derive from the strangest looking little tubers (or tuberous rhizomes, to be more exact) I've ever seen, shriveled up clawlike apparitions that *must be soaked in water overnight* before planting with the little pointy claws *facing down* about one inch below the surface. South of Zone 7, it's okay to plant in fall, but wait until spring if you're in my zone or colder. I kept wondering why every other thing planted in fall bloomed (almost) except anemones till I tried spring planting, which worked like a dream. All the colors are pretty spectacular and are usually sold in a mix, but if you want to concentrate on the vibrant blue, perhaps, or white, McClure & Zimmerman sells them separately. Order in quantities of at least a few dozen or more.

Keep moist and make sure there's some sun. The pleasant leaves die back in summer, so mark your spot if you expect them to return. There are three groups in the *coronaria* group: 'De Caen' (the masterpiece ones); 'St. Brigid', which are double-flowered but pale; and 'St. Bravo', from Holland, which supposedly have bigger flowers in a wider range of colors, including terracotta (which would be really divine with the small dark *Fritillaria*) but I can't find them anywhere! These are the things that drive me mad. [See illustration in Chapter VII, p. 193.]

√√ *Anemone hupehensis japonica* (a-**nem**-o-nee hew-pee-**hen**-sis)
Beautiful border perennial. Hardy to Zone 5.

One of the stateliest perennials, in no way resembling its popular spring-blooming relative—both beautiful in differing ways. In late summer and well into fall it bears cup-shaped dogwoodlike flowers, sometimes double, that are refined and inspiring. My first came from a nearby nursery for the white garden, the classic 'Honorine Jobert', which I've supplemented with 'Whirlwind' from Carroll Gardens; both are healthy and beautiful, reaching three feet in autumn when they flower. A few to many are fine, but even one in the garden as a specimen is engaging because of its elegant habit. The dark green, deeply toothed and divided leaves are always handsome—crepey and crinkled with bronze overtones. The foliage is particularly engaging in spring when it emerges rather early on established plants.

I've since added other varieties in the border in pale mauvey-pinks, and they get more robust every year, with no bad habits. They need a half day of sun and delight in a rich, organically treated soil. As they flower into October, wait until late autumn to cut them to the ground for winter and *mulch well*. The perennial *Anemone* is synonymous with good taste, and you will love it in your garden.

√√√ *Angelica gigas* (an-**jell**-eek-a **gi**-gas)
An astounding biennial. Very hardy here in Zone 7.

A real showstopper. Nothing about this plant is ordinary and can't imagine how it got its celestial name—it should have some name that suggests out-of-this-world, yes—but heavenly, no. Superb celadon-green, large-lobed leaves divided into leaflets have a strange tropical look, plus the inimitable feature of swelling from the branch in a seductive sort of bulbous way. This unique provocative trait makes it fascinating in May and June as it rises to nearly five feet—then in July dense flower-heads of reddish-purple inflate in the same erotic bulging way and last through mid-fall. A center-stage drama piece—even one makes a big statement.

This plant is a biennial, which means it has a short life, so I always make sure to plant in early spring every other year, as it only returns once. Niche Gardens ships big lusty ones, and they're turning up at the nurseries often now. As they command a fair share of space in the border scene—place them fifteen inches apart. Cut the thick stem to six inches in late autumn. Part shade suits them fine here, but they are said to prefer sun. They're great.

√√ *Aquilegia* (ah-kwi-**lee**-jee-uh)
A most cherished perennial. Most Zones 2/3–9.

Commonly called the charming columbine, and a mainstay of English literature for centuries, they're absolutely among the royalty of perennials. With varying versions of them in every garden, I still always want more and prowl the nurseries looking for the most spectacular or new colors. Their range is pretty sensa-

The engaging columbine (*Aquilegia*).

tional, diverging from small species good in the rockery to grand clumps boasting fabulous spurred flowers. I love these soaring flowers that glide like bird's wings and are the reason for both the Latin name, *aquila* for eagle, and common name, "columbine" for dove. Conspicuously upright stalks float above the thrilling foliage. The species *A. flabellata* and *A. vulgaris* are fine plants, too, but lack the drama of the long spurred flowers (found on the hybrids like *A.* x 'Hensol Harebell' and 'McKana's Giants') and produce a chubbier, waxier bloom.

One of the first plants to appear in early spring (actually, it hardly disappears at all except in darkest winter), you will find whorling masses of its dainty scalloped blue-green tinged-with-lilac leaves one of the most enchanting first signs. These divine leaves are incredibly profuse, and if they begin looking scraggly in summer, just shear them off and in a few weeks' time tons of new growth will appear. Depending on the variety, flowering begins in May and persists through July. They want rich, moist soil and luxuriate in sun or light shade. No gardener in her right mind would want to be without this old-fashioned, utterly lovely plant. The more the better.

√ *Arisaema triphyllum* (ar-ih-**see**-muh)
Wonderful woodland jack-in-the-pulpit. Zones 4–9.
A member of the mystical *Arum* family, it truly commands a special place in my heart. Jack-in-the-pulpits burst on the scene in May—large, undulating, hooded, curious flower spathes hover over a spadix—always surprising me in its many variations of green, curiously streaked with purple, on one plant. Tends not to increase in number of stalks and flowers, but magically grows stronger, taller, more robust each year—and lasts longer. The three-part umbrellalike leaves are charming, too.

The trick is to *plant the tuber deeply*—at least to six inches in a fertile spot (heavily enrich with peat and leaf mold) where it can peep out among other garden denizens. The tuber looks somewhat like a gladiolus corm with roots sprouting from its top—plant with the *root side up* in partial to deep shade and doubly enriched soil. As Arisaema die out before summer's end (but you only need to wait for it to pop up again next May), you

A melange of mysterious hooded
Arisaema.

should mark its prescient location lest you unearth it during the fall-planting frenzy. As they are seldom seen at the nurseries, I've ordered mine from various places, but have now hit on the big find! The British Jacques Amand catalog, which takes credit cards and ships just fine, offers ten different varieties, of which I have ordered the most mysterious five—striped ones, inwardly curled apricot with folded mouth, and a purple one with white stripes that has a spadix touching the ground—all fabulous looking. The tubers were just sprouting on arrival and are now all planted deeply—I can hardly contain myself knowing the idiosyncratic *Arisaema* are working their way up to me.

√√√ *Aristolochia durior* (ar-is-to-**loh**-kee-uh)
Exotic twining vine hardy to at least Zone 7.

The common name for this beauty is "Dutchman's pipe" because at one stage its weird and irregular, but fabulous, flowers have the look of a big old leprechaunish pipe. The Latin name from the Greek *aristos,* meaning best, and *locheia,* meaning birth, pertain to some medicinal virtues applied to childbirth it was thought to possess; but to me it simply signifies one of the best climbing plants you can grow and quite the aristocrat.

Although there are many tropical species of this plant, the one mentioned here is the hardy one. Not only am I having great luck with mine, in its second year, planted in a semi-shaded area on the back fence, but an in-the-know guy told me he saw it covering the entire side of a barn in Bridgehampton and looked as though it had been there for years. Mine hasn't flowered yet, but the three-hundred-dollar mature version at Marder's has been bearing miraculous flowers since June; now, in August, there are more weird flowers than ever. Theirs is potted and kept under a lath house. The extraordinary flowers are huge, blotched, deep dark burgundy affairs with a distinct look of otherworldliness.

But even without flowers it's wonderful, as it grows incredibly quickly once it gets started in late spring and bears masses of intertwining heart-shaped crepe-textured leaves. It is said to grow to thirty feet and is a perfect choice for covering buildings, arbors, or fences. At maturity, I've heard, each leaf can be as much as a foot long.

You can order it from Forest Farm or Wayside Gardens as a tiny cutting; but my $18.95 attempt from Wayside didn't succeed—and of course, what they delivered was scarcely there. My bountiful one came from Amagansett Nursery, cost $35 and was already established at eighteen inches when planted in June. You only need one of these as it is so rampant, and you're better off to get a well-started one at your nursery (maybe they can order it).

I've recently read it should be pruned back hard in winter; but this was unbeknownst to me as I let it go during its first cycle, only doing some cutting back of limp-looking shoots in late March, and it thrived just fine. When it's mature, pruning is probably much more in order.

They say it really needs room to grow and somewhere to climb if it is to bear flowers. Robust and great, plus the bizarre flowers will just amaze you.

HM *Arum dracunculus/Dracunculus vulgaris* (**a**-rum drac-**unc**-u-lus)
Strange spatheing tuber. Supposedly Zones 8–10.

The name means "small dragon" and the plant is worthy of a Spielberg treatment. A spotted spearlike projection unfurls into triangularly arranged spotted leaves before the blackish spadix protrudes from a scarlet spathe. Mulch and withhold water. Fantastic. Order from Breck's. Sun or part shade suits it fine.

√√ *Aruncus dioicus* (ah-**run**-kus dee-o-ee-kus)
Terrific large perennial. Hardy to Zones 3–9.

Commonly called "goat's-beard" because of the large showy panicle of white plumes spurting up in June. In habit, it's much like a giant astilbe, though not quite as refined. Its membership in the rose family is only slightly apparent in its finely pleated, often doubly compound ovate leaves. It all adds up to a pleasing feathery appearance. When in full flower it reaches about six feet, so if you're planting young ones—be sure to put them at the rear of the garden because they don't like to be moved around.

Mine came as small plantlings many years ago from Crownsville and became fine specimens by the second year and are very much in evidence today. The bronze foliage powerfully erupts from the ground in mid-April on strong red stems. The rich soil and morning sun of the white garden suits them perfectly. At the slightest sign of withering in autumn, cut it back hard to the ground. Great as a border backdrop and to mix with other feathery perennials. [See illustration p. 234]

√ *Asarum europaeum* (as-**ar**-um)
A glorious ground cover. Hardy to Zone 4. [See Ground Covers.]

√√ *Aster* x *frikartii* 'Wonder of Staffa' or 'Monch' (**ass**-ter fri-**kart**-ee-eye)
Charming perennial wildflower hybrid. Hardy to Zone 4.

Only this singular aster is cited because it's so much more attractive than all the others I've come across or grown. Though the name *Aster* is Latin for star and conjures up nice images, generally, asters can tend to be a bit weedy and their yellow centers so focal the colored petals are obliterated. Not the case with this charmer that only grows to thirty inches, contains itself perfectly, doesn't need staking like all the others, and produces big lavender-blue flower-heads continuously from August till late autumn—probably the longest-blooming aster. A real treasure.

It needs sun, but performs fine for me at the front of the blue border with afternoon sun. A well-drained soil is a must, so it's great for slopes if you've got them. Though it's hardy, apply a good mulch in winter. And of course, for a bushier, more floriferous plant, *pinch back* the growing stems to half their size a few times in June. I've had equal success with nursery plants and the good perennial catalogs. This one is a favorite of all who know it.

√√ *Astilbe* (as-**till**-bee)
Wonderful, dependable perennial. Zones 4–8.

Often called "false spirea," which is an injustice as they are much more regal than *Spirea* and "false" anything is a misleading word in this trustworthy case. This is another of those priceless plants of which you can never have enough. Each year yet another hard-to-fill niche takes on new character by planting a few astilbe. There are many kinds, none bad, but some much more divine than others. All have fluffy flower-spikes ranging from white to pink to red to mauvey-purple and exist in varying sizes to a solid four feet. The individual flowers are minute, but borne in thousands high above the leaves on graceful branches giving a billowy look like colored clouds. Look for *Astilbe* x *arendsii* hybrids, as they are the result of Georg Arends, a German astilbe fanatic who produced many of the best crosses. *A.* x *arendsii* 'Fanal' is dark crimson (gorgeous) and 'Deutschland' is white. Another not to be missed is *A. taquetti* 'Superba'—blooming in mid-July in a gorgeous raspberry color with flower-heads like fluffy stalactites—denser and dreamier than most.

Definitely buy these at your nursery—the biggest ones you can find (though I have a few dwarfs for just right spots I adore). All astilbe foliage is handsome, but naturally some more so than others, so look closely at the intricate leaves, many of which are bronze-toned or definitive burgundy. I've planted countless mail-order seedlings and bare-roots, and none are as rewarding as the stout ones carried home from the nurseries full-blown. Around here they're in abundant supply, I hope for you too. They don't wither in the sun—they luxuriate in the shade—they don't send out any unwanted seedlings—never need staking—pretty close to perfect. By May first, my gardens are filled with several versions of astilbe foliage that stand out like stouthearted sweethearts—dwarfing most other perennials. What they do need is soil rich in organic matter (so amend it well), and moisture because their thin roots need to spread toward nutrients and water. In the border or treated as specimen groupings, they're just splendid. Should be one of the first plants on your list. [See illustration in Chapter VIII, p. 234.]

√√√ *Athyrium nipponicum* 'Pictum' (a-**thir**-ee-um)
The gorgeous Japanese painted fern.

Athyrium is a big group most easily classified as "lady ferns." The one mentioned above is an absolute standout and must-have. Its coloring is probably the most interesting of any plant I've ever seen or grown—dissected fronds are silvery overall, but highlighted with green and brushed with subtle burgundy strokes—like a painting, as 'Pictum' suggests. Too stunning to be simply grouped with the other "ferns." More ground-hugging than erect, they never exceed fifteen inches, but spread far beyond that. They must have a rich, moist, soil in which to luxuriate. Shade suits them fine, and they're the perfect foil to lighten dim areas. A little finicky in their first few years, once they really kick in, you win the prize.

Mark them carefully, as their fronds take their time to materialize in spring. Unfortunately, small scurrying creatures of one sort or another like to dine on the ones in the rockery, but never go near the older ones in the south shade path. For some wonderful reason, the slugs don't seem to like them. Both nursery-bought and ones ordered from Montrose Nursery (good catalogs all have them) have been equally divine. Place them prominently and enjoy them for years. [See photo in Chapter VI, p. 178.]

HM *Bambusa* (bam-**boo**-za)
Good old bamboo. Many need heat, but some tolerant to 0 degrees. [See Chapter IV, p. 123]

Nothing like a dense mound of whispering bamboo for an enigmatic effect, but take care: its invasiveness is rampant and must be controlled with metal, fiberglass, or cement barriers. Evergreen *Fargesia nitida* is the one the BBG endorses as "noninvasive," shade-tolerant, and with a drooping "umbrella habit." Kurt Bluemel has this near-perfect variety.

√√ *Baptisia australis* (bap-**tiz**-ee-a)
Important blue-violet flowering perennial. Zones 3–9.

Known as "false indigo," once it gets started this long-lived perennial is a highlight of the border. After being taunted by Steven Hamilton's description as the "joy of the flower bridge" in Shelburne Falls, Massachusetts (a sanctified spot somewhere in the Berkshires), four summers ago I searched around for not-so-easy-to-find baptisia. Finally planted three bare-root from Crownsville and three potted-in-leaf from McConnell's—both waited till the third summer to produce glorious bloom, but the cloverlike blue-green leaves on three- to four-foot stems were a delight in the border during the anticipation. Happy in our afternoon sun, once they established themselves, racemes of pealike, blue-purple, nodding flowers were displayed at the end of June lasting through most of July.

Rather late to emerge in spring, make sure to *mark their position well* and look for little purple pointed shoots. Choose their location adeptly because once planted, they have a distaste for being moved and a hugh root mass—although they'll probably survive just fine, but procrastinate for a few seasons before flowering again. Their strong stems stand on their own and don't need staking, but a grow-through support keeps them in bounds. It is said baptisia should be cut to the ground after the flowers fade, but that would leave an unspeakable hole in my border, so I allow the charming leaves to persist, only cutting the fading flower stems once bloom is over. In autumn they are cut to the ground, which seems to work just fine. Because of a long, strong taproot they require little feeding or watering, but do prefer a slightly acid soil on the dry side. Include this plant early on in your garden scheme and position it near the rear of the border. Unique among perennials.

√√√ *Begonia,* Tuberous (bee-**goan**-yuh)
The most spectacular flowering tender corm. Not hardy. [See Chapter VII, pp. 190–191.]
It is evident by now how I feel about this magnificent flower. If you can provide a cool and moist place in your garden and want to grow the most incredible of tender flowers to bloom the entire summer—there is no contest—any other annual will pale in comparison, and many bulbs and even perennials will simply be accessories and outshined. Mine grow along the shade path and in the white garden with its few hours of morning sun, where they bloom and bloom and bloom from mid-June till end of September. Before the first frost even thinks of hitting, they should be dug up, dried out for a while, and stored in dry peat moss. June bloom is possible, however, only if you start them indoors in March. The comments they elicit are more than inspired and the pleasure you derive will overshadow any effort they require.

The cool and moist environment they thrive in demands *shelter* (wind is no good, but they want nicely circulating air), *humidity* (but not overwatering—no night sprinklers, in other words), and *bright dappled light* (dense shade is as bad as full sun). I know they sound picky, but they have a right to be, and any shady spot with filtered light where it's not too, too hot should suit them just fine. Out of fifteen plants last summer, every one blossomed like mad and not one was hit by any sort of blight.

There are basically two types: *Begonia* x *tuberhybrida*, which grow upright (the ones you want for planting out in the garden) and the 'Pendula', or cascading type, which are only suited to growing in baskets or pots. A rather spectacular effect was achieved last summer in the shade path by having the gorgeous upright beauties in the sloping ground, as well as hanging baskets of drooping cascading types from the limbs of the overhanging trees. Among these two types: the flowers come in various forms—rose, camellia, ruffled, single, and only one I'm not crazy about—carnation. Colored white, rose, salmon, apricot, scarlet, and red, some also have distinctive edgings of a second color and are termed 'Picotee' or 'Marginata'. 'Bouton de Rose' is particularly beautiful—cream edged deep pink—but they're all beautiful—you can hardly go wrong.

As begonia tubers are relatively cheap, you can buy new ones each year and pot them up in

In my favorite old stone pot, any old terracotta, or in the ground, the tuberous Begonia blossom is the stuff of which sighs are made.

early spring if you don't care to be bothered with the storage routine. But not starting them indoors is unforgivable as it deprives you of weeks of wonderful bloom. Start them in pots, trays, or flats (in a desperate moment, I used a disposable supermarket broiling pan and it did the trick just fine) filled with the usual good soil mix and *plenty of peat moss*. Bury the tuber (round side down, depressed side up) so it is only barely covered by the mix. Put in a sunny place—keep watered—and wait. In a few weeks fat pink eyes (buds) will appear that will shortly after begin to leaf. By the time mid-May rolls around (after all danger of frost, of course, has passed) it is time to plant outdoors (just sink them up to the stems in well-prepared earth) or into whatever comely container you've chosen to show them off—they will be almost ready to flower. I've read a lot of chitchat about removing buds till stems show three pair of leaves, but have ignored it and mine couldn't be lovelier.

If, like me, you can't bear to toss out the beauties in autumn—dig them up at the end of September and put them in a dry place till the foliage dies down. Remove the stems and store in dry peat moss in *marked* cartons in a cool dry place over winter. The Van Engelen bulb cartons are especially good for this. When long-awaited March rolls around—dust off the dirt and peat after their winter's nap—be cautious not to disturb those little specks of white you might see, which are their eyes, or growing points. If they should feel hollow, then something has gone wrong (too cold, too much moisture?). Throw them out, but don't waste a second, and go right out and buy new ones. It's a constant source of stupefication to me that a tuber purchased for $1.49 at the Agway can yield such an abundant, awe-inspiring plant.

√ *Bergenia* (bur-**jen**-ee-a)
Thick-leaved ground-hugging perennial. Zones 3–8.
Gertrude Jekyll, in her wisdom, adores this plant. It flourishes in dry, sunny areas where "*Hosta* will not thrive." Likes poor soil and persists all year. Cut back the homely flowers the second they flag to better appreciate the leathery spoon-shaped leaves.

Betula pendula (**bet**-yew-luh)
Beautiful birch trees. Zones 3–8. [See Chapter III, p. 79.]
I mention only one species of fascinating birch because it is the one jubilantly grown by us—'Youngii' is our beloved variety, with branches that brush the pond's surface—or would reach the ground in another situation. Drifting over our pond, it's a joy all year with its gorgeous white peeling bark (the kind so great for the immortal love letters) and willowy weeping branches festooned with crinkled pale green ovate leaves. In quite deep shade, it persists like a prince.

There are countless others equally divine, and this is a genus of trees definitely worthy of your immersion. Birch fanatics think nothing of washing them with bleach and hosing them down to dispel the mildew that would otherwise mar the whiteness. The whitest-white bark belongs to the *Betula jacquemontii* birches, which are said to be difficult, but are sooo elegant. My first Madison Avenue store opened with huge tubs containing whiter-than-white birches in the front; the look was great, but they perished in a few short years. However, the middle of Manhattan and maintainance by dubious shop girls doesn't mean a thing to me now and I'm avid to try again. White bark, however, isn't the whole story, and other birches are said to be easy to grow and thrive in most soils. There are countless ornamental types, I believe all with the irresistible peeling-bark quality: *B. lutea* has amber peeling bark and turns yellow in autumn; *B. pendula* 'Purpurea' is a weeper with purple leaves; and the fast-growing *B. maximowicizana* has grayish bark and large heart-shaped leaves—just to name a few. The nursery prices around here are pretty palatable for quite grand trees, so I do hope you'll grace your lawn with a birch or two. [See photo in Chapter III, p. 84.]

HM *Brugmansia* (brug-**man**-zee-uh)
Fabulous flowering *Datura*. Hardy only Zone 10.
The apt cognomen of "Angel's Trumpets" does a deservedly heavenly job of describing the pendant trumpet-shaped ten-inch-long white flowers of this evergreen shrub that can be trained as a standard. Keep moist and bring inside for winter. Enchanting.

√√ *Buddleia davidii* (**bood**-lee-uh duh-**vid**-ee-eye)
Wonderful butterfly bushes. Really hardy Zones 5–9.

A shrub (almost treelike) difficult to overrate, and yes, they absolutely do attract butterflies and yes, you should run right out and acquire one immediately if they are not already pervading your garden. In warmer climates than mine, they are said to be evergreen. Don't fool around with mail-order unless looking for a particular species—they're not expensive and will provide a mass of blooms in the first season if bought nursery-started. The long dark-green leaves are only okay; it's the wonderful nodding lilac-shaped flower-spikes and infallible nature of this plant that commend it.

Buddleia is super-hardy—you can move it around—neglect it—never feed it, and it still never quits as long as you remember to *cut it back hard in very early spring.* As new growth and flowers form on new wood, it is a must to shear it straight off—leaving only two to three feet standing at most. Don't be alarmed when it just sits there in this severely cut down state until well into spring—once it starts into growth it grows like wildfire.

My 'White Bouquet' bought at a nursery in the first summer of the white garden has been moved further back each year as it and the garden grew bigger till now it is at the far reaches and towers over even the astounding ten-foot *Cimicifuga racemosa.* Supposedly they require full sun—but this is just not the case. Growing many places in the Benson garden—not one in anything near full sun—they simply grow larger and flower like mad each year. Ultimately, they are said to reach a height of fifteen feet, but there's an old bush at The Bayberry behind their pond easily twenty feet or more. Behind the blue garden grows 'Black Knight' with equally non-sunny success, and under the cedars behind the pool there's a small border of *B.* 'Lochinch', ordered from Montrose for this spot because Nancy said it was more compact (only four feet) and has gray-green leaves that highlight its pale violet flowers—a perfect description for this divine smaller shrub. [See illustration Chapter VI, p. 163.]

All the above benefit greatly by *deadheading the flower-spikes* as they turn brown. This really promotes new growth and keeps them flowering well into autumn. I can't imagine a garden or border not livelier for these foolproof, delightful shrubs.

Another buddleia, more difficult and costly but seriously divine is *Buddleia alternifolia* 'Argentea'. Everything about this species is different—most spectacularly—its weeping fountainlike form. Growing most splendidly at the Villa d'Este Hotel on the magical Italian Lake Como, I was desperate to know the name of these fantastically arching, early-summer blooming shrubs, so the concierge kindly delivered to me the gardener—who, of course, didn't speak a word of English. Another tribute to Linnaeus's botanical nomenclature is that from all the *giardiniere's* excitable gesturing, I was able to decipher *Buddleia alternifolia. B. alternifolia is* available from both WFF and Wayside Gardens, and it was ordered many years ago from one or the other. My struggling one (I think it really needs sun) bears no resemblance to Villa d'Este's beauties, but as of last summer it has begun to approximate this fountain form and there've been pale flowers apparent for two years. Unlike the *davidii* species, its flowers are borne on old wood so it doesn't get pruned until after flowering. If you have space and sympathetic conditions for this lovely one—give WWF your money, order the one they say came from Hillier's great nursery in England, and coddle it for an eventual exceptional display. The Crownsville Nursery has just added it to their list as well.

HM *Caladium* x *hortulanum* (kuh-**lay**-dee-um)
Fancy-leaved old fashioned tuber. Hardy only Zone 10—dig and store.

The white form 'Candidum' and the real reds—'Postman Joyner' and 'Brandywine' are the best, the pink varieties a bit too grandmotherly. They thrive on humidity in dappled shade and adore water (can even be submerged in the pond). Best bought as tubers by mail.

Calla Lilies. See *Zantedeschia*

HM *Calonyction* (kal-loh-**nik**-tee-on)
Moonflowers. Grow as annuals.

The charming white night-blooming versions of morning glories. Give them something to climb on and place prominently where you serve cocktails on summer evenings. Easy to start from seed if you wish. They need plenty of water.

√√ *Campanula* (kam-**pan**-yoo-la)
Perennial bellflowers or canterbury bells. Zones 4–8.

No perennial border should be without this hardy charming perennial. *Campana* is Latin for bell, and certainly its pronounced bell-like flower-form is its most endearing quality. Of 250 species, all in blue-lavender tones (and occasionally white), there are some standouts. Definitely a perennial to be bought at your nursery while in bloom—in order to avoid the more homely ones and concentrate on the big looks. (I find the ground covers unappealing and many of the common forms pointless—all scraggly stems, lousy leaves, and minuscule flowers.) All fare very well in partial shade and seem not to need a thing—no particular feeding, no staking. My favorite, *C.* x *burghaltii* properly, but called *punctata* when brought home from Buckley's many years ago, has self-seeded itself all over the border and fits in everywhere, its very pale lavender (almost translucent) flowers seem to accent everything just right, whether *Filipendula* or *Baptisia*. Tons of these flowers are produced on erect wiry stems. Once it begins to bloom in mid-July it continues through autumn if careful to cut back spent stems, which are rather sad-looking anyway. I know there are many great "bellflowers," the *persicifolia* being another, of the 1,500! cultivars that abound. Check them out as they're great border fill-ins.

Our long blooming *Campanula punctata*. Beautiful, no?

HM *Campsis radicans* (**kamp**-sis)
Woody-stemmed flowering climber. Zones 5–9.

Bought well started at your nursery, it will easily attain ten feet the first season. From dark green toothed, paired leaflets emerge clusters of burnt orange trumpet-shaped flowers from midsummer on. Tidy up in spring and be patient waiting for new leaves—it's a late one, but otherwise easy. Sun helps.

√ *Canna* (**kan**-na)
Rhizomatous showoff. Only Zones 9–10—dig and store.

The first time I ever questioned a canna was when walking with the real-estate doyenne Pat Mason in Greenwich Village where it was growing in a (I thought) grand way out of a pot curiously plopped in the middle of serendipitous Bleeker Street. Answering my bemused "What's that?" with disdain, she replied, "It's *only* a canna," as if to say it wasn't worth the breath it took to say the name. I beg to differ, though I've come to understand how it can be misconceived as it's often used so slavishly in straight rows or silly round circles at shopping malls and on

The tough-as-nails *Canna rhizome*.

various other bureaucratic or institutional settings. It can be spectacular, however, thought of as a lush tropical foliage plant mixed within borders, containers, or highlighting other large-leafers like *Colocasia* and *Gunnera*—particularly if you acquire only the bronze-russet-purple-leaf varieties that I greatly favor—actually canna green is a pretty trite color. From the Greek, *kanna,* it means reed, but that is too slender a word to describe these leaves that are more like banana palms.

In my sunniest spots, 'Wyoming' and 'Black Velvet' elicit all sorts of compliments. 'Red King Humbert' is another good dark-leaved one. So smitten with the foliage, I often all but disregard the flower, which is quite elaborate and in form generally like a loose orchid. All the flower colors are in the bright, warm family, and continuous bloom is more or less guaranteed if you remove the flowering stalk as soon as it's finished.

Of all the dig-and-store plants I espouse, canna is the *undisputed easiest.* Once the edges of the leaves start to turn brown in autumn, dig up the big fat rhizomes (careful to not dig into them) and *leave as much dirt as clings,* plop into a sturdy cardboard box, and store in the warmest part of your basement or garage with the carton left open. *They don't like cold*—either in storage or during the growing season. When it's time to start them into growth in March, shake off the dirt and you will be confronted with a hard rhizomatic root mass with obvious (and probably many) growing tips that look like rocket noses. Divide the rhizomes with your

Two favored exotics: *Hedychium* (hard to find, left) and *Canna* (easy, right).

Felco or a knife, leaving as much tissue as possible to each growth bud—sometimes I even leave two growth buds. Pot them up in nice quart pots (even bigger if necessary) saved from your nursery plants—in a good soil mix—and place in a sunny spot inside till true warm weather rolls around. By then they should be near a foot tall, and once planted out, will shoot up to their stately three- to six-foot height in no time. These seem to be popular in all the wrong ways—use them thoughtfully and the rewards are great.

HM *Cardiocrinum giganteum* (**kar**-dee-oh-krai-nam)
A colossus among fabulous bulbs. Zones 7–9, they say.

Takes years to mature and flower, but when the result is a ten-foot stalk bearing 20 to 30 white, huge lilylike trumpet flowers, this is understandable. It then dies after this taxing exercise. Can be ordered from McClure & Z. and needs dappled shade and lots of fertilizer. Dazzling.

HM *Caryopteris* x *clandonensis* (kar-ee-**op**-ter-is)
"Heavenly blue" shrub. Zones 7–9.

Sparkling blue flowers cover the small shrub in late summer, after a season of fresh gray-green foliage. Cut back to three inches in early spring and position in full sun. Longwood Gardens in Pennsylvania has used it elegantly as a small hedge bordering an allée. Buy big from the nursery.

√ *Celosia cristata* (sel-**oh**-see-a)
Perennial grown as an interesting annual.

Called "cockscomb" and certainly a star among annuals in my book. The fan-shaped rippled flower-heads have more the look of striking sea corals (brain coral, to be more exact) than flowers and a velvety texture that takes them out of the ordinary. They need a fair amount of sun and little else, once you've perused your nurseries and handpicked the best shapes and dark apricot and cerise colors. Other than their look, they have the distinction of each fully formed flower-head lasting about six weeks and can be a real eye-opener in flower arrangements, not to mention at the front of the border. If you're a fan of dried flowers, which I'm not, though I was into them for a while, these dry remarkably. [See illustration in Chapter I, p. 19.]

√√ *Chelone lyonii* (kee-**loh**-nee)
Ideal flowering perennial. Zones 4–10.

Totally trouble-free reliable perennial with subdued bloom looking exactly like its common name of "false turtlehead," as well as its genus title—*chelone* is Greek for turtle. These coy blossoms appear on upright spikes in clusters of a dozen or more in August and persist well into autumn. Deadheading the flowering spikes prolongs the bloom. They grow to just a nice two feet and have a stately presence in the border with pest-free lance-shaped dark green leaves. Semi-shade suits them just fine. Early to break in spring with discernible burgundy-colored shoots, you should definitely insist your nursery order it for you if they don't have it. My first mail-order chelone was temperamental and finally succumbed to something, but my nursery-bought plants are just perfect, and even better with a grow-through support placed over them when only about ten inches into growth. The species *obliqua* is a harsh magenta pink; my *lyonii* is pleasantly pinkey-white. A really fine plant. [See illustration, p. 285]

√√ *Cimicifuga racemosa* (si-mee-si-**few**-ga)
Hardy, exciting perennial. Zones 3–8.

One of my quintet of feathery pluming things in the white garden. They flower after *Tiarella, Aruncus,* and *Rodgersia* and before *Astilbe.* The long graceful spikes of white flowers last for considerable weeks, so it's not disheartening that deadheading doesn't prolong them. They're not even so bad when they turn brown, waving in the breeze a good eight to ten feet in the air. Vigorous and tall, grow-through supports don't help—they need to be staked as they're particularly prone to toppling over after flowering. Tried first by mail order but pulled them out because they looked so spindly—soon after, exuberant five-foot ones were spotted at McConnell's and I grabbed three. They have flourished and are much taller than all the books say they're supposed to be. Naturally, I advise to buy them well-started at your nursery and plant them in the back of the border, although I've just ordered some hideously expensive ones from Kurt Bluemel because they are said to possess black leaves.

The peculiar name comes from *cimex,* a bug, and *fugo,* to flee away from, which has something to do with the cognomen "bug-bane." Assume this means the bugs don't come near them; but they are adored by the bees. Happy in partial shade and normal garden soil, they seem extraordinarily happy chez Benson. Rather late to emerge in spring, they spurt out of the ground glistening and all curled up—something like shiny, dark fern fronds—a real winner.

The feathery perennials: *Cimicifuga,* the tallest; *Aruncus,* the boisterous middle; and *Astilbe,* the demure ground-hugger.

√√√ *Clematis* (**klem-ah-tis**) *not* klem-**at**-is

An incredible assemblage of flowering vines. Most need cool to cold winters. See Chapter III, p. 89.

Where to begin? Unparalleled in beauty and variety. Justifiably mysterious when it comes to how to grow? where to grow? when to prune? Nearly unique in the concept that if planted thoughtfully, one or another clematis can bloom in sequence from spring to autumn. Flowers can be single or double, solid or centrally striped, from a few inches to six inches across, and the most delectable range of color exists. The leaves are dark and attractive, and even the seed pods appearing after the flowers are striking—their sprays prompted Vita to liken them to "Yorkshire terriers curled into a ball." You simply must grow them, even if you take the easy way out and settle only for *C. montana* 'Rubens'.

Since Arthur Steffens (the specialist grower whose crop was afflicted with the Benlate blight) can't ship anyway till he recovers from his clematis catastrophe, I heartily recommend you *buy clematis at the nursery* as well started into growth as you can possibly find. Two reasons: roots must establish themselves before top growth occurs, and second, the vining stems are thin and brittle—susceptible to breakage—so the stronger the plant, the less prone to problems. Better to get it in the ground when under substantial growth, and be careful when planting! Always plant in spring or early summer. Dig a big, deep hole, and don't skimp on composted manure and bonemeal! Bury the plant deeper than you bought it in the nursery pot—look for the first set of buds and set them *beneath the soil's surface.* This is like insurance, as these buds can develop if the top of the vine gets broken or wind-damaged or succumbs to some other tragedy. If a support has not been provided in the nursery pot, make sure a trellis or wire prop is placed right next to the crown—even if appropriately planted next to a tree or fence. The tender, precious (none of them are cheap) darlings need something to attach to in their early stages, and even if in full growth when planted—the support needs to be there next spring as soon as new shoots emerge from the earth.

Be diligent about the clematis you choose. Even in our sophisticated nurseries, many times clematis will not be labeled as to cultivar—try hard to ascertain *exactly what* it is you're buying because all clematis fall into one of three groups. Knowing which group a cultivar belongs to provides the instruction on how to care for them. "Clematis-White" is *not enough* of a description.

All clematis, with the exception of a few mounding species like *C. integrifolia,* are twining climbers and need support of a trellis, wall, fence, or most fetchingly—shrubs, trees, or foliage of other plants. Because their stems are airy and light, they never grow heavy and not a second thought needs to be given about them harming whatever they're capriciously clambering over. Aside from support, they need what I refer to as **COOL ROOTS & HOT TOPS.** The roots they develop are long and deep and prefer to snuggle up in cool and damp dirt, which means they need a consistent mulch or to be covered with a surface-rooting ground cover like ivy or *Lamium*. The vining stems and buds, on the other hand, favor five or six hours of sunlight a day. At first this incongruity made me wince, but now I've established a number of exactly these circumstances, i.e., climbing over a cedar hedge, with ivy as a ground cover, there are three 'Jackmanii'—truly one of summer's most brilliant highlights. It's perfectly understandable you must work a little harder to get these beauties to perform—and perform they will once you get them going. You'll be amazed.

The three all-important clematis groups:

Group I: The clematis species *montana* have smaller and less exotic flowers, but make up for it by producing multitudes of them and are largely known as the easy-to-grow types. Though the cool, moist root zone is still a factor, the stems are thicker, in general the plant hardier, and they grow like mad—as much as fifteen feet in one season. Best of all, no excruciating pruning dictums prevail. Generally, they need only to be pruned—*after* flowering—to eliminate dead or weak stems *or* if you deem it necessary because of space or your desire to train them around an arched trellis or something charming like that.

Group II: The second and third groups are both cultivars (not species). The second group are the large flowering cultivars that differ from the Group III in that the flowers are flatter and often double or semi-double, and most importantly—*bloom on the previous season's ripened shoots* from early to late summer. Therefore, they are pruned in very early spring before new growth starts above a pair of buds that will make themselves known to you if you really look. The most conspicuous Group IIs include the double white 'Duchess of Edinburgh', the striped, bicolored 'Nelly Moser', and the showy lilac double-flowered 'Vyvyan Pennell'.

Group III: The later, large-flowering cultivars with single out-facing blossoms are also herbaceous (not woody) types that produce their flowers on *the current season's shoots* in summer and accordingly, want to be pruned also in early spring. But don't look for buds—look for the base of the previous season's growth, which is a strong stem coming out of the earth that has produced branching. Prune just above the first branching, which will usually be about two feet above ground level. If it's lost in a shrub or so tangled you can't figure it out—snip off any obvious old growth and just leave it be. The obvious Group III examples are 'Jackmanii' and 'Jackmanii Superba' (the rich royal purple climbing all over my pool hedges—so divine); 'Lady Betty Balfour', blue-purple with pronounced yellow anthers; lovely 'Niobe'; and 'Ville de Lyon'.

In autumn, do nothing! Just simply allow them to lose their leaves, and let the tangle of stems stay there through winter, so there will be plenty for you to examine come spring. I know it sounds confusing, but please make it your business to figure it out—if you haven't thanked me for anything else—you'll thank me for nudging you toward the queen of flowering vines, clematis. For a really exotic spectacle, create a proper fence or trellis situation and have them bloom among climbing roses. They out-beauty every other flowering vine, so it is no wonder *clematis* is the Greek word for climbing plant—as this is *the one*. [See illustration in Chapter III, p. 72.]

√√ *Cleome hasslerana* (klee-**oh**-mee)
Spider flower. Definitely among the elite of annuals.

The foliage looks almost exactly like seven-lobed marijuana leaves, so it's a great cover in the event you want to tuck the real plant into your gardening scheme and it makes you nervous. More importantly, cleome bears singular, supernatural, airy flower clusters rising up from prickly stems (be sure to wear your gloves when cutting) which can reach four feet! The big round ball of a flower protrudes from flushed narrow petals with long projecting stamens that have a life of their own—just glorious as their name implies, from the Greek *kleos* for glory. They come in an acceptable deep pink, 'Pink Queen' and 'Rosea', or all white 'Helen Campbell', though the white's not really as fantastic. Cut the main flowering stem for the vase, and more and more flowers will appear from side shoots (though not quite as robust as the first, main bud).

This is also relatively easy to grow from seed, but then you have to wait till August for flowers. Buy a flat (or half a flat) at the nursery in early June for more immediate results, but don't get suckered into buying them by the one-stem-per-pot for ten dollars. One of the best looking flowers in the garden in late summer. Fullest sun you can manage is their preference, and no extra water required. [See illustration in Chapter I, p. 19.]

HM *Clintonia uniflora* (sounds like our president)
Hardy flowering perennial. Zones 4–8.

Listed in all gardening tomes, yet I can find it nowhere. A member of the lily family, it blooms white from a rosette of broad, glossy leaves and likes a woodsy site. Sounds lovely, so I hope some Bill-minded nursery will make it popular. Just doing my part.

√√√ *Clivia miniata* (**klī**-vee-a)
Fabulous bulbous flowering plant. Grow indoors unless Zone 9 or 10.

This exceptional beauty was regally named for Lady Florentina Clive, Duchess of Northumberland, evidently a pretty, chic aristocrat predisposed to a conservatory brimming with the abundant South African "kaffir lily." Not only is the flower to drool over, the leaf structure goes beyond architectural into the realm of royally handsome. Deep, darkest green, smooth, strap-shaped leaves radiate in asymmetric arcs from a central core. This, be assured, is enough to command as much space as you might want to afford it. When it blooms, the to-sigh-for umbels of tubular, pendant salmon flowers with pale butter-colored centers—at least twenty or thirty—are out of this world. I know there is a creamy white version too, but it has not crossed my path. Bio-Quest International now offers the softly colored version.

Though never seen in a nursery around here, I've occasionally spotted them in Manhattan florists at grand prices like seventy-five bucks. Most sophisticated bulb people offer it to plant up yourself (at other varying degrees of expensive prices). Worth every dime. Potted up and kept tenderly inside, mine came from the now-defunct Gladside Gardens and made me wait two years for bloom. Now, kept out of direct sun, in a pot seemingly too small for its great rhizomatous root mass (it likes that—being root-bound), it bloomed like clockwork at the beginning of each spring (until this one, when it waited till May tenth) and grows bigger and more graceful each year. Sans question, no lover of things of beauty could resist this.

√ *Cobaea scandens* (**koh**-bee-a)

Impressive flowering annual vine here. Hardy Zones 9–10.

"Cathedral-bells" or "cup-and-saucer vine" are its everyday names. Aside from gigantic bell-shaped deep violet flowers, it's also blessed with bronze leaves in its younger state. Cobaea supposedly need sun, but after bringing it home and not finding the right sunny place, I planted it toward the rear of the blue garden, hoping it would mingle with clematis on treetrunks here and a trellis there. As summer progressed, it made its way up the trellis and tree but nary a flower was to be seen—at eye-level anyway. Always too busy looking down at the gardens searching out weeds and what needs to be deadheaded—I should've been looking up— way up! Irving arrived for an August weekend and his first question was, "What's going on in the tall cedar by the pond? It's filled with flowers!" Having no idea what he was talking about, I rushed out and beheld the cobaea, which had risen something like twenty-five feet and flourished all through the cedar with gigantic flowers. I was seriously amazed.

Veltheimia (left) and *Clivia* (right) are all the houseplants a good gardener needs.

Needless to say, impressed with this miraculous rampant climber, I now recommend it highly. Am definitely going to try it again this summer in our new clearing that actually does have some sun—where it should be even more astounding. If you live in a warm climate—it's evergreen to boot, but as an annual it's pretty fabulous. If a comely one shows up at your nursery—grab it. The huge blooms supposedly open green and change to mauve, then to intense violet as they age, but seeing only the finished product high in the tree, I missed this probably delightful stage.

HM *Colchium autumnale* (**kol**-chi-um)
Charming autumn blooming corm. Zones 4–9.

Great big wine-goblet-shaped mauvy-pink important flowers in September from huge leaves, which you must take care to bury among abundant ground cover or perennials all summer. Order in spring and plant in July—even six make a beautiful statement.

√√ *Colocasia esculentum* (kol-**oh** kah-zee-a)
Huge-leaf exotic 'Taro'. Dig and store north of Zone 8.

Big, dramatic, and very easy to grow. The gigantic heart-shaped leaves enlarge to as much as three feet long and nearly as wide. This is one time not to ignore the instructions of "Plant at least 2 feet apart." These "elephant-ears" need lots of room to create their divine tropical background. The tubers you will carefully dig up and store in autumn are the stuff of the common tropical food "poi," but there is no flower to speak of. Unfortunately, they lack variety and come in only one shade of green-green, but the overall effect is heavenly. Listed in many catalogs, often by their common name; but as distinctions are nonexistent—seems okay to order them from anywhere. Six of them make a seriously striking statement as they are the ultimate tropical backdrop.

Many horticultural types class them as water plants, as they can be grown in mud or shallow water, but they do just fine in ordinary ground here in East Hampton, and I do try to remember to water them because my "rain forest" is lacking sprinklers—but not going overboard, they still seem quite happy. Otherwise, the digging-and-storing routine is nearly identical to that for *Canna* (which see). When March rolls around and it's time to start your tubers into growth indoors—shake off the crusty old dirt—cut away the dead stem—pull off the dried up roots—what you should be left with is a *hard* healthy-looking tuber somewhat like a turnip. If what you're faced with what looks like mushy leftover oatmeal—your storing hasn't succeeded—throw it out. These need to be kept really warm during all stages. If planting directly into the garden in May, cover with three inches of soil. Not nearly as fast as canna to shoot up, they take more patience and don't really come into their own until late July. They like sun, but shade suits them just fine.

Columbine. See *Aquilegia*

Comfrey. See *Symphytum*

Conifers (kon-if-ers)
Vital evergreen trees and shrubs. Most extremely hardy.
"Conifer" is a synonym for "cone-bearing trees," to put simply what could be a lengthy botanical treatise. The main thing to know about conifers is we gardeners would be lost without them as our hedges, living walls, and "bones" of our gardens. Following is a list of conifers you should deeply consider for your house and grounds. For more particulars, consult the countless books dedicated to this subject.

Abies—"silver firs" come in all shapes and sizes with the most notable attributes being their ornamental cones, bark, and gray-to-blue foliage. These need deep, moist soil.

Araucaria—remarkable symmetrical form with drooping whorled branches—long and spidery. Commonly called "monkey-puzzle," *Araucaria araucana* is the only hardy kind and should be treated as a specimen in a special spot.

Cedrus—the invaluable "cedars," usually conical when young, spread with age and can go on for many decades. Cedars concentrate their color in the blue-green-gray family and can be upright or weeping. *Cedrus atlantica* 'Glauca Pendula' is the fabulous weeping wonder trickling over the edges of our pool like a waterfall, planted early on by us, and *C. atlantica* 'Robusta Aurea' are the thirty-foot "golden" beauties surrounding the pool, in place long before we were (thank God). "Blue atlas cedars" are among the finest specimen trees.

Chamaecyparis—fabulous, diverse, and eclectic "cypresses," ranging in color from gold to blue-gray to darkest green and in form from dwarfs to huge trees. *C. lawsonia* 'Columnaris' brings to mind those great stands of columnar trees on every Italian hillside. 'Minima Aurea' is a dense conical bush of golden yellow; 'Pygmaea Argentea', a rounded bush with dark bluish-green foliage tinted creamy white at the tips; *nootkatensis* 'Pendula' has drooping, spreading, upcurved branches bearing long pendulous branchlets—a beauty; and *C. obtusa* 'Nana Gracilis', known as the divine "Hinoki false cypress," boasts incredibly dense needles packed together in shelllike or cup-shaped sprays—I'm dying for one, but this is a prize specimen and not cheap. The exciting cypress list goes on for days.

Cryptomeria—the beautiful burnished evergreens with a dense, rounded habit that I already extolled as being truly fine and not as expensive as most evergreens, even for substantial twelve-footers.

Ginkgo—one of the few deciduous (leaf-losing) conifers, the prestigious *Hillier's Dictionary of Trees and Shrubs* tells us it's "the sole living representative of a large group of plants which occurred throughout the world in prehistoric times." Notable for its bi-lobed fanlike leaves, graceful Oriental habit, and colorful autumn foliage, the ginkgo can withstand anything—including Manhattan streets and industrial waste dump areas.

Juniperus—the wide, fabulous world of "junipers." Though there are many marvelous tree forms, especially some very stylized columnar ones, junipers are best known as the most elegant of evergreen shrubs: *J. communis* 'Repanda' with densely packed, uplifted stems soft to the touch; *horizontalis* 'Glauca', with long, full, steel-blue branches narrowing to slender tips hugging the ground; 'Pfizeriana' and 'P. Aurea' (the golden version), a wide-spreading shrub with fat, up-reaching armlike branches that drip at the tips. The junipers go on and on *ad extremum* and can grow to be huge old specimens.

Picea—the ornamental "spruces." Shrubs and relatively smallish trees best known for their whorled arrangement of leaves (needles) that gives them an overall fat and globular appearance, though there are heavenly weeping species as well. *Picea glauca* 'Globosa' is the famous chubby "blue spruce" that is so endearing. *P. pungens* 'Pendula', the hanging Colorado blue spruce, is a fabulous look and not so very expensive.

Pinus—our friends, the wonderful long-needled "pines." One of the few conifers that is fussy and demands sun. There are white pines, black pines, lace-bark pines, mountain pines, sea pines, umbrella pines, pines named after every country in the world, every kind of pine you can imagine.

Sequoiadendron—*Hillier's* states, "Not as tall in the wild as the California redwood but more massive and acknowledged to be the world's largest living thing." So if you've room to spare, *S. giganteum* is for you with its dark, downswept branches.

Taxus—especially good for hedging, the "yews" tolerate most soil and situations. There are golden ones and variegated ones, and there is the black-green classic *T. baccata,* the "common English yew."

Thuja—the "arborvitae" I've already applauded this as fast-growing and the most accessible price-wise. It even smells nice. Small scalelike needles thickly arranged in fanlike sprays give it a textural appearance. Its attractive shape has a formal appeal. Hardy to Zone 2.

Tsuga—the "hemlocks." A more open and spreading appearance, usually with drooping or arching branchlets and thin needles. One of the most shade-tolerant conifers.

A few last words about conifers: Unless you want to spend unendurable years waiting for action—start out with trees at least four or five feet tall or as big as you can afford. Never pass up the late-autumn opportunity when all nurseries have sales. And although most conifers more or less take care of themselves, it's advisable to fertilize them in early spring.

√√ *Convallaria majalis* (kahn-val-**air**-ee-a mah-**yah**-lis)
Sweet lilies-of-the-valley. Zones 3–7. [See Ground Covers.]

HM *Cornus kousa* (**kor**-nus)
Divine flowering dogwood. Zones 5–8.

Growing to about fifteen feet in a natural winsome vase shape (no pruning), in June it is laden with white flowers (actually bracts) and stands as one of the unsurpassed glories of early summer. There are many great dogwoods, but this one needs sun and sharp drainage.

√√√ *Corylus avellana* 'Contorta' (**kor**-il-us)
The unreal corkscrew bush. Zones 3–9.

If you want astonishing and strange, then you must have this. "Harry Lauder's walking stick" is its common name and alludes to the twisted cane of some old Scottish comedian. Normal corylus are hazelnut trees, but there is nothing normal about the 'Contorta' type. In summer the corkscrew branches and shoots are covered in broad, deep green, slightly scratchy leaves, but I actually prefer it in winter when the branches are bare and you can really delineate the peculiar, turned, distorted, tangled, strange silhouette.

It is said to need, of course, sun; but our two nursery-bought specimens never got any (sun) buried behind the blue border for years and did just fine, while probably doubling in size. However, two years ago we moved one (and it didn't make a peep, just kept right on twisting) to a new cleared spot where there is a semblance of sun, and it now develops curious golden "catkins" in very early spring before the leaves appear. It takes care of itself and doesn't need any real pruning, though the curvy branches are very nice to use in sparse flower arrangements. Throwing up "suckers," the unwanted stems that sap energy from the main tree is the bad habit you must watch for—take your Felcos to them the minute they rise from the ground around the base. This ultimately will grow to ten feet and be as wide—it deserves a conspicuous place.

√√ *Cosmos* (**kos**-mos)
Among the elite of annuals.

If not for cosmos, it's unclear how I would've got through my first three or four gardening summers. The name is from the Greek *kosmos* meaning beautiful, and although that may be a bit overstated—they are splendid annuals both for the border and cutting. Supposedly simple to start from seed sown directly in the ground where they will grow (like morning glories), it is even simpler to buy the first flat of healthy-looking ones you see at your nursery and plant them in fairly sunny spots. The 'Sensation' mix is the most appealing, with large daisylike flowers in pleasing variations of hot pink, soft pink, and white on strong stems covered with feathery green leaves.

They are fast-growing and bushy and covered in flower-buds; the more you cut, the more the stems branch, and the more flowers appear. Given good sun, they grow to a good five feet here, and I've seen them in the neighborhood as tall as ten feet, dripping with flowers against a south-facing sunny wall. Very good in the cutting garden, but if used in the border surround them with grow-throughs or stake them, as any good wind will knock them flat. Cosmos bloom from June to September and will add a buoyant touch to any garden. [See illustration in Chapter I, p. 19.]

√√√ *Cotinus coggygria* (**kot**-ee-nus ko-**gig**-ree-a)
The mystical "purple smoke-bush." Zones 5–8.

The first time I laid eyes on this in bloom it was as if I was hallucinating—it's such a divine sight. Not only is it a true purple-leaved (and not a crass purple, but divine aubergine) shrub that grows to ten feet, but in mid-summer it shrouds itself in plumed misty, silky flower stalks that form a mauvish haze or "smoke" around it. The species name is from the Greek *kokkugia,* "to smoke," in fact. Quite incomparable—initially you can't quite figure out what you're beholding, it's so unique. Of course, to attain this delirium of dense aubergine cloaked in smoke, you need sun. I resisted buying it for years because of my dearth thereof, but finally succumbed last summer and bought two beauties at Buckley's and dug them in at the rear of the burgundy garden. Well, they looked spectacular anchoring the dark scene—stayed aubergine all summer *but* they never "smoked." Oh well, you can't have everything, and now we've done more clearing in that area, and just maybe enough rays will peep through to kindle it.

They need only ordinary fertile soil and are quite at home in even dry or rocky situations. A good mulch helps, as it does most everything. For some weird reason they are a member of the Cashew Family. The cultivar you want to find at your nursery is either 'Royal Purple' or 'Velvet Cloak'. Don't be misled by others because some have ordinary old green leaves. Carroll Gardens has the former in a two-foot size for seventeen dollars, and Forest Farm has 'Velvet Cloak' for eight dollars, which will probably arrive surprisingly robust, but I would stick to sizable nursery plants. Another bonus is they turn flaming red in autumn. A must-have for any garden with panache.

HM *Crinum* (**kree**-num)
A glorious gigantic bulb. Zones 8–10.

Significant trumpet-shaped masses of flowers (one of the amaryllis family) close the summer on long, strong stems. Roots like to be crowded, so grow in undersize pots with the neck of the mammoth bulb above the enriched soil's surface. A true beauty, to be stored potted in the basement in winter.

HM *Crocosmia 'Lucifer'* (krō-kosmia)
Interesting perennial corm. Zones 5–9.

If a grand clump of fiery red-orange tubular flowers (a bit like freesia) has a place in your scheme—you'll love this. Easy to start from corms planted two inches beneath the surface. Needs some sun, but little else, and is very persistent.

√√ *Crocus vernus* (**krō-kus** vur-nus)
The true harbinger of spring. Zones 3–8. [See Chapter VI, p. 166–167.]

Having experienced two sunny early-April days of crocus in full bloom is without doubt the best inspiration for writing this passage. Yes, the *Galanthus* are really first, the *Hellebores* are sigh-invoking, and my earliest *Iris reticulata* are better than swell, but nothing serves as spring's clarion like crocus. *Vernus* literally means "of spring." The autumn before last, I went on a big crocus binge and planted three or four hundred—throughout a small patch of lawn in the front—around the Hong Kong geese and begonia pedestals, and all throughout the blue border wherever I could squeeze some in. Last year's (the year with no spring) show was pitiful—this year it's a delightfully different story. Crocus crocus everywhere—I love it. Most books say they need sun, but it's just not true. They grow anywhere—in the woods, tucked under shrubs, as well as in more conspicuous places. What they really need is warmth, and they're rejoicing in these fifty-five-degree days. Of course, after they finish flowering I'll love them less because of the messy spent flowers and those grisly leaf tufts left behind that take forever to die back, but it seems most will be camouflaged by other up and coming things.

There are only three things to consider with crocus:

1. Buy big ones—(small ones get lost unless there are thousands) like 'Periwinkle', 'Grand Maitre', and 'Peter Pan'. What you want are the Dutch hybrids, the kinds the catalogs refer to as "giant crocus."
2. Plant them among perennials that will overtake their awful yellowing foliage, which you must allow to die down, as these return for years and will multiply.
3. *Order and plant lots* of them. They need to be only two or three inches under the soil, so it's pretty easy. Less than at least fifty makes no sense. Plant close together.

Of course, there are fall-flowering crocus, but where would you put the tiny things in the garden while summer's imposing munificence is still in full force, and why bother when you can plant the lustier *Colchium*? Crocus is a spring thing. I must admit a double-take upon driving

The endearing *Cyclamen*.

past good old Martha Stewart's house today; her crocus display is quite impressive although it is only a deep row fronting her high hedges. It begins with pale striped 'Pickwick', moves into a big mauve one, and crescendos with a deep magenta-purple. There are tons of them, so the look is striking. The most troublesome thing about crocus is they simply don't last long enough—ten days tops and they're gone—leaving you with all that dreaded aftermath. [See illustration in Chapter VII, p. 193.]

√√√ *Cyclamen* (**sy**-kla-men)

Strange and wonderful tuberous perennials. Hardiness extremely variable.

Almost no plant is quite so striking as greenhouse-raised cyclamen in erect bloom. I've never known a buoyant florist-grown cyclamen, however, that has endured. After a few weeks of splendid flowering, they just wither and die, no matter if watered, not watered, splashed with sun, or coddled in bright light—they perish and that's that. Nevertheless, cyclamen planted in the garden protest the thought of giving in and recur year after year after year, but are of a very different nature. Cyclamen for the garden are smaller and much hardier, but share the magnificent variety of leaf and the dancing blooms of the florist types in miniature. In a dappled, tree-oriented patch between the white garden and shade path I planted two *Cyclamen coum* from Montrose Nursery some four or five years ago. Since then I've all but forgotten about them, planted over them, probably under them, and yet each spring when the salt hay comes up—there are those poignant leaves. For real cyclamen enthusiasts, the various heart-shaped patterned, mottled leaves are as much the point as the beguiling flowers.

Last summer, with the new rockery firmly in place (the kind of environment they need), a very conscientiously thought-out cyclamen order went to Montrose to be *planted in early fall* (my early cyclamen orders were merely an acknowledgement of their specialty). I waited patiently for the arrival of the diminutive plants, carefully dug them in with gravel, sand, and bonemeal exactly as Nancy suggested, and watched over the winter. Since she said nothing about mulch, and little else in the rockery is tender, I left it almost barren of salt hay or anything else and was amazed as the various cyclamen species withstood the onslaught of a freezing stressful winter. I expect most of these

Its counterpart, charming *Dodecatheon*.

ten plants are going to remain with me for a very long time, and one or two have already flowered in their moment (different species flower variously throughout the year). If you are wily enough to find a source of the actual corms, they are to be planted with flat side facing down as both roots and leaves come from the top of the corm, about two to three inches below the surface of well-prepared grainy soil.

Cyclamen-growing is a specialized obsession. They're available from Siskiyou Rare Plant Nursery, but generally difficult to locate. What's clear is cyclamen-growing is a delicate and tasteful pursuit, and if you share my appreciation or are even more taken in, then make yourself known to the Cyclamen Society, to the attention of D. V. Bent, 9 Tudor Drive, Otford, Sevenoaks, Kent, TN17 4LB, ENGLAND.

√√ *Cytisus scoparius* (**sit**-iss-us) (also *Genista*)
Elegant Scotch broom. Zones 7–9.

I'm just crazy about this arching, sumptuous, suave shrub that earns attention by its shape even through winter when leafless. Something subdued yet ebullient catches your eye as it grows in a clumplike form not unlike the most elegant grasses, with a dense mass of ascending branches. Its cognomen hails from the old practice of cutting and trimming the branches, tying them securely to a stick, and using it as a broom. Early on in the gardening mode, fell in love with them in bloom and bought two from L & M (about two feet), which they planted for me (at a surcharge, of course) in the midst of the shade-ridden hammock grove, which was my choice, *but* they should have known better. When the brooms succumbed to their inhospitable circumstance, I didn't know enough then to hold the nursery liable. All brooms need as much sun as you can give them. The nurserymen should have been responsible for their acquiescing to my poor choice of placement. *Remember this short story.*

After the distasteful experience, a few years passed until I found myself caught again by the broom bug, but with enough acquired common sense to plant it myself in a more likely spot. This broom has flourished just west of the burgundy garden with one of Petar's sculptures as its bailiwick. Provides a great show for the better part of June, clothing its debonair branchlets with a profusion of always entrancing pealike blossoms in a mottled combination of mahogany and gold (very Indian in the regal sense). Needs a sheltered sunny position and once in situ will entrance you. Remains evergreenish through winter and in early spring, simply snip off any totally brown branches or stem ends. You will discern lots of buds, and obviously don't cut where they grow. It will begin to throw off its fine leaves in early May. It likes dry, slightly acid soil, and may need some staking or support. Use the thin reedy branches all summer in flower arrangements—they add a perfect touch.

√√ *Dahlia* (**dahl**-yuh or **dayl**-ee-a)

One of Mama's grandest creations. Frost-tender. [See Chapter II, pp. 48–49.]

Having rambled on and on about this mesmerizing genus already, it's now time to clue you into the hard facts. Named for Andreas Dahl, a pupil of Linnaeus's; he surely must have been the teacher's pet. Dahlias lack comparison in the plant world—nothing as diverse and wonderful is so foolproof, cheap, and easy considering the bountiful reward. Take a little time to prepare the earth with your manure mix, peat, and bonemeal, and pick a sunny spot. Dig a hole about four times the size of the tuber, mix the nutrients thoroughly, and lay the homely root not too deep in the ground (four to five inches), but deep enough to *set a big stout six-foot stake alongside the tuber—on the same side as the eye.* Pack the dirt around the tuber (and the stake) firmly but carefully (lest you disturb the eye), and *mulch.* For the first few weeks nothing visible happens while it is down there devouring its nourishment and doing the fantastic photosynthesis thing that will mysteriously transform ugly tuber into gorgeous flowering plant.

When it first bursts through the earth, it's somewhat crumpled; but with a little patience you can almost watch its growth as a strong stalk emerges and large and robust green leaves unfurl. As this is happening, it's important to keep it in bounds by wrapping twine around the stake and gently encircling *(tie the twine to the stake not the stem or you'll choke it)* the main growing stems. As the growth is so profuse and the stems get thicker than broom handles, you must shore it up with twine around its stake a few times as the plant grows. Another dahlia must-do is *disbudding.* If every bud were allowed to flower, the plant would become so heavy it would fall over; and more importantly, to get maximum-size flowers on long stems it is necessary to *disbud* and *disbranch.* After three or four sets of leaves appear (they're arranged in pairs, so it's very easy to count), pinch out the crown, or center. This allows the bush to branch. As the plant matures, continue to pinch off the weakling branches and leave only the strong canes. Each branch will produce buds, and each bud is accompanied by two terminal buds—pinch these out as soon as discernible. If you want really huge blooms—pinch out all buds but the main one on any given stem. A few weeks later, the remaining buds will impulsively open into breathtaking flowers sometimes as complicated as they are wide—as much as twelve inches across. An enigma—yes. A plant to do without—no. If you can't find a dahlia suiting your taste—your space—your budget—your theme—your spouse's offhanded remarks—then you just haven't looked hard enough.

The American Dahlia Society recognizes twelve classifications of cultivars:

Single dahlias—simple strap-shaped petals, pretty ordinary, with open centers.
Anemone dahlias—also known as waterlily dahlias; a less showy, but charming type with
    elongated petals—among my favorites.

Collarette dahlias—I love these; double rows of ray flowers and petaloids in contrasting colors, forming a "collar" around the disk.

Peony dahlias—open centers surrounded by three to five rows of twisted, curling petals—beauties.

Formal decorative dahlias—rounded- or pointed-tip petals arranged regularly; can be a bit stiff, as the name suggests.

Informal decorative dahlias—a looser, more irregular arrangement, fully double, and much more pleasant—this is the class that includes the giants.

Ball dahlias—globose and uptight; remind me of marigolds. I detest them.

Pompon dahlias—a miniature of the above, even worse.

Incurved cactus dahlias—great, spiky tips seem to spiral toward the center; a big favorite.

Straight cactus dahlias—spiky and straight, also double; but the incurved are more interesting.

Semicactus dahlias—pointed tips and a broad base; really nice.

Miscellaneous dahlias—oddballs not fitting into the other groups.

I wish I could be there to see your face when your first dahlia bushes burst into bloom! It's a wondrous event. Another species, for growing in Zone 10 only, is *Dahlia imperialis*, a tree dahlia said to grow to twenty feet and bear six-inch wide flowers, as many as three hundred in a season. Sounds fab for you hot-weather folks. For the rest of you, be sure to include in your first order 'Fascination'—pot this one for your deck or porch. It uniquely has bronze-purple leaves that set off amazing magenta flowers. It's small and perfect. For your cutting garden don't miss 'Alfred Grill', 'Gerrie Hoek', 'Optical Illusion', 'Asama Yama', 'Maltby Fanfare', and 'Vanquisher'. I could go on and on, but it's much more fun to do it yourself. By all means, order your tubers from the dahlia specialists—don't even think of buying them potted at the nursery for three times the price and a scant percent of the selection.

Very frost-tender, they turn a motley shade of black if you don't get to them before the frost does. I've already explained why mine are cut down and tossed out each year—to allow a glorious new selection for the next season, and because storing is a bit tricky. If you choose to save yours, however, here's how:

1. Cut the stalk to about one foot above ground.
2. Dig out the tubers carefully. Most likely they've expanded to immense proportions, so be sure to kick in that shovel far and wide around the base when lifting them out.
3. Knock off the dirt gently, and leave them in the sun to dry for a few hours only.
4. Store in peat moss in a cool (about forty degrees) dry place.

They can't be allowed to dry up, or get so moist they turn to mush—they need a happy medium. If you've succeeded, you should have tubers in spring that have developed "eyes," just like potatoes—separate them from the main stem with a sharp knife, leaving part of the stem intact with the tuber. Now you can pot up indoors and be ready for planting out in May when it is really warm. . . . Good luck.

But believe me, ordering new ones each year makes dahlia-growing a pleasure on many levels. Not the least of which is cutting luscious bunches of blooms for the vase, which you can vary in style and color each season. The best time to cut is in the cool of the morning with dew still fresh. Cut the stems as long as possible (short stems are the bane of dahlia arrangements), often forgoing future budding branches. Shear off all leaves, plunge into fresh tepid water in your gathering bucket, and bring into a cool darkish part of the house to rest for a while. If you cut the flowers just as they've come into bloom—they should last almost a blissful week. [See illustration in Chapter VII, p. 200.]

Datura. See *Brugmansia*

Daylily. See *Hemerocallis*

√√ *Delphinium* (del-**fin**-ee-um)
The bluest perennial. Zones 2/3–8, they say. [See Chapter VI, pp. 174–175.]

As you know, my frustration mounts each season along with other Long Island gardeners because we can't get these to perennialize. However, they are so blue and so beautiful, I freely admit to planting new nursery-grown ones each year. Countless times, ordering from my best mail-order sources to start them as babies in spring has never yielded any luck. They need sun and rich, well-drained earth, and when in flower most definitely demand staking. A sheltered site (wind is a culprit) and generous doses of composted manure are said to be extremely beneficial. True, they sound like a pain in the butt, but the stately spires of their densely petaled cup-shaped or spurred flowers in every imaginable

The old fashioned favorites: *Delphinium* (center), Foxgloves (left), and *Aconitum*.

shade of blue from the palest tint to cobalt to indigo make them well worth the aggravation. The leaping, graceful shape of the spurred variety is the basis of their lovely name, *delphis*, Greek for dolphin.

As soon as flowers diminish, the spike should be cut off to its base, and most likely lateral shoots will spring out and flower again. It's important to me to get as much out of the plant as possible in the one season it stays around. The palmate (hand-shaped) leaves look handsome until flowering, but usually get pretty scraggly after. Even though it never seems to help, I make a special point of fertilizing them with 5-10-5. Cut them down when they turn yellow and it's obvious they're over.

The basic species is the Eurasian *D. elatum*, but there are so many cultivars and hybrids it hardly matters. Scouring your nurseries for the most prolific beauties is the only consideration really, though I find the *belladonna* and *grandiflorum* forms with their spurred flowers even more fetching than most of the hybrids with their dense, flattened flower spires. The hybridizers have busily created magenta, pink, even pale yellow and white forms (which are nice), but for me—no comparison to the breadth of blues.

Sad but true, on May tenth of the spring following the Garden Tour, there is not a sign of any one of the dozen healthy, fabulous ones so diligently planted last June. Not a sign. Regarding them as the most sensational annual of all is my last recourse, but I wish better luck to you.

HM *Deutzia gracilis* 'Nikko' (**doit**-zee-a)
Fat, fabulous shrub smothered in white. Zones 4/5–8.
Already arching branches curve even more downwardly when enveloped in dazzling white flowers. It blooms on old wood, so don't remove a twig until after it flowers in May. Oriental 'Nikko' is dwarf and superb at the front of the white garden. Needs sun.

√√ *Dicentra spectabilis* (dye-**sen**-tra)
Outlandish and fanciful perennial. Zones 4–8. Extremely hardy.
Though "bleeding hearts" may seem a little corny in close-up photos of literally heart-shaped blossoms, in real life I can't extol the virtues of this super one, definitely deserving of its species name, meaning "spectacular." For starters, it is *so easy* as to be unbelievable. My first was sort of an afterthought to a summer-bulb order to Corys Heselton, bulb supplier extraordinaire (now much missed). When the tangle of fleshy roots arrived, not much forethought went into throwing it in the ground, but before the blink of an eye, curious maroon-colored foliage looking like mini celery stalks began to appear in great profusion. Definitely order by mail—much easier to plant, much cheaper, and *results are immediate if the roots are planted in spring*. Plant with about three inches of soil above the roots, and mix in a good dollop of composted

Fritillaria persica rising up among still-young bleeding hearts, then surrounded by their perfect companion, Anna José Triumph tulips.

manure to make them happy. Before long, graceful arching branches covered in deeply cut, fernlike foliage begin to appear, and soon after, tiny little heart-shaped lockets drip from the pendulous branches. "Elated" is not strong enough to describe my happiness. As May progressed, the little locket-shaped buds grew into capricious pink-red hearts with little white teardrops accentuating their tips. These old-fashioned living valentines are at their peak in May, and what could be more perfect to give your mom on Mother's Day than a big bundle of them from your garden. They last beautifully in the vase.

After this great success, which lasts more than eight weeks, mind you, I became a bleeding-heart fanatic and ordered many many more—some in the classic coloring and others 'Alba', which are divine in and around the white garden. Aside being so effortless, they, unexaggeratedly, grow anywhere. In the gardens proper as expected, but pushed way back into the border in the woods and actually *under* hedges, they prosper. Plus they grow into such big showy plants festooned with so many flowers, they never seem to be lost no matter where you put them. My woodland conditions are perfect for them, and think they might wither under the shock of true full sun.

Though early to break dormancy in the spring, you must remember to *mark them well* because they die down by summer's end, and you don't want to dig into their hardy root mass in the frenzy of fall planting. It's imperative you find at least one cozy place to grow these sweethearts, if not many.

Another species, *Dicentra formosa* x 'Luxuriant' (dark pink), and *D.* 'Snowdrift' (white) are not as spectacular, but interesting, as they flower intermittently all summer long. Much tidier and smaller than their bountiful cousins, the charming ferny-foliage is a graceful gray-green and the heart-shaped flowers tinier. Not as facile as *spectabilis,* they can do with more sun and are a bit more finicky (I've lost two), but they do bloom and bloom and also deserve a place in the garden.

HM *Dierama pulcherrimum* (dai-er-**ah**-muh)
Divine "Fairy Fishing Wand." Zones 9–10, dig and store here.
Finally found at Forest Farm after having been intrigued for years by Christopher Lloyd's description. Long, strappy leaves like ornamental grass surround four-foot wandlike arching stems that suspend funnel-shaped deep pink flowers. Treat like *Acidanthera* and give full sun. Very divine.

√√ *Digitalis* (dij-it-**tah**-lis)
The old-fashioned, ever-lovely foxglove. Zones 4–8.
This can't-do-without flower is a biennial, which always flusters me, as once in a while a clump will spring up year after year (I suppose this is self-seeding?). Biennials take a year to mature, flower in the next, and then die out. Digitalis, along with *Angelica,* are the most important biennials. Every year I buy a few either locally or by mail to assure foxgloves are always blooming in the garden. Planted in spring or fall, they begin to flower in latter June and last an unusually long time.

Best success has come with the 'Excelsior' and 'Shirley' strains, and in general the hybrids are more interesting than the species—the flowers encircle the stems and flare out to show the interior coloring more prominently. Foxgloves leave a rosette of hardy leaves that persist through winter, though I'd hardly call it evergreen—more a reminder of its whereabouts in the garden. The cognomen derives from the Latin genus name meaning "finger of a glove"; where the "fox" comes from I haven't the slightest. The "finger" idea comes from the all-over shape of the plant, which is rotund and tapering, and the individual flowers might look like fingers to some, but as they are downward-pointing and tubular, I'd call them more flaring like a trumpet or bell. They droop from a thick main stem and open progressively from bottom to top—lasting for weeks in the garden and gracing it with the spirituality of a charming old church-yard. Moist, well-drained soil and partial shade are its fundamental requirements.

If the main flowering stem is cut, secondary flower spikes will develop. Because they are so engaging, I never had the heart to cut down a main stem from the garden, but during Hurricane Bob—Mama did it for me, and sure enough, strong new spikes developed. Now less fearful of lopping off the abundant dominant stem for a particularly important flower arrangement—they highlight any vase. Once bloom is finished, cut down the flowering stalks.

There are many types, some said to be perennial, all more or less with the same form—the big difference is flower size and color. Here even ones tinged yellow (as it's not a primary yellow, but rather an overripe cream) are appealing. From mauve to white, all colors are pleasing as they are all mottled with crimson or other earthy tones. The 'Excelsior' hybrid strain and *mertonensis* species are particularly beautiful. You don't want to be without foxgloves. Particularly lovely in groups of at least three plants—if you have the space and conditions to naturalize them, that's really a look. Date your markers when planting, so you'll remember to replace them every other year. [See illustration in Chapter VIII, p. 249.]

√√ *Echinacea purpurea* (ek-ih-**nay**-see-a pur-**pew**-ee-a)
Hardy purple coneflowers. Zones 4–9.

Large daisylike flower-heads—each petal distinct—radiate from a prominent burnt-sienna "cone" looking like the hedgehog for which it was named, the Greek *echinos*. Very explicit form and demeanor and easy to obtain and grow, though mine haven't returned year-on-end—about three years seems to be the limit. Though "purple coneflower" is the widespread common name, they also come in white, which reads weirdly on the nursery containers—"White Purple Coneflower." Another color idiosyncrasy is the common ones are not purple at all; but rather an intense, deep lavender-pink. Best nursery-bought in bud.

They really like sun, as befits their showoff attitude. The flowers last and last after smacking your senses toward end July. Deadheading is unnecessary as they won't reflower from the same stem; also, the coppery cone is still interesting in the garden once the leaves fall. Cut back to the ground in autumn and mark well as they are reluctant to emerge in spring. The leaves are nothing to speak of, but the color and form of the flower is intense, and though not so tall (maybe twenty inches), the stem is strong and requires no help to stand erect. Two or three plants make a substantial show as each throws up many stems. Just great in the border.

√√√ *Echinops ritro* (**ek-in-ops rit**-rō)
Metallic-blue globe-thistle. Very hardy Zones 4–9.
Terrific is a tame descrip-

Subtler *Eryngium* or sea holly (left) with its exuberant counterpart *Echinops* or globe thistle (right).

tion. This plant gets better and more floriferous (and bigger) each year it's in the ground. It breaks dormancy very early in spring with jagged insistent leaves leaning toward a gray-green hue, which eventually clump to a sizable twenty-inch spread, so don't plant too close together. Wiry, insistent, branching stems appear in early June and are then crowned in July by perfect, round, spiky (thistlelike) eerie blue flowers with a steely luster—one to a stem. They reminded Mr. Linnaeus of a hedgehog—though the silvery blue color rather thwarts that image.

Mine came by mail as little plantlings and took a few years before they really got going, but are now strong and robust. If you want more immediate action, nursery plants will do the trick. A few will do because they're so individual they appear as specimens, but masses would be even better. (See *Eryngium* for the perfect companion.)

Their intense hardiness requires no particular soil. As a matter of fact most books make a note of telling you they thrive in poor soil, but need lots of sun. 'Taplow Blue', which reaches about three feet, is the cultivar you want. When they've just turned that ghostly blue it's a good time to cut them; not only will this increase flowering, they are also swell as dried flowers. If left in the garden, cut down the flowering stems when they look tired, but maintain the leaves under your winter mulch.

√ *Endymion* (en-**dim**-ee-an)
True bulbous bluebells. Zone—see below.
Oh so Shakespearian. Perfect fall-planting, late-spring-blooming bulb—they flower just after the last tulips and therefore help bridge the gap between spring's profusion and summer's beginning. The bulbs are succulent and white and take only about an inch or two of soil over them, so it's easy to plant them in quantity throughout existing perennials and interspersed with other bulbs. They can take full sun but are happy with some shade. The blue is true-blue (although they can also be had in pink and white), and because of their charm, grace, and important size (twelve to twenty inches) are much more interesting than most other spring-blooming blue-flower bulbs like *Chionodoxa*, *Ipheion*, and *Puschkinia*—all of which are lovely and bloom earlier, but too small and fleeting to be as worthwhile.

The hardy purply coneflower, *Echinacea*.

Sometimes incorrectly listed as *Scilla*, their former botanical name and cause for much confusion, because real scilla are quite different—bloom much earlier, are smaller; and the best kind, *Scilla peruviana*, works only for Zones 9 and 10. Two important species of endymion are readily available from good bulb catalogs: *E. hispanicus* and the ever-so-English *E. nonscriptus*. They both bloom in May and June and produce darling bell-shaped flowers, but the Spanish variety is more hardy and adaptable (Zones 3–9), has no scent, can tolerate *much shade,* and is straighter and taller; while the more delicate English *(nonscriptus)* are divinely fragrant, have lithe arching stems, and are more determinedly English in their climate requirements, so only Zones 5–8. All the books tell me they increase rapidly, but though my few patches return heartily season after season, they don't seem to expand. Perhaps this year. Don't forget to mark them and let the foliage die down. [See illustration in Chapter VII, p. 193.]

HM *Enkianthus campanulatis* (en-kee-**an**-thas)
Special spring flowering shrub. Zones 4–8.
Allan Bush (Holbrook) says this semishade-loving shrub would be more popular if it had a catchy name. I agree. This Japanese specimen sports tufts of shiny, dark green leaves and in late spring drips with lily-of-the-valley-type flowers. Great autumn color and very well behaved.

√√ *Epimedium* (ep-i-**may**-dee-um)
The aristocrat of ground covers. Zones 5–9. [See Ground Covers, p. 268.]

√√√ *Eremurus* (e-ray-**mew**-rus)
Magnificent foxtail lilies. Zones 7–9.
Spectacular members of the lily family grown by fleshy tuberous roots (look like a big star-shaped snarl) instead of bulbs. They are autumn-planted for early- to mid-summer bloom. It is early spring of the first year of *eremurus* planting as I write. Though always adored, never before had we hacked out space where there was enough *sun* to attempt to grow these stellar creations of Mama. *(A rule of thumb: usually the more*

The grandiose foxtail lily, *Eremurus.*

flamboyant—the more they need sun.) More reason for hesitancy, they are to be planted about five inches deep in rich *sandy* soil, which is not exactly our environs here. I have spent more money on these as cut flowers than any single other summer-bloomer (they last an incredibly long time in the vase and are a real statement), and to see them rising up to their six-foot stature out of my own garden will be a new plateau of thrilling. Have strangely never seen them potted at the nursery, but all the books say they're easy to grow, last forever once established, and are available in most bulb-oriented catalogs. You could probably never have too many, but even six would make quite a show.

Along with "foxtail lily" they have the name of "desert candle." Between the two cognomens you get the picture of the flower's stately spire shape covering half the length of the four- to six-foot leafless stem; actually the sinuous "foxtail" is made up of hundreds of tiny cup-shaped florets. The color array is magnificent—the palest of pale cream, salmon, apricot, and banana, although McClure & Zimmerman have a 'Cleopatra' variety in burnt orange that sounds divine and conjures "the barge she sat on like a burnished throne." Awesome and long-lasting as cut flowers, an irislike leaf is left, which must be allowed to yellow. Though hardy they need to be *well mulched* in winter and well-marked, because the entire plant disappears after flowering. Once planted, they like to dig in and stay, so prepare their planting hole well with sand and bonemeal for their supposed long duration. Can hardly wait for summer to bless me with these extravaganzas; as of early May, tufts of long narrow leaves have appeared and I'm beyond hopeful. (Not the grandiose display longed for—not enough sun.)

Erica (heaths and heathers)
Excluded here because they refuse to grow for me, though I find them tempting, charming, and have tried and tried.

√ *Eryngium amethystinum* or *bourgatii* (e-**rin**-jee-um)
Hardy perennial sea-holly. Zones 5–9, though some catalogs say 2–8.
Fascinated by this one, as its unique form is a garden highlight; it's great planted near *Echinops* as they share the same metallic-blue-sheeny quality. Eryngium is not as reliable as globe-thistle, but radiating from its bristly thistlelike center is a spiny metallic collar that juts out in jagged-edged slender spiky—petals? leaves? bracts? The odd flowers are held on stems about two feet above the interesting grayish-green deeply cut leaves that, as on its friend *Echinops,* appear early in spring. Plant a combination of half-dozen sea-holly and globe-thistle in a sunny place and you'll be delighted with the arresting texture and color interest they add to the garden. Any old soil will do—dry and rocky is best. Also good for drying. Sea-holly, however, takes longer to establish and is not quite as easy as globe-thistle, so it's probably best to try to find this one at the nursery going strong. [See illustration in Chapter VIII, p. 254.]

√ *Erythronium dens-canis* (er-ih-**throe**-nee-um)
Tuberous trout lilies. Zones 3–9.

Trout refers to the fishlike markings of the mottled leaves, but these little darlings have the additional common name of "dogtooth-violet," which makes comment on the shape of their toothy-looking tubers, because the flowers resemble tiny little lilies much more than violets or canine molars. These are to be planted in fall three inches deep in well-worked organic soil. There are a number of species of this graceful early-spring-flowering member of the lily family, but I choose *dens-canis* as it has performed and increased heartily for me, unlike my *E. oregonum* 'White Beauty', which just struggles along. Both die down in early summer and rest among my then fern-covered south shade path, which is the woodsy condition they like.

Each plant produces only two wide, blotchy basal leaves, and the upcurved lilylike flowers rise to about ten inches. Lots of them make a great spring show, as their form is so different from almost everything else in bloom at the same time. Most catalogs stick to a yellow version called 'Pagoda', but WFF and McClure & Z have the ones mentioned here. Remember, the flowers are rather small, so only good in a rock garden or other hyper-focal space. [See illustration in Chapter VII, p. 193.]

HM *Eucomis bicolore* (**yoo**-ka-mis)
Engaging pineapple lilies. Zones 8–10, best potted anyway.

Eucomis is "beautiful topknot" in Greek and refers to the sweet tuft topping the rose-tinged green flower spike. Only ten inches, they get lost in the garden but are great potted at eye level with their spotted stems. Bloom lasts six weeks and Dutch Gardens has them. Just adorable running the edge of the exotic pot.

HM *Euonymous* (yew-**on**-im-us)
Lovable evergreen shrubs. Varies, but hardy at least Zones 4–9.

E. fortunei var. radicans 'Harlequin' is my favorite (waxy dark green leaves edged white that trail and climb), but there are many greats throughout the hundreds of cultivars. All are easy, evergreen, and tolerate tons of shade. Choose at your nursery to best suit your color schemes.

HM *Eupatorium fistulosum* (yew-pah-**tor**-ee-um)
Good old Joe Pye Weed. Zones 3–8.

Big and not refined enough for a flower border, it's great for a wild garden—throwing off big terminals of mauve puff-ballish airy flowers in late summer. Clumps become seriously dense over time, okay in sun or shade, cut to ground after flowering, as they look rude and shabby by then.

√√ Ferns
Many genus, species, kinds, and types
Plenty hardy ones and some for every zone.

Few plants carry such a cargo of atmosphere. Ferns are the embodiment of green thoughts in a green shade.
Hugh Johnson (*The Principles of Gardening*)

I'll forgive Hugh for stealing from Andrew Marvell since his sentiment is so nice and his book one of the best. Among the oldest plants in the world (four hundred million years)—there are about twelve thousand species—ferns can be found in every climate of the world, including tropical ferns that can reach two hundred fifty feet, but we'll keep our fern-talk to those familiar and available in most of America—about two hundred. The distinctive features of ferns are the leaves—or *fronds*—in their curled-up charming early-spring stages they resemble the tip of a violin and are thusly called *fiddleheads*. No ferns flower or yield seeds but propagate in their own unique way by producing *spores*, which are the little brown bumps on the underside of the leaves, but you needn't worry about that as ferns are best acquired through catalogs that have already grown them from spores and allowed them to mature a couple years. Of course, they can be nursery-bought, but this can become a very expensive endeavor as big quantities of ferns are desirable to assimilate leafy groves and woodland fantasies. A shady border, a water setting, tucked around shrubs, softening the bases of trees, and mixed in myriad plantings—all situations conducive to the luxurious airy, leafy veil provided uniquely by the fern. Especially beautiful in the spring and early summer with their glistening new shoots, and again in autumn when some turn shades of rust and gold.

The fine, wiry roots are borne by the rhizome, which sends up the fiddleheads at ground level. Therefore, take special care *not to bury the fern's crown*. Also they will benefit from being labeled in a crowded garden because some species lag somewhat in throwing up their engaging fiddleheads in spring. A well-prepared site should eliminate the need for any other kinds of fertilizer, but at planting time be sure the earth is made rich with composted manure and peat—leaf mold is also appreciated. Their natural habitats can range from caves to the wood's floor, so shade and humidity are their preference, though there are some that tolerate dry situations. Also, *do not prune* back the old growth in autumn; allow the old fronds to decompose and enrich next year's plants. They grow denser and lusher every year.

Good sources for ferns are Crownsville, Siskiyou, and Forest Farm, and those to get friendly with:

Athyrium (a-**thear**-ium)—lady ferns—which have their own listing because of the spectacular 'Pictum' variety, but there are many others with delicate and finely divided fronds perfect for the woodland look.

Adiantum (**addy**-an-tum)—maidenhair ferns—extremely vigorous and cold-hardy to Zone 3; not bigger than eighteen inches, with fingerlike fronds on almost black stems.

Asplenium nidus (as-**ple**-nium)—bird's-nest fern—the fronds are solid on this fern (more like a palm)—glossy and bright green with dark stems—very exotic but hardy only to forty-two degrees, so no go here. Too bad. Nice for pots indoors as very stylized.

Cyrtomium (sear-**toe**-mium)—holly fern—Zones 7–9; the dark green leathery fronds should be evergreen where hardy.

Dicksonia antarctica (dik-**son**-ea)—tree fern—not frost-hardy and should be grown in tubs and kept moist-moist-moist; can mature to ten feet across with a glorious, magical, tropical look like a ferny palm tree. If I can track one down I'll try to grow it—though said to be difficult.

Dryopteris (dry-**op**-teris)—shield fern, autumn fern, wood fern—many species, most good Zones 5–9; classic woodland ferns from two to four feet. *D. filix-mas* is tough and suitable for the driest, most hopeless spots, while *D. wallichiana*, the Himalayan wood fern, has great gold-green fronds and is the biggest of the group. Almost evergreen.

Matteuccia (ma-**too**-see-a)—ostrich fern—impressive large fronds to five feet in the garden. I had two nursery-bought that looked just like ostrich feathers. After thriving for three years they inexplicably disappeared last summer. Said to spread and be hardy to as cold as Zone 2—maybe the biggest fern.

Onoclea (ono-**klee**-a)—sensitive fern—Zones 4–8; arching triangular pale green fronds turn to russet in autumn, about eighteen inches; don't know why it's sensitive.

Osmunda regalis (os-**munda**)—royal fern—Zones 4–9; grows in a vase-form with elegant, deeply cut and petaled fronds; has a pale green lighter look than most of its cousins; I grow it by the pond's edge with *Coronilla varia* (crown vetch), which has a similar effect, and they look lush and terrific together.

Polystichum (poli-**sti**-kum)—sword fern, shield fern—most Zones 5–8; varies from leathery to lacy fronds; best known and most easily cultivated is *P. munitum*—western sword fern—making big clumps of long radiating fronds; hardy and evergreen.

√√ *Filipendula camtschatica* or *rubra* (fil-i-**pen**-dyoo-la)
Misty-flowered showy perennial, meadowsweet. Zones 3–8.
You don't need to begin with much "queen-of-the-prairie" *(F. rubra)* because it's a true spreader, but delightfully so if you place it at the rear of the border where it has some room and

a little sun. It shoots up to four feet or better by end June, and because of its heavy leaves and huge irregular plumes of misty flowers, it benefits greatly by being surrounded with *grow-through supports* early on. Frothy flat pinkey-mauve flower-heads begin to appear in early July and will continue through August if religiously deadheaded just as they begin to turn brown. Mixes nicely with *Astilbe* and its cousin *Aruncus*.

The big handsome leaves are lance-shaped and serrated so they almost look pleated, with a tinge of bronze until they really mature. Enjoys moist soil. Cut back to the ground in early autumn as it begins to look tawdry. Buy it at a nursery—after three years two potfuls have made a real show—or order from the good catalogs as it spreads easily from underground rhizomes. Avoid the *F. vulgaris* 'Flore Plena' species—it looks like a weed.

√√√ *Fritillaria* (frit-ill-**air**-ree-a)

Without question, my favorite bulbs. Many are hardy—see below.

My exhilaration over this group of true flowering bulbs is impossible to contain year after year and never wanes. Why they are not more popular is an unsolvable mystery to me. I beseech you, even if you do not heed one other word of advice from this book, to at least grow fritillaria, as they are, without a doubt, some of the most spectacular flowers on the planet, not to mention among the most eccentric—or maybe fiercely independent is more apt. Members of the lily family (and a few books say also related to tulips) they are unquestionably the focal point of the spring garden, and the fabulous large ones can be grown in tandem with all sorts of engaging tulip combinations for a truly breathtaking show. Was just informed recently they even have the therapeutic value of repelling moles and voles. The small ones are real collector's items to be coveted and grown in specific spots where they can be appreciated.

The species vary so greatly it is difficult to make sweeping statements about them—the traits they share in common are glorious pendant bell-shaped flowers, a bloom time of April through mid-May, and all are exceedingly beautiful. Naturally, none of them are cheap, but make it your business to order as many as you can from the fine bulb suppliers. Van Engelen offers the most important at great prices. The not-lovely-enough name derives from *fritullus*, a chessboard, and alludes to the checkered coloring of the species *F. meleagris*, about which I will enlighten you first.

F. meleagris—snake's-head lily—what a delightful sight. These are small (only eight to ten inches) plants perfect for the rock garden or naturalized in shady, cool, sheltered locations, as they grow wild all over Europe and England. Plant the small bulbs three inches deep in a spot *enriched with sand*. Gentle, grassy leaves make way for ovate blooms not marbled or mottled, but actually *checkered* a divine purple and white. All-white can also be had, but the comely checkered are what you want. Mine sadly seem to die out after two or three years, but I'm always happy to replant. They need partial shade in summer so they're perfect under trees. Zones 3–8.

F. michailovskyi—even daintier than *meleagris,* it makes up for in coloring what it lacks in size. The bellflower is deepest glowing claret-red tipped about one-fourth of its length with gold—like the most divine of royal Indian colors. Tiny but fab. Zones 5–9.

F. purdyi—this is native to California of all places, a far cry from Turkey, Greece, Persia, and middle Europe—the origins of most. Another small one, its leaves form a rosette at the base of the stem instead of mini irislike leaves like the snake's-head. For an enormous price you get off-white blooms with a green circle at their base, mahogany stripes on the inside of the petals and dots without! Zones 3–10.

F. imperialis—the "crown imperial"—Wait till you hear this story. . . . Christian lore has it that of all flowers, only the crown imperial stood erect and refused to bow its head when Jesus was carrying the cross en route to the Crucifixion; therefore, to atone for its lack of compassion—it has been weeping ever since! To verify this, peek inside one of the huge, striated bellflowers and you will find six great drops of nectar at the base of each petal surrounded by rich black circles that look precisely like real tears and last the entire three-week life of the flower to prove the point! Also, in Persian it is called "tears of Mary." A magical flower and easily available—it's just crazy not to grow it. When it comes bursting out of the ground in early April you know something akin to the phoenix rising from the ashes is happening. A big multileaved, curled-up, throbbing mass noses out of the ground with great gusto, quickly supported by a thick, strong wine-colored stem. The pulsating flower-bud can be green 'Lutea Maximus'—lemon-yellow, 'Premier'—soft orange and the largest, burgundy ('Rubra Maxima'—burnt-orange shaded with red and purple and the most divine), or celadon and white striped ('Argentea Variegata'). When it brilliantly flowers, the pendant bells arranged in a whorl crown the long stems and are topped with a crest of shiny leaves. Like nothing you've ever seen. Very Alice in Wonderland. Zones 5/6–9.

To grow it, you need good drainage and some sun. Some of mine return year after year, while others die out after one blazing spectacle; maybe it's the drainage??? Plant deeply (at least six inches of soil over the bulb) the minute it arrives in early fall. The bulbs are large and tender like lilies—examine them carefully and you'll note an indent on one side (this is where the stem grew from the previous year)—*plant them tilted on their side with the indentation facing down* so that water does not collect in this cavity. They like composted manure and bonemeal mixed thoroughly into the soil. Mark them well and don't disturb once in the ground. Just sensational. Even three make a proper show—more is fantastic.

Fritillaria imperialis, one of many of its glorious bellflowers I've upturned here, so you can see the "tears."

F. persica 'Adiyaman'—I save my absolute favorite for last. This glorious one, a standout in its two-foot arching form, is much more subtle than its fantastic cousin, the crown imperial, but awesome in its cultured color and unique form—almost thoughtful and solemn, yet extravagantly beautiful at the same time—like a thing of myth or legend. The most exquisite, vague gray-blue tinged purple, regal leaves pirouette from the earth along with the first signs of spring and don't seem to be disturbed by frost that often follows. A thick stem more arching than erect follows, and the broad leaves (which never lose their color over the flowering season, which lasts for a month!) continue to swirl around the stem throughout its long life. The blackish-plum color of the many bellflowers that drape about the stem are relieved by the deep golden nectar and anthers.

Less than three dollars each from Van Engelen; you will be well-served to order as many as possible as they make an awe-inspiring and unexpected spring display in the border, and must be planted deep (like the crown imperials), which makes them perfect for double planting to fill the border in summer. There's no hyperbole using "impressive" and "wondrous" to describe these awe-inspiring plants. Zones 4–9.

All Fritillaria are bulbs, so like narcissus—*plant deep (and tilt them), plant early in autumn, and allow their leaves to die down.* [See illustration in Chapter VI, p. 171 and photo on p. 251.]

HM *Fuchsia* (**fyoo**-sha)
Flamboyant flowers grown as annuals here.

Fancy, flashy tubular flowers usually with petals of one hue and upturned sepals of another. Avoid the magenta and purple combos and seek out the more genteel mauve, pink, and cream ranges to better appreciate the beautiful flower form. Lots of water and no direct sun.

√√ *Galanthus nivalis* (gal-**an**-thus)
Dainty, darling snowdrops. Zones 3–9.

How could you not desire to plant the *very first flower to bloom before official spring even arrives???* Yes, they are small (four to six inches), but they have real staying power. Not only do they flower for an exceptionally long six weeks or more, they increase like mad once you give them a few years to establish themselves. Snowdrop refers not only to the effect of the flowering (if planted in large enough masses they look like snow sitting atop their foliage) but also to their resistance factor, as they are unharmed by late-winter snow. Each stem has a single six-petal flower—three long petals are white-white, while three short petals are sweetly blotched with green. Mine don't bloom till end February, but there's a few old thick patches around here greeting the neighborhood a whole month earlier. Plant in autumn, cover the bulbs with a few inches of soil in sun or shade. Allow the foliage to die down, of course. Order them from any reliable bulb source, and definitely put them somewhere where the whole neighborhood can join you in enjoying the first signs of life!

Gardenia.
One of the finest and most fragrant flowers, which unfortunately can't survive here, but the embodiment of "garden" where they thrive.

One of the splendors of spring, the white brushed green blooms of *Leucojum* (the tall one) following on the heels of darling *Galanthus* (snowdrops).

√√ *Geranium himalayense prat-ense* 'Johnson's Blue' (juh-**ray**-nee-am)

Not those annuals but the "cranesbill" perennials. Zones 5–8.

What is usually referred to as the showy, easy-to-grow annual geranium and a true geranium do not bear the slightest resemblance to one another, and how this mixup occurred I've no idea. The ubiquitous ones you see trailing from planters, growing in every windowbox, spilling off fire escapes, highlighting gas stations—these are *Pelargonium*. Though they are okay for annuals, what I'm endorsing is as different from day to night. First seen by me in the south of France tumbling out of an old stone wall, I was besotted by their frail loveliness. Never attaining much height, they are wonderful for the front of the border (I have them mixed at the edge of the blue border inter-

Charming true geraniums, so unlike the misnamed annual Pelargonium.

mittently with *Nepeta* and they're just great), as an informal ground cover, and in rock gardens because of their mounding, spreading form.

Suffused with open, five-petaled delicate veined flowers of a true, true blue, they will bloom repeatedly if you cut them back after the first big flower flush—which takes careful doing as you have to locate their often long, sinuous stems, which get lost among the pleasant ground-hugging foliage. The leaves are intricately divided, with a fine texture and are especially pleasing in autumn when they turn real red, after which they should be cut back to the ground. Hard to find at nurseries around here for some reason. The rather expensive six planted from Wayside Gardens way back in '87 are still abundantly with me; but I've just received some from Gilson Gardens for only $3.50 each that look terrific. The clump doesn't increase much beyond two feet, so quite a few are advisable for covering any expanse. There's also 'Wargrave Pink'.

HM *Gladiolus* (glad-ee-**oh**-las)
Annually planted corm. Not frost-hardy.

Big, stiff, upright, and predictable in manner, they don't belong in the garden proper; but for cutting they're worthwhile, as they come in every color but blue. When you cut, leave four or five leaves if you plan to store your bulbs and never plant in the same soil twice. 'Krakatoa' and 'Black Lash' are among the more interesting.

√√√ *Gloriosa rothschildiana* (glor-ee-**oh**-sa)
Fabulous climbing lily. Frost-tender; dig and store.

Just as their name implies, these are opulent, rich, and glorious flowers. Being from Uganda, they definitely don't like cold under any circumstance—in storage or outside. They grow from fingerlike tubers *planted horizontally four inches deep* in good organic soil and will make their fabulous display quicker if potted up indoors in March. The resplendent flowers climb by tendrils and need the support of other plants, a trellis, or if tried in the ground—dense shrubs. Also, like clematis, the "cool roots and hot top" mode is their syndrome. They appreciate a hot, humid spot.

One of the most exotic flowers you'll ever see, it doesn't take many to make a statement. From a base of broad lance-shaped leaves, in summer rises a slender stem topped by large, impressive deep scarlet-outlined-with-gold surreal flowers. In a gravity-defying maneuver, the six reflexed undulating petals soar toward the sky while the protruding stamens are earth-bound. Really fab. If given something to climb on and enough sun, they can reach six feet. To save them after foliage dies down in autumn carefully dig up that long tuber and store in a warm place in dry peat moss. When uncovered in early spring, if you perceive two eyes—then separate and you've got two magnificent vines. Available from John Scheepers and Jacques Amand. The *Glorioso lutea* has the same distinctive form but is pale yellow with pink and cream touches. An unforgettable flower that will enthrall everyone who sees it.

√√ **Grasses**
Also Rushes and Sedge
Fabulous Ornamental Grasses. Varying hardiness. [See Chapter IV, pp. 121–123.]

Two incredibly exotic summer bulbs, the fleur-de-lis like *Sprekelia* and the divine *Gloriosa rothschildiana*.

When you see masses of grass in nature, you tend to take it for granted; but particularly graceful and colorful species isolated in the garden scene can be very evocative. Used as punctuation at the bend of a path, effective at the corner of a border, and a garden area devoted to different, but complementary grasses can be fabulous. Already informed about the expert John Greenlee's take on grasses in Chapter IV, you now need to know how to grow this huge and diverse group spanning many botanical families. It's quite easy, as most grasses are very hardy and need little more than some sun. The more sun, the more likely they are to turn in a fantastic late-summer–autumn show of stately plumy tufts wafting in the breeze.

As they adorn the winter landscape so impressively, there is no need to cut them back till early spring. At that time, shear them to within a few inches of the ground, but make sure this is done in *early March, or you will be cutting down new growth.* We've moved various clumps of differing kinds around many times, and they're never been bothered by the uprooting; therefore, grasses are also very easy to divide—just hack the clump in half (or quarters) and spread the bounty around. In two seasons you'll have perfect clumps again; but for a huge, full effect— just leave them alone and let them grow. Mostly they are satisfied with any soil. Your nurseries should have many choices, but Kurt Bluemel has a gigantic selection priced very well. Order right now as they can be planted at almost any time. Some of the more interesting grasses:

Arundo donax 'Variegata'—striped giant reed—Zones 7–10. Strappy green and white striped foliage grows to six feet in a season. Stout canes resemble bamboo. Really great looking and perfect as a specimen.

Carex pendula—drooping sedge—Zones 5–9. A beauty with narrow leaves that grows to three feet and produces catkinlike pendant flower-spikes in summer. Graceful.

Cortaderia selloana—pampas grass—only Zones 7–10, but grows great here. One of the more spectacular grasses, with narrow sharp-edged arching leaves, it can rise from its clump to twenty feet, but most don't exceed seven or eight. 'Sunningdale Silver' bears three-foot feathery panicles of creamy white, and 'Silver Comet' is smaller (overall five feet) with whiter plumes. There are also varieties bearing pink plumes.

Cyperus papyrus—the sacred stuff of Egyptian legend from which historical scrolls that lasted centuries in pyramids and tombs were made. Only for you tropical types (Zones 9–10 only). Grows in water or moist soil. Thick, triangular leafless stems carry huge umbels of spikelets with up to one hundred rays. Can grow to twelve feet. Seen last year at the New York Flower Show in a water garden; it was the stuff of wet dreams.

Festuca—clumping blue fescue grass—Zones 4–8. Among the most charming edging plants; evergreen fountainlike tufts spread to a foot wide and are as tall. Has millions of narrow blue-gray leaves—the sunnier the bluer. I love it.

Helictotrichon sempervirens—blue oat grass—A bigger version of and nice companion to the small tufting fescue grass, it grows to three feet. Full sun, Zones 4–9.

Imperata cylindrica 'Red Baron'—Japanese bloodgrass—Everyone raves about how it gleams when the sun shines through it. Without much sun, it's still nice, with its foot-high red-red blades that get more intense as the season progresses. Wasn't hardy here, though said to be fine in Zones 6–9.

Juncus effusus 'Spiralis'—corkscrew rush—Zones 5–9. Small and divine, twisting and curling, it's a specimen—needs a special sunny spot and tons of water.

Miscanthus sinensis 'Zebrinus'—zebra grass—Zones 5–10. One of my favorites. Grows to about four feet with yellow-ringed leaves having the appearance of a zebra. Have it planted with *Miscanthus strictus* 'Porcupinus', which is striped, and they look grand together.

Pennisetum—fountain or feather grass—Zones 5–9. Loose tuft-forming perennial grass with long-haired stems that give way to autumn inflorescences of coppery-tan featherlike spikelets that behave much like a fountain spray. Very ornamental. One especially divine type is *P. setaceum* 'Rubrum'—a majestic burgundy-leaved grass with pink plumes at the end of summer—one of the few grasses only perennial in Zones 9–10—its big drawback—but I've indulged in it more than once as an annual and had a summer of pleasure.

√√ Ground Covers

A huge and important group of plants. See alphabetical listing for hardiness.

Ground covers are essential to any harmonius garden and, in many instances, far preferable to grass for covering large areas and giving textural contrast. Most are dependable perennials as well as low-maintenance plants, and many of the ten favorites listed here even oblige us further by flowering at some point in their seasonal cycle. As all ground covers are plants you will want to use en masse; buying them in individual pots from your nursery is expensive and unnecessary. Much more practical to order these from Gilson Gardens or any of our preferred catalogs. Most should initially be planted about six inches apart and by the second season will have formed a mat. Here are the best:

Ajuga reptans—semi-evergreen and very vigorous, appropriate in sun or shade, and requires only shearing off shriveled top-growth in spring to liven it up. 'Atropurpurea' and 'Rubra' have bronze and dark purple leaves, respectively, and there are also green-leaved, silver-leaved, and variegated versions—all send up spikes of delightful true-blue flowers in May that last almost a month. Also an 'Alba' version. Terrific.

Asarum europaeum—sumptuous and sophisticated, this "European wild ginger" has wonderful, glossy, heart-shaped green leaves; but the "flower" that buries itself under the foliage is merely a curiosity. Asarum appears early in spring and is one of the last to go in autumn. Likes shade and moist soil, and its luxurious leaves are very delectable to the slugs—so be sure to Deadline. Refined. [See photo, p. 288]

Convallaria majalis—legendary and lovely lilies-of-the-valley take a long time to establish, but after three years or so they begin to multiply like mad. They must have shade and prefer a highly organic soil. Mark your patches as they are very late to emerge in spring. Carroll Gardens has a great deal—twenty-five for $12.85 or, better yet, one hundred for $42.85. Plant next spring for sure.

Epimedium—a subtle and genteel plant, extremely elegant. Leaves are dense, heart-shaped, veined, tinted red-purple in spring, become green in summer, and burst into color again for fall. Tiny flowers on wiry stems hover over the plant in spring. As suits its patrician nature, each plant spreads only about twelve inches and should be cut back to a few inches in early spring to regenerate. Tolerates plenty shade. I really love this one.

Asarum (European ginger).

Heuchera micrantha 'Palace Purple'—don't bother with the green-leaved varieties as the beautiful dark, five-lobed, scalloped leaves of this hybrid make the most exotic ground cover. The clumps, which expand gradually from the center, need some sun. Cut back browned foliage in early spring and it will look great till Christmas.

Lamium maculatum 'White Nancy'—a jewel in the ground-cover crown. 'White Nancy' alludes to the color of both the green-margined silvery-white leaves that look painted and the multitudes of white flowers in whorls thrown off all summer. Its ever-whiteness persists throughout the twelve months. It spreads like mad and is easy to transplant into any dreary corner that needs brightening. Grows anywhere, sun or shade, and is the best be-haved mat-forming plant you could ever hope to

Convalleria, legendary lilies of the valley.

find. Beautiful—a star of the Garden Tour.

Liriope muscari or *spicata*—This hardy evergreen pe-rennial forms a fountainlike tufted mound of nar-row, glossy, dark green leaves. In late summer, it

The elegant *Epimedium*.

throws up wonderful spikes of purple-blue flowers like muscari hyacinths. Needs some sun, and should be cut back in very early spring if it has been damaged by winter. Great as border edging or mixed among hosta for diverging growth patterns.

Myosotis—no one should be without forget-me-nots. Baby-blue flowers bloom in late spring among glossy, small, oval leaves. Likes damp semi-shade and isn't picky. Sweet and sentimental.

Pulmonaria 'Sissinghurst White'—an evergreen ground cover with fuzzy, long, elliptical green leaves spotted white and sweet funnel-shaped white flowers in early spring. Mixes engagingly with *Lamium*, likes shade and moisture, and of course, has Vita's garden to vouch for it.

Tiarella cordifolia—its cognomen "foam-flower" refers to the tiny, star-shaped flowers that look like froth and lather about in May and June. Shady and woodsy, it's a real charmer, with jagged grapelike leaves of a luminescent green. Should be cut

The fountain form of *Liriope*.

Lamium 'White Nancy'—a garden star.

back in early spring for renewed vigor of its dense luxurious clump. Better than its cousin, *Tellima*.

HM *Guara lindheimeri* (**gaw**-ra)
Special perennial plant. Zones 6–9.

Frail pealike blush-pink flowers radiate from long-wandlike leafless stems and brush over their perennial neighbors. Use a support ring and cut back after first flowering. Needs some sun, but the long tap root takes care of everything else. Fairylike.

Heucheria

√ *Gunnera manicata* (**gun**-nur-a)
Huge-leaved perennial beauty. Zones 7/8–10.

This one needs space and the right situation (ideal by water) to be a knockout. Towering, spreading, rough, prickly-edged, lobed leaves said to reach ten feet in Brazil attain the still impressive height of five feet around here. Some shade is okay, and a marshy situation is what it likes. Fabulous in contrast against Japanese maples or any intricately-

Pulmonaria, popular with Vita, too.

leaved tree or shrub. Bears an odd light-green flower in summer that is not significant, but the orangey-brown seedpod is more interesting. As it's of tropical origin, the crowns *need a good winter mulch,* and its own dead shroudlike leaves should be turned upside down and folded on top of it. Have never seen it in a nursery, but tracked it down at Forest Farm (who advises to "feed the brute") and Kurt Bluemel. Only planted last autumn; here in the middle of April it's yet to emerge, so I'm not sure if it made it or not (probably not, because it's in an odd spot that I forgot to mulch). Dammit.

Heaths and Heathers. See *Erica*

√√ *Hedera helix (***hed**-er-a)
Good old ivy. Most fully hardy.

Hard to imagine a world without ivy, let alone my own garden. Ivy does what no other plant can do—it persists through all seasons and climbs and trails wherever you direct it. Of course, if not pruned or steered and focused to your particular image, once it takes root (which takes about a year) it will go wherever it pleases—but that's not so bad. I've never seen one ivy-covered thing (think cottages, campuses, treetrunks, etc.) not benefiting from ivy's appeal, and contrary to many misinformed sources—it's *not damaging* to the trees, walls, or spires over which it clambers. One of my preferred experts, Hugh Johnson, says, "The best authorities agree it does no harm to treetrunks or walls, despite its vigor." Only thing to be watchful of is tiled roofs, but that's hardly a consideration for most.

Most ivies respond perfectly to sun or shade, and around here it's happy as can be in some deep deep shade situations. If it's the gold, cream, or white variegated forms you're after (which I come to like more and more)—they do require bright light or sun and also aren't as energetic as their green-green cousins. Ivy more or less takes care of itself once properly planted. The only maintenance it needs is some pruning in spring to get rid of damaged leaves or control height or spread, if you desire.

Usually available at the nurseries in flats—an easy way to buy it if you want to settle for plain old English ivy or the occasional dwarf form. If you've a barren plot to give texture to, or a new house you want to make look lived-in, bring home a couple flats immediately and rush about planting in groups of six anywhere you want to bring character. Only mail-order from the really reliable sources like Ivies of the World and Gilson Gardens, because most catalogs ship ground covers in the barest slivers of rooted seedlings, and your enterprise will just be unnecessarily dragged out. But if omnipresent green has you down and it's ivy excitement you're after, in leaf shape there are birdsfoot, heart-shaped, curly, fans, miniatures, and more; and in color there are myriad variegations from white, to silver, to gold—so order posthaste from the specialists.

Some beautiful kinds are 'Erecta'—strong upright, whorling form; 'Pedata'—narrow, extreme lobing; 'Deltoidea'—heart-shaped; 'CurlyTop'—wavy-edged; 'Parsley Edged'—crinkled; 'Glymii' and 'Atropurpurea'—bronze-purple; 'Anne Marie' and 'Glacier'—edged white; and 'Goldheart' and 'Angularis Aurea'—alternately variegated gold. I love it as ground cover. It keeps the clematis "cool rooted," and every year find spaces yearning for more. It takes about five years to really scale a wall or cover a treetrunk. You can prune the hell out of it so it doesn't obliterate windows and block the view.

If your ivy is not flourishing, and you live near an ocean or anywhere prone to salt spray, you have run into a natural problem, as there is a complicated but logical chemical reason for ivy's pronounced sensitivity to salt. Definitely be careful with that mean salt-based deicing stuff around your ivy as well. The best you can plant in salty situations is Thorndale. But if that's not your limitation—there's a whole ivy world waiting for you.

√ *Hedychium* (he-**dik**-ee-um)
Ginger lily or garland-flower. Not frost-hardy.

Don't know scads about this as only recently discovered it in the Jacques Amand catalog, but now aware of it—it suddenly seems to be everywhere. Understandably so. Belonging to the ginger family (so they smell good), they are sensational tropical flowering plants with important six-inch, oval, glossy leaves that luxuriate in semi-shade! Sounds perfect for me, doesn't it? The showy flowers have the look of a loose hyacinth suffused with spiky stamens—each flower doesn't last long, but there are many of them, in subtle colors ranging from white to salmon to a scarlet-and-pale-yellow combo on plants that grow to five feet.

The best news is it's easy and should be *treated just like canna* (which see) for the storing routine—which is almost foolproof. Hailing from India, they love humidity and *never like to be cold*—so plant after all danger of frost has passed, and keep warm when in storage. Make sure they stay well-watered, and feed with liquid manure—am sure manure when planting wouldn't hurt either. Just received my roots from Jacques Amand, and they are tough and strong, like canna, but have the distinctive appearance of the male organ, and the growing point looks a bit like a nipple—quite explicit, no? Also available from Bio-Quest International. *Hedys* (sweet) and *chion* (snow) refer to the fragrant white flowers. [See illustration in Chapter VIII, p. 232.]

√ *Heliotropium arborescens* (hay-lee-oh-**trohp**-ee-um)
Evergreen shrub in Zone 10, but great annual here.

Heliotrope is one annual planted every year because it is all the right things. When young the leaves are wonderfully wrinkly and aubergine; as they mature the leaves turn bronzy and are very substantial. In late June they begin to bear dense clusters of flat lavender-blue flowers and continue to do so all summer long while attaining their two- to three-foot height. Mine always come from James Topping's uncle's nursery, and after a few years I learned to cut them back to half about a week after planting; then, instead of being a one-stemmed delight—they get bushier. They don't need as much sun as all the books suggest, but do crave a fair share, as their name suggests: *helios* is Greek for sun, and *trope* is "to turn," meaning the flowers turn toward the sun, as they are rather flattish. I've never noticed this trait. Terrific in the border.

√√√ *Helleborus,* many species (hel-leh-**bore**-us)

A perennial garden delight. *H. niger* Zones 4–8, *H. orientalis* and *H. sternii* Zones 5–9.

The eternally elegant *Hellebore.*

Known as "Christmas rose" or "Lenten rose," without question one of my revered favorites—I strongly urge you to *acquire them immediately* because they take a long time to establish and you want to get them going ASAP. My oldest clump has been going since '88 and only last year reached a nirvanic plateau. The first non-bulb to bloom (for me they begin in late March), and what a plethora of beauty it is, off and on they continue blooming through June. Robust cup-shaped flowers that are tough and fragile at the same time, they smother the chic and dense divided foliage in alluring shades of cream, pale celadon, mauve, old rose, and other similar beauteous colors—all of which are then mottled with tiny darker spots. Everything about the plant is handsome. I have a few *H. corsicus* and *H. foetidus,* which are nice, but the foliage is rougher and not quite as divine as *niger* and *orientalis,* which are the ones you want many of. Look for 'Elizabeth' and 'Little Black', but the entire species are divine.

Best to plant in autumn, the more the better, in dappled shade (under deciduous trees is ideal, but here they're under cedars and couldn't be happier). Prepare the soil well with plenty organic matter, as once in place they don't want to be moved. A top dressing of manure after flowering is helpful. Said to be poisonous, so just because they look so delicious—don't take a bite. Plant in a cool place and make sure to keep *always moist.* Though truly evergreen, cut the old leaves off in earliest spring to give flower-buds room to develop. Not more than a foot high, you want plenty of them. Nursery plants might kick in quicker, but my small plants from Montrose have really flourished. All the good catalogs have them. Really superb.

√√ *Hemerocallis* (hem-er-oh-**kal**-is)

The wonderful daylily. Zones 3/4–9. [See Chapter VII, pp. 197–198.]

Nothing could be more reliable, serve more uses, and be as intriguing because of its staggering variety as the daylily. I plant at least a few dozen every season and will never have enough. Definitely one to order by mail through the fine specialist sources, as you want as many as possible and the roots are much easier to plant and cheaper than full-grown nursery plants. Though they can be planted anywhere anytime, big hearty roots from Daylily Discounters or similar specialists are best planted in autumn for next-summer results. Most spring bulbs in the gardens proper are ideal buried amongst good old diehard daylilies and hosta, as their substantial foliage is the perfect cover for the yellowing foliage. Planting bulbs and daylilies at the same time in fall makes sense—yields a better garden with less work. They grow anywhere in any kind of soil and want some sun, but they're not choosy—actually too much sun will cause the fabulous flower colors to pale. With so many color and form choices (the hybridizers have gone crazy with this one), at all costs avoid the common orange varieties and even the zealously touted yellow 'Stella d'Oro'; even Howard Purcell agrees it's overrated.

One thing you must do is *deadhead after flowering* before the seedpod forms. As each flower lasts only a day ("beautiful for a day" in Greek is *hemerocallis*), there can be as many as twenty flowers on one scape, so this may sound like a daunting task; but snapping them off is easy and really quite pleasurable. Sauntering around the garden, snapping off your seedpods gives a definite sense of purpose. To improve their appearance after flowering, you should even cut down the whole stalk. One of the first perennials to nudge up from the earth in spring (very charmingly so, as they spurt out like little fans), plus their nice strap-shaped leaves are among the last to leave in autumn. It really isn't even necessary to mark them, unless you want to keep track of your cultivars. There are early (June), mid-season, and late (August brushing on September) varieties; there are numerous flower forms with fancy names like diploid and tetraploid; there is a vast selection of color and bicolor—all too numerous to clarify—so many hundreds are good, you must decide for yourself which are the greatest for your enterprise. You be the judge, but don't overlook them, because easy and mediocre is one thing, daylilies are something else—easy and wonderful.

For you evening gardeners and lovers of the cocktail hour, don't despair, as there are night-blooming daylilies, as dichotomous as that may sound. There is a lot of fancy horticultural talk going on about them, as a matter of fact, with phraseology of Noc 1, Noc 2, etc., to indicate exactly during which hours they bloom. A bit too boring for me, but Daylily Discounters has quite a few of these nocturnal varieties. Look for 'Treasured Bouquet', 'Green Ice', and 'American Bicentennial', and surely you'll be hearing more about these as the hybridizers are seriously at work. Study your catalogs carefully for stunning varieties to suit your garden's scheme. Another of the rare breed of perennials of which you can never have enough.

HM *Hermodactylus* (her-moh-**dak**-til-is)
Snake's-head iris. Zones 7–9.
Interesting if you're into bizarre or black, this foot-high odd creature is not an iris at all, but

a tuberous spring flowering perennial in the odd combo of chartreuse and near black. Needs cold winters, a little sun, and a special place, or its curious nature will be lost.

√√ *Heuchera micrantha* 'Palace Purple' (**hyew**-ker-uh my-**kran**-thuh)
Terrific aubergine-leaved perennial. Zones 4–8. [See Ground Covers.]

HM *Hibiscus moscheutos* (hi-**bis**-kus)
A rather gaudy perennial shrub. Zones 6–9.
Not beautiful true *Hibiscus*—the omnipresent bloom of the beguiling tropics—but a woody shrub that bears fascinating dinner-plate-size flowers in late summer that are hardy here. The raggedy leaves aren't commendable, but give them sun and cut back to six inches in autumn and they make a very splashy show in red, pink, or white.

√√√ *Hippeastrum* (hip-pee-**ass**-tram)
Glamorous amaryllis. Tropical beauty to pot. [See Chapter VI, pp. 150–151.]
The habit and flower of amaryllis demand everyone in their path stop and take notice. From gigantic bulbs, magically appear formidable funnel-shaped, perfect flowers as big as eight inches across with often as many as six or eight flowers to a stem. Glistening colors range from pure white through the salmon and pink family to brilliant red and all sorts of stripes and combinations therein. They can be grown outdoors in Zones 9 and 10 (although I think they would look a bit stiff in the garden with their ever-erect stalks), but snails and slugs are said to be a huge dilemma as they not only eat the top-growth but love the bulb as well. For the most part, hippeastrum is a plant for a pot.

Very popular as Thanksgiving and Christmas blooming flowers, the hybridizers have loads of bulbs prepared to emerge into growth during the holidays—although they are charming to plant in spring for May/June bloom as well. For this exercise, let's say you've acquired your amaryllis in time for the festivities. There are many diverging schools of thought on the method of growing potted amaryllis, but the consensus seems to be

1. Pot tightly (only an inch or so of dirt around the bulb or many bulbs to a larger container) with a third of the bulb left bare above good soil mix (compost and peat are most favored by the fleshy roots).
2. Don't forget pieces of broken crockery in the bottom for drainage.
3. Soak the pots thoroughly immediately after planting, and put in a dim place until growth appears (two or three weeks).
4. Move gradually into bright light, and begin watering more heavily as the shoots emerge.

5. Rotate the pot so the stems will not bend awkwardly toward the light, and enjoy the big heady blooms (the cycle from potting to bloom takes about seven weeks).
6. Cut faded flowers and seedpod off, leaving a few inches of stem after bloom is over.

Now the controversy: Some maintain you should keep watering and treat as a houseplant, or even put outside in their pots to bask in the sun during summer—others swear once flowering is finished, you should stop watering completely until first signs of next year's growth, when you should repot in fresh soil and start all over again. I've settled on the middle road of continuing to water through summer and in early September, turning the pots on their sides in darkness and letting them dry out—then repotting in fresh soil about six weeks later—sometimes it works and the bloom is stupendous, and sometimes . . . nothing.

Sorry not to be able to convince you of a foolproof method, but what can I say? There is always the guaranteed way of having amaryllis flowering just when you want them—by simply buying new bulbs every year. Should this be your choice—then definitely order them from Van Engelen (plenty choices and absolutely the best price) and you can't go wrong.

√√ *Hosta* (**hos**-tuh)
The paradigm of perennials. Very hardy Zones 4–9.

The most elegant plant and impossible to overdo, it's obviously very high on my list of both favorites and priorities. Never out of place anywhere, their luxuriant foliage has a place in every garden—can blend in with a formal or untamed surrounding—look great potted in a Parisian courtyard or at a pond's edge—*and* are simple to grow and true long-lived perennials. Because basically they are impossible to improve on, I have them everywhere and so should you: in a shady niche along the driveway there are white-edged *crispula* coupled with white-centered green-edged *undulata* var. *univittata* surrounding clusters of white daylilies—in the golden conifer border I'm anxiously expanding on, 'Gold Standard' and *montana* 'Aurea Marginata' mix with golden ivies as ground cover—in the blue border the big- and blue-leaved, lavender-flowered *sieboldiana* 'Elegans' fills in much space and surrounds one side of the pond—more big-leaved ones along the shade paths—'Royal Standard' is the big white flowering beauty dominating the white garden in August—and then in the back patch, there is a whole garden devoted to all their different shapes, colors, and sizes that is the backdrop for iris and poppies. Every year I plant more because *there can never be enough hosta.*

Acquiring many of them can be very expensive at the nursery; much better to order them bare-root and preferably plant in autumn along with your bulbs (spring planting usually yields a spindly specimen the first year, but the next year they come on strong). Almost every good perennial catalog listed has splendid selections, especially the Maryland growers, Carroll Gardens and The Crownsville Nursery; the latter has a superb list organized by size from dwarf (six inches across and often very textural) through giant (a mature clump can be six feet across and spectacular). Make a nice selection of the cheapest (those expensive "introductions" are for specialists), and look for their distinctive qualities in the descriptions; beyond size, you also choose among color variations, puckeriness, veining, and smooth or undulating edges. And don't forget flowering. The plant is so great unto itself you wouldn't expect it to also produce decorative sprays of charming, nodding lilac or white bell-shaped flowers rising graciously over the leaves on long tall stems—flower time and color depends on the species. Another to note without fail is Hosta *plantaginea*—the only hosta with fragrant flowers (a bit like tuberose) and what flowers!—profuse and each five inches long. Blooms at summer's end and not to be missed.

Although my sister's hosta amaze me by doing perfectly well in full sun without a drop of shade, shade is what they love, although they take longer to reach full size in really deep shade. Maturation is what you're after because hosta aren't static, the clumps increase each year in size and vigor if left alone. Just for the hell of it, a few years ago I tried dividing a few of my oldest—*what a job!* True, the dividing worked fine, and one plant became five or six, but now years must pass before each reaches their big beauteous potential, not to mention it took a *pair* of pitchforks and Irving's help to pry them apart. Sure, plant them well in rich soil if possible, but they're not very picky. The squidlike bare-roots should be sunk into prepared earth about six inches deep. Splay the roots out and pack the earth around them firmly. You can feed them too, if you want, it can't hurt. The only fuss they require is insistent Deadline applications to *keep the slugs away*— their big menace. I suppose the only improvement would be for them to be evergreen, but alas! they shrivel up in mid-autumn and must be cut back to the ground. Don't get nervous in spring if their comely little noses don't emerge with the earlier leafers—around here they wait till almost end April to make their sexy appearance. Elegant, effective, and enduring—well worth waiting for, and the very best plant in a border or around treetrunks to hide the dying foliage of spring and summer bulbs. A plant without equal. [See illustration in Chapter VI, p. 148.]

XXX *Houttuynia* (hoo-**tye**-nee-uh)
Please reread Chapter V, pp. 129–132, as I've not another word to say about this specious, disingenuous cur, although it is very attractive—**BEWARE!!!**

√ *Hyacinthus* (hai-a-**sin**-thus)
Good old hyacinths. Zones 6–9.
Not my favorite among the bounty of flowering spring bulbs, but they do have their admirable traits. The detraction is their ponderous dense flower-spikes get so heavy they sort of slump over just when they ought to be at their peak and remind me of some nice Granny's neglected garden. I love them, however, when just emerging from the soil—compact conoid clusters of dense buds surrounded by seven or eight fleshy green leaves. One of the bluest blues in the flora kingdom is found in 'Delft Blue' and there are many other bluer-than-blue varieties, as well as many other colors. They don't last forever, but begin to peter out after the third or

fourth year—but in a way I prefer the looser look they acquire where you can see each six-petaled flower as an individual.

Easy to force indoors—all sorts of people sell special hyacinth jars that require only water and a little patience—or they can be grown in pots using the good old forcing routine. Outdoors, they need some sun and the bulbs to be covered with a good six inches of soil, and of course, planted in autumn. Their thick, fleshy leaves must die down, so be sure to plant among perennials. Heavenly perfume is discernible in the garden, but when cut and brought indoors (especially the white ones), the scent truly fills a room—perhaps their most divine feature. [See illustration in Chapter VII, p. 193.]

√√ *Hydrangea* (hī-**drane**-jah)
The most lovable shrubs. *H. paniculata* and *H. petiolaris*, Zones 4–8; *H. macrophylla*, Zones 6–9; others Zones 7–9.

You want hydrangeas in your yard just as soon as possible, so don't mince around—but dash out to buy the plumpest ones your best nursery has to offer. All the many species and types are wonderfully and bountifully floriferous and great for cutting. They have discernible buds all winter, usually on whitish branches, strong oval leaves that begin to appear early in spring and crescendo in autumn with brilliant color, plus they grow fast. Much action from these massive bloomers and growers with few problems. They do, however, *love water*, as their name suggests, taken from the Greek *hydor aggeion*, meaning "water vessel."

Though many special kinds abound, you don't want to do without the main three. *H. macrophylla* is the obvious one, producing huge showy flower-heads in mid-summer that can be bluer than blue if you remember to *scratch in the Miracid in March*; or if you want pink to red flowers, use lime. The pale and creamy ones don't need any color help. An important distinction exists within the *macrophylla* group, which otherwise shares all the same characteristics—flower form. The big, globular, heavy, unrelieved flower most commonly associated with hydrangeas is known as 'Hortensia'—naturally these are not my favorite, though nice, too. The more subtly beautiful and delicate, while extremely grand, are the 'Lacecaps'. This flower has a flatter feeling with flower petals interspersed among and surrounding the stamens, which gives a lacework-meshy feeling and really shows off the degrees of blue. A beauty. Make sure you specify you want 'Lacecaps' at the nursery—look for 'Blue Wave', 'Lilacina', 'French Lace', 'Veitchii', or a very special species, *H. aspera*, also called *villosa*. Said to prefer shade, they perform like magicians around here (in the second year my 'French Lace' doubled in size and hasn't stopped), but I've also seen them in incredible bloom all over town in hot sunny spots?? (Maybe the nice cool East Hampton evening air makes them happy.)

Where my experience differs from the usual texts is the pruning method. The year each

The delicate but grand 'Lacecaps' hydrangea.

cane was cut down to a pair of growth buds as advised—I had no flowers, or maybe six instead of many dozen. My version of what should be done is this: after gathering the beautifully colored flower-heads when at their peak in mid-autumn (great for dried indoor arrangements), just *leave them alone*. They look admirable in the winterscape, and come spring—shear off any old flower-heads remaining, snip out any old deadwood, which is easy to spot because the buds on the healthy canes are very prominent, and trim off any damaged growth. Unless you're out to restrain them or shape them into something other than their normal graceful mounding form—don't touch them.

Not such an expert at *H. paniculata* or "pee-gee" hydrangeas, as I lost one for no apparent reason last summer after four years of great performance. These differ from the *macrophylla* in the shape and color of their flowers (conical or domelike panicles that begin white and become suffused with green and pink as summer's end nears), but mostly in their growth habit, which is taller and can be trained as a "standard" or tree-form. Pee-gees bloom later, August and after, and these *should be pruned hard in spring,* but not all the way back. Very gracious. [See illustration in Chapter V, p. 127.]

I can't say the best is last because the other two are pretty hard to beat. *H. petiolaris,* or *anomala,* is just completely different and absolutely terrific. For starters, it's a fabulously climbing, clinging, incredibly rugged yet rarefied woody vine. It takes some years to get it to flower, but when it does, it throws off hundreds of creamy 'Lacecap' type sprays all over its abounding height—which can reach forty feet!! Having seen it in full splendor on the old charming Bayberry building which is half covered in a gnarled old, splendidly flowering wisteria, and the other, shadier side encased by this glorious vining hydrangea, in 1988 I bought three-foot-tall baby versions from them. Five years later it covers great natural-looking (I think cypress?) trellises bought from Smith & Hawken and attached at the bottom to the deck's railing and the top to the inclined roof, creating a sort of staved-in screening device. The most vigorous of the three has already reached the roof (they're planted at the back of the original cutting garden)—and that's a good twenty feet. Diverging from the normal sawtoothed hydrangea leaf, it is instead greener, healthier, shinier, somewhat smaller, and almost heart-shaped. A beauty—everyone comments on it. The only thing it needs once lovingly planted is pruning each spring at strong bud levels to help it branch. Having just read about it scaling a rough-barked tree has given me worlds of new ideas. I feel more must be brought into our enclave.

Once you get into the wonderful world of hydrangeas, you'll be taken with really old-fashioned ones, variegated-leafers, oak-leafs—but will be thrilled by first establishing the fabulous main three. A true summer highpoint and superb in the vase.

√√√ *Hymenocallis* (hi-men-oh-**kal**-is), also *Ismene festalis* and *Pancratium maritimum* (so similar as to be one).

Enchanting spider lilies or sea daffodils. Dig and store, or worth treating as annual.

A vision—an honest-to-God fantasy flower. When it first emerged in the white garden one July I felt as if I had died and arrived in heaven, so otherworldly is it. The name is from the Greek for "beautiful membrane" and alludes to the beautiful green veining in the cuplike base

The out-of-this-world bloom of *Hymenocallis*. This one was ordered from Dutch Gardens and is soaring from the exotic pot.

of the flower. When that revered great source Gladside Gardens was still around, I was bewitched into ordering this radiant flower from the description that sent me scrambling to my books to find it. Pictures can't quite capture its spontaneity or eloquence. Gladys suggested treating it like a gladiolus in the North, meaning dig it up, dry it off, and store it airily. A true bulb, big and tough, plant it out in late spring with its neck slightly protruding above the soil's surface—just a smidge—in a not necessarily too sunny spot.

Three or six make a fine show, more even better—the flower doesn't last very long, but there can be many on a stem and what it lacks in length it makes up for in phantasm. Long, thin, recurving petals lithely jut out from a daffodillike cup and a sweet smell pervades the air. It looks like nothing else in the garden. By the way, the Greek god of marriage, Hymen (who was son to Apollo by one of the muses, no less) is the origin of its name. Legend describes him as such a gorgeous youth and so ethereal he might be conceived as a girl. Telling and appropriate for our androgynous times, is it not?

HM *Ilex* (ai-leks)
The hollies. Surprisingly, only Zones 6/7–9.
Not North-Pole happy after all, but hardy and evergreen where it does grow. These are sexual plants and you must have both male and females to produce berries. Trust your nurseries. Not picky about soil, water, or sun. Many kinds beside the obvious.

√ *Incarvillea delavayi* (in-kar-**vil**-lee-a)
Perennial "hardy gloxinia" Zones 6–8.
Another abundant flowerer almost as easy as *Dicentra*, though not quite as fantastic. Usually not seen in nurseries; my first spring planting was one of those last-minute orders from Spring Hill Nurseries, and no sooner were the gigantic fleshy roots in the ground—signs of life abounded, and before long, thick fernlike leaves emerged. From amongst them, strong eighteen-inch stems topped by exquisite gloxinialike trumpet flowers emerged in a winning pink-red tone.

Said to need sun, mine don't have too much and do fine. Can also be planted in autumn (available from Forest Farm and Dutch Gardens). Incarvillea should be cut back and *mulched heavily* in winter and *marked* as they're extremely late to break dormancy in spring. Bloom begins in late spring and can be prolonged into July if you studiously deadhead all wilted flowers. Plant the fat tubers vertically—they look like a sweet mop-headed girl in a prom gown—with the mop-top level with the soil's surface. Since I can't always count on mine to return, every year I order a few fat roots from Dutch Gardens summer catalog to plant in spring. Delightful.

√√√ *Ipomoea purpurea* (ip-oh-**mee**-a)

Morning glories. Grow as annual, only half hardy even in Zone 10. [See Chapter III, pp. 65–66.]

I couldn't resist a √√√ for this easy-to-grow, so familiar as to be almost trite, flowering vine. Early in my gardening bug, wandering the back streets of St. Tropez early one summer morning I came upon a stone cottagelike house covered in morning glories and was just struck dumb by how enchanting the vision was. They need sun, something to climb on, and lots of water—and, if you remember, are the single thing that can be sown from seed right in the ground without much of a challenge—the seeds are tough, so be sure to *soak in warm water* twenty-four hours before sowing. I love the look of the twirled-up plump buds before they twist and open into captivating saucerlike flowers. Said to open at dawn and close at noon, around here they flower till mid-afternoon and go nonstop till October. If you have a seemly spot—you shouldn't be without them. [See illustration in Chapter I, p. 19.]

√√ *Iris,* bulbous (**eye**-ris)

The delightful spring blooming iris. Zones 4–9.

One of the earliest flowers to bloom in spring are fall-planted *Iris reticulata*. These dwarfs are precursors to the galaxy of iris yet to come as the season proceeds. The *reticulatas* are not much to speak of in size (six inches at most), but range in color from palest blue to deep violet with all the intricacy of their more formidable relatives. Curiously square (read cubist) upright leaves surround the flowers, which last a bit less than two weeks. You need minimally a dozen in one spot to appreciate them at all, but they multiply rapidly once they feel at home. Plant bulbs two inches deep under ground cover or perennials, so as to hide the yellowing foliage and not dig them up later. McClure & Zimmerman offers nine varieties.

The main group of bulbous types are Dutch, Spanish, and English, properly all titled *I. Xiphium* and all much more substantial in size than the early *reticulata*. The most cultivated and easiest to find are Dutch, which are actually North African and European, but named for the Dutch who hybridized them. Quite a charming range of colors for the asking, but the most popular and certainly pretty is self-explanatory 'Wedgewood' that blooms in mid-spring. Not picky about soil, they do like sun, and the bulbs should be covered with three inches of soil. They have a light, airy structure with falls not particularly prominent.

Spanish iris bloom about a month later than Dutch and are taller and more irislike in form. Read somewhere they're called the 'Poor Man's Orchid'. Yellow and purple are their main colors, (like all the bulbous iris), but they also come in peculiar variations of bronze and brownish tones, which of course attract me.

The last of the bulbous iris to bloom are the English, which wait till end June. Larger (about twenty inches) and more important looking than their European cousins, the falls are more pronounced, the colors more varied, and they flower two or three to a stem. Less interested in sun than the others, they prefer dampish semi-shade and want to be planted a bit deeper than the others. 'Queen of the Blues' is a really great one.

Without question, the bulbous iris have their place in the garden, but they can't hold candle to the rhizomatous (which see).

√√√ plus √√ *Iris*, rhizomatous (**eye**-ris)
Fabulous bearded and Japanese iris plus. Zones 3–9. [See Chapter IV, pp. 117–119; Chapter VII, pp. 196–197.]

Iris take their name from Iris, the Greek goddess who carried messages from heaven to earth via the rainbow, hence goddess of the rainbow, which no doubt refers to the splendid palette of markings and colorations abounding in these fantastic flowers. Taking many forms, they are engraved upon the consciousness as the heraldic fleur-de-lis. For ease of understanding, it's important to note *all* iris have three upright, erect, or vertical petals called "standards" alternating with three pendant or drooping petals called "falls." The iris "beard," which is the next formidable distinction, is actually a kind of fuzzy, bushy, well, "beard" on each of the falls and often a different color. The American Iris Society has divided "bearded iris" into six groups, which is basically a breakdown as to size (from MDBs [miniature dwarf bearded] beginning at a few inches to TBs [tall bearded], which can reach nearly four feet) and, more or less, size signals succession of bloom, which culminates mid-June.

All rhizomatous iris like lots of sun (at least half a day), good drainage (a slope or raised bed is best), air circulation, a slightly acid soil (sulfur makes alkaline soils more acidic), and *bonemeal*—also sand if the soil is clayish. Native to almost every country of the northern hemisphere, they can withstand most conditions from hot and dry to cold and wet. A few indelible ground rules abide for all species and varieties:

1. Planting is done in July and August—no later than September as the roots must dig in and establish themselves before the growing season peters out. When your tubers arrive, *soak the roots overnight in water* before planting.
2. Because the fanning out of the swordlike leaves can be so stupendous, this is one plant with which you must follow the directions of planting twelve inches apart (or at least eight) with all leaf fans facing in the same direction—at least three in a triangular group.
3. *Don't plant deep*—you still need to dig a sizable hole to work in the bonemeal and manure (and low nitrogen [like 0-10-10] fertilizer if you want) and to properly compact the basal roots, which must be buried firmly to hold the plant in place, but the rhizome itself (the potatolike growing tuber) should always slightly *show above the soil level!!!*

Since they rarely ever completely disappear, you don't have to label them to find them, but do so to keep abreast of your 'Vigilante', 'Proud Tradition', 'Song of Norway', 'Superstition', and/or all the fetching iris you'll be tempted to plant.

4. Water intensely a few times when first planted until established, after that they take care of themselves—*too much water is bad* for them and can induce (ugh) rot.

5. *Fertilize when the crocus bloom* and again about a month after bloom. This means scratching in bonemeal (or a 0-10-10) as a top dressing, but don't let it actually touch the rhizome.

6. Most iris, especially bearded, are more or less evergreen. The leaf fans might get knocked about and wither a bit in winter, but they never go away. Maintain them by cutting off shriveled foliage on an angle (like they look when you receive them from Schreiner's). Keep iris beds weeded and clean so the rhizomes are always exposed to the sun. During the growing season, *never* cut down the *healthy* green leaves, but in early winter, cut all remaining leaves back to about five inches. A little straw mulch is beneficial for fresh plantings. After blooming, the flowering stalks should be cut almost to the ground.

7. One of the few tough perennials that multiply so fast, you must consider thinning them out after two or three years or the flowers will begin to dwindle. Simply dig up the clump about a month after the tremendous bloom is finished and remove the old tubers at the center. Use a sharp knife to cut off the newer growth (will look exactly like what you started out with)—a tuber with a fan of leaves attached. Replant this in the ground as you did initially.

Now that you know how to grow them, let's talk about how remarkable they are.

Big bearded iris punctuate the gardening year in a flamboyant way, obliterating most other gardening dreams. If you can't find a bearded iris to turn you on—maybe gardening is not your passion after all. Possibilities for exhilarating color combinations are countless, Mama's entire palette is represented except for true red-reds, but the deep scarlets and burgundies are even better. I'm prone toward the bluest, the darkest highlighted with pale counterpoints, and the pure creamy-whites, but having not plumbed the iris depths by any means, often I feel like a welcome stranger in a strange land. Just get that Schreiner's catalog and immerse yourself.

Many other varieties of tuberous iris to scintillate you fall into the category of "beardless," and each has its own aspects and mannerisms to recommend it. With not a qualm about overstatement, the Japanese iris, *Iris kaempferi* is a paradigm of beauty and taste unmatched in the flora realm. Its huge, floating, heavenly blooms rise from stalks reaching four feet with good culture. The falls are horizontal, or levitated somehow instead of drooping, and the effect is sublime. Naturally, because it's so glorious, the Japanese iris have slightly different cultural

The fragile, floating, fantastic Japanese Iris hovering in the
Blue Border.

requirements. These tubers want to be planted *under* the soil about three inches deep as they send up new roots which form *above* the old each year. After three or four years, you will be able to see the roots as the crown grows to the surface—then it's time to dig and divide as detailed above. Plus *water—water—water*; these delight in water and need to always be wet from early spring till bloom, and moist thereafter. Also, this iris desires *plenty composted manure and organic humus* be dug into the soil, prefers a slightly acid soil, and is always happy when mulched. Don't stint on these requirements, or the bloom might be stunted, which is the last thing you want from these breathtaking babies.

Other terminology which you will find related to Japanese iris are *I. laerigata* (the bog version that *really* needs to be wet), *I. ensata*, a beauteous species with standards usually darker than falls, giving a bi-tone effect to the buoyant flower; and 'Ise', 'Edo', and 'Higo', which are the various strains of these iris hybridized in different areas of Japan. All you need do is plunge into the Ensata Gardens catalog and restrain yourself because you will want them all. Japanese iris utopia.

D I A N N E   B E N S O N

Siberian irises are effortless to grow and easily found in every nursery. Slenderer straplike foliage makes impressive grasslike clumps appealing all summer long. The color range is not as spectacular, hovering primarily around purple, blue, and white. The clumps increase noticeably each year, producing more and more flowers—and need for division is less rigorous than the others—maybe every six or eight years. Though not as fabulous as the others, they are very dependable in the garden scene, and can be planted in either spring or fall.

Other iris to note are *I. cristata*, a smaller iris great for rock gardens, without a beard, but instead a "crest," which is a cockscomb like a ridge on the falls; "remontant" iris, which are rebloomers and good if you're in a mild climate; Louisiana iris, which favor damp, acid soil; and the truly charming *Iris tectorum* that I absolutely adore. *Tectorum* is the "Japanese roof iris" that throws off lilac-blue or white flowers and has wonderful curved foliage that spreads in a shorter, more graceful fan and looks terrific at the very front of the border as a sophisticated edging plant. And lastly and particularly lovely, *Iris pallida,* which means pale, and can refer to either the pale lavender-blue flowers or the light creamy-white variegation that streaks and outlines the leaves. The foliage is truly handsome in the garden all year and deserves a focal point right in the front of the border.

Ismene festalis. Great. See *Hymenocallis*

Ivy. See *Hedera helix*

√ *Ixiolirion* (iks-ee-oh-**lir**-ee-on)
Lovely spring-blooming bulb. Zones 6–10.

Deep blue, almost purple, tubular flowers tumble from an umbel on foot-high stems in late spring lasting almost through June. The grasslike foliage dies down quickly, so it's easy to find a spot for them. A hundred from Van Engelen at $9.75 is a good deal and makes just the right show in a comely not too sunny corner (need bright light more than real sun). Though from Siberia, it's still advised to give them a good winter mulch. Known as "Tartar lilies," and "Siberian lilies" they should be planted at three inches deep and enjoy being fertilized in spring.

Mine are buried under *Ajuga,* and they complement each other like a charm.

√√ *Kirengeshoma palmata*
(keer-en-**gesh**-im-a)
Surprising sophisticated perennial. Zones 5–8.

The subtle perennials:
Kirengeshoma and
Chelone. (false turtle
head, right)

Even the boys from know-it-all Marder's asked me, "What's that?" It is simply one of the most forthright, yet tame and subtle, perennials—actually closer to a shrub in growth habit— of any I know. My first try from Milaeger's Gardens waned, but bought two great-looking ones at McConnell's three years ago that are flourishing beyond any reasonable expectations in the shadiest nooks of the main shade path. Strong maplelike leaves whorl from thin but strong *ebony* stems; they support themselves and need no help of any kind. All they need is moist, rich, lime-free soil.

Without an enticing common name, kirengeshoma should be called something like "the dignified wax plant." Its flowers are strange but wonderful. They never really "open"; the rounded, convex, cool, creamy-yellow buds just grow plumper and plumper till they reach about two inches, when they finally drop off after considerable time. The peak is reached early in September when the bush is smothered with these waxy tubular buds. There is a certain harmony and carriage about the plant difficult to describe, but if you have a shady moist nook—please find kirengeshoma (Carroll Gardens has it) and grow it. Emerging like little swollen arrows relatively early in spring, it should be cut to the ground in late autumn and mulched. Elegant and easy.

HM *Kniphofia* (nip-**hoh**-fee-uh)
Self-explanatory "red hot pokers." Zones 6–9.
A real showoff and sometimes called *Tritoma*. Great accent because of its flaming huge flowerhead. Needs lots of sun and, mainly, room because it throws off tons of long leaves that must not be cut back till spring (braid and tie off with raffia).

√√ *Lamium maculatum* (**lay**-mee-um)
A favorite ground cover. Zones 4–8. [See Ground Covers.]

HM *Lavandula augustifolia* (la-**van**-dyoo-luh)
Fragrant and lovely lavender. Zones 6–9.
'Hidcote' and 'Munstead' are backbones of English and French gardens. Most effective massed in fields. Let the flowers dry on the plant over winter. Cut it down and grind up for the potpourri bowl in early spring. Usually found with the herbs.

√ *Leucojum aestivum* (**loo**-koh-jum)
Lovable "summer snowflakes." Zones 4–10.
Don't be misled by the common name, as this sweetheart actually blooms in late April and lasts through most of May. I have it planted with *Galanthus* (the snowdrops), and it follows their dainty flowering cycle with a much showier allusion to snow. Masses of them are welcome

as their refined white flowers (with adorable little green polka dots on each petal's tip) nod on short arching stems off the fourteen-inch stalk, two or three to each one. Plant in fall with about two inches of soil over the bulb. Seems to be happy with some shade and generally not fussy about anything. Strap-shaped leaves, of course, need to be allowed to die down, and after a few years, there is noticeable increase. Order in quantity because you'll love them. [See illustration in Chapter VIII, p. 263.]

√√√ *Lespedeza thunbergii* (less-puh-**deez**-a)
Adored late-summer flowering subshrub. Zones 4–10.

Nancy's (Montrose Nursery) eloquent description made me fall in love with this one because never found it pictured anywhere (not even listed in the American Horticultural Society's *Encyclopedia of Garden Plants*, only in old *Hortus*) and dearly love it I continue to do. This is another everyone asks about because it's so charming and unfamiliar. (Forest Farm has it and so does Niche Gardens.) In autumn, just leave it alone and it graces the border through winter in a sort of crepey beige vertical mass. Cut back to a few inches above ground at end February (along with the *Buddleia* it pairs engagingly with), and don't worry when the woody stump just lies there dormant till late May, because then it explodes forth to six feet in the blink of an eye, or so it seems. The soft gray-green-leaved arching habit is lovely all season, and at summer's end, fountains of long racemes of white (or pinkish mauve) flowers are produced in great profusion on wandlike stems "giving the plant an unequaled elegance," says Nancy. It's big, beautiful and another true beauty from Japan that makes a wonderful statement in the back of the border, where it luxuriates with little sun, though the books call for full sun. Definitely worth your attention—it's a charmer. [See illustration in Chapter VI, p. 163.]

√√√ *Ligularia dentata* (lig-ew-**lah**-ree-a)
Treasured dark-leaved perennial. Zones 4–8.

Crazy about this one and especially entranced by my favorite varieties, 'Desdemona' and her Moor, 'Othello', although for the life of me I can't find out how they acquired these portentous names. Must have something to do with the divine but foreboding gigantic, glossy heart-shaped leaves in a rhapsodizing shade of deepest green changing to mahogany with shiny burgundy veins and stems. If this plant never flowered, it would be fine with me, as it's so perfect and architectural in its dark and mounding form. Reaching beyond three feet and just as wide, it needs room, and it's another that faithfully returns each season bigger and better. When it does flower in late summer, big bunches of airy daisy-like burnt-orange flowers branch to almost four feet. Worried the flowers might intrude on the bold, elegant plant, I cut them down quickly for meadowy flower arrangements.

The singular drawback is slimy slugs love them, so *Deadline the minute the coppery*

A prized garden nook on the shady south side of the pool. From left to right: grasses and daylilies, *Asarum*, *Ligularia* 'Desdemona', and a smidge of our Bloodgood Japanese maple.

darlings start to unfurl from the earth in early April, and continue as their leaves reach out to their wide stature. They are just fine in shade (but okay in sun, too) and like to be kept moist. You don't need many of them to make a very important statement. Have always bought mine at the nurseries, but they're so thriving and hardy, am sure they'd take fine if ordered from the good perennial catalogs. *Ligularia przewalskii* is quite a different beauty, but also very effective. More or less the same habit but with deep gold flowers that rise like spires and insipid green leaves that are deeply fingered on black stems. Both need to be cut to the ground in late autumn. Don't miss out on these if it's drama you're after.

Lilac. See *Syringa*

√√√ plus √√ *Lilium* (**lil-ee-um**)
The garden queen—the lily. At least Zones 4–9. [See Chapter IV, p. 117, and Chapter VII, pp. 198–199.]

Singing the praises of lilies is easy as they are an indulgence to savor. Said to be in cultivation longer than any other plant, in five thousand years they certainly have amassed their share of fanatics (and rightly so) as there are nineteen lily societies in North America alone, and at least that many in the rest of the world, including two each in Czechoslovakia and South Africa, which give you a small taste of their diversity. Through countless ages the lily has been a symbol of purity and beauty in literature and in art, and even served as the Anglo-Saxons' version of a sonogram—a pregnant woman choosing a lily over a rose supposedly was assured a male child. Because of their long blooming season, fascinating panoply of shapes, sizes, colors, and types, and their prolific tendency to increase, the lily enthrallment is easy to comprehend. The advantages of lilies go on and on and on because of their stately size, wondrous color, and demure habit. In a shrub area, a perennial border, a water garden, any spot that needs accent—lilies will rise up and shine against or above the other plants. The slender stalks don't take up much room, and the lily roots benefit from being planted among companion plants as they are much like clematis in their preference for cool roots and sunny tops.

Lilies, to boot, are quite easy to grow if you know *which* lilies you are dealing with—the fundamentals from specie to specie often vary greatly, so sweeping generalizations are not in order. The one thing they all appreciate is *good drainage and plenty of organic material* mixed in the dirt. So when you plant them, remember they will be with you a long time, and fill those deep holes chock-full of composted manure, peat, and bonemeal or bulb food and swish it around really good. If drainage is a problem in your swampy garden, you'll have to be content to grow your lilies in containers, which isn't so bad as they make marvelous potted plants.

The last thing they all have in common is a tender, scaly bulb that must be treated with delicacy—planted quickly—and *not be allowed to dry out.* If your bulbs arrive with roots on them, which they probably will if ordered from the good growers, be careful not to break them off or disturb them—they are just itching to get in the ground and begin doing their stretching routine. Because of the tender nature of the bulb, a few scales might appear mildewy or mushy—simply pick them off or scratch off the mildew and everything will be fine. If the whole bulb looks bad, however, call and scream for new ones. Once planted, *water* thoroughly, even if it's raining—very important the roots get used to their new home quickly because most lilies are planted late and there's not much time before the ground freezes.

If you begin by planting a dozen lilies from each of the groups illuminated, you will have gorgeous flowering from early summer through September and avidly go back for more year after year. Always make a hole large enough to plant at least three in a group, making room for the big bulbs and ample space between them—I say four inches is plenty, but the big-time lily enthusiasts would have my head. *With the exception of L. candidum,* the pure Madonna lily, which only gets covered in one inch of soil, *all lilies want to be planted deep—three times the depth of the bulb. And for some of those big ones, that's pretty deep.* One more planting tip—slightly tilt the bulb so the water doesn't collect among the scales.

The Royal Horticultural Society has decreed nine divisions. Here they are:

Division 1—Asiatic Hybrids
The earliest and the easiest of all. Plant these in groups of at least a dozen in as much sun as you can find, although my shade-ridden ones do fine and have multiplied as early as the second

year. Most ordinary catalogs offer these in pretty garish shades of red and orange, but the better bulb people and lily specialists offer much more appealing dusky roses, pinks, lemons, creams, and whites. Try 'Unique'—it's a beauty. There are upfacing (most of them), outfacing, and downfacing Asiatics, and most grow to about thirty inches. These can be planted in autumn, or even spring, for a nearly immediate show.

Division 2—Martagon-Hansonii Hybrids or Turk's-Cap Lilies

Taller lilies with pendant, strongly reflexed petals like Tinkerbell toe-shoes. They are woodland plants liking neutral or acid soil and light shade. The cocky flowers and whirled leaves make quite a show. The first season may be disappointing till they settle in, but after that, you're in for a treat. *L. martagon album* is all white, but they can be had in yellows and oranges, as well as lavender and deep dark red, usually with odd speckles and dots.

Division 3—Candidum Hybrids

The Madonna lily and her hybrids. Ancient art, sculpture, and literature are engulfed with lily imaging, and this is the sacred one stirring up so much allusion. All bulbs in this division are planted *close to the surface* and almost immediately send up a rosette of leaves when planted in August—the *only* summer-planted lily. Flowering a year later in early summer, they are a vision of white and purity. They favor a limey heavy soil, so I've haplessly not had much luck with them in acidic East Hampton.

Division 4—American Hybrids

Native to the West and East Coast and a few from the South, these are wonderful big ones—up to seven feet tall, with many pendant flowers per stem, often reflexed, they bloom in July. Dappled shade is their metier, and it's obviously best to grow the ones geographically associated with your area, though the 'Bellingham' hybrids of California are said to be the easiest. The famous "tiger lily" is *L. columbianum* from the West Coast, and many others are easy to place, with species names like *canadense, philadelphicum,* and *michiganense.* Most are colored lively yellow, orange, red, and spotted.

Division 5—Longiflorum Hybrids

These are the "Easter lilies" florists force into bloom for the big day but don't expect yours to bloom at Easter. The natural bloom time is midsummer. Pristine, white, and beautiful. Although a peachy-color hybrid has broken through, 'Casa Rosa'. Six or more bulbs in a big container make a great show.

Division 6—Aurelian and Olympic Hybrids

The trumpet lilies, easy to grow, fragrant, and fabulous—to many (I am one), these are what lilies are all about. Only meticulous exercise needed is to heed the cool-root syndrome, so keep these *mulched* if not grown among other plants. The aurelian lilies have been bred from an old rugged strain, *L. henryi,* and are extremely hardy. Mostly from China and a few from other parts of Asia, these bloom in late July and August on stems of five to six feet. One of the most exciting gardening experiences is waiting (it seems interminable) for their long plump buds to open and unfurl into a pyramid of waxy bloom—stately, serene, and magnificent. Some of the most divine lily colors are present here—chartreuse, apricot, dusky pinks, and a divine plum— often backed with maroon, purple, and even an iridescent green. Look for 'Amethyst Temple' and 'Black Dragon'; there are a fantastic panoply of great choices.

Division 7—Oriental Hybrids

Originally from Japan, these are the glamor girls of the lily world, incredibly exotic and, of course, not so easy to grow as some others, though I've had quite great luck and the blooms are astounding. Stick with acid soil and a cool leafy mulch, for sure. These bloom the latest, bringing the lily season to a spectacular climax. Trumpet-shaped, immense flattish bowl-shaped, and some recurved, everything about them is huge and heavenly. *L. speciosum,* the great old 'Rubrum' lily, and *L. auratum* are the parents of most hybrids, which get more dependable all the time. You must try 'Imperial Gold', 'Early Beauty', 'Geisha', and 'Journey's End'. The most marvelous white, pink, and red flowers of them all. Delve into the B & D Lilies catalog and acquiesce to these wonders.

Division 8—All Other Hybrids

These are for lily aesthetes..

Division 9—All Lily Species

The true lilies that are parents to all the hybrids and more difficult to grow. You might want to try *L. regale* 'Album' and *L. speciosum* 'White Angel' just for the hell of it—both breathtak-ing whites.

I'm sure you are by now a confirmed lily-grower. Three more thoughts. Fabulous tall lily stems bearing masses of flowers naturally need help to stay upright. Any old stakes will do, but without a doubt Walt Nicke's "Loop Stakes" are the best.

When cutting for the vase, be sure to leave at least eighteen inches (or more, depending on the height) of the stem, as the plant will be weakened too much if you take the entire stem. If left to reach fruition in the garden—*remove spent flowers before seed can set.*

Lastly, at the ends of the anthers of all lilies there is that fuzzy, annoying orange-colored stuff called pollen that gets all over your hands and stains clothes. There is the school of thought saying all pollen should be purposefully removed, but if you're growing lots of lilies as you should, this would be very time-consuming and deny the insect kingdom its due. Instead, if the pollen gets on your skin—wash it; if it gets on your clothes—let it dry and take it off with a stiff brush, or cellophane tape does wonders. A mere microbe of bother from such overwhelming wonders of the flowering world. [See illustration in Chapter II, p. 49.]

√√ *Liriope muscari* or *spicata* (leer-ee-**op**-ay)
Better than a ground cover. Zones 5–10. [See Ground Covers.]

HM *Lisianthus russellianus*, actually *Eustoma* (lis-cee-**anth**-us)
Among the most sophisticated "annuals." Not hardy.
Beautiful twirling buds flower into tuliplike apparitions having the unique characteristic of lasting almost two weeks when cut. Need plenty sun. Mauvy-pink, lavender, and white, all spray from pleasant gray-green leaves.

HM *Lithodera diffusa* 'Grace Ward' (lith-oh-**dor**-uh)
Deep true blue perennial flowers. Zones 6–8.
Too small and special for the border, needs a rockery or its own space. Likes sun, hates lime, and flowers off and on all summer. Color is matched only by delphiniums. Order from Forest Farm and carefully choose its site.

√√ *Lobelia erinus* 'Crystal Palace' (loh-**beel**-ya)
Not the perennials, the great blue annual.
I have toyed with the perennial lobelias, but in the end can't really recommend them, as both *L. cardinalis,* the red one, and *L. syphilitica,* the blue one, remind me more of weeds than cultivated plants. This low-growing beloved blue annual is another story entirely—as blue as *Lithodora* or the bluest delphiniums—this (extra bonus) bronze-leaved plant spreads into a mat of blue by end of June—thick and great and blue-blue-blue. About the middle of May, I do a mad dash to the nurseries to buy my flat of 'Crystal Palace'—occasionally not finding it, I settled for 'Blue Moon' once and 'Sapphire' another time. Forget it. 'Crystal Palace' is the one creating a literal carpet of blue. Undeniably great at interstices in the border, between stepping-stones, trailing out of containers, and really great by the blue of the pool (my pool is not that everyday aqua color, but an indigo blue). It needs some sun, but not that picky. Don't pass it up if it confronts you—bring it home and you will find plenty places to plant it. Lasts all summer, too. Beautiful.

The incomparable Lotus doing its dance over the
water's surface.

Lotus (**loh**-tŭs), actually *Nelumbo,* but how would you ever find it in this list?

The sacred water plant. Definitely not hardy here. [See Chapter III, pp. 85–86.]

How not to include Buddhism's metaphor for virtue and purity triumphing over wickedness? Rising from foul mud through polluted waters, the lotus is a miracle of perfection and the choice seat of the Buddha himself in many religious icons and artworks. And rightly so; such beauty of form, fragrance, texture, and color could come only from a plant whose seeds can remain fertile for hundreds of years encased in an inviolable pod as beautiful as the flower and leaf. Idolized for centuries, the lotus has even inspired such ancient artistic architectural treasures as the Angkor Wat in Cambodia. The five central towers of this, the *largest religious monument on earth,* were designed to resemble lotus buds as they are about to bloom.

So much significance. . . . but if you haven't a pond or water garden of any kind—it's futile to read further unless you are into total fantasy or empyrean images. Standing from a few to seven feet out of the water, the giant perfect celadon umbrellalike leaves radiate an otherworldliness and provide a grand backdrop for the spectral flowers that waft even higher. If you do have a pond with the virtue of at least four hours of direct sun a day—spend your last dime to acquire lotus (see *Nymphaea* for other necessary cultural tips), and plant them in the richest soil you can concoct. A paragon in God's achievements, as ideally and dreamily painted by Botticelli. [See photo in Chapter III, p. 84]

HM *Lycoris squamigera* (lye-**kor**-iss)
Exotic spider lilies. Supposedly zones 6–10.

Long stamens jut out and dance around the flower head, giving it a "spidery quality." Leaves appear in early summer just after planting with the tip of the dark bulb at the surface, then disappear making way for the gem of a flower. Needs a dry, sunny spot.

√√ *Lysimachia clethroides* (lye-sim-**mayk**-ee-a)
Dear Mr. Gooseneck Loosestrife. Zones 4–9. [See Chapter I, p. 13.]

You've got to find room for this plant, and bought at the nursery, one is truly all you need as it clumps and spreads with the vigor of few other plants. Fortunately, the profuse flowering is so lovely it deserves its space, and by the second year gives the border real heart and that eternal look we all seek. Hundreds of tiny white flowers clothe a spike that gracefully nods like a "gooseneck," or better still—a swan's neck. Deadheading spent spikes gives way to incredibly dense flowering. To control it, simply pull out the rosettes of leaves (which have a burgundy cast about them when young) from the spots where you don't want it. Begin to do this as soon as the leaves emerge; as the larger they grow, the harder it is to be gone with them. In the white border, which has a modicum of morning sun, it is extremely happy. You can try to contain it somewhat with grow-through supports, but I love its wild look and don't even bother. Cut to the ground in autumn. Requires a bit of sun and ordinary dirt.

Beware, however, of any other lysimachia! This is the *only one* you want. Others look like weeds and deserve the connotation of their common name, which was originally "louse-strife" as they were grown in the Middle Ages to repel the then ever-present louse. [See photo in Chapter I, p. 14.]

√√√ *Magnolia grandiflora* (mag-**nol**-ee-a)
The grandame southern magnolia. Zones 7–9. [See Chapter III, p. 76.]

How can I rave enough about this magnificent tree, now with us for six summers and more enchanting each year. It amazes me it grows so splendidly here as it's so associated with the best old southern gardens, but we have it in a *sheltered spot* (between the huge cedar hedges), and it gets as much sun as possible on our plot. Around it as a ground cover there are hosta and spring bulbs like 'Thalia' daffodils and *Endymion*—important to *smother root base in ground cover* as magnolias are shallow-rooted and need protection not only from sun, but lawn mowers as well. Also, I mulch it really well in winter, stacking the salt hay a few feet deep around its trunk. Other than preferring acid soil, it seems to take care of itself. Ones I've seen in South Carolina were gigantic affairs, and I've read it can reach eighty feet. Evergreen as can be, it remains beautiful all winter, but come spring the old leaves get a bit tatty in April as they mottle and discolor, and by May it looks like a shriveled up wrinkly brown mess. But never fear, it's only making way for the fabulous new growth that will have arrived in full force by early June. The large ovate leaves are so glossy they appear to be lacquered and in winter have a bronze sheen underneath.

White and gigantic, the many-petaled, dinner-plate-size blooms begin in June and periodically recur throughout summer. Can't say it smothers itself in flowers—that would be too much—but each flower is an event and smells divine. Following on the heels of the flowers are fantastic dark red seedpods, also huge, that I just leave there as they're so interesting and no scholarly tome has ever suggested removing them. This native American tree is the ultimate and very hardy—to Zone 6 if well protected.

Other magnificent flowering magnolias abound, but we haven't acquired them yet. If we ever move the driveway as I'm yearning to, my vision is to line it with the spring-flowering magnolia hybrids, the fabulous saucer *Magnolia* x *soulangiana* with its huge cup-shaped creamy pink/purple blooms being my favorite; *M. tormentosa* widely known as the "star magnolia" that densely blooms white; and even the incomparable Chinese tulip tree, *Magnolia campbellii*. The magnolia is the preeminent flowering tree. Make it one of your first important gardening purchases from your finest nursery and, honey, you'll be pleased as punch.

HM *Malva moschata* (**mal**-va)
Congenial musk mallows. Zones 4–8.

Airy and charming perennials best bought at the nursery—look for bushy, bud-laden ones. Flowers June through August if religiously deadheaded. Needs sun and grow-through supports. Cut woody stems to a few inches in autumn. The *alba* variety is especially nice.

HM *Mandevilla* (man-da-**veel**-uh)
Great flowering vine. Annual here. Zone 10.

From Buenos Aires and very ooh-la-la Evita, deep rose-pink trumpet flowers bounteously bloom their hearts out all summer. Can be trained as vine or trail into a pool. They needs lots of water and sun, but make a big tropical statement. Terrific.

√√√ *Mertensia virginica* (mer-**ten**-see-a)
Adored Virginia bluebells. Zones 4–9.

These beautiful little perennials are hard to find for some reason, unless you want to pay the extravagant price of three for $18.55 at WFF, which is a fortune considering you want lots of them. Twenty-four for $39.75 from Van Bourgondien is much easier to take for this small spring-flowering beauty because they don't make much sense unless they're massed. Plant the fleshy roots in fall with the tops only an inch below the soil's surface. Mix with *Muscari* and daffodils for a real treat. In early spring, dusty purple leaves emerge that soon turn gray-green, and in April the darlingest crinkled tubular violet-blue flowers appear and prolong into mid-May. After that, unfortunately, the plant dies out (goes dormant) and looks awful, so it makes sense to place this joyful spring scene among hosta or ferns or an equally reliable choice. Mertensia love a rich, moist, woodsy spot. The grand garden on Lily Pond Lane has hundreds of them mingling with white and yellow daffodils, and it's a sight producing oohs and aahs for days.

HM *Monarda didyma* (mon-**nard**-uh)
Perennial bee balm. Zones 4–8.
Bees and hummingbirds love it. Dense heads of spiky tubes provide lots of color (they come in many) in August. It's a spreader, so control in spring. To avoid powdery leaves, douse with Wilt Pruf when young. Use flower supports. Try 'Mahogany'.

√ **Moss**
You know, plain old moss. I guess it's everywhere.
Don't know exactly what moss is botanically, but along with the Japanese, I just love its tranquillity and velvety appeal. You don't have to go out and buy moss—although you can order it from We-Du Nurseries with very detailed descriptions, and one nursery around here sells tiny little pots for about seven dollars—because I'm sure if you give it a little thought you can find plenty all around you or somewhere in your neighborhood. Look in north-facing areas or on treetrunks—that's where it grows. Just lift up the sheet, or lump, or sliver, or whatever you find, and place it on moist ground and stick it down with those rounded old hairpins where you want to establish it. Keep watering till it settles in.

I'm trying desperately to create a moss ground cover in my rockery, carting it there from all over the property, but the problem is weeds keep popping up and spoiling the serene scene. Hugh Johnson says, "Happily, moss is encouraged rather than killed by contact with weed-killers, which will keep down any competition." I just went out with my RoundUp and blasted all the spoiling weeds, so we'll see if erudite Mr. Johnson is right. (I've still got some weeds but the moss does seem thicker.)

√√ *Muscari* (**mousse**-kuh-ree)
Beloved grape hyacinths. Zones 2–9.
Of the many species, all are wonderful except *M. comosum* 'Plumosum', which is a hairy-

looking mess. Oh, but the others are divine—the blue-blue flowers spring from narrow grass-like leaves in grapelike clusters a few weeks after the crocus and literally carpet the spring garden if you plant enough. They are cheap (about twelve dollars per one hundred from Van E.) and easy to plant (only a few inches beneath the soil in fall)—so why not indulge in a few hundred for great reward next spring. The die-hard Brit institutions, like Oxford in spring, think nothing of planting thousands upon thousands—and it's a cherished sight.

The long, narrow leaves appear soon after planting in autumn and persist all winter, so you always know where your muscari are, except for a few months in summer when they go dormant. I have them in both sun and shade and they do equally fine in either situation, but of course the sunny ones bloom first. They are also extremely charming in pots, where they can be better examined, as at the max they're only eight inches high. You will adore them. Cut and bring them inside and place in a *kenzan* or somewhere you can really appreciate the subtlety of the colorations—some have tiny white edgings, others are paler blue in the middle than at the bottom or top; all are truly lovely. [See illustration in Chapter VII, p. 193.]

√ *Myosotis* (mai-oh-**soh**-tus)
Forget-me-nots. Zones 5–8. [See Ground Covers.]

√√ *Narcissus* (nahr-**kis**-us or nahr-**cis**-us)
And daffodils and jonquils. Zones 3–9 at least; they need frosty winters.

The beautiful vain young man of Greek mythology, Narcissus, was so enamored by his own reflection in glassine ponds he pined away because he couldn't embrace himself. Eventually he was changed into a flower, and thus the fetching tale of the narcissistic but beloved daffodil. Singularly the most endearing trait of this huge family of bulbs is they literally last forever (at least, many of them), unlike their fleeting spring friends, the tulips. Without question, the often giant bulbs are a pain in the ass to plant, but once done they are your devoted companions for a long, long time. You can tell how many flowers to expect from each bulb by counting its "noses," or separations. The gigantic ones, needing such big deep holes, usually have three. My trusty three-inch flower auger doesn't work for these big bulbs; the only method is to dig suitably large trenches (you want to plant at least a dozen bulbs in any spot for a decent display)—*deep enough so the bulb rests underground at twice its depth*, figure about eight inches at least. Because the bulbs will increase and bear new noses over the years, you must not plant them too close together—leave a few inches between, but not six or eight inches as so many books attest, which would produce an unfulfilling, scattered planting. Beef up the soil with peat moss and bonemeal when planting, but they're not very persnickety about kind of dirt, or anything else for that matter.

Contrary to most opinions, they bloom equally well in sun or dappled shade, and actually shade is better for the pink-apricot ranges. The only other cultural requirement is that, of course, their many leaves must be allowed to die down naturally, which takes an agonizingly long time in May and June. Where I don't have them situated among jubilant perennials that rise up and cover the yellowing foliage, the tedious task of braiding the leaves and tying them off with raffia (or one of their own strong leaves twisted round the bunch) becomes necessary—the aftereffect is so improved, the chore is worthwhile. And please, as the flowers fade, *deadhead* by snapping off the top inch of the stem to conserve their energy for next year's growth instead of going to seed.

Botanically speaking, all daffodils and jonquils are technically *Narcissus;* commonly those with more obvious trumpets are termed daffodils and all the doubles, specials, and those with flatter "faces" are called narcissus. Jonquils are a specific late-blooming group of narcissus. Unlike the interesting and defining horticultural divisions of iris and lilies, the eleven divisions of daffodils are boring: e.g., Division II—the cup is more than one third, but less than the length, of the perianth segment. See what I mean? So let's not bother with the exalted societal divisions. The vast array of daffodils available to you is staggering, and new ones are introduced each year. It makes more sense to discuss the great ones.

Beginning with the many beguiling kinds of dwarfs, those only reaching eight inches max, most are in the *cyclamineus, triandrus*, and *bulbocodium* group. Usually dwarf forms of flowers don't interest me too much, but dwarf daffodils are another story as many are extremely pronounced and quite glamorous. Place them purposefully near rocks, along a path, or at the garden's edge for best effect. *Bulbocodium obesus*, only five inches high, has a wonderful hoop-petticoat-like, widely flaring trumpet structure; the *cyclamineus* 'Dove Wings' has a long, slender pale-yellow trumpet that turns white and curved, narrow white petals arching straight back—a real look; and *triandrus* 'Ice Wings', pure white, would make a very auspicious beginning dwarf daffodil collection.

There are hundreds of standard narcissi to choose from—scan the brightly colored bulb catalogs and choose your favorites. Don't think you need to make your daffodil splash all at once—an abundant spectacle of flowering can be *achieved over several years*. I find adding a hundred or so to my collection each year has been the way to go as they are not easy to plant and expensive as well. Among my preferences are the gigantic flowered 'Fortissimo', with the yellowness relieved by a blazing orange-red trumpet; 'Ice Follies' soft lemon ruffly trumpet on white petals and one of the very first to bloom; 'Ice King', which is gigantic and extraordinary—a fully double pale-cream trumpet (looks quadruple to me) with petals that flare back; 'Mount Hood', the classic all-white; 'Mrs. R.O. Backhouse', a very pretty all-pink; and 'Barrett Browning', with white petals and a wide short cup of brilliant orange. All yellow daffodils are not my cup of tea, but if they're yours there are tons of varieties, with 'King Alfred' reigning supreme.

Unquestionably in the common trumpet-cupped narcissi, I greatly prefer the doubles (Division IV). The trumpets here are not pronounced and instead there is a profusion of usually ruffled and crimped petals that yield fuller and fancier flowers. 'Obdam' and 'Ice King' are all-white and both beauties. 'Tahiti', as its name implies, is a commingling of all warm colors, and 'Lemon Beauty' and 'Broadway Star' have ruffled and shirred striped middles. 'Cheerfulness', one of the antique *poeticus* group, is simply wonderful—many flowers to a stem bloom in clusters, white petals with creamy centers, and they smell heavenly—twenty of these make a very significant statement. You'll want many doubles.

But most of all, it's the split-coronas (Division XI) that really ring my bell. Also known as "butterfly daffodils." The trumpet or cup is "split" in such a way it almost gives the impression of two flowers—one being superimposed on the other. The unusual "collar" narcissus 'Tricollet' has an atypical triangular salmon cup against white and the breathtaking 'Palmares' (Dutch Gardens has it) is peachy-pink and ravishing. Another it's a cinch you'll adore is 'Parisienne', known as "orchid-flowering" because of its intense fluting and ruffling—a beautiful combination of apricot and cream.

Even in a first-year garden you'll not want to be without the sixteen-inch *triandrus* 'Thalia'. This icy white beauty flowers at least two to a stem with petals that reflex backward and a hoop-shaped cup. Another must-have is the *poeticus* (Division IX) daffodil 'Actaea'— whiter-than-white rounded petals frame a tiny sophisticated "eye" of yellow edged in red with a green center. Just one more to round out the daffodil array no garden should be without, the *tazetta* 'Geranium'. Produces masses of flowers on each strong stem, frilly creamy-white petals with bright orange cups, and it smells fabulous. For not being my absolute favorite spring-flowering bulb, what would spring be without them?? And the minute you veer off the tried and true path of the ubiquitous yellow ho-hum varieties—splendors are in store. Why grow ordinary daffodils when so many are extraordinary!?! Gather the fine bulb catalogs around you and strike out any looking like the packs populating every pedestrian daffodil display you've ever seen. Order the exotics, and thank your lucky stars you didn't get snookered into the too-obvious too-yellow prosaic presentation. [See illustration in Chapter VI, p. 151.]

Nasturtium. See *Tropaeolum*

√√ *Nepeta mussinii* or *faassenii* (ne-**pet**-a)
Catmint. Zones 4–8.

What a great perennial for border's edge or spilling over pathways. Of course, it smells like mint, and although supposedly irresistible to cats, a few of my friends delight in eating it, but we've not acquired any stray cats. I simply adore the way it looks in the garden. Perfect foil for blue-border edging as the gray-green leaves with a blue sheen billow and tumble in just the right manner on arching stems all summer. To make it even finer—loose spikes of small tubular lavender-blue flowers envelop the plant in June through July. Around mid-July, *if all flowers are sheared off*, it reblooms like crazy and lasts through September. Three plants densely cover about eight feet. Always bought mine from nurseries (they look so appealing), but they're very hardy and I'm sure would be easy to start from catalog plantlings. Early to emerge in the spring, they should be cut back hard at autumn's end. All they really require is well-drained dirt. I tried some in the shade and they're not performing as handsomely as the blue-border ones with afternoon sun, but still possible. A wonderful plant for sure.

√√√ *Nerine bowdenii* (nay-**ree**-nay)
Exotic bulb. Zones 8–10.
Akin in its shooting-stamen tendencies to *Lycoris*, the spider lily, this beauty from South Africa is at home here as a potted specimen or its big fat bulbs must be dug and stored for winter. Back in my penthouse days, I managed to grow these with great luck in pots and was especially enthralled with the staying power of the exciting flowers that bloom at the tail end of the season—the perfect time for pink spidery blooms. It wants sandy soil, full sun, and nice hot climates, and needs to be interplanted among hosta or something eternal as the leaves die down in summer. I've just received some giant bulbs from Dutch Gardens abounding with signs of life, so a quasi-sunny spot was prepared deep (cover with six inches of dirt) and the bulbs buried well, and if I can grow it in the ground—'twill be a great thrill.

√√√ *Nymphaea* (**nim**-fee-uh)
Glorious waterlilies. Hardy and tropical. [See Chapter III, pp. 83–85.]
Without a pond, a pool, or at least a big Oriental fish urn, there's no point in going ga-ga over waterlilies, although you are well advised to establish some sort of method by which you can enjoy these lovely creatures. Both hardy and tropical waterlilies need at least twelve inches of still water (no gurgling fountains or gushing brooks can be too close) in which to grow and the *more sun the better*. They all have big fat roots and need large underwater containers (cover the surface with gravel and rocks to keep the dirt in and the plant down) and frequent doses of fertilizer (Lilypons Water Gardens calls theirs Lilytabs). Though flowering is the highlight of waterlilies, there is something exquisite to be said about their leaves—the lilypads. No water scene could be said to be complete without them, and if the occasional frog decides to alight on

one and pose—don't fight a bit of Hollywood. It's the intricate network of veins in the flowers and the leaves that keeps them afloat—so handle gently.

"Hardy" waterlilies are okay, but smaller, less floriferous, and lacking the gorgeous blue and violet colorations of their more divine cousins, the tropicals. But the "hardies" even withstand our coldest winters at the bottom of the pond along with the sleeping fish and faithfully return at the end of spring. However, the allure of the tropicals draws us back to the water nurseries each summer to purchase expensive new ones. Always try to buy plants already in flower so you don't have to wait forever for the first magical bloom, which naturally occurs later than with the hardy types. The tropicals also have the divine distinction of holding their flowers high above the water's surface, like the lotus, and have larger lily pads than their temperate cousins. No water gardener in his/her right mind would choose to be without extraordinary waterlilies. Considering seventy new hybrids were introduced in 1992 alone—it's certain there is one for your pool or pond.

Oenothera. (ee-no-**thera**)

Evening primrose, charming pale cup-shaped flowers, but the foliage is scraggly and they just don't last long enough.

√ Ornithogalum (or-nith-**og**-uh-lum)

Star-of-Bethlehem and chincherinchee. Zones vary.

A striking group of diverse spring flowering bulbs from Europe. All are easily planted in autumn to a depth of only two inches in organically amended soil, and all basically flower white. Actually, egglike white, like its name, from the Greek for "bird" and "milk." Sun or some shade is fine, and they have no funny quirks or special needs except, as usual, the leaves must be allowed to die down. An application of manure when flower-buds appear is recommended. As they're late to break through the ground in spring, be sure to mark them. Supposedly bulbs increase quickly, but I'm still waiting for this blessed event.

O. *nutans*—Zones 6–10—this little beauty doesn't have the glistening white flowers that are the trademark of the genus, but instead curious downy, celadon-green–edged ecru flowers that slightly resemble a daffodil and look different from anything else in the garden—almost ghostly. It's supposed to naturalize but my little patch on the outskirts of the shade path haven't been happy enough to do that.

O. *thysroides*—Zones 7–10—the chincherinchee of South Africa has a few remarkable traits. The white six-petaled flowers open from the bottom up in a conical form and last up to three weeks! In water. More quaint is their ability to absorb color when the stems are put in a pot of ink or dye. Of course, the minute I read this I ran right out to pluck some out of the garden and try them in my indigo ink—and yes, after about twelve hours, they more or less became indigo.

- *O. arabicum*—Zones 7–10—the tallest of the genus, these sparkling white flowers are centered with a black-green bead that looks mineral-like. Originating in the Middle East and Bethlehem justifies its common name, star-of-Bethlehem. Also very good and long-lasting for cutting, though a dozen make a terrific exhibition in the garden.

HM *Oxypetalum caeruleum* (ok-see-**pet**-uh-lum)
Darling blue-flowered perennial. Zone 10, grow as annual north.

The subtle flower's unusual shade of waxen baby blue with a turquoise center is different from all else in the garden. Flowers in summer and needs full sun. Can be trained as a vine with the proper support. Special.

√√√ *Paeonia* (pee-**oh**-nee-uh)
The royalty of perennials. Zones 4–8 generally.

Incomparable isn't strong enough a word for these silken-bloomed, overwhelmingly beautiful flowers suffused with dense petals and petaloids. A sight to cure any ills and dispel gloom, the name commemorates the physician to the Greek gods, Paeon. In cultivation for centuries and hailing from hard-winter parts of the world like Mongolia, Tibet, and Siberia—their most important cultural requirement is a *cold winter.* So while you Zone 9 and 10ers have all your exotic tropicals—*we* have peonies. Aside from magical flowering, the deeply divided compound leaves, often in comely shades of dark red, almost purple, stay lovely all summer and are suitable as a hedge once flowering finishes. Peonies last through generations, so consider your choices carefully and plant them well.

Bare-root peonies should be planted in autumn, but if you'd rather deal with nursery grown potted plants, then spring is okay, too. For some reason the peony is always a plant I've bought from nurseries—must have something to do with my patience level, as they take a legendarily long time to become established and reach blooming size. Now that I've come to better understand the specialist growers, come to think of it—their mature roots might bloom even quicker. Even my most carefully selected nursery plants have taken three to four years to really produce satisfying flowers—this standard of perfection not something miraculously happening overnight. All the books say once planted they hate to be disturbed, and I've always taken this as gospel and therefore have a pink flowerer in the dark-red garden, etc. Much to my surprise, however, as I write this on a mid-April day, the three peonies I was forced to move from the white garden last summer because of the dreaded *Houttuynia* scourge have flourished from the ground this spring in a grander way than any of the other peonies on the property??? I don't get it; and of course, I've yet to see flowers—but I find it curious, and perhaps this "do not disturb" syndrome is a bit hyperbolic. One of the very first plants to break through the ground each spring, the peony rises in a dark crimson color with leaves forming when they are only about six inches out of the ground. They shoot up quickly and must be *surrounded early with grow-through supports* (the small size is best) as the heavy flowers will cause the branches to topple, which is the last thing you want.

Something not to be alarmed about is ants, which tend to crawl over the buds when they plump up and are about to bloom. Terribly unnerved by this ant infestation and whining to Steven Hamilton—he quelled my anxiety with a story springing from his "primal memory of peonies at his natal home in Indiana." It seems that he, too, as a child was unsettled by ants slithering over the peony buds and began methodically knocking them off, bud by bud, from a hedge stretching some thirty yards, when his adored great grandmother, Minnie Meier, came rushing to the defense of the ants (or the peonies) and insistently told him to "stop at once!" She agreed the ants *appeared* to be dining on the buds, but maintained that if denied their little meals the buds would fail to bloom properly, if at all. As I understand it, the long peony hedge in question is still blooming—so don't touch the ants.

When planting your peonies, if bare-root, deeply dig and heavily enrich the dirt with twenty pounds of composted manure and a good pound of bonemeal well worked into the soil. Remember these are eternal plants, so this extra work is mandatory. Bonemeal scratched into the soil each spring doesn't hurt either. Make sure the crown of the tough, thick, tuberous root mass is no more than *one and a half inches below the surface*, and be careful not to damage the eyes. Peonies are very long-lived and might well be around for generations, so plant them well and don't be stingy. The more peonies the better—they are plants worth every dime of their expensive prices.

Flowers should be *deadheaded quickly* once faded and stems cut directly to the ground in autumn. For the first few winters at least, mulch well. Use only salt hay or evergreen boughs as mulch, as air needs to circulate around the crown. If you are growing enough peonies to afford to cut some for the vase—they are one flower that *doesn't like being immediately plunged* into water. Let them rest in a cool dark place for twenty-four hours before trimming the stems *again* and immersing them up to the flowering point. They only last three or four days, but these are special and glorious cut flowers. However, *don't cut any* in the first few years of bloom until the plant is truly established, and when you do cut—leave at least half the flowers on the plant and three complete leaves on each cut stem.

Flowers are either single, semidouble, completely double, rose, bomb, crown, or anemone as form—all relatively self-explanatory and not a homely one in the bunch. The plants themselves are either standard herbaceous bush form (normal peonies) or "tree peonies." Tree peonies are actually shrubs that can reach three to five feet and be trained as a standard. Ideal for growing in containers, their culture is much like that for herbaceous peonies, except they're a bit more tender and need a somewhat sheltered spot. Of the myriad cultivars, surely you'll latch onto a strain or hybrid that awes and engulfs you. *P. suffruticosa* 'Rock's Variety' is semidouble creamy white with nuances of burgundy in the center; 'Sarah Bernhardt' is a vision in pink; 'Auguste Dessert' is semidouble deep pink tinged golden; 'Festiva Maxima' is the must-have huge rose-form—all-white flecked with crimson; and *P. tenuifolia* is a "laceleaf peony"—a fragile single white, breathtakingly lovely. They're all stunning—you really can't go wrong.

Pancratium. Gorgeous. See *Hymenocallis*

√√√ *Papaver orientale* (pah-**pay**-ver)
Gigantic and fabulous perennial poppies. Zones 4–9.
Oh, do I love these! There is a superb poppy garden on the funnily named Highway Behind the Pond that makes me swoon each June. Perfectly positioned on a slight hill (good for drainage) to entrap every ray of sun (which they need tons of), these splendid crepe-papery crowning-achievement blooms nod and dance in the air in a brilliant combination of white, salmon, vermillion, and deep mahogany. The true source of opium, it's appropriate these scintillating blooms are so potent, almost intoxicating.

I tried and tried to establish them at the beginning of the border and in the white garden, and though I've a few diehards—there just isn't enough sun. Now I've planted a slew of them in the new cutting garden, where they're apt to make it. Mounds of their rather unattractive foliage have already appeared and June flowering seems almost certain. Order the fleshy bareroots from a good perennial catalog and *plant them deep* in autumn—you may have bloom the next year. Poppies don't like to be crowded, transplanted, or kept damp. Soon after planting, hairy foliage will push up from the earth and persist to one degree or another all winter; in spring the coarse fernlike leaves really sprout. The first of the big thrills comes as a giant whiskered ball of a bud noses out of the ground and rises on wiry leafless stems. The prickly, funky stems are unusually strong and never need to be supported although they can reach over three feet. When the silky, richly colored (or gorgeous white with a black-splotched base) petals unfurl—the flower can be as wide as eight or ten inches across. The center of the flower-cup bristles with zillions of little purple-black stamens to protect the seedpod. Even though this many-sided seedpod is quite attractive, too, after the flowers fade you want to pluck it off. Once flowering finishes, the leaves, which are not that pleasant anyway, yellow and die down and look lousy, so you want to plant your poppies among other perennials to hide this tattered aftermath (mine are among hosta).

If you have cold winters, this is a flower to definitely not ignore. Start with a minimum of six grouped together and I guarantee you'll want more the moment the exhilarating

The Oriental Poppy in all its heady glory.

bloom graces your garden. When you've acquired enough and can bear to cut them for the vase—sear the ends of the stems with a match before the water plunge. Fabulous ones are 'Barr's White', 'Curlilocks' deep salmon pink, 'Mahogany', and 'Allegro Viva'—the classic scarlet.

√√√ *Passiflora caerulea* (pass-ih-**flor**-uh)

The passionate "passion flower." Zones 9–10, but great indoors. [See Chapter III, pp. 93–94 for the whole story.]

The Spanish Jesuit missionaries who discovered passiflora in the jungles of South America and scrutinized the flower to come up with its powerful religious significance must have also been mesmerized by the flower itself—as it's a wondrous thing. Each of its parts—the stamens, corona, petals and sepals—are so pronounced, perfect, and otherworldly that it possesses a definite surreal quality. All my mail-order attempts to grow this failed (they were from lousy sources), but when I found it in full form in a hanging basket at Marder's all my dreams came true. The original plants have been with me for four years of nonstop flowering all summer long and green green leafing and vining indoors all winter. Incredibly resilient, a housekeeper once neglected one in winter and on return to East Hampton I found what looked like a dead plant. After maniacal cursing of the housekeeper, I immediately removed all the withered leaves and stems and was left with a woody base; but (thank God) within days green shoots were everywhere and it fantastically returned to its normal vigor.

In Florida and California this amazing vital plant can be grown outdoors where it will climb to thirty feet and is said to be incredibly rampant, and how divine to have excessive five-fingered leaves and celestial flowers clambering over a fence or up a tree??? In cold-winter climates, you must settle for bringing it indoors to your nice toasty house at the first sign of frost in autumn and make sure to keep a trellis in the pots so it has something to climb on. We bring it outside in May, *water it religiously*, and feed it occasionally. In the latter months of summer, ours even bear strange-looking plump eggplant-shaped (but not sized) green fruits that turn orange. This just began happening last summer and was a first. This summer I want to track down another and plant it outdoors to twine around our pillared cherub in the latest cleared-out space—I will just dig it up and bring it indoors in a pot for the winter. (It was beyond divine.) In the midst of whatever else is high priority on your list, make it a point to locate this magnificent plant. Crownsville offers something named *Passiflora incarnata*, which is probably divine, but was sold out when I tried to order this year. Can't tell you a definitive source for the real thing, so you must insist your favorite nursery order it for you. Don't be without it in any case. [See illustration and photo in Chapter III, pp. 94 and 95.]

√ *Peltiphyllum peltatum* or *Darmera* (pelt-ee-**fye**-lum)
Umbrella plant—a giant. Zones 5–9.

This huge leafy plant is said to bear flowers on a hairy stalk in spring before the leaves emerge, but I've got leaves emerging like crazy on my two plants in the would-be rain forest and assure you no flowers preceded them. Anyway, the canopy of green leaves is what this plant is all about so who cares? The round, scalloped, glossy ten-inch-wide leaves rise up (to five feet supposedly; mine made it to about forty inches last year), one to a stem. Dark green, the shape of the leaves looks more like an inverted umbrella than the traditional parasol the name suggests. Mr. Linnaeus thought they resembled a shield, from the Greek *pelte* (a shield) and *phyllon* (a leaf).

Takes sun, but prefers shade. This is a perfect waterside plant as it likes rich boggy soil, so it must be *always kept moist* and planted in enriched soil. It grows by large rhizomes and is said to multiply if happy. Cut to ground in autumn and mulch.

HM *Perovskia* (pe-**rof**-skee-uh)
Russian sage, a subshrub. Zones 6–9.

An overall delicate, silvery presence imbues this charming border plant which can reach three feet. Needs plenty of sun and a dry location. Lavender flowers billow from tall spikes in late summer. Leave the whitish woody stems in winter and cut to the base in spring.

√√ *Petunia* (puh-**tyoo**-nee-a)
The dear annual.

Of all the profusely flowering bedding annuals, this is my favorite, as the hybridizers have made a science of producing great form and glorious colors and combinations thereof. I've little to say about petunias, except they need to be deadheaded constantly and grow well for me in shady spots, even though they're said to be sun-loving. They don't have that sprawling, leggy habit of pansies, for example, but still need to be revitalized by cutting back in midsummer. Useful in just the right spots in the garden or in a potted arrangement where you want a particular color accent. The 'Picotee' series can be very glamorous. It's simply a matter of searching the nurseries for the most engaging. [See illustration in Chapter I, p. 19.]

√√ *Physostegia virginiana* (fai-soh-**stee**-gee-a vir-jin-ee-**ah**-na)
A divine perennial. Zones 4–8.

Called the "obedient plant" because its flowers have the curious ability to respond to being twisted round the stem and stay where put. The gorgeous flowers, which individually look something like a sophisticated snapdragon, rise in tall spires in mid-July and last through September if you keep cutting off the ones that fade—or better yet, cut for the vase as they begin to open—superb cut flowers. The stems are a bit weak, and you must put your *grow-through supports in place early on*. They are late to emerge in spring, and as the leaves are ordinary, they could be mistaken for weeds, so please mark them. The usual color is a vivid purplish-pink, though I also have a stunning clump in the white garden, which increases ever year. Both my nursery plants and bare-root ones have thrived.

Half sun suits them just fine, though I'm sure they'd be tickled pink in full sun, too. Physostegia has a fondness for moist, slightly acid soil and are assisted in spring by a generous sprinkling of that great old composted cow manure. Cut them back hard in autumn not long after the thrilling bloom finishes.

√√ *Pieris japonica* (pee-**air**-iss), syn. Andromeda
A shrub to love. Zones 6–8, though there are other more cold-hardy species.

East Hampton is awash with these heavenly shrubs; some old ones are huge, at least fifteen feet high and almost as wide, and in early to mid-spring they are all covered with masses of drooping racemes of urn-shaped white (or white tinged with red) flowers that look like fulfilled lilies of the valley. Therefore a drive round town in April is a vision of whiteness and daffodils. Virtuosity of this shrub is expressed in its name, derived from Pierides, suggesting Muses who were goddesses of the arts. Young leaves have a bronze cast, and the bush is insistently evergreen, with whorling, glossy, lance-shaped, deep green leaves that revert again to bronze in winter. Andromedas are rounded and dense, and mine have grown amazingly fast. Planted three years ago from healthy nursery starts of about fifteen inches, they are now approaching five feet and full as can be.

They like moist, peaty, acid soil and are said to prefer a sheltered site. Come to think of it, most all the big fabulous ones around here are nestled against houses. Dappled or real shade are their preference, though mine get morning sun and seem content. Deadheading after flowering improves growth, which is a big chore as the flowering racemes are so numerous. I'm not too fastidious about it but they don't seem to care. I'm sure you have a perfect spot for wonderful andromeda. Oh, and the flowering lasts weeks and weeks on the shrub and holds up pretty well in a vase too. Don't miss this one.

√√ *Platycodon grandiflorum* (plat-ee-**koh**-duhn)
An adored perennial. Zones 4–9.

Impossible to have too many of these. Every time a vigorous one is spotted at the nurseries I bring it home and it invariably graces another spot. Never tried it from the catalogs, but the nurseries here are teeming with them, and rightly so. Commonly called "balloonflower" because of its divine buds that swell up like a six-sided balloon, but instead of just being filled with hot air, they develop into dreamy strong, star-shaped flowers from end July and into September. From the Greek, *platys* for "broad" and *kodon* for "bell," most are blue-purple, but the Japanese have cultivated pink, mauve, and white. I planted a white one between the Buddha heads in '87, the first gardening summer, and it has surpassed any wildest visions of perennial glory. Each year it increases until last year it threw off maybe three dozen abundantly ballooning and flowering stems at least thirty inches tall, draping all over Buddha. Every book says this plant would rather die than be transplanted, but I was naturally forced not to heed this advice when faced with the *Houttuynia* pestilence, so I lovingly moved it to a holding ground in the cutting garden.

Because this great plant is very late to materialize in spring, I don't know yet whether I've lost the beloved white or not, but am suspicious the "would rather die than be transplanted" is a fact of life, as now into May all I see are some dreaded *Houttuynia* leaves and not a trace of platycodon pushing up. Damn. Damn. *DAMN.* Anyway, be sure to *carefully mark* your precious platycodon. I use small grow-through supports on my older bushier ones to keep them erect as who wants to miss out on a single bloom? Never attempt to divide them, but do deadhead the flowers—it *really* promotes more bloom. Give some sun and you will be rewarded with spectacular plantings. Even the bluish-green leaves are nice. [See photo in Chapter I, p. 14.]

HM *Polemonium caeruleum* (pol-eh-**moh**-nee-uhm)
Jacob's ladder, a fine perennial. Zones 4–8.
One of the first perennials to bloom in late May from a lovely clump of fernlike foliage. Mauvy cuplike flowers last a month. Likes sun and good drainage and needs fertilizer, as its fibrous roots tend to quickly deplete the soil. Lovely.

√√√ *Polygonatum odoratum thunbergii* (pol-ee-gon-**ah**-tuhm)
I have a fetish for Solomon's-seal. Zones 4–8.
First saw this in my single garden summer on MacDougal Street where an old colony of them in a shady dell mesmerized me. This decisively arching perennial is a graceful and serene sight in spring, and the winglike pairs of pale green foliage curve lithely till summer's end. In spring it produces clusters of green-tipped white floral bells hanging at intervals from the underside of the long, strong, wandlike stems that can reach two feet, absolutely enchanting

An idyllic plant, Solomon's seal.

hovering over lilies of the valley, or in any moist shady place for that matter. Seldom see these lovelies at the nursery and first failed with expensive ones from Wayside, but hit the jackpot with six gorgeous variegated (creamy-edged borders along the leaves) from Holbrook. It even seems the long tuberous rhizomes are already (three years) doing their colonizing and matting thing because I just went out to give a look and counted eleven pointy projections rising from the earth instead of the original six!! Bravo!!! Once they surface, it's only a matter of a few weeks till the flowering bonanza, but the leaves stay beautiful for months.

Solomon's-seal needs a woodsy or cool shady place. Plant the roots in autumn two to three inches below the surface and mix in all your enriching friends. It needs cold winters to initiate its dormancy and moisture when in growth. It's a charming old-fashioned plant. You'll just love it drooping along a path or hovering over a shady scene.

Primula. (**prim**-u-la)
The masses of primroses in my favorite garden on Lily Pond Lane are inspiring, but they're just not one of my things.

√ *Pulmonaria* 'Sissinghurst White' (pull-moh-**nay**-ree-uh)
A Vita perennial. Zones 4–9. [See Ground Covers.]

√ *Puschkinia scilloides* (push-**kin**-ee-a)
A darling spring bulb. Zones 3–8.

It's tiny, but its creamy-white flowers striped with blue cluster so charmingly I just had to include it. Planted in masses in my favorite L. P. Lane garden they are enchanting, but of course, there are hundreds of them there. Less than a few dozen wouldn't make any sense anywhere. Great for a rock garden or along a stone path. Plant in fall about three inches deep in sun or shade. The bloom time and their life span are both long, so you might want to add sand to the soil as they like a gritty environment. They need cold winters. There's a pure white version, but what would be the point? I think the blue stripes are part of the Lilliputian allure. [See illustration in Chapter VII, p. 193.]

HM *Rhododendron* (roh-doh-**den**-drun)
Majestic flowering shrubs. Zones vary, but mostly 7–9.

Prowl your nurseries in May and June, when they're in flower, to choose your favorite of the five hundred species (including azaleas) and thousands of hybrids and cultivars. All evergreen, they need acid soil, cold winters, cool and moist springs, and warm summers. Very happy in shade under tall trees, some becoming huge trees themselves. Prolific and very useful.

√√ *Rodgersia aesculifolia* or *pinnata* (rod-**jer**-si-a)
Very impressive perennial. Zones 5–8.

A true beauty. The books always chat about their exemplary place on pond banks, where they look swell no doubt, but they are stupendous hardy plants for the moist garden and are great both in my white patch and along the shade path. Their striking architectural form— seven or eight long, crinkled bronzed-green leaves radiating in a circular pattern from each strong stem—is grandly imposing, as each leaf-head is about eighteen inches across, like the leaves of the splendid horse-chestnut tree. Planted in sunnier spots, in early summer, plumes of fragrant pinkey-white astilbe-like flowers hover like a mist over the plant—but in shade, you've still got the great leaves. Very special and a standout anywhere, especially stunning rising over hosta.

Rodgersia, named for some tasteful fellow named John Rodgers, are happy in either sun or dappled shade and want an enriched acidic soil, but are otherwise a snap. Be sure to *keep them moist*. Quite late to sprout foliage in spring, so mark 'em. Always bought mine at nurseries till now, but this spring tried to order species *tabularis* from Crownsville, but was devastated to learn they were Sold Out! These are strong plants, and I've a real feeling that planting the creeping rhizomes bare-root will yield fab results. This one has huge circular pale green leaves and is a knockout as pictured in *Large-Leaved Perennials*. One more for next year. Rodgersia are terrific plants no gardener should overlook. [See illustration in Chapter VI, p. 148.]

√√√ *Rosa* (**roh**-za)
Roses, of course. Mostly Zones 4–9.

I've no business writing about roses as they've been written about for centuries by zealots and scholars of all kinds. Chinese history alludes to them in 3000 B.C.; the historic Greek island of Rhodes is named after them; Cleopatra dispersed sixty pounds of gold to procure a cushy twenty-inch-thick carpet of rose petals to smother the decks of her barge on the eve of the famous banquet at which she seduced Marc Antony; and Shakespeare, as we know, was entranced by them. There are wild roses, shrub roses, hybrid teas, floribundas, grandifloras, miniature China roses, ramblers and climbers, polyanthas, briars, musk, French, cabbage, and damask roses, to name some. Since my knowledge of them is little more than an infinitesimal seed, I prefer to quote an old missive from True Brit Timothy Andreae, quite the plantsman.

> 24 May, 12 or 14 years ago
> Went to Suffolk Friday soir to design the garden of a friend who has just inherited a tangled jungle together with large early Jacobean mansion c. 1600—what fun—topiaries, knot garden all silver and grey & other visions of burgeoning flora, including the ubiquitous rose patch. Also took in the Chelsea Flower Show which was v. flashy. At 5PM the bell rings and 10,000 demure old ladies smelling genteelly of blue grass and clad in respectable twin sets suddenly go through a particularly English Jekyll & Hyde routine and become all teeth, elbows, foul language, knees, and heels. *FOR* the great flower loot is on; they dive for the stalls and drag, carry, or pilfer anything they can lay their acquisitive green fingers on. A sight worth filming for posterity.
> Being rather recherché about things floral, I headed for an obscure stall showing obscurer Victorian flora and carried away two ten-foot tall rose bushes, among the new ones being spliced every year, and three giant thistles: which are not only apposite 'au jardin', but, being thorny and scratchy, are positively the best exit card from 10,000 Bacchae in twin sets on the rampage. Many a pinstriped sedate City businessman was left, trampled and bloodied, a self-deprecating carpet of blue and chalk stripe serge for the harried ranks of English jardinières to methodically abuse with their sensible shoes.

You see, much more entertaining than a big blah-blah-blah from me about roses, no? However, there is one big idea I must impart, recently retrieved from *The Avant Gardener*. Rose pruning is the subject of many debates, scholarly tomes, etc., and the tried and true method has always wound up being to meticulously prune all stems just above outward facing buds on a slant, plus cutting back weak stems, thinning out centers and on and on. Seems the American Rose Society, after much trial and testing, is advocating "rough pruning"—cutting all shoots straight across with a pruning shears or hedge trimmer, which sounds much easier. They've only tested floribundas and hybrid teas, but I thought this a tidbit worth passing on.

One more fashion hint gleaned from numerous sittings and stylings including roses. If your vase full begins to look dowdy or wilted—take your hair dryer to them and give a few quick gusts and they will perk right up.

And a recent boon from the Brooklyn Botanical Garden newsletter: two thousand members of the American Rose Society, all experienced, have benevolently made themselves available to give advice to us novices. Referral to a "Consulting Rosarian" can be had by simply phoning 318-938-5402 for free. That's the best advice I can give.

HM *Rudbeckia fulgida* 'Goldstrum' (rud-**beck**-ee-uh)
Maybe the only yellow-flowered perennial to consider. Zones 4–9.
A big, bold, golden statement with a fat black center inspires smiles with its oomph and perkiness. Likes plenty of water and lots of sun, but otherwise easy if not besieged by the rabbits, who absolutely love it.

HM *Ruta graveolens* (**roo**-tuh)
Rue, herb of grace. Zones 5–9.

The truest, bluest cloverlike foliage of any plant I've ever seen. Never reaches more than fifteen inches, but gets bushy and can form a delicate but dense mat for the border or herb garden. Cut back to old wood in early spring to maintain its ever-blueness.

√√√ *Sanguinaria canadensis* 'Multiplex' (san-gwi-**nay**-ree-uh)
A woodland wonder. Zones 3–8.

The old plantings at The Bayberry are much more captivating than the nursery stock they currently offer. I don't understand why they don't capitalize on their own beautiful gardens and make it a point to stock what they grow. Anyway, a beautiful patch of Sanguinaria grows there (but not for sale there) that I've finally tracked down through Carroll Gardens catalog (also at WFF but always sold out and three bucks more per plant). The three- or five-lobed leaves—looking like butterfly wings but bigger, up to six inches across—of a fresh water-green, shoot up from underground stems in early May. Then in a unique and charming manner, they encapsulate, or cradle, a delicate, waxen, double white flower as exquisite as a waterlily in miniature. The leaves unfurl as the flower blossoms. A really breathtaking sight—the white white against the green green. The handsome foliage covers its ground till August when it goes dormant. I am infatuated, really, with this one.

Its spurious common name, "bloodroot," has to do with the red sap in its roots and stems, which is nothing to bother with, but does stain your hands. Sanguinaria likes an *enhanced acid soil,* moist but never dripping, augmented with an overdose of manure/humus. The root of the ground-hugging plant should be planted horizontally two inches below the surface in just the right amount of shade. Am waiting impatiently for my first six to really establish—the first leaves and flowers are just heavenly. Among the most elegant bits of flora ever seen, I think there could never be too much.

√√√ *Sauromatum guttatum*
(sow-**roh**-ma-tum)

Incredibly prolific bulb (corm?). It's hardy for me??? Sauromatum is more vividly known as "voodoo lily or "monarch of the East," giving you some idea of

The stuff of gardening dreams—
Sanguinaria 'Multiplex'.

how strange it is. *Arum cornutum* seems to be the name most often incorrectly attributed to this ultimate favorite of mine, so much so I think of it as my "signature plant". Once used even as a motif for a Dianne B. Resort collection print when I became smitten with it four or five years ago. However, according to my cherished encyclopedia and *Hortus*, it is actually Sauromatum.

I've decreed it my signature as I've never seen it growing anywhere and neither had any of the thousand people on the Garden Tour. It elicited much inspection and interrogation, though

The fabulous circular summer leafing of my *Sauromatum* distinguishes it from everything else in the garden.

The "flower" of my signature *Sauromatum* is in the monkey's hands.

it hadn't even come close to reaching its peak that fated June day. Its flower, though hardly recognizable as such, provides for the name, as *sauros* means lizard, which can refer either to its divine spotted arching stalk or to the weird appearance of the sterile taillike appendage that is the "flower." This odd thing reaches about eighteen inches and is bronze on the outside; inside it's an incredible panoply of maroon and pale yellow markings that put most animal skins to shame (as far as pattern goes, that is).

Everything I've read says they are tender plants, but this has definitely *not* been my experience. They exist as a large flattish corm or tuber (like a big bulb). The voodoo-like quality stems from the fact they need no soil or water to produce the strange tubular spathe. Placed on a windowsill in strong light in a warm room around the end of March this intriguing oddity just appears without the benefit of being planted in dirt or watered. Strange, huh? However, this is by far not the most interesting aspect of this plant. It claims my highest honors because of its wondrous foliage, which looks like a miniature palm tree of the most exotic kind.

You are supposed to plant the bulbs in pots or in the ground after this strange blooming when the ground has warmed in May to achieve the palmlike state in the ground—and then dig them up and bring indoors at the summer's end to rest and prepare their cycle again. Well, a few years ago I missed taking up some from the garden, where I had barely buried them with no particular fussy procedure. For the last two years, in that very spot is a most miraculous sight. By end July there is a literal tropical jungle of thirty or forty stalks of these incredible palms held erect on fleshy, strangely *spotted* stems. The individual frondlike leaves can reach twenty inches each, and there are as few as seven to as many as fifteen of them on each stalk, radiating from a *circular* stem to boot! This is a magical incident I pass on to you.

However, it is unfortunately harder to find them than grow them. My original source, Gladside Gardens in Massachusetts is sadly no longer in existence, as you know. Once I received them as a substitute from Breck's marked *Arum cornutum* when I ordered *Arum dranunculus*, which had a crop failure; although they don't list them now. Last year I found them at the New York Flower Show at the booth of an exotic bulb-grower from Pennsylvania whose name I stupidly neglected to record.

Since I've discovered they are perfectly happy being left in the ground in East Hampton, I now take only some of them up from the garden when they begin to die back in September and bring them indoors (just to be on the safe side). Left in a basket in the kitchen, they begin to show signs of growth early in March when I set them out on a particularly focal table in the living room for winter entertainment. In their most spectacular positions in the garden, I cut the foliage off end September, mulch, and leave in the ground. Each year the palm-tree show, which begins in early June, is more spectacular. Definitely make it your business to find them.

√√ *Scabiosa caucasica* (skay-bee-**oh**-sa)
Beautiful floriferous perennial. Zones 4–9.

A real treat in the border, this frilly, heavily ruffled pale blue flower blooms for at least a month in late summer, smells delightful, and is great for cutting. Too bad its name is related to the disease "scabies," which it was said to cure in the Middle Ages. "Pincushion-flower" is the common name and relates to the pollen-tipped central filaments that look like a golden well-stuck pincushion. Must have *alkaline soil.* For a few years I kept failing with my nursery-bought plants until discovering the addition of lime to my more acidic soil did the trick. Needs sun. Three are scattered throughout the blue border and give real punctuation when in bloom. They should be deadheaded religiously and cut to the ground in autumn. Terrific for cutting too.

Scilla. Small early-spring bulbs. See *Endymion*, and forget mentions of "hyacinthoides"; they don't appear in *Hortus* (once in a while I do use it as the definitive reference) and are actually *Endymion*.

√√ *Sedum* (see-duhm)
Many kinds of succulent perennials. Most zones 4–9.
Low-growing, ground-hugging, and rosette-leaved describes most sedums, but others are tall and erect like the invaluable 'Autumn Joy'. Mainly they are great for edging the border or rockery, particularly valuable because the gray-green (often maturing to a rich, glossy burgundy) leaf whorls of established plants never seem to disappear all year, or at least are one of the absolute first sights in spring. I never cut them back in autumn, but leave them to do their thing and then clean up the old stems in spring. All sedum are succulent, which means they have thick fleshy leaves and add textural contrast to any garden scene. Every book I've ever read insists they need full sun, and perhaps they would be lusher, but thrive just fine here with never more than half a day, at best. They like any old well-drained soil and are not that thirsty for water.
Sedum spectabile 'Brilliant' and 'Autumn Joy' both are erect, produce flat dusty-rose flower-heads in late summer that last through autumn and undergo a thrilling mutation of color, finally winding up coppery bronze. They should be allowed to dry out and left in the winterscape. By the time they are cut down in spring, tons of pirouetting rosettes will have appeared. 'Autumn Joy' grows large (to thirty inches or more) and benefits from a grow-through support to keep it tidy. Of the ground-covering types—*S. roseum's* blessed with explicitly blue foliage and showy chartreuse flowers. *S. purpeum* 'Vera Jameson' is a low-grower with a beautiful wine-colored leaf that spews forth nice rosy-pink flowers in mid-August; and *S. purpureum* 'Live Forever' has been with me from the first days of the garden and I have the singular feeling it might do just that. Scout your nurseries, usually flush with many varieties, and see what strikes your sedum fancy. Carroll Gardens has a huge list too. If you're heir to one of those grand unmortared stone walls, sedum are great for growing in the crevices.

√√ *Sidalcea* (sye-**dal**-see-uh)
Profuse perennial. Zones 5–8.
Would like to think the hybrid of my dear sidalcea is the 'Oberon' or 'Puck' that I've read about, but don't know actually what it is except wonderful. Another with me since the first

summer, I remember buying it to echo the look of cosmos, but now realize the flower is more like a mallow and the plant much better than cosmos. Christopher Lloyd snobbily refers to the flower as "a very good pink," which it is—slightly mauve-toned and charming in the blue border. Related to the hollyhock, but much better—instead of sending up one heavy towering spire, it is many-branched and fully adorned with flowers that bloom for weeks on end from mid-July through September if you remove the faded flower branchlets. The stems are a bit weak, however, and grow-through supports should be used when the plant is relatively young each season. The dark green, scalloped leaves are among the first to surface in spring. Once again, I must differ with the avid full-sun requirement. In the bluish border it does get good afternoon sun, but because it has the habit of springing up new bushes around it (though you would never call it invasive), I have stuck some in the shade of the woodsier part of the garden—and what can I say? Seems perfectly happy. Each year the forty-inch high bush increases in width a little and gets better and better. Cut back hard in late autumn. It's easy and charming.

Malva moschata is equally appealing, but not as long-lived. Growing on woody stems, it demands grow-through supports, deadheading, and cutting back to the ground in autumn. Buy the most bud-laden at your nursery.

√ *Spirea japonica* (spy-**ree**-uh)
Generously flowering shrub. Zones 4–9.

The first silly Benson garden, put in by a landscape person who shall go nameless, at least contained three nice spirea. Since moved around many times to their final position on the north shade path where they mix enticingly with small, pale blue *Buddleia* 'Lochinch', they're extremely agreeable to being uprooted. Not the most handsome shrub in winter and spring, they're very woody and branchy and don't really begin to leaf till mid-May. But all summer are clothed in delicate lance-shaped pale green leaves and bloom all through July with abundant flat fuzzy flower-heads of rosy pink. If you take the time to shear off the spent flowers, I guarantee they will bloom again before summer's end. Whatever gardening books were my founts of knowledge early on told me to cut them to six inches in early spring, which I dutifully did for a few years. In '89 I forgot this springtime chore and they bloomed better than ever, so now I cut them back about a third and clean out any dead branches in spring. They require some sun and don't seem to be particular about anything else. There's a beautiful arching version bearing white flowers called 'Bridal Wreath' I've only planted last fall which already is making quite an impression.

√ *Sprekelia formosissima* (spreck-**kee**-lee-uh)
Aztec or Jacobean lily. Zones 9–10. Dig and store for the rest of us.

This striking beauty would merit a triple check if the flowers lasted longer, but alas—these dramatic beauties are a fleeting thing. A grand six-inch waxy crimson flower looks curiously like a fleur-de-lis and seems much too sophisticated to have originated in Mexico. Its name doesn't have very glamorous origins—seems J. H. van Spreckelsen was Linnaeus's lawyer in Hamburg. The true bulb is burgundy-colored and has a very long neck that should protrude from the surface of the soil slightly when potted. If grown outside, they are said to bloom and rebloom all summer and must be a magic garden sight, but my experience with them in a pot has been quite different. Soon after planting (a month at most), the amazing flowers burst forth and last maybe a week—but it is a spectacular week indeed. Last year, combined with canna, lilies, *Glorioso*, pineapple lilies, and *Haemanthus*—it was far and away the first thing to bloom in the exotic pot. Dig up at the end of summer and store in dry peat moss till potting up again the next summer. [See illustration in Chapter VIII, p. 265.]

HM *Stephanotis floribunda* (stef-uh-**noh**-tas)
Madagascar jasmine. Zone 10, or indoors in a pot in winter.
Gleaming dark green leaves vine beautifully all year long, and when brought outdoors for summer, scented small waxy white flowers are produced all season. This is the traditional "Hawaiian Wedding Flower." A beauty. Needs sun, sun, sun.

HM *Stewartia pseudocamellia* (stoo-**ar**-tyuh)
A fabled flowering tree. Zones 4–8.
The best alternative to camellias for cold winter climes, this slow-growing tree produces its white flowers in July. Likes morning sun, fertile acid soil, and a cool root zone—so mulch well. Wayside always has it, but prepare to be patient.

√√ *Stokesia laevis* (**stohk**-see-a)
Brilliantly flowering perennial. Zones 5–8.
Another great blue one, not quite as pretty as, but more reliable than *Scabiosa*. From sort of dreadful narrow green leaves (that hang around all winter) rise an incredibly dense profusion of mauvy-blue fancy flowers. Though a member of the aster family, these flowers have much more depth and dimension. They grow singly at the tip of many stems and are great for cutting, *as cutting encourages dormant buds into bloom*. If these are in your border and you can't bear to mar the scene by cutting, at least deadhead often. Sun or light shade suits them fine and they like well-drained soil, but otherwise are nonchalant. They also come in white, but whites dragged home from the nursery haven't been as robust. Belongs in every border.

√ *Symphytum caucasicum* (**sim**-fit-uhm)
The comfy and charming comfrey. Zones 4–9.

This would get a much higher rating if it didn't take up soooo much room! As it is, in flower the plant is thirty inches high tops, but its big, rough leaves swirl out of the clump nonstop all summer and cover at least a three-foot diameter—maybe more—and they're not so gorgeous. The flower, however, couldn't be more charming—blue as the sky they hang down in clusters—bell-shaped and crimped something like *Mertensia*. If you have a big meadow garden or a wild garden you'll covet these reliable old friends. Initially planted in the sunnier parts of the blue border, but after seeing this tremendous leafing action—I thought "What the hell" and moved them back into the woods line where they seem almost as happy shrouded in shade. Quite nice back there, to tell the truth. Bought them around the corner at Buckley's and they're available in the Carroll Gardens catalog. They're totally independent and don't need a thing.

√√ *Syringa* (si-**rin**-juh)
Lilacs!!! Mostly Zones 3/4–8

Perhaps too exhausted from a childhood spent enduring much oohing and aahing over the late spring-flowering lilac bush. It highlighted our yard otherwise sprinkled with cherry trees (inedible) and plantings around a brick walk totally immemorable, except for my Daddy's attention to them when he was there, which wasn't often enough as he was a merchant seaman. At any rate, a few years ago during a late-spring nursery haunt I was suddenly spellbound by lilacs and hauled home three straightaway to tolerably sunny spots. Now I love them. One of the first plants to break into bud in late winter in preparation for the masses of May blossoms that fill the air with the dowager scent of lilac. Only at home in places with cold winters, and responsive to alkaline soil, lilacs otherwise will be around for generations. All thirty-some sweetly scented species produce dense panicles of countless small tubular flowers in lilac, of course, as well as purple, red-violet, white, and even yellow if you are so inclined. The unremarkable oval leaves always drop in winter.

Pruning is the big issue with lilacs. There's lots of talk about buying them on their own roots (which seems preferable to me) or grafted onto plants like privets so they will be more contained. The big issue is suckering, which is an unwanted shoot arising from the below ground roots. Lilacs don't want suckering, nor does anything else for that matter, because it saps energy from the main growing system of the plant into loathed side shoots that spoil the look anyway. If your lilac has suckers, grafted or not, *dig down and cut them hard* with your trusty Felco. More lilac pruning: *immediately after flowering* cut off most branches producing flower-heads. Remove all flower clusters and generally prune for shape; in winter cut out weak or damaged shoots. Lilacs are a lovely, persevering old-fashioned thing to be cherished. I'd buy healthy ones at the nursery if I were you. There are oh so many cultivars, the best being those

grown at the Lemoine Nursery in Nancy, France—so
look for their offspring.

Tacca chantreiri
(**tak**-ka)

Bat-flower or devil-
flower, also devil's-tongue, cat's-
whiskers, and jew's-beard.

Hot Zone 10, of course, and if
you aren't bewitched by those common names, then in the end we might not
have much in common except a general love
of things floral. Definitely a weird, eerie, and
fabulous-looking creature, the flower which rises
on foot-high stalks is not really black, but even a more
sinister shade of deep purple-brown. Looked to me like a
beardless iris sprouting out of a dark, veiny calla lily when I
saw it in the Caribbean—with the added attraction of long,
pendant maroon threads, or "whiskers," that seem to have no botanical reason. It springs from large, oval, wrinkled leaves and is
evergreen.

You can be sure I'll make an all-out effort to track it down
and give it a go in my living room in winter (when it takes very
little water), and pot it up in a prominent spot on the deck in summer (when it
needs lots of water) with regular applications of fertilizer. It should be shaken
free of old soil when new growth begins in spring and repotted in a fresh mixture of
sand, loam, and peat. Sounds like the perfect infidel for my summer scene.

√ *Tellima grandiflora*. Ground cover. [See Ground Covers.]

√√ *Thalictrum aquilegiifolium* (tha-**lik**-truhm)
"Meadow rue." Big, beautiful perennial. Zones 4/5–9.

As you might expect from its species name, it has something to do with the charming
columbine. Their shared characteristics are their nearly indistinguishable lovely leaves and their
growth habit. Among the most delicate divided and subtly colored filigree foliage in the plant
kingdom—so that's saying something. The plant stays fresh blue-gray-green all summer, but

unlike the smaller columbine, grows to a heavenly five feet with terminal sprays of airy, misty flower clusters, not unlike *Astilbe*, that rise even higher. 'White Cloud' is an especially floriferous white one, but most of this species flower lavender-pink. Didn't have much luck with mail-order bare-roots, but my earliest ones from Warren's Nursery have been going strong for four years.

They break dormancy much later in spring than columbine. To look at them now on April 22, you would think *Aquilegia* the bigger plant, though that's not the case at all. With a look so weightless and elegant, you might expect staking to be required, but in any slightly sheltered position (as in any border grouping) they don't need any help at all. I've read advice to cut them down after the first flush of bloom for rejuvenation, but mine bloom from early June to mid-August, so I just deadhead occasionally if the flower is reachable. Perfect in part shade, in sunnier positions they need to be kept constantly moist. Cut to the ground in autumn. Thalictrum make a lovely contrast in the garden to other large perennials, which are usually coarser—and look beautiful flowering with *Astilbe* and *Aruncus*.

√√ *Tiarella cordifolia* (tee-ah-**rell**-uh)
Great shady ground cover. Zones 3–8. [See Ground Covers.]

HM *Tigridia* (tai-**grid**-ee-uh)
Spectacular fleeting flower. Not hardy except zone 10.

If you're looking for something to flaunt—this is it. Plant the tiny, crusty bulbs in May for dazzling spotted flowers lasting only one day. A huge range of flashy colors exist and bulbs can be dug and stored like *Acidanthera* (which see). Unique and radiant.

√√ *Tradescantia andersoniana* or *virginiana* (trad-es-**kan**-shi-a)
Beloved perennial. Zones 4/5–9.

Multitudes of common names adorn this must-have perennial, though many species are relegated to the dominion of "house plants." It's impossible you can't conjure up a vision between "wandering Jew," "creeping Jesus," "speedy Jenny," "inch plant," and the least en-thralling, "spiderwort." The perennial-garden version indicated above is a wonderful plant, sharing the spontaneous leafing habit of the just named "house plant" varieties—long, narrow boat-shaped leaves that tumble over the stems in architectural pairs, but also bearing, for long periods in summer, wonderful three-petaled triangular flowers in abundance. Extremely hardy and easy to please, tradescantia bounces forth early in spring with dark foliage jutting from its clump in little spikes. The cultivars and hybrids offered in the catalogs and at the nurseries (equally successful sources) are refined and not as vigorous (invasive) as the house-plant varieties might lead you to believe. Especially look for 'Zwanenburg Blue'—heartbreakingly big, tender, blue blossoms that never quit; 'Snowcap'—glistening and gleaming nonstop white; and 'Red Cloud'—a bit smaller and more restrained in a blushy-pink.

Just great toward the front of the border, as they like a little sun but no overdoses. They need good moisture and soil turned over with the enriching nutrients, but so do they all. This is one that responds to deadheading particularly well, or even more drastic— fully cutting back just at the nadir of the flowering season— note when the flowers begin to wane in size—grit your teeth (I always find this very hard) and cut it back to at least half and it will tumble forth and reward you with another complete cycle of full-blown bloom. Individually each flower lasts only a day, but at each leaf joint on every vigorous stem there are great umbels of buds. You'll love this plant if you pay attention to it. It looks really great with arching *Liriope* nearby.

The prolific *Tradescantia*.

√√ *Tricyrtis hirta* (try-**ser**-tis)
Forget the unbecoming common name "toad Lily." Zones 4–9.

What a great perennial! All summer long a well-behaved clump of statuesque, arching stems grace the garden with a lithe Oriental effect. Pointed, ovular, dark green leaves clasp the stem in an out-pouring horizontal fashion difficult to describe, but great looking. In early September, senses are heightened when from the leaf axils on top of the stems, hundreds of little spotted flowers looking for all the world like orchids appear. I have it growing near *Physostegia* 'Vivid', and when both are in bloom—it's quite a sight! Though members of the lily family, these flowers look exactly like creamy orchids sprinkled with little purple spots. Architectural, enchanting, and extremely reliable all at once—this plant is a treasure.

Needs no staking or special coddling. As it grows to a good three feet and spreads even more after a few years, it is a standout in the woodland garden, where it basks in dappled shade. Said to also take sun if the soil is rich and moist. Tends toward acid soil, so amend yours with sulfur or Miracid if on the alkaline side. Spreads by stoloniferous (horizontally spreading roots) rhizomes, but not invasive, and forms handsome, healthy clumps. Mine have been growing strong since '88, planted bare-root from a catalog (can't remember which, maybe Holbrook) and my nursery plants, at the woods' edge of the serpentine border are great, too. Cut to ground in late autumn after flowering finally ceases, and mulch well. [See drawing next page.]

√ *Trillium grandiflorum* (**tril**-lee-uhm)
"Wake-robin" or "trinity lily." Zones 5–8.

Another sweet woodlander, it has the distinction of all its parts being trinary: three leaves to a stem, three petals, three sepals, plus style divided into three. All parts are balanced, a bit pointy and veiny, and appear whorly and buoyant. *T. grandiflorum* is taller than most species, to fifteen inches, and bears fairly large white flowers in late April that last through beginning June, by which time they've turned a subtle pink. Avoid *T. erectum*, even though it has great maroon flowers, it really smells bad, which has earned this species the common name of "stinking-Benjamin."

As I've found it a bit difficult to establish, buying at your nursery is probably the best route if you can find it, or order fresh healthy ones from Carroll Gardens. Whatever you do, do not even think of digging this one from the wild as it is a bit endangered, though native to America. Prefers the shade of deciduous trees and moist humus. Dies down at summer's end, so if you're planting bare-root rhizomes—do so when it's dormant in autumn and only plant them two inches deep. Don't forget to mark them. Very charming.

√√ *Tropaeolum majus* (trop-eye-**ohl**-uhm)
Great bushy annual nasturtium. Frost-tender.

A big winner on the annual hit parade. Just love it, even though some golden and orangish flowers sneak in sometimes, they are countered by dark crimson and scarlets. As I'm not the seed-starting type, I'm stuck with these mixtures of color, as they are the only ones found in the nurseries here, but there are strains of single-colored varieties to be had. The joyous flowers are ruffly, petally, and fantastic, nestled among pale green, round leaves looking like masses of little lily pads. Bushy and cascading, they are great for containers, windowboxes, or baskets and need to be exposed to sun. Never tried them in the ground, but probably would be a great vine. They also need a dry spot, which I'm sorely lacking here in moist East Hampton. They need continual deadheading and shearing of sagging leaves, but just snap them off—it's easy. Unlike many of my other more wily and dramatic favorites—these are bright and cheerful.

√√√ plus √√ *Tulipa* (**tyoo**-lip-uh)
Tulips. The Blessed Event of spring. Need cold winters or simulation. [See Chapter IV, pp. 115–116.]
Tulipa is the Latinized version of an Arabic word

Little orchids and great architectural leaves are the treasures of *Tricyrtis*.

meaning "turban," alluding to the shape of the flower the whole world knows and loves, I am absolutely one of its most enraptured devotées. If around in the early seventeenth century at the height of "Tulipomania," I'm sure I would've gladly traded my jewelry, horse and carriage, pound of flesh, or whatever I happened to have around to fanatically acquire my tulip bulbs. Today, fortunately, so many hybridizers and growers are in on the tulip act that there's enough to go around for universally everyone and a staggering roster of species, classifications, cultivars, types, and kinds from which to choose. Making my tulip decisions each summer, with at least two dozen bulb catalogs spread around me, is one of my most congenial gardening chores.

How to Grow Tulips:

1. Meticulously choose them.
2. Figure out how to pay for the hundreds you've managed to narrow your choice down to.
3. Examine them when they arrive, and if any mildew or shriveled up bulbs are spotted—call and insist on replacements.
4. Store in the refrigerator or somewhere cool until planting time. You can wait till all other fall planting is in the ground—okay till at least Thanksgiving—as the earth must be cool to receive them.
5. Haphazardly plant them about five or six inches deep and *very close together* with bonemeal mixed into the trenches—artfully arrange some in the garden scene to accentuate other spring-bloomers—and plant many for cutting.
6. Label them so you will know which tulips came from whom and what to order more of the next year.
7. Wait impatiently for April.
8. Luxuriate in their beauty for the glorious six weeks or so they are with us. Fill your house, office, your lover's vases, bring some to an unfriendly neighbor, share them. Everyone will love you for it.
9. Plunge them in *cold water* immediately after cutting.
10. Except for Darwin hybrids and species tulips—pull them out of the ground after flowering and discard—replace with summer-flowering bulbs, plants that get dug and stored, etc. I am a firm nonbeliever in spindly second-year tulips with half the luster (if that) of ones planted freshly every autumn. Tulips are worth every ounce of effort required for annual planting.

All scholarly gardeners will be up in arms over my tulip-growing instructions and think me quite the philistine I'm sure, but for me *this method works* and will undoubtedly perform for you too.

In the case of majestic Darwin Hybrids, and the exhilaratingly diverse species tulips or "wild tulips," it's worth your effort to cater to them a bit. Place these returning types in your sunniest spots (all tulips are said to like sun, but I've grown the beauties I treat as annuals in all sorts of spots) and plant among other perennials because you, of course, need to allow the leaves to fully ripen and die down. Be sure to *plant late in fall after the ground has cooled* (important for all tulips). Plant deep—at least eight inches underground (less for the smaller, species bulbs)—and be especially conscious of properly mixing in considerable amounts of bulb food or bonemeal. Tulips to be left in the garden should be deadheaded when bloom is over. In early spring, just as they begin to emerge, top dress with a balanced commercial fertilizer and scratch in some bonemeal. Following these rules, a modicum of success has greeted me with decent tulips returning for three years—by the fourth year it's real stragglesville, but three years is not so bad. If you have a pervasive belief that all your tulips will return year after year—following the above instructions is how to best extract longevity from the supposed perennial bulbs. White Flower Farm offers five different tulips it calls "perennial," but are actually Darwin Hybrids, I'm sure. So why not buy your Darwin hybrids from John Scheepers? After all, it was they who perfected the original cross.

Any tulips, however, will gloriously bloom the first year if you follow my ten-step quick-gratification method and order from reliable sources who export the bulbs from Holland—tulip capital of the world. According to the fine catalogs, the Dutch government severely regulates bulb exports to America, and only three degrees of size (measured in centimeters around the widest part of the bulb) are allowed for export—all of which have blooming capacity. How can you go wrong? But wouldn't you know, of the near seven hundred tulips I planted last autumn all but a few dozen are now in full leaf with buds swelling everyday and the Fosterianas will probably burst open this weekend. And guess where these tulips showing absolutely no sign of life came from??? If you're on to me by now, and said White Flower Farm, you would be absolutely right! I called them this morning, very politely, to question this non-event—explaining hundreds of other tulips from varying sources, including some others from them, were abounding like mad—but 'May Wonder' and 'Angelique' were nowhere to be seen. Unfortunately for them, they were quite short with me, said they'd had no other complaints, told me to wait (which is ridiculous—by now they'd be there), and intimated, basically, that I didn't know what I was talking about. Hah! Won't they be sorry? Of course, the bulbs looked perfectly fine when planted, and perhaps have been eaten underground by one of our furry friends, but *isn't it odd* that the tulips all around them and plants like lilies (also very delectable to the fuzzy creatures) are bursting forth. What can I say?

Okay. You've perused your catalogs, everything looks divine, and you have no idea what to order. Well, I shall help you. To have the fullest, most sensational tulip season lasting as long as possible, we'll examine the precious flowers by category and order of bloom. Never order less than a dozen of any given kind, else you won't be able to appreciate a decent vase or a memorable show, and order as many as your means and space allow. The classification system dreamed up by the Royal Horticultural Society of England in cahoots with the Royal Dutch Bulb Growers Society has twenty-three divisions, which is a bit of a lengthy bore. The major classifications used by the good catalogs make much more sense—so here they are:

Species or Wild Tulips

These are not the big dreamy beauties that jump to mind when tulips are invoked. Different in form and habit, they are small and can really only be appreciated in a rock garden or some such deliberate planting—and they come and go very quickly and are mostly delicate. But they are definitely among the earliest to bloom, and some are quite intriguing, like *T. saxatilis*—rosy-lilac true tulip form and good for rocky soils; *T. eichleri*—intensely scarlet with bright yellow base, multiflowering, really early, one of the biggest (eight inches); *T. praestans* 'Unicum'—another biggish one, real red with nice cream edges, strong leaves, among the best. But truly, the ones you think might be really interesting like *T. acuminata* and *turkestanica* are nothing to write home about and more a botanical curiosity than a tulip.

Greigii Tulips

Also a species tulip, but gutsier. Though on short stems, the true-tulip-like flowers are large and showy and will brighten up any dull spot with happy blooms in dreary early spring, but not as early as the former. Do definitely try the hybrids. All have sturdy (and very interesting) leaves mottled and striated with splotches and stripes of purple—their distinguishing feature: 'Corsage'—apricot-rose with pale yellowy-cream edges and appropriately named, as some Greigiis flower many stems to a bulb; and certainly, the quite special 'Red Riding Hood'—you can really see that big wolf trying to snatch her away when you gaze into its deep black center.

Kaufmanniana Tulips

Still on short stems and most with plain old green foliage, these boast big flowers with slightly reflexed petals, truly looking like waterlilies. When they quickly open at the end of March, it's slightly akin to a dream. Mine unfortunately never last very long as they are very close to the ground (never more than four or five inches) and are perfect dining-table height for the rabbits. If you are rabbitless, however, you will want to get in on this display. Order 'Waterlily'—it's a creamy-white one with a golden base—very surprising and surreal, and 'Shakespeare'—outside red, interior and edge salmon—and you can't go wrong.

Fosteriana Tulips

Now we're talking. These are the earliest of what we presume to be real tulips (though still a species, but not one you should expect to perennialize like the first three categories), and they're just incredibly great! The giant-size flowers are the most astounding thing—some of the biggest petals in the entire *Tulipa* genus. When you arrive to inspect your garden on a dewy April day and suddenly are saluted by the satiny unfolding of 'Red Emperor' or 'Madame Lefeber', you will truly concede the majesty of spring and its queen, the tulip. Each petal is about three inches long and sort of concave; when it opens and dreamily dances at some six or more inches across, the velvety ideal red is backdrop to an intense black eye. It's fabulous and the stems are long enough to cut. You can't ever have enough of these. Also exists in gold—but pale-yellow-edged-white 'Sweetheart' is nicer—pink, and all-white, but nothing tops the reds. You can ignore everything mentioned before—but not this one—a must-have.

Single and Double Early Tulips

Now we move out of true species categories and into those hybridized and cosseted by man. Not as fabulous as Fosteriana, the single and double earlies would be easier to appreciate if they *really* bloomed early, but what they do is provide a sweet interlude between the earliest bloomers and the glories yet to come. The double earlies look a bit like small peonies on stubby stems of only ten inches; mixed with *Muscari* they are quite splashy and springy, if a bit erect and not particularly graceful. They last an incredibly long time in the vase and open wide and willowy as they age. 'Schoonoord' is all white and my favorite, and 'Peach Blossom' a rosy pink and probably the "sport" (spontaneous mutation in the tulip fields rather than a deliberate hybrid) most resembling 'Murillo', its classic parent. All catalogs offer a mixture of colors as well—the mixture from Dutch Gardens is especially nice—all crimson, pink, and lavender with very few yellows. The single early is especially good for forcing, and is best exemplified by the ever-popular 'Apricot Beauty' which is a dreamy light salmon/pink/apricot combo and very pretty. More poised and bigger than the double earlies, some reach eighteen inches. Other charmers in this group are 'Coleur Cardinal'—brilliant scarlet flushed plum, and 'Princess Irene'—an exciting color blend of burnished orange with purple-red flames, though it's a bit short.

Triumph Tulips

This is an important and meaningful group as it's saturated with energetic colors and color patterns, which have an important place in your spring garden. Substantial at sixteen to twenty-two inches, these belong in front of the big Darwins and Cottage tulips that come lustily later. Triumphs bloom at the very beginning of May here and are the first tulip subjects to *really* fill an inspired vase. You will definitely want to sparkle your yard with: 'Anna José'—plant this pinky-red edged with cream all around your bleeding hearts (*Dicentra*) for a perfect garden picture; 'New Design'—rather tall blush-pink edged in soft fushia, has nice white-edged foliage as well (though tulip leaves are not really the point); 'Margot Fonteyn'—as fiery as the wonderful dancer, vermillion edged palest yellow. Two great ones to plant together are 'Negrita'—dark purple with bluish veins—and 'Shirley'—creamy white edged with fushia-purple. 'White Dream' is exactly what its name implies, and don't forget 'Dreaming Maid'—lavender-pink edged white. Rather short but with the intense colors of the Imperial Raj—'Indian Maid' is gold with burgundy embellishment. 'Bestseller'—which is sort of mottled and coppery—is absolutely divine planted with *Fritillaria* 'Crown Imperial Rubra'—don't miss out on this fabulous look.

Darwin Hybrid Tulips

Tall (some to twenty-eight inches!), stately, true, huge goblet-shaped tulips. Fill your garden with these beauties for sure. This is the tulip so perfected by the hybridizers it deserves your extra attention and thoughtful planting as it can be counted on to return for at least three years. A cross between *T. fosteriana*, from which it gets its huge flower, and the regal, last-to-bloom Darwins, from which is derived the imposing long stems. It comes in a huge range. Some of the best are the classic 'Apeldoorn'—spectacular red with big black base and two feet tall; 'Pink Impression'—no ordinary pink, but a clear soft rose turning deeper as the flower ages and maybe the most enormous flower-head of all; 'Silverstream' and 'Gudoshnik'—not quite as tall but just divine—a few dozen of them in combination is a symphony of pale creamy yellow brushed randomly with pink and red nuances—each tulip slightly different; and 'Daydreamer' (also great with *Fritillaria*)—a big warm pastel carroty color with hints of apricot and yellow—a great one. For you fans of white, 'Cream Jewel' is tall and elegant and lasts an abnormally long time.

Viridiflora Tulips or Green Tulips

Not very tall, but with nicely shaped flowers, the Viridifloras all have prominent green markings on their petals. I feel ambivalent about them, even though they are a great favorite of many, and would much rather wait for the sensational show of the parrot tulips for the really impressive markings.

Peony or Double Late Tulips

These put the double earlies to shame, and almost everything else as well—not only do they really look like their namesakes, the heavily petaled flowers on strong stems come in a fabulous selection of form and color. These are perhaps the most magnificent as cut flowers. Arriving in early May, they are the first of the unusual tulips. Beauties abound in this division. You don't for a minute want to be without 'Angelique'—in a class by itself, looking more like an old-fashioned China pink rose than a peony, its ruffly creamy-white petals are flushed with divine degrees of pink, and often there are three to a stem. 'Mount Tacoma' is beyond white, so fully double it is nearly indistinguishable from the classic peony 'Festiva Maxima' except it's pure white and boasts so many petals they would be impossible to count—lasts forever in the vase. Plant together with 'Carnavaal de Nice', which is creamy white with gorgeous red stripings, and to add extravagance—round out the look with parrot tulips 'Estella Rijnveld' and 'Firebird' and you will want to hold a garden party just to show them off. 'Wirosa' is another exceptional beauty—wine-red petals with a generous cream edge. 'Maravilla' and 'Lilac Perfection' are both in the lavender-violet family, fully double, and very divine. In a vase, these tulips will make anyone swoon. [See photo in Chapter IV, p. 116.]

Single Late or Cottage Tulips and Darwin Tulips

These are the real classics of tulip visions. Darwins are more cup-shaped, Cottages veer to the egg shape—all are fabulous and the tallest tulips of all. Proud and majestic in the garden scene with a spectacular color range—from purest white to blackest purple. From vast choices, it's difficult to highlight a few, but make sure to include 'Queen of the Night'—the darkest tulip, velvety and superb in a vase with white tulips of almost any kind; no matter how many I plant, there's never enough. For purity of form and color, 'Maureen' is the white delight. To keep your tulip story going emphasizing the *Dicentra*, now in full bloom, plant 'Sorbet' along with the Triumph 'Anna José'. 'Bleu Amiable' is an almost metallic, silvery lavender-blue. 'Black Diamond' approaches blackness, but is more purple than 'Queen of the Night' that gets its blackness from the maroon family. Plant 'Black Diamond' with *Fritillaria persica* for an incomparable moody garden vision. In the world of salmon-rose-apricots-'Temple of Beauty' and 'Blushing Lady' will make you drool. And for a knockout giant beauty, plant 'Grand Style'—its dazzling shade of deepest pink shimmers in the garden scene and is gorgeous mixed with the black ones.

Lily-Flowered Tulips

Pointed petals usually bending outward (reflexed) culminate the elegant long and narrow flowers for which I have a special devotion. Tall and noble, these seductive beauties are perhaps the longest lasting tulips—often up to four weeks. Important you order enough for cutting and the garden. The mixes are usually a bit homely and replete with too many yellows and whites—the white in this case is not quite so fabulous and usually smaller than the others. Revel in: 'Queen of Sheba'—fabulous glowing deep scarlet with burnished golden edges, 'Ballade'—deep lilac edged white, 'Marilyn'—white feathered red, and 'Mariette'—an unforgettable shade of luminous pink. And don't forget the fantastic 'Picture', which is really just that—pink-lilac and different in form than all the others, its wavy petals appear to be made of wax. You will adore the grace of the lily-flowerers, which have a vague resemblance to lilies, but really are a thing unto themselves.

Fringed Tulips

These actually fall into the lily-flowering category, but for me are more of a novelty and not as lovely. The petals are edged with tiny glassine fringes with a very delicate appeal. For some reason I haven't had much luck with them, which is probably why I'm not more vociferous at singing their praises. 'Cobalt Violet' and 'Burgundy Lace' are the ones from which I expected more.

Rembrandt Tulips

These oddities surprisingly leave me a bit cold. Also known as "broken tulips," their strange featherings and fancy markings are said to be a by-product of a centuries-old virus. In the heady days of Tulipomania, these stubby flowers were much prized and appear in many seventeenth-century paintings, but the ones I've grown are not nearly so exotic. If it's fascinating and wondrous you're after, forget these and hop right on the parrot tulip bandwagon.

Parrot Tulips

My enthrallment with these approaches fetishism. As different from the stately Darwins and lily-flowerers as day from night, these overwhelming beauties must be planted with care suiting their unique and spontaneous stature. Some must be placed in the cutting garden, for you surely don't want to be without these highlighting a vase or two, and for the garden, search for special spots you want to fill with high drama. Solidly colored, the most resplendent are 'Black Parrot', 'Firebird' or 'Red Sensation', and the divine 'White Parrot', which is never solid white, but delicately garnished with light red and green markings. Of the outrageous and wonderful multicolored parrots, rejoice in 'Estella Rijnveld'—she must have been quite some chick as this white brushed with crimson and a little green is a showstopper; 'Amethyst'—blends of lavender and rose with silvered edges; and 'Flaming Parrot,' an explosive yellow and red combination. Parrot tulips last a wonderfully long time in the garden and vase and get more relaxed as they age. The long twisted and cut petals open widely and lay flat, lending an almost bizarre, but purely ornamental quality to any scene they enhance. The last tulips to linger into June, you must find a home for them in your garden.

So, gardening friends, now you have my tulip treatise. Bear in mind, as the season progresses the tulips get better and better, but you can't ignore the early ones and not have any April bloom—it would just be too sad. Don't forget to thoroughly search your bulb catalogs to come up with the choicest selection. No one catalog has all the great ones, and to put together inspired pictures, you must motivate yourself to make a plan including bulbs ordered from different catalogs that will arrive at varying times. No exercise is more worth your effort than this one.

HM *Valeriana officinalis* (vall-eer-ee-**ay**-nuh)
Perennial garden heliotrope. Zones 4–9.

Healthy, old-fashioned, wild-flowery plant that grows easily to five feet and fills out the back of the border with flower clusters in midsummer among deeply toothed leaves. Light shade is fine. Cut to ground in autumn. Attracting butterflies is its bonus.

√√√ *Veltheimia* (felt-**hī**-mee-a)
A gasp-provoking South African bulb. Zone 10, but takes to pots.

Like the *Clivia*, this flower is so spectacular it is worth fussing with and growing indoors, plus it has long, tapering, waxy, dark green leaves forming a rosette all year. The difficult-to-describe flower of the "Veldt lily" rises on foot-tall leafless spikes in early spring. Drooping tubular *penne*-like (as in pasta) petals a glorious shade of pinkish-mauve tinged with bright spring-green at their tips are clustered in an inverted spire shape. The sight of *Clivia* and *Veltheimia* in flower at the same time is almost more than you can bear. My first spotting of this visual feast was at the New York Flower Show a few years ago and emulating it became an obsession. [See illustration in Chapter VIII, p. 238.]

They can be acquired from McClure & Zimmerman or Bio-Quest International and should be planted in fall with the tip of the bulb at the surface of the well-prepared soil mix— sandy and rich in compost. Not much water until growth appears, and keep in a bright spot but never in full sun—outdoors they like filtered shade. Very exquisite.

HM *Viburnum plicatum* 'Watanabei' (vai-**bur**-num)
Huge group of floriferous lovely trees and shrubs. Zones 5–8 for 'Watanabei'.

This one flowers white in early summer and looks like a "lace-cap" hydrangea. Only one of 120 beautiful and varied species. Most fine in sun or semishade and need deep, fertile, moist soil. Many evergreen. Check them out at your nursery.

Viola. Violets. Of course I appreciate them, but had no luck with my few nursery tries, and don't like them enough to push the issue.

√√ *Vitex agnus-castus* (**vy**-tex)
The chaste tree. Zones 6/7–9.

First spotted in the neighborhood in bloom at the end of summer in one of the finer roadside gardens, I couldn't rest till acquiring it the next spring. The Bayberry sold me two that doubled in size the first season to about four feet, and now five years later in full growth, they reach seven feet. Pleasant all summer with pale gray-green, much divided leaves that are quite aromatic—come end August it bursts into bloom. Steely-blue flowers are in form like a lilac, but instead of pendulously nodding, they are erect, upright panicles. My flowering never reaches the crescendo of the bushes I first saw, as it doesn't have full sun as it should, but the bloom is very impressive anyway.

Though frost-hardy, in cold areas it needs a sheltered position and a good winter mulching. No boggy spots for this one, it needs to be well-drained. As it blooms on new growth each year, *cut it back hard in early spring* to about two feet, just like *Buddleia*. For some reason, Irving is not a fan of this one and we have an ongoing argument about moving it to a less prominent spot—not on your life.

√√√ *Wisteria* (wis-**tear**-ee-uh)
The most spectacular flowering vine/tree. Zones 4/5–9/10. [See Chapter III, p. 90.]

If you've never seen a mature wisteria in full bloom hugging a house or festooning a fence, there's little I can say to conjure up the heavenly vision. Depending on the species, flowering racemes (a hanging-flower cluster) from eight inches to four feet! are suspended in massive profusion from the twisted and bent vining branches. On a developed plant with something sturdy to climb on, the branches take on a gnarled and thick aspect, as if they've been in place for centuries. Most of the intense flowers are a pale shade of lilac or white, whether a *floribunda* (Japanese, with the longest racemes), *chinensis, sinensis*, or *formosa*. The species vary little, all capable of easily reaching thirty feet, but can be treated in many methods. Free-growing as a vine covering houses, trees, fences, and pergolas is a natural, but they can also be grown as "standards" (tree form), and can even be potted. Aside from the elaborate flowering, the leafing is worth noting as well. Leaves can be very long and are comprised of oval leaflets, so the overall look is something like a huge fern.

Controlling wisteria is a never-ending chore, as it must be pruned and pruned and pruned some more as it throws off whiplike leaf stalks constantly from the twining branches and thick runners from the roots—all of which must be kept in bounds unless you're in an entirely wild and overgrown situation. Heavy pruning should be done after flowering in spring and again in late winter—and quite a few snips here and there in between. I suppose they are the fastest growing thing encountered in my gardening experience. They need sun and fertile, well-drained, *acid soil*. All are leaf-losing (deciduous), and though they bud early in spring, the big leafing outbreak doesn't take place till after flowering, which is an immediate and breathless occurrence—if you can get them to flower, that is—but I've already told you about that. The quickest route to success is buying nursery grown ones *already in flower*—you can still go wrong but are less likely to. And water, *lots of water*, especially during the flowering period. I wish you great success with your wisteria experience, after balancing on pins and needles through early spring hoping for flower-buds, now in mid-May *two* of my wisteria are loaded with them!! So exhilarating when your efforts are not in vain. Now I'm certain it's just a matter of time till the other three grace us with their flowering presence. [See illustration in Chapter III, p. 65.]

HM *Yucca gloriosa* (**yuk**-kuh)
Evergreen architectural plants. Zones 5–10.
Bold, stiff, sword-shaped leaves don't blend in a border, but *Yucca* make a strong statement on their own or complementing bamboos or grasses. With enough sun, they send up huge showy panicles of flowers in midsummer. Significant if deftly placed.

√√√ *Zantedeschia aethiopica* (zan-tee-**desh**-ee-a)
The legendary calla lily. Zones 8–10, but fine for pots.
This is the classic calla and the one you want—not *albomaculata, elliottiana,* or *rehmannii*—these all have spotted leaves, a much smaller stature, and everything but the pure, pristine, and perfect white flower of your dreams. Without a doubt, order *Z. aethiopica*—which is not what most catalogs touting calla lilies are trying to sell you. McClure & Zimmerman has the real thing. From arrow-shaped, vertical, deep solid-green leaves, a magnificent succession of trumpet-shaped flowers (actually spathes) encircle themselves in the most comely manner. The prominent golden spadix relieves the whiteness. 'Green Goddess' is a fabulous cultivar in the *aethiopica* species; here the spathe—or what we think of as the flower—is almost as green as the leaves, with a huge white blotch in the center. Very divine and special.

What the true callas need is *very moist to boggy soil,* a muddy situation would suit it just fine, also soil amended with *lots of cow manure.* The aforementioned garden-variety callas like regular well-drained soil, so if you can't provide dirt moist enough or don't want to be a slave to watering, then settle for the modest others; but if you can—plant the real four-foot wonders where the glistening flowers appear at the ends of tall, tall stems. Flowering in early summer for a long period, they, of course, need real sun, but perform after a fashion for me with not much of it. Biweekly feedings of manure dug into the soil in the growing season is a big boon too.

Planting callas outdoors north of Zone 8 is a difficult situation unless you have lots of time and space. I've always read they *can't stay out of the ground* or they will dry out—so must be moved from the garden into individual earth-filled pots. Not thrilled with this technique, but loving them so much for their fabulous garden show, I've tried two methods. The first is easy and expensive—buy new callas each year, plant them in the garden, then toss them out like annuals in fall. But two years ago, I dug them up and stored them in damp peat moss, starting them inside in March, and planted them out in summer. Although flowering wasn't overwhelming, I had flowers and big beautiful green plants—so what can I say? The same tubers are in my living room right now leafing like mad—will they bloom again? Who knows? (They did.)

If you've kept your callas potted, when you bring them in for winter keep in a cool place and water moderately—as spring arrives, beef up the watering and fertilizing and move them into the sun. Repotting every few years is helpful. Regardless of how you choose to grow them—plant the thick rhizome *vertically with its growing tip just protruding* from the soil. If outside, wait till the ground is warm, but be sure to start the dormant tubers into growth inside so you have the plethora of beauty earlier.

I once saw a stand of them, maybe a hundred or more, on a shady bank in a coastal garden near Portofino, and the sight was so dazzling and unforgettable that I'll do practically anything to succeed with calla lilies in my garden. Once you become a fanatic, I'm sure you'll find a way, too.

One last word to all you gardeners out there, seasoned or beginning, every word of this book has come from my heart. I hope it made you laugh, made you think. . . . but most of all made you want to run right out to your garden and plant, and on that note I should conclude with Dianne's Favorite Helpful Planting Tips:

1. When planting nursery potted plants or shrubs that necessitate digging a big hole in an already crowded garden space—a big dilemma was always what to do with the dirt. The trick is to carry in your garden cart a nice strong piece of burlap (or any sturdy material like an old feed bag)—shovel the dirt onto the burlap—and once the plant is in the ground, pick up the burlap by the edges and pour the dirt back into the hole to pack around the plant. Always plant your nursery buy at least as deep in your garden as it was in their pot.

2. Save your plant containers from the nursery when they are the nice, strong green or black polyurethane ones. They become working tools when transplanting, receptacles for extra dirt, and vessels for the potting up indoors that takes place in March. You will find myriad uses for them, you've already paid for them, and watching them pile up gives a sense of your garden's history.

3. At the end of a big gardening day,

Zantedeschia aethiopica, the romantic calla lily. Don't settle for anything less alluring.

who feels like lugging around the hose to water all your new plantings? **DO IT**. It's the only way to really drive out the air pockets and bring the soil into a oneness with the roots.

4. When planting bare-roots it's absolutely unnecessary to dig a hole and enrich the earth for each one. Dig a much bigger hole than would accommodate one root, enrich it thoroughly with peat moss and composted cow manure (which is the same thing as organic humus—at least that's what it says on our Agway bags) and lay three or four bare-roots against the sides of the hole. Spread the root out against the perimeter, hold the root with one hand while backfilling the enriched soil against the side wall of the hole with the other, and after all roots are in place—pack the remaining dirt into the center. This way is much easier and creates a natural plant grouping to boot.

5. Never leave as much space between plants or bulbs as the instructions insist on, but use good judgment and note the eventual size of the plant.

6. Whether planting a bare-root or a nursery plant, the job isn't done until you've tamped the dirt solidly by a succession of judicious steps around the new planting to pack down the dirt. Another reason for sensible outdoor shoes, and the chance to do a little garden dance.

7. Don't worry if you haven't followed every single edict for every single plant—doing what comes naturally and logically, with a little affection thrown in, will probably yield more than sighed-for results.

That's all the dirt for now. I hope you've dug it.

SOURCES & CATALOGS FOR TOOLS, EQUIPMENT, & CLOTHES

A. M. Leonard, Inc.
6665 Spiker Road, P.O. Box 816
Piqua, OH 45356
800.543.8955
A real no-nonsense catalog, no four-color photo spreads, no *nothing* except everything from stakes and ties to garden carts.

Cabela's
812 13th Avenue
Sidney, NE 69160
800.237.4444
Sporting and outdoor gear, more authentic-looking than L.L. Bean, if you can believe it.

Dirt Cheap Organics
5645 Paradise Drive
Corte Madera, CA 94925
415.924.0369
I can't vouch for how cheap they are, but if you are not blessed with an Agway or honest fertilizer and mulch supplier, these people will gladly send anything from BatGuano to bonemeal to shredded fir bark.

Gardener's Eden
P.O. Box 7307
San Francisco, CA 94120
800.822.9600
A combination of useful things and fluff; but they have *The Gloves!*

Gardener's Supply Company
128 Intervale Road
Burlington, VT 05401
802.863.1700
Full line of Gardena and those great Bosbags.

Gardens Alive
5100 Schenley Place
Lawrenceberg, IN 47025
812.537.8650
This catalog offers lady beetles and praying mantis, Weed Barrier Mats and bluebird food, every organic fertilizer you could ever want and all the things you will ever need to wage combat with the unfortunate pestilences. This one is printed on newsprint and seems more real because of it.

Hermès of Paris
Personal Shopping Services
745 Fifth Avenue, Suite 800
New York, NY 10126-0287
If you cannot resist spending a small fortune, they have their gardening side, just like their horsey side.

J. Crew
One Ivy Crescent
Lynchburg, VA 24513-1001
800.562.0258
Those great rain shoes and generally good honest clothes.

The J. Peterman Company
2444 Palumbo Drive
Lexington, KY 40509-1102
800.231.7341
Fax 800.346.3081
An interesting selection of quasi-functional things, plus those real riding boots if you can bear them.

Langenbach
P.O. Box 453
Blairstown, NJ 07825
800.362.1991
The undisputed couture of tool catalogs with the largest planting auger I've come across, as well as a plethora of stainless-steel tools.

Merrill's Manure, Ind.
P.O. Box 708
Millerton, NY 12546
518.789.4123
This company actually sells nicely packaged manure in easy-to-lift five- and ten-pound boxes; I in no way suggest you should spend $14.95 for ten pounds; but the concept of someone marketing couture manure was so absurd, I had to include it.

Museum of Modern Art.
11 West 53rd Street
New York, NY 10019
800.447.MoMA (6662)
Fax 212.708.9891
The snazzy Japanese saw as well as other adeptly designed garden tools.

Paw Paw Everlast Label Company
P.O. Box 93C
Paw Paw, MI 49079
Garden-marker heaven.

Phelan's
10 Liberty Ship Way
Schoonmaker Building #184
Sausalito, CA 94965
415.332.6001
Riding clothes, good ones.

Smith & Hawken
25 Corte Madera
Mill Valley, CA 94941
415.383.2000
Fax 415.383.7030
Good tools, buckets, the *best* small pruners, along with all those plain-Jane clothes.

State Line Tack Inc.
P.O. Box 1217
Plaistow, NH 03865-1217
Fax 603.382.8471
A true horseman's catalog with a complete line of riding breeches, both imported and their own brand. Very interesting 30–40%-off sale in January and February—a perfect time to stock up.

Voice of the Mountains Catalogue
The Vermont Country Store
P.O. Box 3000
Manchester, VT 05255-3000
802.362.2400
Fax 802.362.0285
A sweet, loving, hands-at-home idea with wonderful cashmere socks and silk underwear, among other curious things.

Walt Nicke Company
36 McLeod Lane
P.O. Box 433
Topsfield, MA 01983
The finest frank and trustworthy catalog, with almost every tool, weeder, and accoutrement you could ever hunger after. Charmingly written, well-priced, plus those nice handwritten "Thank you, Dianne's" on the box or invoice reassure you they appreciate your business. I love this one. Don't forget Loop Stakes.

Wathne
1095 Cranbury So. River Road, Suite 8
Jamesburg, NJ 08831
800.942.1166
A big fancy color catalog with a few useful things.

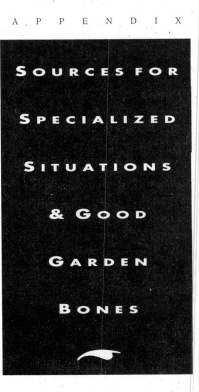

SOURCES FOR

SPECIALIZED

SITUATIONS

& GOOD

GARDEN

BONES

Asian Artifacts
P.O. Box 2494
Oceanside, CA 92054
619.723.3039
If it is a Chinese pagoda, Japanese lantern, or
stone bridge you seek to indulge your Oriental
serene theme, this charming brochure has it, as
well as a self-possessed seated Buddha. Everything is handcrafted from granite, so it's not
cheap—but quite nice.

Bamboo Fencer
31 Germania Street
Jamaica Plain, MA 02130
617.524.6137
Fax 617.524.3596

Woven bamboo, bamboo pickets, split
bamboo—fences, gates, arbors, planters—you
name it and these people will supply it in existing modules or custom made to your specs.
Some designs are pure Japanese, others could
blend in anywhere. Surprisingly well-priced.

Blue Ridge Stone Company
Arch Hathcock, owner
1930 N. Salem Street
Apex, NC 27502
919.362.4700
This man is an expert on dry-stack stone walls
and a supplier of "gorgeous boulders" and all
types of stone. He can design and build your
wall (or water garden) for you, or if you happen

to be in the area, he teaches classes on how to build a fabulous unmortared wall yourself and insists if you can lift a ten-pound rock, that's all it takes.

Bow House, Inc.
Randall Road
Bolton, MA 01740
508.779.2271
Fax 508.779.2272
$3

Too-cute names for very nice products. Their "Belvedeary" is actually a quite charming gazebo or garden house you assemble yourself (they say it's easy) and their "BowBends" range from interestingly patterned wooden fencing to prebuilt wooden bridges—some very pleasant. They also custom-make and stock treillage and arbors.

Chilstone Garden Ornaments
Sprivers Estate
Horsmonden, Tonbridge
Kent TN12 8DR ENGLAND
Brenchley (089 272) 3553

The most intriguing of all the stone catalogs. Stated in their preface: "Each Chilstone ornament is handmade in reconstituted stone by a special process . . . virtually indistinguishable from natural stone. Its composition encourages the spontaneous growth of mosses and lichens, which rapidly gives it the aged quality of the original." Exactly what you want, yes? Certainly what I wholeheartedly endorse. They have the exclusive right to reproduce all sorts of eccentric English garden ornaments, and vouching for their reliability and shipping practices are some of my very favorite bones: my two benches with acanthus-leaf legs, the round French pedestal highlighting the hammock grove, and my beloved blackamoor stools serving as tables. They all look as if I had inherited them.

Country Casual
1317 Germantown Road
Germantown, MD 20874-2999
800.284.8325

THE source for classic wood garden furniture, a great color catalog reminds you they've supplied their furniture to the Folger Shakespeare Library, the Met, Harvard, Yale, many important botanical gardens, as well as the Dog Museum in St. Louis—so the prices are obviously honest. They will also inscribe the furniture for you—very nice gift idea. Plus a good modular architectural trellis selection and a spattering of real wrought iron—very New Orleans.

Design Toscano
15 East Campbell Street
Arlington Heights, IL 60005
800.525.0733

Gargoyle-engrossed people with faithful Florentine and French reproductions spanning the gamut of bizarre carvings and griffins. Aside from their gargoyle specialty, they offer classical columns and friezes and other architectural items in four different finishes plus an assortment of garden sculpture from a life-size Bacchus to a Beethoven bust.

House Parts, Inc.
479 Whitehall Street, S.W.
Atlanta, GA 30303
404.577.5584
Fax 404.525.6708

This curious mimeographed catalog is filled with all sorts of fascinating things made of reliable cement or industrial plaster (which really holds up though they suggest it for indoor use). Among the fetching items they offer (you must spend a minimum of two hundred dollars—but all the prices quoted are actually 40 percent less!! when you place your order) are eerie but divine "piano hands," dolphin pedestals, finials, and all sorts of great statuary like "pan garden seat" or "girl with sleeping cat." This is not the usual junk, but really great stuff weathering with the best of them. The only thing ever disappearing (stolen, I guess) from my garden was my divine House Parts "Pig: Fat. #6224." I suppose it was just irresistible.

Kenneth Lynch & Sons
Box 488
78 Danbury Road
Wilton, CT 06897
203.762.8363
Fax 203.762.2999
Some catalogs free, some as much as $35; but we are speaking here about proper bound books suitable for your library. They carry perhaps the epitome of easily purchaseable garden bones. Not only is there the main catalog with catagories ranging from lead fountains through animal statuary (in lead, bronze, or stone); there are even specialized books that can be ordered dealing in sundials & spheres (my favorite), weathervanes, clocks, picture hanging rods, benches, and topiary. Though this unique purveyor supplies institutions and the like, they are perfectly happy to furnish you and me with almost any garden bone imaginable. Clearly it's not cheap, and the prices they quote with each catalog are the real prices; but when you opt for the *real thing,* it's usually never a bargain. Anyway, you'll love the books.

Lilypons Water Gardens
P.O. Box 10
Buckeystown, MD 21717
Maryland: 800.999.5459, Fax 800.879.5459
Texas: 800.765.5459,   800.766.5459
California: 800.365.5459,   800.283.5459
$5, but worth it.
This is truly a complete source for any and all types of water gardening from one lily in a ceramic pot to the makings of a fountained formal pool, if you are so inclined. Tad-

poles, fish, snails, and everything you need to maintain your pond in a natural or chemical way. Better than a textbook, too.

Michigan Grindstone
1110 Seneca
Lake Orion, MI 48362
313.693.4960
If you can't find rocks to make your pond or path, they supposedly can do for you what no one else can.

New England Garden Ornaments
38 East Brookfield Road
North Brookfield, MA 01535
508.867.4474
$6.50, also worth it but for different reasons. Not only are these people the USA distributor for Chilstone (which is probably much easier than importing from England, but I didn't know they existed at the time), they also carry American-made mahogany trellis in predetermined modules or custom-made. I am at this very moment contemplating ordering a Gothic obelisk from their "Agriframes" group, which are made from black-coated tubular steel and appear to look like wrought iron. The shapes are more charming than classic and the prices are not breathtaking. However, if you *are* into spending a small fortune, they can accommodate you with a huge range of English lead statuary (some quite whimsical), sundials, planters, and troughs.

Mr. Robbie Haldane
North Mountain Road
Copake Falls, NY 12517
518.329.0383
The New York Times recommends him as a landscape gardener who will build your stone wall for you in the tradition of his grandfather, and estates in Ireland. He stacks the real thing with field stones and no mortar.

Old World Garden Troughs
P.O. Box 1253
Carmel, IN 46032
317.465.9117
A very specialized little catalog offering hand-crafted troughs perfect for particular Alpine and container gardening.

Simple's Creative Quality Trellis
RD #2, Box 69G
Honeybrook, PA 19344-9222
215.273.3938
$1
And simple is too elaborate a word to describe the endearingly awkward homemade drawings; but the product appears good. Various trellis configurations—all made from cedar or cypress—good prices—and anxious to produce trompe l'oeil or any custom effect you can conceive of to turn your garden into a Parisian wonderland.

Southampton Brick & Tile, Inc.
Montauk Highway
Wainscott, NY 11975
516.537.1106
Fax 516.283.8349
I just had to include our huge local rock store. You can spend hours there conjuring all sorts of visions from the many stones they offer, every-thing from gravel to river rocks to gigantic boulders. They are very cooperative, but they must be able to drive their big rock truck up to exactly where you want the stones dumped. Once dumped, you're on your own.

Topiary, Inc.
41 Bering
Tampa, FL 33606
813.254.3229
Another hand-drawn offering packed with top-iary shapes and hints—also great prices. Since they have cross-legged bunnies, standing alliga-tors, poodles, dashshunds, and schnauzers—I'm contemplating commissioning an English sheepdog. Very Edward Scissorhands.

Warren F. Broderick—Books
P.O. Box 124
694 Fourth Avenue
Lansingburgh, NY 12182
518.235.4041
$1.50
An intriguing catalog of rare and out-of-print books—only gardening or subjects dear to gar-deners. I've fallen for a few old Gertrude Jekylls and some wonderfully illustrated idyosycratic tomes. All sorts of prices.

Wind & Weather
The Albion Street Water Tower
P.O. Box 2320
Mendocino, CA 95460-2320
800.922.9463
Barometers, cupolas, gazing balls, great weather vanes, all sorts of sundials and beauti-ful wind chimes—most made from honest ma-terials like bronze, copper, brass, and stone. There's invariably something I want.

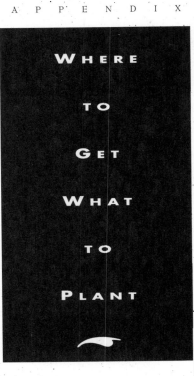

WHERE

TO

GET

WHAT

TO

PLANT

(Your Gardening Dreams Come True)

Amaryllis Incorporated
E. M. Beckham
P.O. Box 318
Baton Rouge, LA 70808
504.924.4521
$1
They sell only amaryllis, so you can be sure these will flower like mad. Most things come in a normal seven-dollar size and a jumbo (exhibition) nine-dollar size, and of course they offer expensive theatrical treats as well.

Ambergate Gardens
8015 Krey Avenue
Waconia, MN 55387
612.443.2248
Fax 612.443.2248
$1
Good perennial list conveniently arranged by sun and shade groupings, with a specialization in Martagon lilies, plus a list of the major dozen plant societies.

B & D Lilies
330 "P" Street
Port Townsend, WA 98368
206.385.1738
$1
The big catalog ($5) displays 248 hybrids and species—all the most sensational kinds and then some. You receive huge, plump bulbs dripping with roots. Good prices, too.

Bedford Dahlias
65 Leyton Road
Bedford, OH 44146
216.232.2852
Please send a stamp.
This catalog has no pictures, but an eccentric sense of humor to go along with its estimable dahlia offerings. Prices are the best I've found, e.g., $6.75 for the dazzling 'Optic Illusion' as compared with Swan Island's full-color catalog's $15.00 price. The names are *hand-written* on the tubers in ballpoint ink.

Bio-Quest International
P.O. Box 5752
Santa Barbara, CA 93150-5752
805.969.4072
$2
Most of the delectable offerings of this source are "Cape Bulbs" (referring to the Cape of South Africa), and not suitable for outdoor culture here; however, there is a grand choice for growing indoors like *Clivia* and *Veltheimia*. The offerings in this catalog will make a dweller in Zone 9 or 10 drool.

Breck's
6523 North Galena Road
Peoria, IL 61632
309.691.4616
This is a counterpart of Spring Hill Nurseries— the two not requiring payment in advance. Basically, Breck's specializes in bulbs and Spring

Hill makes its claim with perennials and some shrubs. Selection and quality aren't bad and they come in handy when you're short on funds.

Caladium World
P.O. Box 629
Sebring, FL 33871-0629
813.385.7661
Almost nowhere can you pick and choose among caladium colors, but here. They also sell them in indiscriminately mixed colors for incredibly cheap prices. The hitch is you have to order twenty-five bulbs of one kind—but if these Victorian lovelies move you—this is the place.

Carroll Gardens, Inc.
444 East Main Street
Westminister, MD 21157
800.638.6334
$2
One of two good Maryland nurseries (perhaps I'm a little partial to my home state)—a no-nonsense catalog with a profound perennial list, good clematis selection, and sizable shrublings (they don't ship twigs). Lots of hard-to-find plants like *Sanguinaria* 'Multiplex', which actually arrived bare-root, but in bloom!

Charles H. Mueller Co.
7091 River Road, Star Route Box 21
New Hope, PA 18938
215.862.3696
Well-organized bulb catalog arranged by bloom-time and color. No pictures, but easy descriptions and some special tulips.

Connell's Dahlias
10216 40th Avenue East
Tacoma, WA 98446
206.531.0292
Another fine dahlia specialist. Ships unusually fat tubers (not that it seems to really matter)

nicely packed in cedar mulch. Long, long list with about half pictured—catalog divided by dahlia size and easy to read.

The Crownsville Nursery
P.O. Box 797
Crownsville, MD 21032
410.923.2212
$2
This bounteous catalog is all business—no jokes, no quotes—but hundreds of good perennials, grasses, ferns, and herbs very well described and equally well priced. Everything arrives very hale and hearty due to gigantic plants shipped in scrupulous packing. An especially good hosta list and, overall, a very fine source.

Cottage Gardens
11314 Randolph Road
Wilton, CA 95693
415.387.7145
50 cents
Only iris—hundreds of iris—good descriptions, no pictures. Unlike Schreiner's, also has good list of *median* Iris (intermediate and dwarf).

Daylily Discounters
Route 2, Box 24
Alachua, FL 32615
800.DAYLILY
$2
A fantastic selection of daylilies. They ship real clumps with fat roots and inspire tremendous confidence because *you just know* bloom will occur the first season after planting. Also, this is where you can order the primordial muck. Don't forget the September Sale!

Dutch Gardens, Inc.
P.O. Box 200
Adelphia, NJ 07710
908.780.2713
Fax 908.780.7720
There is also a Holland address, so you know it's the real thing. You're already been informed how Howard Purcell feels about this one, and it's where I spend many of my considerable planting dollars. Their spring (fall-planting) catalog is superb, their spring-planting-for-summer catalog is pretty good too. This is the one, for sure, when you are just beginning, as the pictures are completely telling. And don't dismiss their perennials—they ship big healthy roots. Prices are among the best on all offerings. For an obviously big business—the consistency of their quality is almost awe-inspiring.

Ensata Gardens
9823 East Michigan Avenue
Galesburg, MI 49053 (only six miles east of Kalamazoo)
616.665.7500
$2
The source for heavenly Japanese iris. Fat, healthy roots arrive with at least six inches of top-growth. Each iris wrapped in a wet paper towel and moisture preserved with plastic—it's obvious this was done by loving hands.

Forest Farm
Ray and Peg Prag
990 Tetherow Road
Williams, OR 97544-9599
503.846.7269
$3
A wonderful catalog for grasses, ferns, and perennials that arrive healthy and robust. Also, a miraculous selection of trees and shrubs if you

have the patience to wait for even the best mail-order results. I've received three or four shipments from them and each time am amazed by the quality and *huge* size of the plants. There are no pretty colored pictures, but lots of interesting chitchat. A very wide range and extremely good prices. They tend to sell out early, so don't waste too much time in deliberation. Very nice people.

Forevergreen Farm
70 New Glouster Road
North Yarmouth, ME 04097
Fax 207.829.6512
Of all the rose specialist catalogs I have seen, this is the easiest to decipher. No pictures, but dreamy descriptions. Emphasis is on hardy growers, and the selection of old-fashioned and uncommon roses is bountiful.

French's Bulb Importer & Garden Shop
Route 100
Pittsfield, VT 05762-0565
802.746.8148
Specialists in bulbs for forcing. If you are a crazed apartment gardener, make sure you receive this one.

Gilson Gardens, Inc.
3059 U.S. Route 20
P.O. Box 277
Perry, OH 44081
Thorough selection of ground covers, many ivies especially, with terrific multiple prices if covering a lot of ground. I almost didn't include them because they make a point of boasting *Houttuynia*, that devil plant, with no warning; but otherwise—big fat rooted plant stock arrives. This is a good one.

Henry Field's
415 North Burnett
Shenandoah, IA 51602
605.665.9391
This is one of those old loving-hands-at-home catalogs, the one I like best of this multi-offering sort, but can't say I've ever used it. Every fruit tree—every radish—every bush wax bean you could possibly ever hunger after—is available here.

Holbrook Farm
Allen W. Bush
115 Lance Road, P.O. Box 368
Fletcher, NC 28732-0368
704.891.7790
$2
Great selection of perennials. Catalog has just a few photos but a very interestingly descriptive text. Plants arrive in perhaps the best packaging of all and I've always been pleased with the contents. Most everything is shipped in a four-inch pot, which means it's of good size and you can believe in it.

Holland Bulb Farms
354 Old Hook Road, P.O. Box 127
Westwood, NJ 07675-0127
215.253.9160
On the cover of the latest edition of this catalog, "No Gimmicks—Just Value" is proclaimed. I like that. Lots of pictures—very good prices—a few unique tulips—generally, a worthwhile catalog.

The Iris Pond
7311 Churchill Road
McLean, VA 22101-2001
703.893.8526
$1
A mimeographed no-picture list boasting "reblooming" bearded iris as its specialty, along with a nice selection of most all other iris types.

Of course, I'm fascinated by the idea of showy iris *twice* in one season and am about to order.

Ivies of the World
P.O. Box 408
Weirsdale, FL 32195
904.821.2201,2322
$1.50
Ivy is a great thing—evidently loved by the whole world because it's everywhere—making Oxford ivied, festooning Florentine brick, outlasting everything else in Grecian stone graveyards, even a mainstay in Burle-Marx's Brazilian schemes. Every ivy you could hope to covet is here.

Jackson & Perkins
P.O. Box 1028
Medford, OR 97501
800.292.4769
Forget their "Designer Gardens," their "Old-Fashioned Favorites," if you will; but how can anyone deny them their rose credentials.

Jacques Amand
The Nurseries, Clamp Hill
Stanmore, Middlesex HA7 3JS
ENGLAND
081.954.8138
Fax 081.954.6784
$2 U.S.
This source, who happily exports, gives credence to the English gardening elite. Never before have I seen so extensive an offering in such delectable categories as ten *Arisaema* (lovely woodland jack-in-the-pulpits), five trillium, seven calla lilies, and a phalanx of previously unknown bulbs like *Hepatica* (looks good), *Hedychium* (looks great), and *Curcuma* (looks fantastic). My order arrived promptly on May first—perfect timing for summer planting—with everything healthy (including temperamental lily bulbs) and well-marked (most by

hand) after their trip across the ocean. I'm impressed.

John D. Lyon Co.
143 Alewife Brook Parkway
Cambridge, MA 02140
617.876.3705
A true specialist in only dwarf bulbs (corydalis, crocus, iris, narcissi, and species tulips)—a really intriguing selection of these dainty and intricate wonders. Some odd, glorious *Fritillaria* are described, but at ten and twelve dollars a bulb, I haven't gotten around to taking the plunge yet—after all, you need at least twelve!

John Scheepers, Inc.
P.O. Box 700
Bantam, CT 06750
203.567.0838
Fax 203.567.5323
A revered catalog, beautiful pictures, a nice selection of bulbs, and as expensive as they get. A good reference source.

Kartuz Greenhouses
1408 Sunset Drive
Vista, CA 92083-6531
619.941.3613
A no-pictures catalog abounding with tropical beauties, perfect for your Zone 9 and 10ers, but equally enthralling for we who are content with summer outdoors and wintering inside. An amazing selection including *Brugmansia*, *Mandevilla*, and *ten* species of passion flowers!!!

Kelly's Plant World
10266 E. Princeton
Sanger, CA 93657
209.292.3505
$1
An expensive canna specialist, but if you can't live without unique purple lance-shaped leaves and an orchidlike flower that grows to ten feet—you've happened on the right source.

Kurt Bluemel, Inc.
2740 Greene Lane
Baldwin, MD 21013-9523
410.557.7229
Fax 410.557.9785
$2
This guy has a very tasteful catalog grounded in
a series of specialties—grasses—lots of them—
ferns, and perennials majorly parading as
ground covers or big-leaved important plants.
I've just received various *Rodgersia* and irresistible *Cimicifuga racemosa* 'Brunette' I couldn't
pass another season without, "almost black
leaves/fabulous specimen." Very straightforward bare-roots with some top-growth arrived
without fanfare, but made me feel assured.

Mary Mattison van Schaik
P.O. Box 32
Cavendish, VT 05142
802.226.7653
A Chinese sacred lily daffodil here, a different
strain of *Galanthus* there. Interesting. No pictures. Only bulbs.

McClure & Zimmerman
108 West Winnebago Street
P.O. Box 368
Friesland, WI 53935-0368
414.326.4220
Fax 414.326.5769
Beautiful collection of spring bulbs with the
most diversified miscellaneous bulb selection
I've unearthed in America. Few sketches, no
pictures, but great descriptions. Blooming results have been fantastic.

Milaeger's Gardens
4838 Douglas Avenue
Racine, WI 53402
414.639.2371
$1

Another reliable perennial source; particularly
good selection of shade plants and wildflowers.
They adoringly call it "The Wishbook"—many
items, well photographed.

Mountain Maples
5901 Spy Rock Road (which is way off the
beaten track, they say)
Laytonville, CA 95454-1329
707.984.6522
The irrefutable source for Japanese maples.

Niche Gardens
1111 Dawson Road
Chapel Hill, NC 27516-8576
919.967.0078
$3
These, too, are concerned, environmentally correct people from North Carolina specializing in
native plants of their region. Even though their
packing method is a bit annoying—shredded
paper really flies around—they have a very interesting catalog touching on a plethora of unusual finds. Most important, they ship big,
healthy plants in at least four-inch pots—
usually even larger—everything labeled by
hand. Extremely gardener-friendly. Will probably replace Montrose as my favored source for
special plants.

Potterton & Martin
The Cottage Nursery
Moortown Road, Nettleton, Caistor,
Lincolnshire, ENGLAND LN7 6HX
0472.851792
$3 U.S.
Happy to export—a Brit specializing in dwarf
bulbs, e.g., *Colchium*, crocus, *Allium*, twenty-
two kinds of *Galanthus!* and species tulips. No
experience yet, but am definitely placing my
first order this year as they have longest *Fritillaria* list I've yet to see.

Reath's Nursery Hybrid Peonies
County Road 577, Box 247
Vulcan, MI 49892
906.563.9777
$1
Heart-stopping selection of both herbaceous and tree peonies. Emphasis is on shipping three- to four-year-old plants so you won't wait an eternity for bloom. Prices are steep, but this is an extreme specialist with a very precious preoccupation.

Rex Bulb Farms
P.O. Box 774
Port Townsend, WA 98368
206.385.4280
$1
A fine lily catalog—where another will give a few paltry choices in each of the species, these people offer an enormous selection. They also cost a bit more, but if you are very discriminating about lilies—get this catalog to satiate your glorious lily hunger.

Russell Graham
Purveyor of Plants
4030 Eagle Crest Road, N.W.
Salem, OR 97304
503.362.1135
$2
This one is big on native American plants. Interesting perennials and great fern list. Many things shipped bare-root, which is often preferable.

Schreiner's Iris Gardens (since 1925)
3625 Quinaby Road, N.E.
Salem, OR 97303-9720
800.525.2367
Fax 503.393.5590
$2

The bountiful bearded iris treat—no need to even consider buying Mama's June extravaganza anywhere but here.

Shady Oaks Nursery
112 Tenth Avenue, SE
Waseca, MN 56093
507.835.5033
$1
A fine specialist in hosta and other enticing, shade-loving ground covers like Japanese painted fern and *Epimedium*. Am just trying them now, but have a good feeling.

Sheperd's Garden Seeds
30 Irene Street
Torrington, CT 06790
203.482.3638
$1
If you insist on starting from seed—this is where to buy them.

Siskiyou Rare Plant Nursery
2825 Cummings Road
Medford, OR 97501
503.772.6846
$2
For you lovers of minutiae and those who aspire to alpine gardening—this is your source. Also a good selection of ferns, dwarf conifers, and Japanese maples.

Spring Hill Nurseries
6523 North Galena Road
Peoria, IL 61632
309.691.4616
The most distinguishing feature of this catalog is not having to pay until well after your plants are in the ground. They will establish an account for you no matter who you are. At the last minute, when cashed out, without an open credit card line to turn to, bereft of a check, I've

turned to them; but also, their perennial offering is plentiful and the quality not bad.

Steffen's Clematis
1259 Fairport Road, P.O. Box 184
Fairport, NY 14450
716.377.1665
Fax 716.377.1893
$2
Soon Arthur's crop will be back in shape. Get the glorious catalog and wait with me through this excruciating interval.

Steve Ray's Bamboo Gardens
909 79th Place South
Birmingham, AL 35206
205.833.3052
$2
If you happen to live in the area, you can repair right to the groves and choose your own plants. If you must have bamboo by mail or are looking for exotic types, might as well order from Steve Ray's 250 varieties on fifty acres. Black-and-white photos and great descriptions.

Summerville's
R.D. #1, Box 449
Glassboro, NJ 08028
609.881.0704
The only gladioli specialist I've ever come across. Near-encyclopedic descriptions, but no photos. As I've had spotty luck with my cutting-garden glads, this year I'm going to get my bulbs from these all-out enthusiasts.

Swan Island Dahlias
P.O. Box 700
Canby, OR 97013
503.266.7711
$2
The Dahlia Center of America, they proclaim. Every homely tuber ever received had a perfect eye and was true to description or picture. They

have the best labeling method yet—the name indelibly stamped right on the tuber—and all they do is grow dahlias on forty acres, so how can you go wrong? They are very specific.

Trans-Pacific Nursery
16065 Oldsville Road (love that name, Oldsville)
McMinnville, OR 97128
503.472.6215
$1
Am just placing my first order—have very high hopes. They call it a collector's list and their byline is "Rare and Exotic Plants." Not a picture to be seen, but cover and intermittent artwork is dense and moody and makes me believe we have the same taste. The listings are riddled with things I've never heard of—always a turn-on. A real hands-on operation, just called to track whereabouts of my order and was told the "brains of the operation was out in the field grafting." (What arrived was sensational.)

Van Bourgondien
245 Farmingdale Road, P.O. Box 1000
Babylon, NY 11702
800.622.9997
Fax 516.669.1228
Bulbs and perennials and occasionally things difficult to find elsewhere. Good pictures, fair prices; for some reason I always resort to it as an afterthought, although I like it and have never been disappointed.

Van Engelen, Inc.
Stillbrook Farm, 313 Maple Street
Litchfield, CT 06759
203.567.8734
Fax 203.567.5323
A truly great one—a bulb catalog to be consumed—where I spend my main fall-planting money (along with Dutch Gardens). These two are the main stories—with them you

reap the cream of the springtime crop at the best price and with the most satisfaction. Make sure to carefully check out the last pages of the catalog where the quantities are not so over-whelming. Have just discovered this is the wholesale arm of John Scheepers. Now I'm even more impressed.

Veldheer Tulip Gardens, De Klomp Wooden Shoe and Delft Factory
12755 Quincy Street & U.S. 31 North
Holland, MI 49424
616.399.1900
The spring catalog is fairly predictable, but the for-summer-planting selection is quite nice—good *Caladiums* and begonias.

Wayside Gardens
1 Garden Lane (Isn't that sweet?)
Hodges, SC 29695-0001
800.845.1124
$1
The grandame of the catalogs. It's a fabulous learning tool and there's always a must-have nobody else offers, so you're sure to stay on their mailing list. However, I generally avoid them for most things as they are drastically overpriced and have such a wide audience that what you receive may not be as developed as expected. Caution is the keyword; but absolutely peruse it for all its good information and great pictures taken from enough distance you get a real idea of how the plant actually looks.

We-Du Nurseries
Route 5, Box 724
Marion, NC 28752
704.738.8300
$1
Another honest North Carolina catalog with an attitude and descriptions reminding me of my beloved Montrose, but they ship very tiny plants, so will never really take Montrose's

place. All sorts of interesting perennials and ferns, even mosses, which is a first for me.

Wheel-View Farm
212 Reynolds Road
Shelburne, MA 01370
413.625.2900
I feel sad about this one because I can't share the real thing with you any longer. Three seasons ago this catalog was named Gladside Gardens and presided over by a fabulous eccentric lady named Gladys Heselton who prided herself in offering the most obscure of everything bulbous one could plant. I won't go on and on about what doesn't exist anymore. Carolyn and John Wheeler have bought her nursery and con-tinue in a less interesting, but still commendable pursuit. You can acquire here a canna that grows to fourteen feet and the cheapest *Crinum* lilies in America. I really miss Gladys, but these people are okay, too.

White Flower Farm, Plantsmen
Litchfield, CT 06759-0050
203.496.9600
5 bucks, no less
The grandpère. A scholarly tome grounded in a properly color-separated hundred-page catalog and another must-read, but be aware of Amos Pettingill's giddy anecdotes, which are often better ignored. However, as with Wayside, you're sure to find something irresistible here not existing elsewhere. Most recently, I was swayed by *Lithodora* 'Grace Ward' that turned out to be as blue as they promised—but, again, be wary as they are extremely computer-driven and very expensive.

York Hill Farm
271 N. Haverhill Road
Kensington, NH 03833
603.772.8567

For iris other than magnificent bearded and magical Japanese (like *I. Louisiana* and *I. tectorum*)—this is the place to order. Also, hosta, daylilies, and that important obsession, Heritage (or Old World or English) roses.

To the best of my knowledge, the catalogs with no dollar amounts listed below their information are free for the asking. Where a small contribution is requested, it's usually deductible from the first order you place. Of course, once you become a viable customer—it's all gratis.

Yucca Do Nursery
P.O. Box 655
Waller, TX 77484
$2
The grass expert, John Greenlee, says this is the absolute best source. Who am I to argue?

The American Horticultural Society. *Encyclopedia of Garden Plants.* Ed. Christopher Brickell; horticultural consultant, John Elsley. New York: Macmillan, 1990. When I need an academic tome, I consult this. At least it has pictures.

Barbara J. Barton. *Gardening by Mail.* Boston: Houghton Mifflin, 1990. This is where to find everything available through the trusty U.S. Postal Service, as well as all the plant societies.

Jane Brown. *Sissinghurst: Portrait of a Garden.* New York: Harry N. Abrams, 1990. Vita and Harold's celebrated house and grounds, including of course many views of the quintessential "White Garden."

Myles Challis. *Large-Leaved Perennials.* London: Ward Lock, 1992. We share similar tastes and so I've devoured this book, which frustrates me as I'm unable to locate a few spectacular entries therein.

T. H. Everett, ed. *The New Illustrated Encyclopedia of Gardening.* New York: Greystone Press. (My volumes range from 1964 to 1967—I found them at the East Hampton Ladies' Auxiliary Society.) Mr. Everett, a curator at the New York Botanical Garden, and his contributors, "twenty horticulturists and authorities in the United States and Canada," have been an indispensable fount of knowledge for me.

Nicola Ferguson. *Right Plant, Right Place: The Indispensable Guide to the Successful Garden.* New York: Summit Books, 1984. I would have been lost without Nicola in the early days.

The Gardener's Calendar. Published each year and filled with tips and hints for your very own zone. If you can't find it, you can order direct from the publisher: Starwood, P.O. Box 40503, Washington, DC 20016; telephone 202-362-7404.

John Greenlee. *The Encyclopedia of Ornamental Grasses.* Emmaus, Pa.: Rodale Press, 1992. The comprehensive, illustrated reference on this beguiling topic.

Rhonda Massingham Hart. *Bugs, Slugs, and Other Thugs: Controlling Gardening Pests Organically.* Pownal, Vt.: Storey Communications, 1991. Often silly or untenable solutions, but a plethora of information.

Hillier Nurseries (Winchester) Ltd. *The Hillier Colour Dictionary of Trees and Shrubs.* London and North Pomfret, Vt.: David & Charles, 1981. Hillier's is a Brit nursery of note, and this guide is fundamental.

Gertrude Jekyll. *Colour Schemes for the Flower Garden,* seventh ed. London: Country Life. A classic—and don't forget to pronounce her name Jee-kul, *not* as in Dr. Jekyll and Mr. Hyde, or you will be boo-hooed right out of the bookstore.

———. *On Gardening.* New York: Random House, Vintage Books, 1985.

———. *Wall and Water Gardens.* Salem, N.H.: The Ayer Company, 1983. See also the book on Gertrude Jekyll by Tankard and Van Valkenburgh listed below.

Hugh Johnson. *The Principles of Gardening: The Classic Guide to the Gardener's Art.* A Fireside Book. New York: Simon & Schuster, 1979. The most intelligent gardening book I've ever come across.

Christopher Lloyd. *The Year at Great Dixter.* New York: Viking Press, 1987. If you want to read about a gardening year as seen through the eyes of the landed gentry, this is the one. Great Dixter boasts a horse pond, lower moat, high garden, orchard garden, long border, topiary lawn—you name it, they've got it, and it's been in the family forever.

Ann Lovejoy. *Three Years in Bloom: A Garden Keeper's Journal.* Seattle: Sasquatch Books, 1988. You can order it from the publisher at 1931 Second Avenue, Seattle, WA 98101; telephone 206-441-5555.

Stirling Macoboy. *What Flower Is That?* New York: Portland House, 1986. A great pictorial compendium full of exactly the kind of information intriguing to me and chock-full of extraordinary flower photographs.

William C. Mulligan. *The Adventurous Gardener's Sourcebook of Rare and Unusual Plants.* A Running Heads Book. New York: Simon & Schuster, 1992. Filled with beautiful photographs of many favorites included in the DB Greatest Hits list, as well as some others I'd give anything to find.

Bill Neal. *Gardener's Latin: A Lexicon.* Chapel Hill, N.C.: Algonquin Books, 1992. Amusing and helpful.

The Old Farmer's Almanac, 1993. Robert B. Thomas. Dublin, N.H.: Yankee Publishing. It has a certain undeniable charm.

Jane Owen. *Eccentric Gardens.* New York: Villard Books, 1990. Follies and allées, surrealism and egotism, and all sorts of fabulous animal indulgences.

Michael Pollan. *Second Nature: A Gardener's Education.* New York: Dell Publishing, 1992. Without question, my favorite contemporary gardening treatise.

The Royal Horticultural Society. *Gardener's Five Year Record Book.* Compiled by Donald McKendrick. London: Eubury Press Stationery. You can order it from The Secretary, Royal Horticultural Society, 80 Vincent Square, London SW1P 2PE, England.

Vita Sackville-West. *The Illustrated Garden Book.* Ed. Robin Lane Fox. New York: Atheneum, 1986. Although Vita didn't write this precisely as a garden book—it is a compilation of her garden articles in the *Observer*—'tis a real joy to read her down-to-earth account.

George Harmon Scott. *Bulbs: How to Select, Grow, and Enjoy.* Los Angeles: HP Books / Price Stern Sloan, 1982. The most comprehensive modern book I've come across about both spring- and summer-blooming bulbs—it really gives you the dirt.

Mrs. Charles H. Stout. *The Amateur's Book of the Dahlia.* New York: Doubleday, Page & Co., 1922. This taught me everything I needed to know when the dahlia bug bit.

Judith B. Tankard and Michael R. Van Valkenburgh. *Gertrude Jekyll: A Vision of Garden and Wood.* A Ngaere Macray Book. New York: Harry N. Abrams / Sagapress, 1989. Luscious black-and-white photographs of her stunning grounds and gardens.

The Unique Horticultural News Service. *The Avant Gardener.* Published monthly, $18 per year. By subscription only from Horticultural Data Processors, P.O. Box 489, New York, NY 11028. Occasionally a ho-hum issue but more often a tidbit I'd be lost without.

J. D. Vertrees. *Japanese Maples.* Portland, Ore.: Timber Press, 1987. The classic illustrated book of the genus, a beauty.

Note: All italicized words, other than genus or specie names, indicate a cross-reference in the glossary to other terms that make the meaning more significant.

acid soil—largely what we have in East Hampton—without *lime* or chalk—a spongier, more "open" kind of dirt—add sulfur or Miracid to make it more acid. On the famous pH scale, acid is 7 or more.

alkaline soil—the opposite of *acid*—a dryer, more desertlike dirt, the kind that exudes with little rain—generally more fertile. Add lime if this is what you seek.

allée—a walk or wide path cut from massed trees or ponderous plantings, originated in Napoleonic France.

alpine—refers to plants native to the Alps or other high rocky slopes, usually small and precise flora suitable to crevices of rock gardens or maintained *troughs*.

annual—a one-season idea, a plant with an entire life span from seed through flowering through demise that occurs within the cycle of one year or less.

anther—the male organ of a flower, usually protruding (wouldn't you know).

arboretum—one of many spellings for a "tree collection."

armillary sphere—a divine decorative sculptural object made up of hoops to show the heavenly bodies in their place, while in motion, see the *Wind & Weather* catalog.

aroid—many of my favorite plants are included in this *Arum* group where the "flowers" are formed into a central phallic protruberance sheathed in a shroudlike mantle, the former known as the *spadix* and the latter as the *spathe*.

axil—a poignant point between a stem and a leaf; often a bud forms within it.

balustrade—a very fancy or formal fence appropriately made of stone with various columns, or pillars, that support the railing.

bare-root—a plant's growing system (root, tuber, etc.) with no soil surrounding the roots, usually dormant when planted, and the best method for planting many *perennials*.

bark—the protective outer covering or sheath of a tree, shrub, and certain vines; often valued for its ornamental quality, as in birches.

basal leaves—leaves that remain at ground level, the lowest leaves occasionally differing in form from the rest of the plant.

beard—an *Iris* term, refers to the funny little "hairs" on the upper surface of the *falls*.

bed—in gardening, refers to a predetermined space set out for flowers particularly focal in a garden; in a way—unnatural and to be avoided.

bedding plants—an old-fashioned terminology, but put in practice in an arbitrary way these days more often than it ought to be. Usually *annuals*, these are plants put in place for one season to add vivacity and color and at the end of the season tossed out—better to concentrate on nonbedding plants.

belvedere—aside from being the papal name of the holiest villa in the Vatican gardens, it is a pavillion or any raised structure in the garden scene that is open and permits air to waft about and is well situated enough to provide a view.

berm—a low, rolling, artificial hill used in landscape design to create a feeling of different levels or to highlight a *specimen*.

biennial—somewhere between an annual and a perennial, this sort of plant can be expected to last a few years; the first with robust leafing and growth—but no flower, and the second with stupendous flowers and seeds.

bog plants—those happy in permanently wet ground, like some iris, cattails, mosses *et al.*; a bog is a stretch of low-lying, wet, spongy ground containing a great amount of decomposing plant matter—usually the transition between a pond or stream and dry land.

bonemeal—organic fertilizer made from ground-up animal bones, and the most expensive thing per pound at the Agway—great for most bulbs and tubers, it is mainly a source of *phosphate* and *nitrogen*.

border—much more desirable than a garden "bed"—a border is usually a more natural planting that edges a path, skirts a wall or woods, and generally serves as a margin, boundary, or perimeter; it can be tame or wild, formal or casual.

bract—a modified leaf, often encircling or replacing a flower, many times showier than the flower itself, occuring at the base of the flower stalk; many times the glory of the plant, as in *Bougainvillea, Zantedeschia,* and my beloved *Arums.*

Brooklyn Botanical Garden—one of New York's proudest assets, a walk through it in any season is a gorgeous learning experience: woodland gardens, Shakespeare garden, Japanese garden, and almost any other specialty that comes to mind.

bud—what we wait for in winter, the rudimentary, embryonic offshoot containing the leaf and/or flower.

bud blast—or "die-back," the death of the tips of the shoots or buds due to frost or disease.

bulb—usually, an underground swollen stem serving as a storage system during a rest period, often with fleshy scales (as in lilies and *Fritillaria*), or sometimes tight and compact as in tulips and daffodils; from this incredible creation of Mama Nature develops above-ground fantastic flowers.

Burle-Marx, Roberto—(1909–) the preeminent Brazilian landscape architect, greatly influenced by Le Corbusier, who is responsible for the fantastic cubistic-colored concrete and planted beaches of Rio and many famous Brazilian gardens; the only plantsman ever honored by a retrospective at the Museum of Modern Art.

calyx—the outermost ring of modified leaves that form—or surround a flower. It encloses the *petals.*

catkin—looks a bit like a cat's tail, usually found on *deciduous* trees or shrubs, a unisexual pendant petal-less "flower" found on willows, birches, and "Harry Lauder's walking stick."

Chelsea Flower Show—The Brit Royal Horticultural Society has been hosting this magnificent springtime event since 1913, except during the crisis of war, on the grounds of the Royal Hospital in Chelsea—the ultimate flowering event of the western (or maybe the entire) world.

climber—a non-self-supporting plant, one that needs a wall, *trellis, tuteur,* tree, or other plants for support—may climb by twining leaf stalks, aerial roots, suckering pads, tendrils, or coiling stems—you want many of these to give that vertical zing to your garden.

compost heap—decomposing plant remains piled up or put in a pit to decay together, with help from bacteria and other microorganisms, resulting in a precious form of organic enrichment for the soil. Not a composter myself, I much prefer to buy Composted Cow Manure & Organic Humus already decayed and bagged.

compound—plant parts composed of several units; e.g., a compound leaf is comprised of several leaflets.

conifer—any cone-bearing tree, a cone being the flowering or fruiting spike of a conifer, usually containing the seeds; as well as yews and junipers that bear fleshy fruits—most are evergreen.

conservatory—differs from a *greenhouse* in that it is comfortable and people-oriented, a part- or all-glass structure housing your plants in winter (summer too) that can be decorated and divine—I'd give anything for a nice cozy conservatory attached to the house.

corm—performs the same function as a *bulb,* but unlike a bulb it isn't layered and the whole is covered with papery scales, as in crocus and gladioli.

corolla—the part of the flower formed by the *petals,* usually a different color than the *sepals.*

corona—the outgrowth between the *petals* and *stamens* of a flower, for example, the "trumpet" of a daffodil.

crown—part of the plant usually just below the soil's surface from which the shoots grow and to which they die back in autumn; the very top of the *root stock.*

cultivar—short for "cultivated variety." Horticulturally selected by man after the botanic *genus* and *species* of Mama Nature.

deadheading—the removal of spent flowers from a plant at their base—important to keep the plants alluring, prevent the sapping of their energy by seed production, and, often, to promote another cycle of bloom; a significant garden chore.

deciduous—leaf-losing, the opposite of *evergreens*—an annual occurence at the end of the growing season, usually autumn.

disbudding—removing side *shoots* or flower-*buds* from a stem to promote larger flowers from the remaining buds.

division—the only method of propagation that I've occasionally indulged in. Any clump-forming plant (*perennial*) can be divided into several parts, each of which will form new plants; the plant must be mature for you to do this.

dormancy—a period of rest when the plants die down and withdraw into the ground, or before the *bud* blooms; also appropriate to *bulbs* after their leaves die down.

double, semidouble—usually *hybrids* of flowers

having a second or third (or more) row of *petals;* typically some of the sexual organs (the *stamens* or *carpels*) are turned into petals.

drainage—the running off of water from the surface and below the soil. In soggy environments this can be corrected by planting on a slope or hill (which can be concocted) or by an underground system of pipes—good drainage is a must for many plants.

drift—usually a random mass of flowers (best just a few kinds of flowers, e.g., daffodils and muscari) meant to conjure up a look of massing and naturalness.

dry wall—a freestanding stone wall without mortar joints, usually not more than three or four feet high, and another thing I'm dying for.

espalier—an elaborate means of training appropriate trees (fruit trees, crab apple, etc.) on latticework or walls to grow flat against them in a very stylized manner, quite formal.

evergreen—can be tropical or temperate. These are plants and trees that lose their older leaves or needles slowly and unnoticeably throughout the year, are always green, and usually their discard becomes a fine *mulch.*

eye—a very young *bud,* most noticeable on dahlias, potatoes, *et al.*

falls—the downward-hanging *petals* of iris, these are the ones that sport a *beard* and differentiate the bearded from the beardless.

fertilizer—fertility boosters, may be liquid or powdery or earthy. They add the essential minerals or humus-producing qualities to the *dirt:* bonemeal composted cow manure, dried blood, *lime,* etc.

flora—Mama Nature's huge group of plant life, as opposed to the animal world (fauna).

foliage—the leaves. Foliage plants are those more interesting for their leafing, as opposed to flowering.

folly—a particularly English contrivance, and an endearing one at that—a garden edifice with no reason for being other than its ability to charm or intrigue you, and set your *garden* distinctly apart from all others.

forcing—thrusting a plant into bloom prior to its natural cycle by enclosing it in a predetermined atmosphere of heat and light swifter than Mama's plan. What the bored gardener does in winter.

frond—the leaflike, feathery, *compound* structure found in ferns and palm trees.

garden—the pleasure-ridden goal we're all striving toward, a planted, tended, and cultivated patch of land meant to rouse the senses and provide artistry where there was none.

gazebo—a charming *garden* edifice that unlike a folly is meant to serve a function, a necessarily covered and open-air structure meant to encapsulate a view and provide a platform for picnics or political speeches.

genus—plants with collective characteristics, the first and most important part of the Latin name and the one you want to get familiar with first.

glaucous—bluish-white, green, or gray; commonly used to describe leaves.

greenhouse—a glass building dedicated to protecting plants from the natural milieu of Mama, a manmade environment sanctified for the indoor growing of plants under controlled conditions that can take on many shapes and sizes, attached to the house or not—I have my eye on a separated, iron and glass, concave-roofed, Victorian kind of structure . . . but think I'm more likely to wind up with a sort-of *conservatory.*

ground cover—ground-hugging, low-growing plants meant to enhance the garden scene by replacing the basest horizontal level with something more charming than spotty grass, weeds, or plain old dirt; they can vary from ivy to lilies-of-the-valley, *Lamium* to hosta—any ground cover makes an estimable difference.

hardiness—the indication of a plant's susceptibility to frost damage (though in tropical lands, it may be a warning of the plant's sensitivity to drought), the ten hardiness zones in North America are the gardener's barometer for recognizing what plants one might grow in any given area.

herbaceous—not *woody;* any *perennial* that dies back to the ground at the end of its growing season.

Hillier Nurseries—around since 1864, the preeminent tree and shrub nursery located in mythical Hampshire, the heart of the English countryside; someday I plan to garden there. If they say it's from Hillier's—take note.

Hortus—beginning in 1930 (*Hortus I*), the most definitive plantsman's dictionary, extremely horticulturally correct; *Hortus III* is the most recent update (1976) for the fecundity of flora cultivated in the USA and Canada—you don't really need it.

humus—the vital source of nutrients resulting from the decay of organic matter, found in and generally applied to the soil to make it richer, more water-retentive, and helps to break down the soil's natural chemicals so it is more easily absorbed by the plants—my favorite fertilizer is Composted Manure & Organic Humus, costs $2.49 for a forty-pound bag, and I go through dozens of bags in a planting season.

hybrid—when you see an x following the *genus* name—it is a hybrid; this means it was conceived from human cross-breeding between two *species*—taking the best qualities from each, usually. Hybrids are often the best form of the plant as we know it today.

incurved—a flower part bending upward and inward, best seen in some dahlias.

inflorescence—made up of many small flowers (florets, actually); usually branching clusters of flowers variously termed corymb, *panicle, raceme, umbel,* and *spike.*

insecticide—chemical combinations formulated for plant groups and used to kill insects and other pests with no harm to the plant; usually dusted or sprayed on. "Systemic" insecticides also available that are applied to the soil and taken up by the sap stream of the plant.

invasive—a plant too prolific for its own good, or the garden's good anyway; increases quickly, customarily by underground roots—an extreme example is the loathed *Houttuynia.*

Jekyll, Gertrude—(1843–1932) the reknowned Surrey gardener who approached her garden-making and writing as an art, collaborated importantly with the classic garden architect Edwin Lutyens, and introduced the idea of "controlled wildness" on the gardening panorama of Edwardian England—highly revered and exceedingly influential; even Vita was a disciple.

kenzan—Japanese flower display method using a small, heavy, spiked arranger to highlight one or a few worthy flowers.

Kew, Royal Botanical Gardens at—founded in the eighteenth century by the royal family and located in Surrey; hailed as the paradigm of great botanical institutions, with a vast collection of plants. Both historically and horticulturally important.

knot garden—a Renaissance *garden* in which *ground cover,* dwarf *evergreens,* and low *shrubs* were designed in tenuous twisted designs resembling *knots*—extremely ornamental.

lath house—a building for storage and coddling of tender plants, usually made of wood framing and glass (or less desirable, plastic).

leaf mold—a great source of *humus* formed by the piling of autumn leaves in deep piles until they decay and become shredded.

lime—compounds of calcium that neutralize *acid* in the *soil.* The amount of lime determines whether the soil is *alkaline, neutral,* or *acid.*

Linnaeus, Carolus (Carl von Linné)—(1707–1778) dear Carl, the father of the scientific system (a *generic* and *species* name) of naming twelve thousand species of plants and animals; his major works *Species Plantarum* (1753) and *Genera Plantarum* (1754) are commonly used to identify plants the world over.

liquid manure—horse or cow manure mixed with water and dispersed for concentrated plant feeding.

loam—well-structured, fertile soil that is moisture-retentive but well-drained—the ideal dirt.

loggia—originally a shaded walk in Italian gardens, now recognized as an arcade open to the air on one or both sides.

moss—nonflowering tiny plants that form mats and thrive in deep shade under damp conditions; their velvety texture is delightful in a rockery or near a water garden.

mulch—a layer of organic matter (usually) applied to the *soil* around trees and plants to conserve moisture, keep down *weeds,* protect the *roots* from frost, and enrich the soil—decorative, too.

naturalize—to establish and grow plants as if in the wild, based on informality and best achieved with *drifts* of spring bulbs or wildflowers.

nectar—a sweet liquid secreted by the "nectary," a gland usually found in the flower.

neutral—as regards soil, with a *pH* value of 7, the point at which the *soil* is neither *alkaline* or *acid.*

nitrogen—supplied in fertilizers as ammonium sulphate or sodium nitrate, one of the three most essential elements for plant growth and health—mainly affects the *vegetative,* or green, leafy, part of the plant.

node—the point on the stem from which the leaf or leaves arise.

nursery—in horticulture, a plant-growing and display house—to us, the local valuable source for in-growth purchase of flowers, *shrubs,* and trees.

offset—a new plant developing naturally from a side stem of the mother plant, usually at its base.

opposite—leaves arising in pairs from the *nodes* directly opposite one another, as opposed to alternate leaves, which are pairs at different levels.

pagoda—an Oriental *garden* structure with a pyramidlike form.

palmate—a leaf with five lobes in the manner of a "hand."

panicle—form of flower-head known as a branched *raceme*.

pealike—with the same look as a pea-flower (a member of the Legume Family, which is the third largest family of flowering plants). The flowers have two side *petals* that look like wings hovering over two lower petals that combine to form a "keel." Usually small and always charmingly profuse.

peat or peat moss—a dark, partially decomposed organic substance found in *bogs*, usually developing from sedges or sphagnum moss, importantly used as an enrichment of the soil, not for fertilizing purposes as much as for improving the physical structure of the *soil*, its tilth and water-retention capacity—easily available and absolutely a planting must.

perennial—a plant living more than two years, and in many cases, for decades; usually associated with *herbaceous* plants that produce stems that die down to the ground every year—although can be applicable to *woody* plants that die down only partially, leaving a woody stem at the base.

pergola—a (usually) wooden *garden* structure supported by posts with an overhead *trellis* or formation, routinely used to grow vines over a walk or pathway and provide a shaded passage—a lovely garden feature.

pesticide—see *insecticide;* same thing.

petal—often the showiest and most highly colored part of the flower, a petal is one of the modified leaves forming the *corolla*.

pH—the measure of *acidity* and *alkalinity* of the *soil*, ranging from zero to 14. Zero through 7 indicates degrees of acidity; 7 through 14, alkalinity. The ideal pH for most gardening is about 6.5.

phosphate—the chemical form of phosphorus—another of the essential nutrients in the soil—and the one most responsible for the plant's beauteous flowers or fruit.

photosynthesis—the magical conversion of solar energy arranged by Mama Nature to transform the sun's potency into the vital life-giving, greening power (aided by chlorophyll) of plants, causing carbon dioxide to be extracted from the air and water sent up from the roots; the major by-product of photosynthesis is the oxygen that permeates the atmosphere of Earth.

pollen—the miniscule male grains produced by the *anthers* (male organs) of a flower; actually the flower's sperm, which in pollination (or fertilization) is transferred to the *stigma*, the female portion of the flower found at the tip of the *style;* plants can either be self-pollinating, or cross-pollinated by the wind or insects carrying the pollen from one flower to another—another amazing feat of nature.

potash or potassium—another of the three essential minerals (nutrients) of the *soil;* largely adds to the strength of the overall plant, especially its *roots*, and provides resistance to disease and cold.

potting up—in any cycle, the first time a plant is taken from the seed tray or the *dormant* state (as in *bulbs, corms,* and *tubers* wintered over by storing) and transferred to a pot of its own (brimming with enriched *soil,* of course).

propagation—the multiplication of plants, either sexually by seed, or vegetatively by layering, grafting, cutting, *division, tuber or rhizomatic* growth or any other means; for the most part—easiest to leave this job to the catalog growers and nurseries.

pruning—the selective cutting of tree, *shrub,* and plant branches or stems (and sometimes *roots*) to improve the plant's shape, rid it of diseased or damaged stems, increase its vigor, or stimulate fruit and flower production; depending on the plant, the method and time of pruning varies greatly.

pubescent—as pertains to plants, any part covered with downy, tiny hairs.

quagmire—soft, sticky, boglike earth that yields under foot, or a precarious predicament we can find ourselves in, i.e., if one wants to garden and neglects to ammend the *soil* or water the plants.

quarry—an open mine from which stone is extracted in blocks.

raceme—a projecting, unbranched flower cluster, or *inflorescence,* bearing many short-stemmed flowers along an extended *axil;* the lower flowers open as the top continues to produce new *buds.*

rambler—much the same as a *climber,* usually describes a rose with long sprawling stems.

recurved—turned backward or downward delicately or gently.

reflexed—abruptly turned downward or backward, as is the case with Turk's-cap lilies.

rhizome—like a *bulb,* a rhizome is an organ of storage; an underground, swollen, creeping stem that bears roots, leafy shoots, and flowering stems—the most obvious rhizome is that of the bearded iris.

rock garden or rockery—usually on a bank or slope (often created by man) an interplanting of low-growing plants amidst rocks and often gravel integrated to form a harmonius composition; a careful choice of accent plants providing color, form, and texture contrast or harmony—either massed or singled out; the perfect place for highlighting dwarf or miniature plants. Mixed within my small rockery are many things, including Japanese painted ferns and tuberous begonias and it's just lovely.

root—usually underground, the part of a plant that stores food, takes in water and minerals from the soil, and serves as an anchor for the plant; most plants are either fibrous-rooted (many fine roots) or taprooted (a single long fat swollen root that looks like a carrot); aerial roots, such as those found on orchids and ivy, are formed above soil level and take their nutrients and water from the air.

root-bound—an overgrown plant in a restricting container; usually an unhealthy condition, but there are the exceptional plants that like this status such as *Crinum* and *Agapanthus*.

rosette—circular or radial, usually basal, plant growth equidistant from the center; in appearance like a classic rose.

runner—a horizontally spreading, slender stem that forms *roots* at each node, usually underground.

Sackville-West, Victoria (our Vita)—(1892–1962) Woman of many talents: poet, novelist, journalist, gardener extraordinaire; and of great style—perhaps her grandest achievement was the garden she created at Sissinghurst Castle in Kent from 1930 on with her husband Harold Nicholson—dominated by the Tudor Tower (at the top of which was her private room), the engaging gardens were divided into "rooms," each with different themes or color plans. For more on Vita, read all of this book.

scree—a garden bed or *trough* filled with small stones and a little *loam*, providing extremely sharp drainage for *alpine* plants, or any plants that are offended by water at their base.

self-seed—the natural production of seedlings by the parent plant.

sepal—a single part of the *calyx* of a flower, usually green and low-profile, but occasionally the showiest part of the flower as with clematis; mainly they help protect the lower *bud* before it opens.

shoot—the aerial part of a plant that robustly bears leaves, a side shoot can arise from a main shoot.

shrub—a plant with *woody* stems, all usually arising from the base of the plant; the value of most shrubs is their flowering.

soil—the *dirt;* a medium suitable for plant growth, consisting of air, minerals, water, and organic material; depending on the minerals, soil is generally sandy (holds the least water), clay (usually hard and holds the most water), and *loam*—the ideal.

spathe—a large bract (or modified leaf) enclosing (wrapped like a cloak) the *inflorescence,* or flower (*spadix*), like the "hood" in jack-in-the-pulpits or the strange construct of the *Arum.*

species—the natural botanical unit; one or more (often dozens) species are grouped to form a genus. The species are individuals exhibiting like characteristics distinguishing them from others; they breed true from generation to generation.

specimen—unique or fine enough individual example of a *species* to be treated as a separate and singular display to create an accent or highlight, often containerized, but also very nice planted within due space upon a lawn—they should be intriguing from all viewpoints.

spike—an elongated flower-head in which the flowers grow directly against the main stem—always unbranched, with the lower flowers opening first.

spur—a particularly engaging flower part found in columbine and delphiniums—a hollow, gracefully pointing extension of the petals, usually producing *nectar.*

staking—a bamboo cane (or imitation thereof), stick, or stout stake (depending on the size of what needs staking) placed on the side of the main stem of a plant or the trunk of tree or shrub to give support and direct growth; whatever is used as a tie must always be tightly wound around the stake itself and loosely encircle the stem or trunk in order to allow growth.

stamen—see **pollen**.

standard—not only the three upright petals of an iris, but importantly "tree form"—a tree or *shrub* with an upright single, main stem or trunk bearing no branches for a considerable length; this doesn't often happen in nature and is a result of *pruning* and training; roses and wisteris, for example, may be disciplined as standards.

stigma or style—See **pollen**.

stolon or stoloniferous—a horizontally spreading or arching stem, usually at ground level, that *roots* at its tip to produce a new plant.

succulent—a plant with thick and fleshy leaves, or stems with absence of leaves and odd shapes; these usually contain juice or sap and are at home in arid environments (like cactus).

sucker—a shoot that arises from below ground level directly from the root; they are usually robust and unwanted as they interfere with the look of the main-stemmed stance of the plant and they sap energy from the primary growing system—take your Felcos to them as deep in the ground as you can manage.

symbiosis—an intimate relationship between two different kinds of organisms that results in a mutually beneficial life together; an *alga* and a *fungus* living together as lichens are a botanical example—but a sweeping generalization could take in many forms of marriage—in the garden and out.

tendril—a threadlike, coiled growth that helps a plant climb by twisting around any available support.

toothed—with indented edges, as refers to any plant part but most commonly to describe leaves.

topiary—the strictly decorative practice of *pruning* trees and shrubs into exotic and ornamental shapes, usually practiced on *evergreens* such as yew and box, can be highly formal as it was with the Romans or imaginative and whimsical as in *Edward Scissorhands*—I love it and am anxious to incorporate it somewhere.

transplanting—moving a plant (initially) from its place of origin to a cultivated situation, and any act of moving a plant from place to place—a real testament to the hardiness of nature.

trellis or treillage—light, overlapped, (usually) wooden *laths* used as a plant support, normally one-inch wide and a quarter-inch thick and used as a screen—to add height, or the illusion of depth, or provide a backdrop; in elaborate French treillage architectural features and trompe l'oeil effects are recurrent themes.

trompe l'oeil—foreshortening and other deceptive devices of exaggerated perspective usually carried out in *trellis* work, used to modify and heighten the apparent depth, length, or width of a landscape.

tropical—between the Tropic of Cancer and the Tropic of Capricorn—the torrid zone.

trough—a container usually made of stone, brick, or concrete and suitable for growing miniatures and *alpine* plants.

tuber—a thickened plant stem or root found underground, functioning as a storage unit (also like a *bulb*); tubers usually bear *eyes* from which entire plants and new tubers are generated, as in dahlias.

umbel—the type of flower-head on which the individual flowers are born on stems arising from a single point and form a rounded flower cluster, like the spokes in a wheel if it were drooping.

variegated—having marks, stripes, outlines, or blotches of some color other than the basic groundcolor—green—usually white, cream, or yellow.

vegetative—describes reproduction not involving the sexual organs of plants or seeds, such as found in *bulbs* and *tubers*, etc.

veranda—a roofed-over porch.

weed—anything you do not want in your garden.

whorl—the arrangement of three or more flowers or leaves arising from a single point on a stem and radiating out from it in a radial or circular pattern.

woody—a stem composed of woody fibers that do not die back, as opposed to soft-stemmed and *herbaceous*.

x—when located between the *genus* and *species* names, indicates a hybrid plant derived from the crossing of two or more botanically dissimilar plants.

zone—in gardening, the omnipotent regional classification defining a plant's ability to grow and thrive (its *hardiness*). The American Horticultural Society recognizes ten zones from Arctic (Zone 1) to subtropical (Zone 10).

Toying with the idea of writing a book and actually writing one are two very different concepts. For making it a reality as opposed to a daydream, I deeply thank:

Hansa and Guido for the gift of a wondrous laptop computer, I realize the best writers carried on before electronic devices; but this book, humble as it is, might never have come to fruition if not for this machine.

Clara Gyorgyey and Erin Clermont, who put me on the right textual track in the beginning phase.

Jimmy Stein, my agent . . . after all our travels, so much fun, and all these years . . . that's what friends are for.

Emily Reichert, my editor, who got hold of the idea in Beverly Hills and liked it, then had to teach me what the publishing process is all about; special thanks for your patience and being as eager to see this book in print as I.

Michael Gabriel, who took dribs and drabs of my conversation, and said *DIRT*, honey, name it *DIRT*.

Timothy Andreae, who showed me beautiful gardens and planted the seed.

Steven Hamilton for acquainting me with the best of written words, having a unique understanding of my aspirations, and introducing gardening basics.

For important inspiration over the years: Rei Kawakubo, John Glover, Issey Miyake, Paul Sinclaire, Annika Held, and Bill Cunningham for being the epitome of perseverance and friendliness.

For inspiration thwarted: Peter Hujar, John Dolf, Robert Mapplethorpe, Howard Reitzes, Andy Tse, Tim Dlugos, Bob Currie, and Ron Doud—only the good die young.

For ideas secretly stashed in this book: Gerry Kamitaki, Stella Ischii, and Mari Gyorgyey.

Peter Jevremov and Elizabeth Hardwick for their artistic input into this book and the garden.

Howard Purcell for deeming my garden tourable.

All the good folks of East Hampton who've had a hand, a saw, a tree, a plant, an inspiration, or good advice for the Benson garden.

Our pooch, Dylan, who never figured out why I tied myself to a machine in this green, green room not nearly so divine as the outdoor greenery we normally share.

Marc and Wendy, our children

. . . and most of all, my Irving, for making all my dreams come true. I love you.

PREVAILING WOODS

 GARDENS, ALL ONCE WOODS

 BURGUNDY GRAVEL DRIVE

 HAPPY HOUSE

GRASS

 STONES (PATHS)

SPECIAL/SPECIMEN TREES

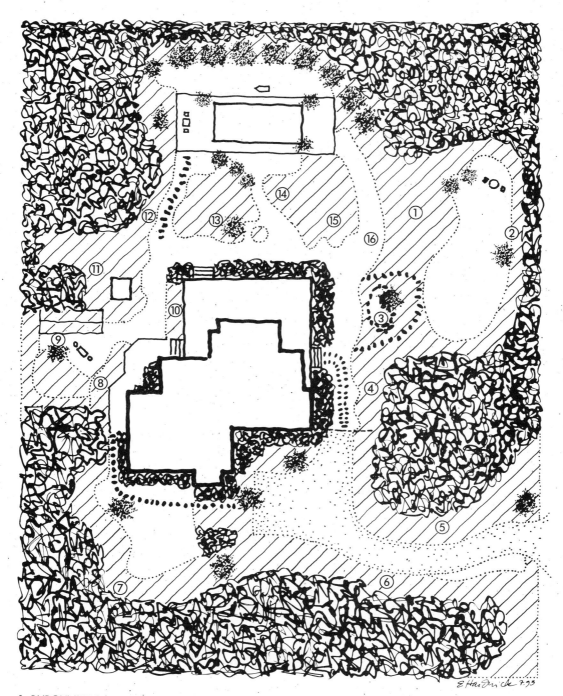

1—BURGUNDY GARDEN
2—CLEMATIS FENCE
3—IRVING POND
4—BLUE BORDER
5—NARCISSUS & DAYLILY DRIVE

6—GROUNDCOVER & SHRUB
   MELANGE
7—IVY & RHODODENDRONS
8—HOSTA GARDEN
9—CUTTING GARDEN
10—MORE CUTTING & HERBS

11—WOULD-BE RAINFOREST
12—BROKEN POTTERY PATH
13—WHITE GARDEN
14—ROCKERY
15—HAMMOCK GROVE
16—NORTH SHADE PATH

Designer, writer, lecturer, and once-owner of four highly successful design stores called Dianne B., DIANNE BENSON has been called "A woman of fashion, a fabulous purveyor of words, stance, and attitude . . . a woman with a brilliantly developed sense of design, business, and marketing." She took up gardening with a fervor seven years ago at the East Hampton home she shares with her husband.